AF763635

INTERNATIONAL ECONOMICS

Dhurata Hajdini

Toronto Academic Press

INTERNATIONAL ECONOMICS

Dhurata Hajdini

Toronto Academic Press
4164 Lakeshore Road
Burlington ON L7L 1A4
Canada
www.tap-books.com

Email: orders@arclereducation.com

ISBN: 978-1-77956-324-8

ABOUT THE AUTHOR

Dhurata Hajdini is a graduate of the University of Prishtina and holds an MA in Banking & Finance. Inspired by her economist father since childhood to pursue economics, she now has a particular interest focusing in international economics. When she's not working, she can usually be found walking in nature or reading.

Table of Contents

List of Figures *xi*
List of Tables *xiii*
Preface *xv*

1 THE INTERNATIONAL ECONOMY AND GLOBALIZATION 1

Introduction **2**
1.1. International Economy **3**
1.1.1. International Trade 3
1.1.2. Global Economy and Human Resources 7
1.1.3. International Finance 8
1.1.4. Exchange Rates and Capital Mobility 8
1.1.5. Migration 10
1.1.6. Globalization 11
1.1.7. Trading Blocks Concept in International Economics 12
1.2. International Trade and Economic Growth **17**
1.2.1. Benefits of World Trade Organization 18
1.3. Barrier of International Trade and Economic Growth **19**
1.3.1. Terms of Trade 20
1.3.2. Aspects of International Trade 20
1.3.3. Dispute the Trade Barriers 21
1.3.4. Role of International Trade Center 22
1.3.5. Patterns of Trade 23
1.4. Globalization and International Marketing **25**
1.4.1. Designing Global Market 27
1.4.2. Importance of Trade 28
1.4.3. Problems Arising from Free Trade 30
Summary **37**
Review Questions **38**
References **38**

2 FOUNDATIONS OF MODERN TRADE THEORY: COMPARATIVE ADVANTAGE 41

Introduction **42**
2.1. Historical Development of Modern Trade Theory **43**
2.1.1. Why Nations Trade: Absolute Advantage 44
2.1.2. Why Nations Trade: Comparative Advantage 45
2.1.3. Production Possibilities Schedules 47
2.1.4. Trading Under Constant-Cost Conditions 48
2.1.5. Changing Comparative Advantage 50
2.2. International Trade and Development **53**
2.2.1. Patterns of Trade 54
2.2.2. Invisible Trade 55
2.2.3. Trade Sanctions 55
2.2.4. Trade Between Developed and Developing Countries 56

2.2.5. International Trade Law 57
2.2.6. State Interference in International Trade 58
2.2.7. Methods of International Trade Regulation 61
2.3. International Trade Services 63
2.3.1. Methods to Measure the Gain from International Trade 64
2.3.2. Role of International Trade 67
2.3.3. International Trade Strategies 68
2.3.4. Advantages of International Trade 69
2.3.5. Terms of Trade 70
2.3.6. Facets of International Trade 70
2.4. Barrier of International Trade 72
2.4.1. Dispute the Trade Barriers 73
2.4.2. Tariff Barriers of International Trade 74
2.4.3. Objectives of Tariffs 75
2.4.4. Tariff Reduction and the Growth of International Trade 77
2.4.5. Nontariff Barrier 78
Summary 83
Review Questions 83
References 84

3 TARIFFS 85

Introduction 86
3.1. Concept of Tariffs 87
3.1.1. Types of Tariffs 87
3.1.2. Effective Rate of Protection 89
3.2. Tariff Escalation 92
3.2.1. Outsourcing and Offshore-Assembly Provision 93
3.2.2. Dodging Import Tariffs: Tariff Avoidance and Tariff Evasion 94
3.3. Postponing Import Tariffs 96
3.3.1. Bonded Warehouse 96
3.3.2. Foreign-Trade Zone 97
3.3.3. FTZ's Benefit Motor Vehicle Importers 98
3.4. Tariff Effects 99
3.4.1. Tariff Welfare Effects: Consumer Surplus and Producer Surplus 99
3.4.2. Tariff Welfare Effects: Small-Nation Model 101
3.4.3. Tariff Welfare Effects: Large-Nation Model 103
3.5. Arguments for Trade Restrictions 108
3.5.1. Job Protection 108
3.5.2. Protection Against Cheap Foreign Labor 109
3.5.3. Fairness in Trade: A Level Playing Field 111
3.5.4. Maintenance of the Domestic Standard of Living 112
3.5.5. Equalization of Production Costs 112
3.5.6. Infant-Industry Argument 112
3.5.7. Noneconomic Arguments 113
3.5.8. A Supply and Demand View of Protectionism 114
Summary 118
Review Questions 119
References 120

4 NONTARIFF TRADE BARRIERS 121

Introduction 122
4.1. Non-Tariff Barriers 123
4.1.1. Origin of Non-Tariff Barriers 123
4.1.2. Types of Non-Tariff Barriers 124
4.1.3. Examples of Non-Tariff Barriers 124
4.2. Import Quota 126
4.2.1. Trade and Welfare Effects 127
4.2.2. Allocating Quota Licenses 129
4.2.3. Quotas Versus Tariffs 130
4.3. Tariff-Rate Quota: A Two-Tier Tariff 132
4.3.1. Sugar Tariff-Rate Quota Bittersweet for Consumers 133
4.4. Export Quotas 134
4.4.1. Japanese Auto Restraints Put Brakes on U.S. Motorists 134
4.5. Domestic Content Requirements 136
4.6. Subsidies 138
4.6.1. Domestic Production Subsidy 138
4.6.2. Export Subsidy 140
4.7. Dumping 142

4.7.1. Forms of Dumping 142
4.7.2. International Price Discrimination 143
4.8. Antidumping Regulations 145
4.8.1. Smith Corona Finds Antidumping Victories Are Hollow 146
4.8.2. Canadians Press Washington Apple Producers for Level Playing Field 147
4.9. Antidumping Law Unfair 148
4.9.1. Average Variable Cost Be the Yardstick for Defining Dumping 148
4.9.2. Antidumping Law Reflect Currency Fluctuations 149
4.9.3. Antidumping Duties Overused 150
4.10. Other Nontariff Trade Barriers 151
4.10.1. Government Procurement Policies 151
4.10.2. Social Regulations 152
4.10.3. CAFÉ Standards 152
4.10.4. Sea Transport and Freight Regulations 154
Summary 157
Review Questions 157
References 158

5 TRADE REGULATIONS AND INDUSTRIAL POLICIES 161

Introduction 162
5.1. Basics of International Trade 163
5.1.1. Trade 163
5.1.2. History of Trade 163
5.1.3. Globalization and Contemporary Trade 164
5.1.4. International Trade 165
5.1.5. Factors Affecting International Trade 166
5.1.6. Benefits of International Trade 167
5.1.7. Need for International Trade 167
5.1.8. Common Barriers to International Trade 167
5.2. U.S. Tariff Policies Before 1930 169
5.3. Smoot-Hawley Act 171
5.4. Reciprocal Trade Agreements Act 173
5.5. General Agreement on Tariffs and Trade 174
5.5.1. Trade Without Discrimination 174
5.5.2. Promoting Freer Trade 176
5.5.3. Predictability: Through Binding and Transparency 176
5.5.4. Multilateral Trade Negotiations 176
5.6. World Trade Organization 179
5.6.1. Settling Trade Disputes 180
5.6.2. Does the WTO Reduce National Sovereignty? 181
5.6.3. Should Retaliatory Tariffs Be Used for WTO Enforcement? 182
5.6.4. Does the WTO Harm the Environment? 183
5.7. From Doha to Hong Kong: Failed Trade Negotiations 186
5.8. Trade Promotion Authority (Fast-Track Authority) 188
5.9. Industrial Policy 189
5.9.1. Industrial Policy Resolutions 189
5.9.2. New Industrial Policy, 1991 193
5.10. Industrial Policies of the United States 198
5.10.1. Export Promotion and Financing 199
5.11. Industrial Policies of Japan 201
Summary 206
Review Questions 207
References 207

6 TRADE POLICIES FOR THE DEVELOPING NATIONS 209

Introduction 210
6.1. Developing-Nation Trade Characteristics 211
6.2. Tensions Between Developing and Advanced Nations 213
6.3. Trade Problems of the Developing Nations 215
6.3.1. Unstable Export Markets 215

6.3.2. Worsening Terms of Trade 217
6.3.3. Limited Market Access 218
6.3.4. Agricultural Export Subsidies of Advanced Nations 220
6.4. Stabilizing Primary-Product Prices 222
6.4.1. Production and Export Controls 222
6.4.2. Buffer Stocks 223
6.4.3. Multilateral Contracts 224
6.4.4. Does the Fair-Trade Movement Help Poor Coffee Farmers? 224
6.5. The OPEC Oil Cartel 226
6.5.1. Maximizing Cartel Profits 226
6.5.2. OPEC as a Cartel 228
6.6. Aiding the Developing Nations 230
6.6.1. The World Bank 230
6.6.2. International Monetary Fund 231
6.6.3. Generalized System of Preferences 232
6.6.4. Does Aid Promote Growth of Developing Nations? 233
6.7. Economic Growth Strategies: Import Substitution Versus Export-Led Growth 235
6.7.1. Import Substitution 235
6.7.2. Export-Led Growth 236
6.7.3. Economic Growth Good for the Poor 237
6.7.4. Developing Nations Achieve Export-Led Growth 238
6.7.5. East Asian Economies 238
6.7.6. Flying-Geese Pattern of Growth 239
6.8. China's Transformation to Capitalism 241
6.8.1. China's Export Boom Comes at a Cost: How to Make Factories Play Fair 243
6.9. India: Breaking Out of the Third World 245
Summary 253
Review Questions 253
References 254

7 REGIONAL TRADING ARRANGEMENTS 255

Introduction 256
7.1. Regional Integration Versus Multilateralism 257
7.2. Types of Regional Trading Arrangement 259
7.3. Impetus for Regionalism 261
7.4. Effects of a Regional Trading Arrangement 262
7.4.1. Static Effects 262
7.4.2. Did the United Kingdom (UK) Gain from Entering the European Union? 264
7.4.3. Dynamic Effects 265
7.5. The European Union 267
7.5.1. Pursuing Economic Integration 267
7.5.2. French and Dutch Voters Sidetrack Integration 269
7.5.3. Agricultural Policy 270
7.6. Economic Costs and Benefits of a Common Currency: The European Monetary Union 275
7.6.1. Optimum Currency Area 276
7.6.2. Europe as a Suboptimal Currency Area 277
7.6.3. Challenges for the EMU 277
7.6.4. Does the Eurozone Need a Bailout Fund? 278
7.7. North American Free Trade Agreement 280
7.7.1. NAFTA's Benefits and Costs for Mexico and Canada 281
7.7.2. NAFTA's Benefits and Costs for the United States 282
7.7.3. NAFTA and Trade Diversion: Textiles and Apparel 285
7.8. Free Trade Area of the Americas 288
7.9. Asia-Pacific Economic Cooperation 291
7.10. Transition Economies 291
7.10.1. The Transition Toward a Market-Oriented Economy 292
7.10.2. Russia and the World Trade Organization 294
Summary 300
Review Questions 301
References 301

8 INTERNATIONAL FACTOR MOVEMENTS\ AND MULTINATIONAL ENTERPRISES 303

Introduction **304**

8.1. The Multinational Enterprise **305**

8.1.1. Reasons for Being a Multinational Corporation 305

8.1.2. Models of MNCs 306

8.1.3. Advantages of Being a Multinational Corporation 306

8.1.4. Disadvantages of Being a Multinational Corporation 306

8.1.5. Examples of Multinational Corporations 307

8.2. Motives for Foreign Direct Investment **308**

8.2.1. Types of Foreign Direct Investment 308

8.2.2. Reasons for Foreign Direct Investments 308

8.2.3. Importance of Foreign Direct Investment 309

8.2.4. Ways to Attract FDI 309

8.2.5. Advantages and Disadvantages 310

8.3. Supplying Products to Foreign Buyers **311**

8.3.1. Direct Exporting Versus Foreign Direct Investment/Licensing 311

8.3.2. Foreign Direct Investment Versus Licensing 312

8.4. Country Risk Analysis **315**

8.4.1. Types of Country Risk 315

8.4.2. Managing Country Risk 318

8.4.3. Managing Political Risk 318

8.4.4. Managing Exchange Rate Risks 319

8.4.5. Managing Industry Risks 320

8.4.6. Country Risk Strategies 320

8.5. International Trade Theory and Multinational Enterprise **322**

8.6. International Joint Ventures **323**

8.6.1. Basic Elements 323

8.6.2. Reasons for Forming 324

8.6.3. Due Diligence 325

8.6.4. Advantages 325

8.6.5. Structure 325

8.6.6. Management 326

8.6.7. Finance 326

8.6.8. Potential Disputes and Agreements When Entering IJV's 327

8.7. Multinational Enterprises as a Source of Conflict **329**

8.7.1. Elaboration and Analysis 329

8.8. International Labor Mobility: Migration **332**

8.8.1. Importance of Geographic Mobility 332

8.8.2. Importance of Occupational Mobility 333

8.8.3. Labor Mobility: Two Perspectives 333

8.8.4. Types of Labor Mobility 334

8.8.5. Restrictions Placed on Labor Mobility 334

Summary **337**

Review Questions **337**

References **338**

9 THE BALANCE OF PAYMENTS 341

Introduction **342**

9.1. Balance of Payments: The Global Phenomena **343**

9.1.1. History 343

9.1.2. Exchange Rate Regime 344

9.1.3. Components 344

9.1.4. Uses 347

9.1.5. Imbalances 347

9.1.6. Balancing Mechanisms 349

9.1.7. Post-Washington Consensus Developments 351

9.1.8. Economic Policy and the Balance of Payment 353

9.2. Purpose of Balance of Payments **355**

9.2.1. Balance of Payments Accounts 356

9.2.2. Significance of Balance of Payments (BoP) Data 358

9.2.3. The Current Account Component in Balance of Payments (BoP) 359

9.2.4. Balance of Payments (BOP) and Exchange Rates 362
9.3. Balance of Payments (BoP) Accounting 364
9.3.1. The Capital Account Component in Balance of Payments (BoP) 365
9.3.2. Use of Exchange Controls 367
9.3.3. Disequilibrium in Balance of Payments 369
9.3.4. Correction of Balance of Payments (BoP) Deficit 372
Summary 378
Review Questions 378
References 379

10 FOREIGN EXCHANGE 381

Introduction 382
10.1. Meaning of Foreign Exchange 383
10.1.1. History of Foreign Exchange 384
10.2. Functions of Foreign Exchange Market 387
10.2.1. Transfer Function 387
10.2.2. Credit Function 388
10.2.3. Hedging Function 388
10.3. Types of Foreign Exchange Market 389
10.3.1. Spot Markets 389
10.3.2. Forward Market 394
10.3.3. Future Markets 397
10.3.4. Option Markets 398
10.3.5. Swap Market 400
10.4. Forex Market Participants 402
Summary 407
Review Questions 407
References 408

INDEX 411

List of Figures

Figure 2.1. Trading under constant opportunity costs
Figure 2.2. Trading environment of international trade
Figure 2.3. Ricardo's approach
Figure 2.4. Mill's approach
Figure 2.5. The modern approach
Figure 3.1. Tariff escalation on industrial countries' imports from developing countries
Figure 3.2. Consumer surplus and producer surplus
Figure 3.3. Tariff trade and welfare effects: small nation model
Figure 3.4. Tariff trade and welfare effects: large nation model
Figure 4.1. Non-tariff barriers
Figure 4.2. Import quota: trade and welfare effects
Figure 4.3. Trade effects of tariffs versus quotas
Figure 4.4. Welfare effects of a domestic content requirement
Figure 4.5. Trade and welfare effects of subsidies
Figure 4.6. International price discrimination
Figure 5.1. The flows of globalization
Figure 5.2. Example of the effects of trade barriers
Figure 5.3. Smoot-Hawley protectionism and world trade, 1929–1933 (millions of dollars)
Figure 6.1. Export price instability for a developing nation
Figure 6.2. Trade barriers limit export opportunities of developing nations
Figure 6.3. Buffer stock: Price ceiling and price support
Figure 6.4. Maximizing OPEC profits
Figure 6.5. Openness and economic growth
Figure 7.1. Static welfare effects of a customs union
Figure 7.2. Variable levies
Figure 7.3. For the former soviet bloc countries, freer economies grow faster
Figure 8.1. The choice between direct exporting and foreign direct investment/licensing. When the Canadian market's size is large enough to permit efficient production in Canada, a U.S. firm

increases profits by establishing a Canadian production subsidiary or licensing the rights to a Canadian firm to produce and market its product in Canada. The U.S. firm increases profits by exporting its product to Canada when the Canadian market is too small to permit efficient production
Figure 8.2. The choice between foreign direct investment and licensing. The decision to establish foreign operations through direct investment or licensing depends on (1) the extent to which capital is used in the production process, (2) the size of the foreign market, and (3) the amount of fixed cost a business must bear when establishing an overseas facility
Figure 10.1. The structure of the foreign exchange market constitutes central banks
Figure 10.2. Functions of foreign exchange market
Figure 10.3. Types of foreign exchange market
Figure 10.4. A spot market is a financial market
Figure 10.5. Types of spot markets
Figure 10.6. An organized market exchange
Figure 10.7. The forward market is the marketplace
Figure 10.8. The types of forward market that exist in the financial sector
Figure 10.9. Forward market refers to a market that deals in over-the-counter derivative instruments
Figure 10.10. A futures market is an auction market
Figure 10.11. The concept of options trade is a bit complicated than stock trading
Figure 10.12. Modern financial markets employ a wide selection of such derivatives
Figure 10.13. Some countries with transition economies there are currency exchanges
Figure 10.14. Brokerage firms are bringing together buyers and sellers

List of Tables

Table 2.1. World output possibilities in the absence of specialization
Table 2.2 Examples of comparative advantages in international trade
Table 2.3. World output possibilities in the absence of specialization
Table 3.1. Selected U.S. tariffs
Table 3.2. Examples of tariffs for selected countries (in percentages)
Table 3.3. The effective rate of protection
Table 3.4. China's nominal and effective tariff rates in forestry products, 2001
Table 3.5. Effects of increases in U.S. tariffs on the world price of imported goods
Table 3.6. Hourly compensation costs in U.S. dollars for production workers in manufacturing, 2007
Table 3.7. Productivity, wages, and unit labor costs, relative to the United States: Total manufacturing, 2002 (United States = 1.0)
Table 4.1. Examples of U.S. import quotas
Table 4.2. Examples of U.S. tariff-rate quotas
Table 4.3. Domestic content requirements applied to automobiles in selected countries
Table 4.4. North American content of automobiles sold in the United States, 2007 (sales weighted)
Table 4.5. Normal value and the margin of dumping: delicious apples, regular storage, 1987–1988
Table 4.6. Dumping and excess capacity
Table 5.1. US tariff history: average tariff rates
Table 5.2. US tariffs on imports from nations granted, and not granted, normal trade relation status: selected examples
Table 5.3. GATT negotiating rounds
Table 5.4. Uruguay round tariff reductions on industrial products by selected countries
Table 5.5. Examples of loans provided by EXIM bank of the United States (in millions of dollars)
Table 6.1. Basic economic and social indicators for selected nations

Table 6.2. Structure of output for selected advanced nations and developing nations, 2007 value added as a percent of GDP
Table 6.3. Developing nation dependence on primary products, 2007
Table 7.1. Government support for agriculture, 2007
Table 7.2. Advantages and disadvantages of adopting a common currency
Table 7.3. Winners and losers in the United States under free trade with Mexico
Table 7.4. Gross domestic product, employment and labor productivity, 2007
Table 7.5. Trade effects of NAFTA: Trade creation and trade diversion (thousands of dollars)
Table 7.6. Major western hemisphere regional trade agreements
Table 9.1. The Current account of balance of payments
Table 9.2. Actual Process of measuring BoP activity

PREFACE

With regard to the theories of growth, the flow of trade has a significance in determination of the rate of economic growth because trade allows the progress of technology in a region that ends up playing a crucial role in productions and gains of competition. This eventually fosters both the development and growth of a given economy. However, there are several arguments that claim that only trade cannot bring about economic growth and development and thus there are other factors like the political stability, the extent to which the rule of law is enforced, the population growth rate and the level of secondary and tertiary enrollment among other critical issues.

Economics helps us identify the policy measures that encourage prosperity and avoid inefficiency, making it a crucial driver in the search for sustainable growth. The human race's curiosity has expressed itself in the creation of various fields of study that examine specific aspects of the world around us. The 'natural' sciences like physics and chemistry study the behavior of the basic particles and elements of the universe and their interactions with each other. The 'humanities,' on the other hand, study the creations of humans, such as literary texts and the arts. Interspersed between these two is economics—a 'social science' which deploys a highly quantitative, data-driven, problem-solving approach towards understanding the behavior of human beings. Economics, therefore, is the field of study that is best placed to track, study, project and predict human behavior; and as such is one of the most important and relevant skills for the world today, helping us choose wisely when it comes to our personal, social and professional lives. Understanding humans, and their motivations, is critical to designing initiatives that can have social and economic impacts upon society at a local, regional and national level.

Content/Structure of the Book

This book encompasses 10 comprehensive chapters that examines various facets of the international economy and globalization, providing a thorough understanding of the dynamics shaping global trade and economic interactions.

Chapter 1, The International Economy and Globalization, sets the stage by examining the interconnected nature of economies worldwide, exploring the drivers and consequences of globalization on trade, finance, and development.

Foundations of Modern Trade Theory: Comparative Advantage are explored in Chapter 2, elucidating the principles established by classical economists like David Ricardo. It explores how nations benefit from specializing in the production of goods and services where they have a comparative advantage.

Chapter 3, Tariffs, examines the role of tariffs as a trade policy tool, discussing their impact on international trade flows, consumer prices, and economic welfare.

Nontariff Trade Barriers are the focus of Chapter 4, addressing regulatory measures such as quotas, subsidies, and technical standards that countries employ to restrict imports and protect domestic industries.

Trade Regulations and Industrial Policies are analyzed in Chapter 5, exploring how governments formulate policies to promote industrial development while navigating global trade rules and agreements.

Chapter 6, Trade Policies for the Developing Nations, examines the unique challenges and opportunities faced by developing countries in integrating into the global economy, addressing issues of trade liberalization, development aid, and capacity building.

Regional Trading Arrangements take center stage in Chapter 7, investigating the proliferation and impact of regional trade agreements like NAFTA and the EU, exploring their implications for member states and global trade dynamics.

Chapter 8, International Factor Movements and Multinational Enterprises, explores the mobility of capital, labor, and technology across borders, analyzing the role of multinational corporations in global production and investment.

The Balance of Payments is scrutinized in Chapter 9, providing a detailed analysis of a country's transactions with the rest of the world, including trade balances, capital flows, and exchange rate impacts.

Finally, Chapter 10, Foreign Exchange, examines the mechanisms of currency markets, exchange rate determination, and the implications for international trade and investment.

Together, these chapters provide a comprehensive framework for understanding the complexities of the international economy, globalization, and the policies that shape global trade and economic relations across diverse nations and regions.

Audience

This book is tailored for a diverse readership, including undergraduate and graduate students studying economics, international business, and related fields. It serves as an essential resource for academics and researchers seeking a comprehensive understanding of global trade dynamics and economic interactions. Policy makers and professionals working in government, international organizations, and financial institutions will find this book invaluable for its in-depth analysis of trade policies, tariffs, and international economic regulations. Additionally, business leaders and entrepreneurs engaged in international trade or contemplating global market expansions will benefit from its insights into comparative advantage, regional trading arrangements, and multinational enterprise operations. The book also caters to informed general readers interested in understanding the complexities of the global economy and the factors influencing international trade and finance. With its clear explanations, rigorous analysis, and practical examples, this book is an indispensable guide for anyone seeking to navigate and comprehend the intricacies of the international economic landscape.

Learning Features

- Start-of-chapter learning objectives
- Key terms in each chapter
- Summary Points at the end of each chapter
- Review Questions at the end of each chapter
- Case Studies and Activities in each chapter for solving real problems
- References at the end of each chapter

CHAPTER 1

The International Economy and Globalization

LEARNING OBJECTIVES

After studying this chapter, you will be able to:

- Discuss on international economy
- Learn about the international trade and economic growth
- Examine the barrier of international trade and economic growth
- Determine globalization in international marketing

KEY TERMS FROM THIS CHAPTER

Economic activity	Economic integration
Economic nationalism	Economic theory
Global economy	Global value chains (GVCs)
International agreements	International finance
International institutions	International monetary
International relations	Macroeconomics
Multinational corporations (MNCs)	World Trade Organization (WTO)
	Traditional marketing

INTRODUCTION

The international economy refers to the economic activities and transactions that cross national borders, encompassing trade, investment, and financial flows between countries. Globalization, on the other hand, is the process by which these interactions and integrations are accelerated and deepened, leading to a more interconnected and interdependent world economy.

Globalization has been driven by a combination of technological advancements, policy decisions, and the liberalization of trade and investment. Technological innovations, particularly in transportation and communication, have significantly reduced the cost and time of moving goods and services across the globe. The internet and digital technologies have revolutionized the way businesses operate, allowing them to manage global supply chains more efficiently and reach consumers in distant markets. Policy decisions, such as the reduction of tariffs and non-tariff barriers, the establishment of free trade agreements, and the creation of international economic organizations like the World Trade Organization (WTO), have facilitated easier and more predictable international economic exchanges.

One of the key features of the international economy under globalization is the rise of multinational corporations (MNCs), which operate in multiple countries and leverage global efficiencies to enhance their competitiveness. These corporations play a critical role in global trade and investment flows, often driving economic integration by establishing production facilities in different regions, sourcing components from various countries, and marketing their products worldwide. This has led to the development of global value chains (GVCs), where different stages of production are located in different countries, adding to the complexity and interconnectedness of the global economy.

1.1. INTERNATIONAL ECONOMY

The study of international economics focuses on how variations in consumer preferences and productive resources across borders, as well as the international institutions that influence these differences, affect economic activity. It aims to clarify the trends and outcomes of interactions and trade—including investment and transaction—between the citizens of various nations.

The study of international trade examines the movement of goods and services across national borders as a result of supply and demand dynamics, economic integration, international factor movements, and changes in trade policies like tariffs and quotas. The study of international finance focuses on the movement of capital across global financial markets and how it affects exchange rates. International money flows and their impact on national economies are the subject of research in international macroeconomics and international monetary economics. As a subfield of international relations, international political economy examines the problems and consequences raised by, among other things, international negotiations, international conflicts, international sanctions, national security, economic nationalism, and international agreements and observance.

1.1.1. International Trade

The relatively restricted international mobility of capital and labor is the primary reason that the economic theory of international trade is distinct from the rest of economic theory. That seems to set it apart from trade between isolated areas within a single nation more in terms of degree than in principle. As a result, there are not many differences between the methodology of international trade economics and other branches of economics. However, governments have frequently attempted to impose restrictions on international trade, and the desire to ascertain the effects of such restrictions has frequently motivated the development of trade theory, which has influenced the direction of academic research on the subject. The traditional definition of classical trade theory is the area of trade theory that focuses primarily on the application of deductive logic. It began with Ricardo's Theory of Comparative Advantage and evolved into a variety of theorems whose applicability depends on how realistic their postulates are. On the other hand, empirical analysis is the primary source of data for modern trade analysis.

1.1.1.1. Classical Theory

International trade makes sense because of the comparative advantages resulting from inter-regional differences, regardless of how those differences occur, according to the theory of comparative advantage. Since David Ricardo first introduced it, neo-classical economics methods have been used to simulate the trade patterns that would arise from different theorized sources of comparative advantage. However, to make the problem amenable to theoretical analysis, some very restrictive (and often unrealistic) assumptions have had to be made. The Heckscher-Ohlin theorem (H-O), the most well-known of the resulting models, is predicated on the notions that there are no cross-border variations in productivity, technology, or consumer preferences, as well as no barriers to free trade or pure competition and no scale economies. By making these assumptions, it creates a model of the trade patterns that would result from variations in the relative abundance of labor and capital (also known as factor endowments) across international borders alone. According to the ensuing theorem, a nation with a relative abundance of capital would import labor-intensive goods and export capital-intensive goods. The discovery known as the Leontief Paradox—which showed that America was exporting labor-intensive goods while importing capital-intensive ones—evidenced that the theorem had very little predictive value. Nevertheless, the theoretical methods and many of the underlying presumptions employed in the H–O model's derivation were later applied to the derivation of other theorems.

Often regarded as a corollary of the H–O theorem, the Stolper–Samuelson theorem was one of the first. The simplest explanation of this is that when the price of a good increases or decreases, the price of the factor that is used heavily in that industry will likewise rise or decrease, while the price of the other factor will decrease (rise). In the framework of global trade in which it was developed, it indicates that while trade barriers raise the real wage of the scarce factor of production, trade itself lowers it. Samuelson's factor price equalization theorem is another corollary of the H–O theorem. It asserts that as trade between nations tends to equalize product prices, it also tends to equalize the prices paid to their factors of production. Certain theories have occasionally been interpreted to suggest that trade between an industrialized and developing nation would result in lower wages for the unskilled workers in the industrialized nation. As mentioned below, however, that conclusion is predicated on the improbable supposition that productivity in the two nations is equal. Several academic papers have been written in an effort to expand on the Stolper-Samuelson and H–O theorems. Although many of these papers are thought to offer insightful information, they have rarely shown to be directly relevant to the task of explaining trade patterns.

1.1.1.2. Modern Analysis

Instead of adhering to the H–O theorem's narrow assumptions, modern trade analysis investigates how a variety of factors, such as scale economies and technology, affect trade. It heavily utilizes econometrics to determine, from the available data, the relative importance of various factors among the myriad variables influencing trade. The gravity equation is one instance of an econometric model of this type. Numerous studies have assessed the contributions of disparities in technology. According to one study, the short-term benefit that results from a nation developing new technology is a contributing factor. Other researchers have discovered that the amount spent on R&D, the number of patents granted, and the availability of skilled labor are indicators of a nation's technological leadership, which allows it to generate a steady stream of technological innovations. These researchers have also discovered that nations that lead in technology typically import more conventional goods from other nations and export high-tech goods to others. A correlation was also found by another econometric study between the size of a country and the proportion of its exports that consist of goods produced using scale economies. According to the study, goods that are traded internationally can be classified into three groups, each of which has a distinct comparative advantage.

Items produced through the extraction and routine processing of readily available natural resources—like coal, oil, and wheat—that tend to migrate to countries with adequate factor endowments—like Heckscher-Ohlin goods; low-technology goods—like steel and textiles—that are produced by developing countries—like Ricardo goods; and high-technology and high scale-economy goods—like computers and airplanes—whose comparative advantage comes from the availability of R&D resources and specialized skills as well as the proximity to large sophisticated markets.

Although there is a strong assumption that any freely undertaken exchange will be advantageous to both parties, it is still possible that it could be detrimental to other people. Nonetheless, Paul Samuelson has demonstrated that it will always be feasible for the winners from international trade to make up for the losers (based on assumptions such as constant returns and competitive conditions). Furthermore, Samuelson neglected to include in that proof the benefits that others would receive from increased consumer choice, from the global specialization of productive activities and the ensuing economies of scale, and from the dissemination of the advantages of technological innovation. Further dynamic gains may arise from improved resource allocation, deeper specialization, higher returns to research and development, and technology spillover, according to an OECD study. The authors concluded that while there is conflicting data regarding growth rates, there is compelling evidence that a 1% increase in trade openness raises GDP per capita by a range of 0.9% to 2.0%. They proposed that the expansion of the most productive companies at the expense of the less productive accounts for a large portion of the gain. Economists generally agree that trade confers very significant net benefits and that trade restrictions are generally detrimental, thanks to these and other findings.

1.1.1.2.1. Factor Price Equalization

However, there are a lot of people who are concerned about how global trade will affect middle-class wage earners in developed nations. According to Samuelson's factor price equalization theorem, trade would result in wage rate parity if productivity were the same in both nations. The aforementioned theorem is sometimes interpreted to imply that trade between an industrialized and developing nation would result in a decrease in the wages of the unskilled within the industrialized nation. It is illogical to believe, nevertheless, that productivity in a developing nation with low wages would be equal to that in a developed nation with high wages. International variations in wage rates are roughly matched by corresponding variations in productivity, according to a 1999 study. Such remaining disparities were most likely caused by labor market rigidities or an over- or undervaluation of exchange rates. It has been suggested that, despite the fact that developed-country wage rates may occasionally face temporary pressures, wage competition among employers in developing nations will eventually force wages to reflect their workers' marginal products. There wouldn't be a difference in unit labor costs between developed and developing nations, nor would there be any downward pressure on wages in developed nations; any remaining differences in international wages would then be the result of productivity differences.

1.1.1.2.2. Terms of Trade

Concerns have also been raised about how trade might work against the interests of developing nations. Significant research by British economist Hans Singer and Argentine economist Raul Prebisch, published in 1950, revealed that agricultural product prices have a propensity to decline in relation to manufactured good prices, shifting the terms of trade against developing nations and resulting in an unintentional transfer of wealth from them to developed nations. Numerous later studies have confirmed their findings, despite suggestions that the effect could be the result of manufacturers' market dominance or quality bias in the index numbers used. The Prebisch/Singer findings are still debatable, but they were used then, as well as later, to support the idea that developing nations should build barriers against manufactured imports to support their fledgling industries and lessen their reliance on exporting agricultural goods. The arguments in favor of and against such a policy are comparable to those made generally for the protection of emerging industries.

1.1.1.2.3. Infant Industries

A new industry that has the potential to acquire a comparative advantage over time but would not be able to withstand competition from imported goods is referred to as an infant industry. This circumstance may arise when more time is required to acquire potential learning curve economies or to realize potential economies of scale. Import substitution industrialization, a policy that involves successfully identifying a situation like this and temporarily imposing a barrier against imports, has the potential to yield significant benefits for the nation implementing it. The ability of governments to select winners—with realistic expectations of both successes and failures—will determine whether or not such policies are successful. There has been a claim that the automobile industry in South Korea is a direct result of early import substitution policies. However, an analysis of protection for emerging industries in Turkey shows no correlation between the level of protection and productivity increases. Descriptive evidence from another study indicates that attempts at industrialization through import substitution since the 1970s have generally failed, but the empirical data on the subject has been inconsistent and ambiguous. It's been stated that the argument against import substitution industrialization isn't that it will fail, but rather that tax breaks and subsidies work better. Furthermore, it has been noted that trade restrictions cannot be expected to address the flaws in the domestic market, which frequently impede the growth of emerging industries.

1.1.1.3. Trade Policies

The conclusions of economists regarding the advantages of trade have frequently been disregarded by government officials, who have consistently aimed to shield domestic industries from foreign rivalry by constructing obstacles, such as tariffs and import limits. The average tariff rates, approximately 15% in late 19th century, escalated to around 30% in the 1930s after the implementation of the Smoot–Hawley Tariff Act in the United States. Primarily due to international accords under the supervision of the General Agreement on Tariffs and Trade (GATT) and later the World Trade Organization (WTO), average tariff rates were gradually lowered to about 7% during the latter half of the 20th century, and several other trade restrictions were also lifted. Despite these reductions, the remaining restrictions hold significant economic impact: for instance, the World Bank estimated in 2004 that the elimination of all trade restrictions would generate annual benefits exceeding $500 billion by 2015.

In response to quotas, foreign suppliers raise their prices to match those of the importing nation. This reduces the competitive pressure that local suppliers face, and while both they and the foreign suppliers benefit, there is a cost to consumers, the domestic economy, and the global economy as a whole. Following the General Agreement on Tariffs and Trade's (GATT) prohibition on quotas, the US, the UK, and the EU implemented comparable measures known as voluntary export restraints (VERs) or voluntary restraint agreements (VRAs), which were negotiated with exporting nations (primarily Japan) until they were also outlawed. Tariffs have been viewed as less detrimental than quotas, despite the fact that evidence suggests that their welfare effects only change in response to notable increases or decreases in imports. A vast array of non-tariff barriers, some of which are governed by WTO agreements, are also imposed by governments and function similarly to quotas. Applying the precautionary principle to exclude innovative products is one recent example [when?].

1.1.2. Global Economy and Human Resources

Globalization has significantly impacted the management of human resources. As the world gets smaller due to globalization, there are more challenges to deal with. These include managing talent from foreign countries, dealing with legal and cultural differences, outsourcing, and international assignments. Since any business is only as good as its employees, small businesses are equally impacted by these developments as large corporations.

- **Anticipating Future Needs:** Considering how labor markets have changed, one of the biggest challenges businesses face is forecasting their talent needs. It's difficult to find and hire bright people who can pick up new skills as needs in the workplace change. If you or one of your managers has a better idea of what your company needs to expand, your HR manager might not be in the best position to anticipate future needs. Globalization has increased the pool of talent available to you, whether you choose to grow your company internationally or hire foreign workers for your domestic office.
- **Nurturing Talent:** Small businesses must embrace technology and the employees who can use it in an endless quest to stay competitive. Small businesses need to think outside the box when it comes to employee training and consider it an investment rather than a cost. When welcoming foreign workers to your company, try to find ongoing ways to involve staff members. To stay up to date with industry trends, employees should be encouraged to take part in real-time training with expert consultants, many of whom are from abroad, in addition to conventional seminars and continuing education.
- **Overseas Assignments:** An extended assignment abroad with

the chance to work with a global division of your company sounds exciting on the surface. However, things are not always as easy as they seem. It can be challenging to integrate corporate procedures and knowledge with foreign employees. Your staff members may view business differently when they return from assignments abroad than when they work from home. This situation poses concerns for human resource managers who are responsible for incorporating overseas assignments into talent management and development initiatives. One issue that needs to be resolved is how to balance hiring local talent with taking on overseas assignments.

- **Outsourcing in a Global Market:** A growing number of small and medium-sized businesses are using outsourcing to meet their demands for human resources in international markets. Talented freelancers in almost every industry, from virtual assistants to highly technical specialists, make up the vast pool of contract workers. Make careful plans if you decide to outsource your work. While some websites offer protections for both parties, no guarantees are made. Language and cultural barriers may cause issues, and the low bidder on your project might not have the necessary expertise. Globalization has, however, made it possible to control the costs associated with human resources while maintaining productivity.

1.1.3. International Finance

There are notable distinctions in focus between the economics of international trade and international finance, but fundamental differences remain. Because the assets that are traded are claims to returns flows that frequently stretch many years into the future, the practice of international finance tends to involve greater uncertainties and risks. Because decisions are made more quickly and are revised more frequently than markets for goods and services, financial asset markets are typically more volatile. There is a shared assumption that a freely entered transaction will be advantageous to both parties, but the likelihood that it will be detrimental to others is far higher. Sudden reversals of international capital flows have frequently resulted in damaging financial crises in developing countries. For instance, in 2008, mismanagement of mortgage lending in the United States caused banking failures and credit shortages in other developed countries. Additionally, the comparative statics methodology is less applicable in the theory of international trade due to the prevalence of rapid change, while empirical analysis is used more frequently. Furthermore, there is less agreement among economists on its main concerns than there is on international trade, leaving room for debate.

1.1.4. Exchange Rates and Capital Mobility

In the last decades of the 20th century, there was a significant shift in the structure of global finance that economists are still discussing today. The Bretton Woods Agreement's signatories pledged to keep their national currencies fixed at a fixed exchange rate with the US dollar ($) at the end of World War II, and the US government committed to buying gold on demand at a fixed price of $35 per ounce. To uphold their commitments, the majority of signatory countries have enforced stringent regulations on their citizens' use of foreign currency and transactions involving global financial assets. However, a progressive transition to the current regime of floating exchange rates occurred after the US government announced in 1971 that it was suspending the dollar's convertibility. Under this regime, most governments no longer make an effort to control their exchange rates or impose restrictions on citizens' access to foreign currencies or to international financial markets. The global financial system started acting differently. There was a protracted string of devastating financial crises, and exchange rates became extremely volatile. According to one study, there were many times more banking crises at the end of the 20th century than there had been in the preceding post-war years, with an estimated 112 banking crises in 93 countries, 86 currency crises, and 27 mixed banking and currency crises.

Milton Friedman had argued in the 1950s, when he made a significant case for flexible exchange rates that any resulting instability would primarily be the result of macroeconomic instability; however, an empirical analysis conducted in 1999 found no apparent connection. They had assumed, based on neoclassical theory that capital would move from developed economies with large capital stocks to developing nations with small capital stocks, as the returns on investment would be greater there. Financial capital flows tend to lower the cost of capital for developing nations, encouraging more investment there. Direct physical capital investments encourage specialization and the transfer of knowledge and technology. But the final result of these measures was not what was anticipated. Empirical analysis has been required to address the issue of how to weigh the benefits of volatility against its costs, as theoretical considerations alone are insufficient. An overview of the empirical data can be found in an International Monetary Fund working paper from 2006. The benefits of liberalizing capital movements and claims that it is to blame for the recent wave of financial crises were not well supported by the authors' research. They contend that while certain nations may experience net gains if they are able to meet the requirements for financial competence, others may experience delayed benefits and increased susceptibility to disruptions in capital flows.

1.1.4.1. Policies and institutions

Even though most developed nations now have floating exchange rates, many developing nations and some of them still have nominally fixed exchange rates, typically relative to the US dollar or the euro. Adopting a fixed rate necessitates the central bank of the nation to intervene in the foreign exchange market and is typically accompanied by some level of control over the citizens' access to foreign markets. While some governments, like Denmark, have kept their national currencies but have pegged them at a fixed rate to an adjacent common currency, other governments have given up on their national currencies in favor of the common currency of a currency area like the Eurozone. The International Monetary Fund's (IMF) economic policies have had a significant impact on global affairs, particularly for developing nations. In order to promote global cooperation on monetary issues, stabilize exchange rates, and establish an international payments system, the IMF was established in 1944. Its main function is to make loan payments to member nations in order to assist them in reestablishing their depleted currency reserves and overcoming balance of payments issues. However, the introduction of economic policies by recipient governments that the Fund's economists deem to create recovery-friendly conditions is a requirement for their loans. Their suggested economic policies, known as the Washington Consensus, are essentially those that have been implemented in the US and the other major developed nations and frequently involve eliminating all barriers to foreign investment. Joseph Stiglitz and other critics have harshly criticized the Fund for what they see as the improper enforcement of those policies and for neglecting to alert recipient nations to the potential risks associated with the volatility of capital movements.

1.1.4.2. International Financial Stability

Regulators and their economic advisors have known since the Great Depression that financial crises can have severe economic repercussions and that they can spread quickly from one nation to another. Governments implemented stringent regulations on the operations and behavior of banks and other credit agencies for many years after becoming aware of this. However, in the 1980s, a number of governments adopted a deregulation strategy, believing that the efficiency gains that would ensue would exceed any potential systemic risks. The article on financial economics describes the wide range of financial innovations that ensued. One of their main effects has been to make the financial markets more globally interconnected and to build an international financial system that possesses the traits that control theory refers to as complex-interactive. Analysis of the stability of such a system is challenging due to the multitude of potential failure scenarios. The October 1987 stock market crash, the 1990s Japanese asset price collapse, the 1997 Asian financial crisis, the 1998 Russian government default (which brought down the Long-Term Capital Management hedge fund), and the 2007–2008 subprime mortgage crisis were among the globally systemic crises that followed. Typically, the signs have been asset price collapses, rises in risk premiums, and overall decreases in liquidity. Several international institutions have proposed measures aimed at mitigating the vulnerability of the international financial system. The Financial Stability Forum, which was established in 1999 to identify and address systemic weaknesses, has made some recommendations in an interim report. The Bank for International Settlements made two consecutive recommendations (Basel I and Basel II) concerning the regulation of banks, as well as a coordinating group of regulating authorities.

1.1.5. Migration

The assumption that there is a net increase in economic welfare as a result of international migration stems from basic considerations. It has been discovered that the primary cause of wage disparities between developed and developing nations is productivity discrepancies, which are likely primarily caused by variations in the availability of physical, social, and human capital. According to economic theory, moving a skilled worker from an area with relatively low returns on skill to one with relatively high returns on skill should result in a net gain (even though it would likely drive down skilled workers' wages in the receiving nation). Numerous econometric studies have been conducted in an effort to measure those gains. According to a Copenhagen Consensus study, there would be $675 billion in annual global benefits by 2025 if the proportion of foreign workers in wealthy countries increased to 3% of the labor force. Nonetheless, a House of Lords committee concluded after reviewing the data that there aren't many economic advantages to immigration to the

UK. Evidence from the US also points to comparatively minor economic gains for the receiving nation and a negligible local wage decline as a result of immigrants' presence in the labor market.From the perspective of a developing nation, the brain drain—the exodus of skilled workers—represents a loss of human capital, depriving the remaining workforce of their assistance. The remittances that emigrants send home, along with the increased skill and education that some of them bring with them, partially offset this effect on the welfare of the parent country. According to one study, there is an additional compensating factor that makes migrating advantageous because it encourages education enrollment, which can lead to brain gain and offset the loss of human capital associated with emigration. However, depending on the purposes for which remittances are used, these factors may be counterbalanced in turn. Remittances have the potential to further encourage emigration by acting as a resource to ease the migration process, as evidence from Armenia suggests, rather than as a contractual tool.

Although certain research indicates that emigration of skilled workers can be advantageous to parent countries, emigration of unskilled and semi-skilled workers typically benefits countries of origin economically by relieving pressure on employment creation. When highly skilled emigration is concentrated in one industry, like medicine, the effects can be dire and even catastrophic. In some cases, about half of the trained doctor population has left the country. The important issue is that the migrants themselves must return to and reinvest in their home countries, as the OECD recently acknowledged. As a result, European government policies are increasingly centered on facilitating skilled temporary migration in addition to migrant remittances. Government policies have attempted to restrict migration flows since 1973, often without any economic justification, in contrast to the movement of capital and goods. Due to these limitations, the vast majority of migration flows have been diverted toward illegal immigration and fictitious asylum requests. The gain from labor migration flows is actually greater than the minimal gains calculated for legal flows because these migrants work in unskilled industries for lower wages and frequently for free social insurance costs. However, there are significant side effects as well, such as diminished political support for immigration, lower wages for the host population in unskilled industries, and higher policing expenses in addition to lower tax revenues.

1.1.6. Globalization

Although the term "globalization" has many different connotations, in the context of economics, it describes the process by which capital, labor, and their products are moving toward complete mobility, i.e., the world's economies are moving toward complete integration. Reductions in politically imposed barriers and transportation costs are the process's driving forces. This is a long-term process that has picked up steam in the last five decades, but it is far from finished. Eventually, as investors, wage earners, corporate and individual taxpayers threatened to leave in search of better terms, interest rates, wage rates, and corporate and income tax rates would all become equal due to competition. In actuality, there aren't many indications that tax, wage, or interest rates are convergent globally. While there are some areas where the world is more integrated than before World War I, many middle-eastern nations are less globalized than they were 24 years ago, and overall the world is less integrated than it was before the war. The financial markets have seen the largest integration efforts out of all, with globalization there estimated to have tripled since the mid-1970s. According to recent research, it has only improved risk-sharing in developed nations; in developing nations, it has increased macroeconomic volatility. Globally, it is estimated to have increased net welfare, but there have also been losers. Recessions have also spread more easily between nations as a result of increased globalization. One of the ways the business cycle spreads from nation to nation is through the reduction in demand for exports resulting from a decline in economic activity in one nation, which in turn causes a decline in activity in its trading partners. Empirical studies verify that a country's business cycles are more coordinated the more trade links it has with other nations. Macroeconomic policy conduct can be significantly impacted by globalization as well. Paul Krugman also used the Mundell-Fleming model and its extensions to provide a basic explanation of the Asian financial crisis. These models are frequently used to analyze the role of capital mobility. In certain cases, globalization can be blamed for a portion of the rise in income inequality that has occurred within nations.

According to a recent IMF report, globalization and technological change were equally responsible for the rise in inequality in developed countries, while globalization alone was partially responsible for the increase in inequality in developing countries between 1981 and 2004.

1.1.6.1. Opposition

Most economists, though not all of them, believe that globalization promotes economic welfare. Joseph Stiglitz, a professor at Columbia University's School of International and Public Affairs, has defended emerging industries in developing nations against aid conditions set by the International Monetary Fund. The advantages of globalization are not evenly distributed, as noted by Harvard Professor Dani Rodrik. It has also resulted in income inequality, negative losses of social capital in the parent countries, and social tensions brought on by immigration in the receiving countries. Martin Wolf has provided an in-depth critical analysis of these claims, and Professor Jagdish Bhagwati has summarized the discussion among economists in a lecture.

1.1.7. Trading Blocks Concept in International Economics

Interest in regional economic integration of national economies has grown since the end of World War II. Political squabbles and unanticipated economic obstacles have frequently caused the formation of regional alliances, trade blocs, and treaties to fail. The desire to expand one's market to include multiple national economies stems from realizing the constraints imposed by national borders and the potential advantages of doing so.

Through the implementation of similar trade policies toward outsiders and the reduction of direct and indirect trade barriers, regional trade agreements represent an attempt by a group of countries to increase trade and investment flows. Multinational trade blocs are a significant worldwide trend. Geographically adjacent nations make up the majority of these blocks, which are centered on a select few more developed economies. This demonstrates even more how crucial proximity and closeness are in creating network structures. In this context, proximity refers to a country's geographic proximity as well as its economic and social affinities. Smaller member nations are protected from marginalization through such trade and economic conglomerations, which also give the group a larger role in the global economy. Global trade and regional trade blocs like ASEAN, the EU, and NAFTA will drive economic growth, according to a recent study on future high growth areas.

A trade agreement's common trading policies and member-only preferential treatment have the dual benefit of fostering intraregional trade and disadvantageously affecting outsiders. For investors, this has two important ramifications. First, many businesses choose to locate inside a trade area in order to take advantage of the intra-regional preferential arrangements because doing so entails liability as an outsider. Second, most nations strive for increased trade and economic integration rather than just standardizing their trade policies. This is further demonstrated by the degree of economic integration among Western European nations, which is steadily rising. Due to regional standardization of laws and business practices, these trends increase market similarities. The literature has shown that market similarities play a significant role in influencing decisions about which foreign markets to pursue. Additionally, since harmonization of trade practices eliminates the need for different trade approaches for different markets, costs related to international commerce can be lowered when conducting business in similar markets. Concerns about how regional trade relationships in Europe, Asia, and Latin America will affect excluded nations and the global trading system have come up as a result of their rapid growth. Concerned observers believe that discriminatory regional blocs may be forming within the multilateral system. Others believe that regional accords will surpass the outcomes of the Uruguay Round and serve as foundational pieces for additional global liberalization and WTO regulations in uncharted territory. Through in-depth empirical research, Jeffrey Frankel demonstrates that the new generation of preferential trade agreements is, in fact, regionally concentrating trade. Subsequently, he evaluates the "natural" or "supernatural" nature of regional blocs, i.e., if they increase or decrease global welfare. He comes to the conclusion that the trading system would be forced into the supernatural zone of excessive regionalization if there were a move toward total liberalization within blocs without a corresponding decrease in barriers between blocs. However, more balanced liberalization patterns produce positive results. He examines regionalism from two perspectives: the formal trading agreements that are currently in place and the more expansive continent-sized groupings (the Americas, Europe, and the Asia Pacific) that are being discussed. In addition, Frankel's research evaluates the political and economic aspects of regionalization and its consequences for public policy and global economic prospects. Frankel concludes by outlining various policy recommendations for pursuing partial regional liberalization among blocs as a first step toward free trade on a global scale.

1.1.7.1. Conditions for Success of Trading Blocks

Whether the World Trade Organization, the European-Mediterranean agreements, and the Arab common markets are complementary or substitute arrangements is one of the questions that is brought up these days. This is a provocative and relevant question, but it's also intriguing because it lacks a clear answer. For example, a common belief is that nations could be forced to abide by the terms of regional trade agreements and not necessarily feel compelled to expand their market openings. All of the Middle East's and North Africa's countries are currently dealing with it or will soon have to deal with it, making it relevant and not just academic. As a matter of fact, these nations have been working to liberalize their trade policies while also seeking to join the Arab common market and engaging in negotiations with the EU. Furthermore, it is provocative because many people who attempt to respond to it may wind up endorsing the Euro-Med accords over an Arab common market, which would enrage others. Whether trade agreements are stepping stones or obstacles toward complete liberalization will determine whether they complement or replace the WTO. It also depends on how beneficial these agreements are to the development of the respective nations. In this regard, these agreements appear to be advantageous under three circumstances. Initially, these accords function best when nations possess the financial and political motivation to finalize them. The fundamental problem here is that political realities may outweigh economic incentives even when they exist, and vice versa. For instance, nations in the Arab world have been attempting to establish a common market for a while now. It's possible that the economic incentives are insufficient to move nations in that direction, despite the likelihood of the existence of political incentives. There isn't an Arab common market as a result. Simultaneously, during the past 24 months, trade agreements have been inked by Morocco, Tunisia, and Egypt with the EU; additional Arab nations are in the process of negotiating similar agreements. The rationale behind these nations' signing of trade agreements with the EU is the existence of economic incentives plus the absence of political constraints. Stated differently, it is difficult to come up with strong justifications for these nations to refuse to sign trade agreements with the EU. Additionally, the close proximity of Europe and the Middle East to one another as well as the absence of competition between their disparate production structures are favorable factors for trade cooperation; the latter is lacking among Arab nations, where production structures are strikingly similar.

Second, when complementary domestic reforms are implemented concurrently with trade agreements, they are successful. For example, if Egypt signs a trade agreement with the EU, its domestic industry will face increased competition from European producers as tariff barriers are removed. Even as European inputs become more affordable, the transaction costs of domestic production may eventually prove to be too high, even though the nation may initially have a comparative advantage in labor costs, to the point where Egyptian exporters would not be able to penetrate European markets. Therefore, in order for Egypt or any other nation to fully benefit from a trade agreement with the EU, these transaction costs—which include processing, shipping and communications, and even bribery—must be decreased. Furthermore, investment concentrations will occur in regions with low production costs and sizable export markets. Investors will therefore typically search elsewhere to the extent that transaction costs are high and domestic reforms are not implemented to lower them. To summarize, the accomplishment of trade agreements requires the implementation of domestic reforms. Third, some trade agreements might prove advantageous in the long run even if they don't seem like they would be in the short term. This has to do with the ability to reconcile "horizontal integration," or trade agreements amongst countries in the region, and "vertical integration," or trade agreements between countries in the region and the EU. It might seem that a nation like Egypt would benefit from opening its economy first to a major trading partner like the EU rather than to other nations in the region given the current political and economic incentives. Ultimately, roughly half of Egypt's total exports and imports are made to and from the EU, respectively.

Conversely, less than 10% of the nation's total trade is with other countries in the region. Therefore, it doesn't seem that integration within the region is currently nearly as desirable as integration with the EU, based on strictly revealed preferences. Furthermore, investors from the EU and possibly all three countries will choose to locate where they can serve a larger market, namely the EU, as Egypt, Morocco, and Tunisia move toward greater economic integration with the EU. This will further lessen the appeal of horizontal integration. But eventually, as these nations open up and become more appealing to investors, it will be advantageous for them to integrate horizontally since it would expand their market and draw more investors to the area. Put another way, even though horizontal integration might not seem appealing from an economic standpoint in the near run, it is likely to prove advantageous in the long run due to the benefits that come with vertical integration with the EU.

1.1.7.2. Forms of Trading Blocks

There are four different forms of trading blocs:

- **Free Trade Area**: A free trade area (FTA) is created when the parties to a preferential trade agreement remove all tariffs and quantitative import restrictions among themselves (also known as 100% preferences). They usually keep different degrees of tariffs and other restrictions on goods from non-member countries. It is possible that the more powerful member nations' uncompetitive industries will exert enough influence to keep their shields from being lowered to the same extent as those of the less powerful nations.
- **Customs Union**: When an FTA's members remove trade barriers among themselves and establish a common level of trade barriers against outsiders, they reach the next level of integration. This requires a common external tariff, at the very least. In addition, quantitative limits, export subsidies, and other trade distortions would be harmonized under a complete customs union. In fact, it would establish trade policy for all of its members collectively. For instance, it would speak with one voice in any upcoming trade talks with other nations.
- **Common Market**: A common market includes the free movement of labor and capital, the two factors of production, in addition to the unrestricted exchange of goods and services among its participants. It is true that there are instances when it is difficult to distinguish between the free movement of factors and the free exchange of services: capital includes banking and other financial services, while labor includes services like consulting and construction. Both portfolio capital and foreign direct investment (FDI), which is the buying and selling of real estate, machinery, and equipment across international borders, are covered by the free movement of capital.

This is deep integration because, even with a high degree of trade integration, it affects certain laws and institutions that could have remained as domestic prerogatives.

- **Economic Union**: Economic union goes beyond the free movement of factors, products, and services. It entails coordinating national economic policies, usually involving taxes and a single currency. A single central bank and a single currency are in place. Both the monetary and fiscal policies are well-coordinated, with the central bank making some decisions. The European Community's decision to become the European Union in 1994 signified a commitment to moving forward with this more advanced level of integration. In exchange for the central decision-making authority, the member nations of an economic union must give up a great deal of economic and social freedom.

1.2. INTERNATIONAL TRADE AND ECONOMIC GROWTH

The concepts of international trade and economic growth are complementary to one another because trade has multiple positive effects on a nation's economy. Import and export effects, specialization, higher productivity, and better infrastructure are a few of these methods. By boosting that nation's income, exporting goods to other nations can aid in the development of the exporting nation. Some nations' national economies even rely on and are supported by their exports. For example, the financial support of their countries comes from the export of crude oil and its derivatives in certain oil-producing nations. A number of these nations truly base the planning of their national budgets on estimates or computations of the anticipated revenue from oil exports. In addition to crude oil, other nations also rely in part on revenue from precious stones, agricultural products, and even technology to fund their national budgets. This illustrates one connection between global trade and economic expansion.

In addition to commodities, another consequence of globalization is the international labor market. Skills that are greatly needed are brought to countries by immigrants. The majority of immigrants from less developed countries send money to family back home, boosting the economies of those nations. By boosting productivity, they also aid in the economies of the nations in which they reside expanding. For example, migrant laborers are frequently employed on farms as laborers who assist in preparing food items for sale both domestically and abroad. More competent immigrants help their host nation's economy flourish by bringing in engineers, physicians, and nurses, among other professions. The growth in productivity is another factor that links international trade to economic growth. The countries that manufacture a given product will automatically increase production to keep up with demand when there is a high demand for it. This rise results in increased income and a strengthening of the national economy. The development of an infrastructure needed to support trade is facilitated by a thriving culture of international trade. For example, a nation's need for groundnuts may drive the construction of roads and better transit infrastructure to support the crop's production. In the event that groundnuts are grown on farms situated in villages with inadequate road systems, it is possible that the government or other corporate entities will construct improved roads.

1.2.1. Benefits of World Trade Organization

The World Trade Organization (WTO) states that its mission is to facilitate trade between importers, exporters, and producers of goods and services. This multinational organization primarily does this by assisting nations in creating and approving trade regulations. Trade relations between foreign entities could be challenging, unfair, and inconsistent in the absence of such an organization. Three official languages of the World Trade Organization are Spanish, French, and English. The organization was founded in 1995. Nonetheless, the organization strives to act in the best interests of all of its hundreds of members worldwide. The majority of WTO decisions are reached by consensus. This indicates that they are accepted by all members. The rights and obligations of the parties to a trade agreement are typically included. In general, there are two types of WTO agreements. Multilateral agreements are those to which every member of the World Trade Organization has consented. Agreements that only a few members have signed are known as bilateral agreements. Cultures vary widely amongst different nations. Many in the business world are aware that culture can play a significant role in influencing how things are handled. Other elements, such as prior experiences—both positive and negative—can influence the choices made in business. If such business agreements were left up to the whim of individuals, these are just two of the numerous examples of factors that could result in trade barriers or trade inconsistencies. Normalizing trade is one of the objectives of the World Trade Organization. This implies that some procedures need to be followed consistently. For instance, the group might negotiate agreements with trading partners that forbid politics from being involved in the imposition or escalation of tariffs. The World Trade Organization seeks to end discrimination in international trade in addition to facilitating trade. This may have the dual advantages of giving consumers access to international goods and giving producers access to international markets. This can also keep some people from experiencing significant economic growth while unfairly or unethically stifling it for others. The World Trade Organization's role as an agency for monitoring is another one. In other words, the organization aims to make sure that parties that reached a consensus respect their choices. Despite the agreements they sign, members frequently have a great deal of freedom and flexibility to create their own policies. The WTO has the authority to examine national policies and collaborate with members on matters that could impede trade, stifle development, or possibly go against agreements.

1.3. BARRIER OF INTERNATIONAL TRADE AND ECONOMIC GROWTH

Language, cultural, legal, and regulatory barriers are a few things that prevent goods from being traded internationally. Trading companies may also run into miscommunications regarding the terms of contracts, which can cause issues with freight, insurance, or payment for goods. Different countries have different laws pertaining to land, employment, intellectual property, and public health, which can be problematic for multinational corporations. Unsuspecting traders may fall victim to fluctuations in currency exchange rates, as well as increases in inflation or interest rates in the foreign nation. In many nations, the odds are stacked against foreign companies by import tariffs and quotas along with subsidies for home industries. One of the historical obstacles to global trade was the movement of goods, but these logistical issues have diminished with the advent of contemporary cargo ships, containerization, and advanced container ports, including inland dry ports. Standardized contract terms have helped minimize misunderstandings in international transactions, and governments frequently provide guarantees to businesses seeking export funding. Businesses may need to seek guidance in order to protect themselves from foreign exchange rate fluctuations, inflation, and other financial risks associated with doing business abroad. Businesses must deal with licensing laws, company law, investment regulations, and tax laws when opening a branch or subsidiary abroad. To handle such issues, they typically require local business advice; however, there might also be opportunities, like free zones or special economic zones, in the other nation. Businesses in some sectors, such as the food and children's product industries, may run into issues with health and safety regulations. Certain businesses might have to adjust their products to accommodate regional preferences and customs.

Tariffs and quotas are the most obvious obstacles to international trade. Developed nations frequently impose high tariffs on agricultural imports and sometimes pair these measures with support for their own domestic farmers. They may also set quotas that restrict the annual import of a particular category of manufactured goods. To defend their own pioneer producers, developing nations may erect tariff barriers against imports of goods in specific industries. Even though it is widely acknowledged that protectionism harms both national incomes and international trade, nations typically prioritize their own national interests when deciding on trade matters. Talks and negotiations on trade barriers are held by international organizations like the World Trade Organization (WTO). These frequently focus on touchy subjects like tariffs and subsidies on agricultural products, tariffs and quotas on manufactured goods, and obstacles to the international provision of services. The protection of intellectual property is another delicate topic in international trade since foreign businesses frequently lament the inadequate patent laws in some nations.

1.3.1. Terms of Trade

Terms of trade are the differences in price that a nation pays for its imports and the prices it sells its goods for. A nation's terms of trade are said to have improved if the prices of its exports increase in relation to the prices of its imports. This is because the nation now effectively receives more imports for every unit of goods exported. The terms of trade specify how the profits from international trade will be divided among trading nations and are based on the global supply and demand for the goods involved. Additionally, the idea is applied to various economic sectors (e.g., the manufacturing and agricultural sectors). A sudden modification to a nation's trade terms (e.g., a significant decline in the price of a primary product that is a nation's principal export) can result in major balance-of-payments issues if the nation depends on the foreign exchange received from its exports to pay for the import of its capital equipment and manufactured goods. A thorough analysis of trade statistics has not revealed any evidence to support any of the numerous theories that have been proposed to explain changes in the terms of trade. A long-held misconception was that less developed nations' exports were mostly primary goods (like coffee or rubber), while their imports were mostly manufactured and, thus, more expensive goods from developed nations. This led to the idea that the terms of trade tended to move against less developed nations. More recent research has looked at the potential effects on a nation's terms of trade of labor inflows (via immigration) and capital inflows (through foreign investment).

1.3.2. Aspects of International Trade

Businesses in different countries typically specialize in different sectors; for instance, industrialized countries may have companies that specialize in high-tech manufacturing or financial services, while developing countries may export primarily agricultural products. Businesses in different countries conduct international trade when they are efficient enough to be competitive on the international market. International agreements and organizations have attempted to increase trade by reducing tariff barriers and providing dispute resolution procedures. Governments impose tariffs or quotas to protect specific domestic industries from foreign imports. Improved transportation methods, containerization, and uniform terms for international contracts have all benefited world trade. International agreements and organizations like the World Trade Organization (WTO) have made it easier to trade internationally. Negotiations have resulted in the removal of quotas and tariffs that were impeding global trade. In the event that disagreements arise regarding the application of tariffs, a dispute resolution process exists that entails the imposition of fines on nations that violate regulations. WTO negotiations guarantee that international trade issues are carefully considered, despite the fact that international agreements are frequently difficult to reach. Reducing farmer subsidies in developed nations and taking into account the need for protection for agriculture and other sectors in less developed nations are among the issues pertaining to global trade that still need to be resolved as of 2011.

The advent of containerization has greatly simplified the logistics of shipping goods internationally. International trade has been boosted by the growth of large container seaports, inland dry ports, and quick docking, loading, and unloading procedures. Larger ships can carry heavier loads and are guided to ports by radar. The ports have grown in size to handle the cargo and have built the necessary infrastructure to move it quickly.

The efforts of groups like the International Chamber of Commerce (ICC) have harmonized terms used in international contracts. Standard contracts lessen the likelihood of misunderstandings regarding the division of freight and insurance expenses between buyers and sellers. In order to ensure that financial matters are completed as quickly and smoothly as possible, letters of credit have been modified in response to the decrease in payment concerns brought about by the increased use of electronic means of payment.

The implementation of dispute resolution mechanisms by organizations like the United Nations Commission on International Trade Law (UNCITRAL) may facilitate the resolution of disputes pertaining to international trade. By establishing bilateral investment protection agreements that offer specific guarantees to investors and provide for dispute resolution, nations have made it easier for businesses to conduct business internationally. In a similar vein, bilateral agreements aimed at preventing double taxation of companies engaged in international trade also serve as a means of resolving tax disputes between nations.

1.3.3. Dispute the Trade Barriers

Trade barriers are any of several limitations on international trade imposed by governments. The most prevalent ones include embargoes, tariffs, quotas, duties, and subsidies. The theoretical elimination of all trade restrictions, enabling totally unrestricted trade, is referred to as "free trade.." In actuality, though, no country fully supports free trade since every country uses a variety of barriers to further their own interests. Tariffs, which are essentially taxes on goods as they cross national borders, are a fairly common type of trade barrier. Although they occasionally apply to both imports and exports, tariffs are almost always imposed on goods that are brought into the nation. Because tariffs were a simple way to levy taxes on ships as they arrived in the country, they historically constituted a significant source of income for the government. Tariffs may be applied for a variety of purposes. Certain tariffs are merely imposed to generate revenue for the government. This could be a fixed price for a certain item or it could be determined by the item's market value. As a kind of protectionism, other tariffs are in place to raise the price of imported goods relative to their normal value in order to shield domestic industries. For instance, the cost of manufacturing a single gadget might be about 10 units if the nation has high labor standards and a fairly high wage. Imports of that nation's widgets could easily put the home industry out of business if a neighboring nation can produce a widget for three units. In order to ensure that domestic widget prices always remain competitive, the nation may impose a restrictive tariff on widget imports or even make it impossible for widgets to be imported at all. Another common form of trade barrier is subsidies, which are frequently implemented to safeguard home industries. Even though the primary goal of subsidies may be to lower the cost of some essential goods for the country's citizens, the ultimate effect may still be to render imports non-competitive. For instance, a lot of food crops receive significant subsidies to guarantee that the public always has access to reasonably priced food. To guarantee that a country always has a domestic steel supply—which can be vital in times of war when regular shipping routes may be cut off—steel is also frequently subsidized. The strongest form of trade restriction is an embargo. Embargoes essentially forbid the import or export of goods into or from another nation. This is frequently carried out as a kind of punishment or in an attempt to compel the nation to go through an internal radical transformation as a result of its fragile economic situation.

Because the embargo was historically employed as a military strategy, it was frequently interpreted as a declaration of war. Even with the most severe of barriers, a declaration of war nowadays is typically not seen as an act of overt aggression, even though it is frequently followed by an embargo.

There are numerous free trade organizations worldwide that work to reduce the use of trade barriers by countries. The World Trade Organization is arguably the most expansive of these organizations, enforcing stringent regulations against its member countries that limit the permissible application of measures like tariffs. Because of this, some nations have started implementing trade restrictions that function similarly to tariffs but are not the same. For instance, the bulk of food imports from the United States are essentially prohibited by European Union regulations prohibiting the importation of numerous genetically modified organisms. Organizations like the WTO have started to examine these types of trade barriers in recent years and remove them when practical.

1.3.4. Role of International Trade Center

An international trade center uses cooperative and instructional initiatives to promote global trade. Usually, the purpose of these centers is to support business interests with practical assistance and to promote active international trade. Centers can help on a regional, governmental, or worldwide scale. An international trade center also helps by providing a networking space for government representatives and business people. An international trade center's duties also include advising national and local governments on how to promote global trade.

There is an intricate network of interactions between different business entities all over the world. When attempting to ship or receive goods internationally, a single business—regardless of size—may run into obstacles and other problems. Businesses looking to trade internationally may find guidance and useful support from the staff at an international trade center. For example, a U.S. business in Washington State may seek to increase exports of wood products to Japan, but the business owner might have insufficient knowledge of trading customs and legal requirements that may be involved.

These trade centers provide assistance to companies in establishing trade relations with foreign trading partners. Understanding the traditions and business practices of another nation may be part of the training. For instance, in the U.S. Spending a significant amount of time socializing prior to starting a business negotiation is frequently regarded as impolite. However, it might be impolite to enter trade talks too soon in many Middle Eastern nations as certain social cordialities need time to materialize—hours or even days.

Though not always, a local international trade hub is located close to a national border. These hubs are usually found near the world's largest ports, where exporters' and importers' agents may have offices. These establishments might also be found in cities with foreign airports. An international trade center's amenities frequently include meeting spaces for business trade professionals to connect with one another. Individuals who have gained some experience in trading relationships can impart their knowledge to beginners, resulting in cooperative partnerships. Referrals to freight forwarding firms or attorneys who specialize in drafting contracts for trading partners are examples of information that could be shared. Because building trade relations with other countries is time-consuming and expensive, it is frequently advantageous for individual companies within a nation to join a trade delegation. An international trade center's employees may also instruct and counsel decision-makers on how to strengthen fruitful trade ties. A small but embarrassing slip-up could ruin a fruitful business relationship. Should a politician make the mistake, it could have serious consequences.

1.3.5. Patterns of Trade

1.3.5.1. Degrees of National Participation

Countries differ greatly in how much they trade internationally. In general, a country's involvement in foreign trade decreases with increasing physical size and population, primarily due to the greater variety of raw materials available within its borders and the larger size of its internal market. Therefore, in terms of the percentage of GDP that the United States and the former Soviet Union have contributed, they have done so at relatively low rates. The U.S.S. Nonetheless, the United States continues to be one of the most significant trading nations in the world due to its enormous GDP in comparison to other nations. The combined export and import amounts of a few of the smaller Western European nations, like the Netherlands, come close to matching their GDPs.

1.3.5.2. Trade Among Developed Countries

Trade between developed, capital-rich nations accounts for the majority of trade volume; these include major industrialized nations like Australia, Belgium, Canada, France, Germany, Italy, Japan, the Netherlands, Spain, Sweden, the United Kingdom, and the United States. A nation's participation in international trade typically increases faster than its GDP as it becomes more economically developed. The benefits of increased trade between these nations are aptly demonstrated by the EU. It is highly likely that the elimination of trade barriers is responsible for a significant portion of the increases in real income in EU member states. However, since EU members impose tariffs on goods coming from outside the Union, the EU's formation cannot be seen as unqualifiedly embracing the free-trade principle.

1.3.5.3. Trade Between Developed and Developing Countries

Trade between developed and developing nations often gives rise to challenging issues. The economies of the majority of less developed nations are based on agriculture, and many of them are tropical, so they are largely dependent on the export of one or two commodities, like sugar, coffee, or cacao. These products are subject to fierce competition on the market, as defined by economists, meaning that price changes are highly responsive to shifts in supply or demand. On the other hand, the costs of manufactured goods, which are developed nations' usual exports, are typically far more stable.

As a result, the tropical nation's "terms of trade," or the ratio of export prices to import prices, fluctuate greatly in tandem with the price of its export commodity, frequently having detrimental effects on the home economy. Price stabilization and output control have been attempted for almost all significant primary commodities. The results of these efforts have been mixed. There has been much debate over trade between developed and developing nations. The exploitation of foreign labor, the environment, and the needs for domestic labor are cited by critics as multinational corporations from developed nations shift their operations to less developed nations with cheaper labor pools and less political or economic clout. The work of the WTO came under increasing scrutiny from its critics, particularly after 1999, when trade talks were interrupted by anti-globalization protestors during the WTO ministerial conference in Seattle. The most serious criticisms focused on issues like the rights of domestic workers, the democratic nature of the WTO, national sovereignty, the impact on the environment, health and safety, and the wisdom of supporting free trade and commercialism at the expense of other values. These critics raised a variety of concerns about the authority and reach of the WTO.

1.4. GLOBALIZATION AND INTERNATIONAL MARKETING

In relation to the business operations of large multinational companies, it is imperative to address and discuss the concepts of globalization and international marketing. The integration of economies on a worldwide scale is known as globalization, and it has two primary components. The majority of trade in the global economy occurs between multinational corporations, according to the first main feature of globalization. The second main feature highlights that money moves around the world economy primarily through foreign investments, derivatives, and other financial transactions. To put it simply, globalization is the opening up and interacting of various economies worldwide in response to the need for a more expansive and varied market. This means that the idea of an international market then becomes pertinent because the goal of globalization is to widen and diversify its market. International marketing is the practice of promoting goods and services across national boundaries. In this context, the environment in which goods and services are supplied varies from nation to nation, as do the costs associated with those goods and services. In certain nations, certain goods and services are completely unavailable. This definition makes it clear that the goals of international marketing and globalization—market diversification and expansion—are comparable. The distinction, though, is that globalization might result from international marketing.

With the aim of increasing profits, sales, and consumer recognition, many business organizations and companies concentrate on and participate in international marketing. Additionally, business organizations can further develop and improve their products, services, strategies, systems, and operations through the use of international marketing. This is due to the fact that global markets present enormous business opportunities for companies that have highly sought-after goods or services that are in line with their uniqueness, ability to adapt to different cultures, attractiveness, and effective marketing techniques. Additionally, companies that concentrate on international marketing have the opportunity to learn more about their industry and gain the ability to offer their customers more cutting-edge services and goods.

This opens the discussion of international marketing strategies. Multinational corporations employ international marketing strategies and techniques in an effort to broaden and diversify their customer base. Exporting is primarily a company's first approach to entering a foreign market. Exporting entails marketing goods that have been manufactured or assembled in a target nation. It also refers to the process of producing a good in one nation and selling it to another. Since exporting involves few investments and is a low-risk strategy, this is where international businesses start. The second tactic is to forge a long-lasting presence in the foreign nation through contract manufacturing, which entails having a third party produce goods while a particular company handles some of the marketing duties to save money. The third strategy involves licensing and franchising local businesses' products. These are low exposure methods of entry because they give other people or groups of people the ability to use the company's trademarks and accumulated expertise, giving them little control over how the business is run. Additionally, companies can build their brand and reputation in a foreign market by importing raw materials and other equipment or sourcing components from other countries. This would help the business in some way build its name and reputation in the other nation, giving it ample opportunity to be recognized by its intended market. The final approach or technique for entering the market is direct entry, in which the company either establishes operations with the greatest exposure or buys a company. By using direct entry strategies, the company maintains more control over its information and resource management while learning more about the target country's local market.

Businesses and organizations employ these tactics to guarantee their place in the target nation's market. By employing these strategies, business organizations and firms are able to concentrate on their objectives, which increases their focus when it comes to seizing opportunities that they may view as giving them an advantage over rival businesses in the same sector. Additionally, by using these tactics and approaches, multinational corporations and firms would be able to gather sufficient and pertinent data about their target market and nation, which would be helpful for the development and enhancement of their products and services. By employing these tactics, they are able to contribute to and further the process of globalization. Global strategies share the same objectives as international marketing strategies and techniques employed by businesses in their global marketing endeavors. The majority of businesses view globalization as simply taking an excellent business model and expanding it geographically while making the required adjustments to optimize the business's economies of scale. According to this viewpoint, the main strategic challenge is simply figuring out how much of the business model to localize in response to local differences and how much to standardize across national borders. The harmony between standardization and localization does not, however, ignore the reality that no two businesses are the same, including in terms of their potential for growth. On the other hand, national differences are seen as challenges that must be overcome.

Companies today understand that differences can be both a benefit and a disadvantage for their business and sales. This is demonstrated by the sizable international corporation Coca-Cola. Almost everywhere in the world, The Coca-Cola Company is the most well-known producer, marketer, and distributor of syrups, concentrates, and non-alcoholic beverages. Since it can appreciate and acknowledge the cultural variations across nations and continents, it is regarded as a global company that actively engages in the globalization process. Through product innovation and development, Coca-Cola was able to educate and learn from its mistakes in order to continue serving, meeting, and satisfying the demands of its customers. This allowed the company to play a major role in the globalization process, as building their brand and reputation on a worldwide scale not only increased sales and profits but also allowed them to support and encourage education and learning through the Coca-Cola Foundation. The main objective of the Coca-Cola Foundation, which was established and is currently active in almost 200 nations, is to assist those in need, particularly those who do not have access to formal education or knowledge. This indicates and proves that the Coca-Cola Company has been successful in its pursuits and has thereby aided in the globalization process.

Furthermore, the idea that going global does not require a company to have a global presence similar to that of Coca-Cola runs counter to the company's global strategy. This essentially means that the business has to understand global markets and competition and have chosen the optimal course of action to thrive in those conditions. Although the term "global" refers to the entire world, it actually refers to a collection of smaller, more distinct geographic entities that start with a market in a specific state or province and go farther; as a result, it does not only refer to the involvement of major manufacturers. Numerous furniture producers have established themselves in the European market. Once more, it's critical to realize that a global strategy need not include every continent but rather can be regional in scope, placing a high value on planning above all else. In summary, it appears that the ideas of international marketing and globalization have an impact on each other when it comes to how multinational corporations operate. Developing international marketing strategies helps a multinational company to take part in the globalization process, which improves its capacity to handle any issues or challenges that arise. Moreover, developing international marketing strategies helps a multinational company to acquire pertinent and supplementary information about its target market. Utilizing this knowledge would be beneficial for both the actual process of creating a product or service and its day-to-day operations.

1.4.1. Designing Global Market

The world of the 21st century is portrayed as flat. It's not flat because the earth is getting smaller; rather, it's flat because of advancements in communication. Information, goods, and services are moving more quickly. Developed nations like the United States and the developing economies of China and India sell branded goods like Gucci. The quantity of multinational corporations has grown exponentially. While not all businesses are amenable to the concept of globalization, it is wise for them to think about doing business internationally at some point. Businesses can become global through research and analysis. The first thing that businesses need to ask themselves is: Is globalization necessary? Going global presents certain difficulties, from product mix and design to hiring personnel with experience in international marketing. If foreign markets are more profitable than the home market, a business may choose to expand internationally. A business may choose to enter the global market in order to take advantage of economies of scale or if competitors from other countries are increasing competition in the home market. If a company's customers are moving across national borders, it may choose to become a global player. Being a global player, however, comes with some dreaded consequences if businesses disregard local customs, laws, political climate, foreign exchange policies, and rivalry in the targeted international markets. The next step after deciding to go global for the business is deciding which market to enter. Businesses may decide to enter multiple markets and spread their risk, or they may decide to start small and work their way up from just one market. For instance, with access to 15 countries, the European Union is one of the world's largest markets.

Assessing the potential markets is the next stage. Businesses typically choose to expand internationally by selling to nearby nations. For instance, US businesses favor conducting business in Canada. One of the causes is a deeper comprehension of the market due to similarities in language, culture, and legal systems. Businesses decide to enter markets where they have a competitive advantage, a high market attractiveness rating, and minimal risk. There are several approaches to breaking into foreign markets. One approach to expand internationally is through direct and indirect exporting. Seling goods to domestic export agents is the first step towards becoming a global player in indirect exporting. Direct exporting businesses establish foreign subsidiaries or sales branches. Another strategy for breaking into international markets is licensing, in which a company (the licensor) signs a contract granting another company (the licensee) the right to produce and sell the product in the designated market. Licensing and indirect/direct exporting involve very little investment and risk. A joint venture is an additional method of market entry. The business partners with the regional player to enable direct market entry. The joint venture may have political as well as financial motivations. Direct investment is the final method of entry. Through direct ownership, a business enters the international market through direct investment. Purchasing a nearby business or establishment can accomplish this. Additionally, businesses can establish their own manufacturing facility.

The company should develop a marketing strategy after deciding on the market and the format for entering it. The company must decide whether to develop a fully new strategy for the new market or use standardized, one-size-fits-all marketing. As an alternative, businesses may decide to combine different products, promotions, prices, and locations. At the product level, a business may decide to launch entirely new products, alter the product to suit the tastes and preferences of the local market, or decide to enter the global market with no changes to the original product. A promotion company may select a standard option or alter it to suit the needs of the local market. Costing is a difficult topic. As a result, businesses have three options for setting prices: using a cost-based strategy, introducing market-based pricing in each market, or setting a uniform price across the board. Companies must determine the most effective approach to market at the distribution channel level.

1.4.2. Importance of Trade

1. **Make Use of Abundant Raw Materials**: Certain nations possess an inherent abundance of raw materials, such as fish (Iceland), butter (New Zealand), metals, oil (Qatar), and diamonds from the Congo. These nations would not profit from their natural resources of raw materials without trade. Eli Heckscher and Bertil Ohlin created a theoretical model for

this. The Heckscher–Ohlin model, or H–O model, predicts that nations will focus on manufacturing and exporting goods that make use of plentiful local factor endowments. In places with limited resources, countries will import those goods.

2. **Comparative Advantage**: According to the comparative advantage theory, nations ought to focus on producing goods where the opportunity cost is comparatively lower. One nation shouldn't produce everything, even if it can produce two goods at a lower total cost. India could be at a competitive advantage in labor-intensive production due to its lower labor costs (e.g., call centers, manufacturers of apparel). India would therefore be well served by exporting these products and services. Though the UK economy might have a comparative advantage in the creation of video games and in education. Trade enables national specialization. Further information about how economic welfare can be raised by comparative advantage. Despite its flaws, the theory of comparative advantage can explain at least some parts of international trade.
3. **Greater Choice for Consumers**: Relative input costs and comparative advantage are given less weight in the new trade theory. According to new trade theory, providing customers with a wider selection of unique products is one of the main factors driving trade in the real world. We import BMW vehicles from Germany due to their high quality and reputable brand, not because they are the least expensive. Trade in music and movies allows the greatest selection to satisfy a variety of tastes. The Beatles were exporting British music when they embarked on their US tour in the 1960s, so labor costs were irrelevant. Clothing is a prime example of a good example. Certain apparel (e.g., Value items from Primark are likely imported from Bangladesh or other nations with lower labor costs because price is a major factor. But we also import clothing brands like Chanel (France) and Gucci (Italy). Here, choice—rather than the best deal—benefits the consumer. Economists contend that monopolistic competition is a good fit for the model of international trade. The key component of this model is brand differentiation. We like to purchase a lot of products with well-known brands. e.g., popularity of McDonald's, Addidas, Nike, Coca-Cola, and so forth.
4. **Specialization and Economies of Scale – Greater Efficiency**: Another aspect of new trade theory is that it doesn't really matter what countries specialize in, the important thing is to pursue specialization and this enables companies to benefit from economies of scale which outweigh most other factors. Sometimes, countries may specialize in particular industries for no over-riding reason – it may just be a historical accident. But, that specialization enables improved efficiency. For high value-added products, multinationals often split the production process into a global production system. For example, Apple designs their computers in the US but contract the production

to Asian factories. Trade enables a product to have multiple country sources. With car production, the productive process is often even more global with engines, tires, design and marketing all potentially coming from different countries.

5. **Service Sector Trade**: Trade typically evokes images of tangible goods, such as cars and bananas imported. However, as the economy becomes more service-oriented, trade in invisible goods like banking, insurance, and IT services will increase. Even in the process of creating this website, I occasionally contract with foreign developers for IT services. Maybe for jobs worth as little as $50. In addition, I might export a revision guide for £7.49 to all nations worldwide. A pre-internet era would not have allowed for as many microtrades as it does in a global economy with modern communications.
6. **Global Growth and Economic Development**: Economic growth has been significantly aided by international trade. The rate of absolute poverty has decreased as a result of this growth, particularly in south East Asia, where growth has been rapid since the 1980s.

1.4.3. Problems Arising from Free Trade

Given the importance of free trade to an economy, it is unsurprising that people are concerned about the potential negative impacts.

- **Infant Industry Argument**: There is concern that "free trade" may lead to nations specializing in basic goods with unstable prices and low income elasticity of demand. Restrictions on imports and economic diversification may be necessary for economies to grow. This is not a critique of trade in general; rather, it raises the possibility that trade may require "management" as opposed to merely depending on free markets. View more at Infant Industry Debate.
- **Trade Can Lead to Cultural Homogenization:** Some worry that trade benefits multinational corporations, which could harm regional goods and customs. Proponents contend that if local goods are superior to international brands, they ought to be able to carve out a niche for themselves.
- **Displacement Effects**: Uncompetitive domestic industries may close as a result of free trade, creating structural unemployment. The issue with free trade is that while there are many winners, there is no compensation for the losers. Free-market economists, on the other hand, might argue that since economies always experience some degree of creative destruction, a static, closed economy is unavoidable. Positively, if the uncompetitive businesses close, new jobs will eventually be generated in other industries.

CASE STUDY

INFLATION IN INDIA

By inflation one generally means rise in prices. To be more correct inflation is persistent rise in the general price level rather than a once-for-all rise in it, while deflation is persistent falling price. A situation is described as inflationary when either the prices or the supply of money are rising, but in practice both will rise together. These days economies of all countries whether underdeveloped, developing as well developed suffers from inflation. Inflation or persistent rising prices are major problem today in world. Because of many reasons, first, the rate of inflation these years are much high than experienced earlier periods. Second, Inflation in these years coexists with high rate of unemployment, which is a new phenomenon and made it difficult to control inflation. An inflationary situation is where there is 'too much money chasing too few goods.' As products/services are scarce in relation to the money available in the hands of buyers, prices of the products/services rise to adjust for the larger quantum of money chasing them.

Inflation in Indian Context

Inflation is no stranger to the Indian economy. The Indian economy has been registering stupendous growth after the liberalization of Indian economy. In fact, till the early nineties Indians were used to ignore inflation. But since the mid-nineties controlling inflation has become a priority. The natural fallout of this has been that we, as a nation, have become virtually intolerant to inflation. The opening up of the Indian economy in the early 1990s had increased India's industrial output and consequently has raised the India Inflation Rate. While inflation was primarily caused by domestic factors (supply usually was unable to meet demand, resulting in the classical definition of inflation of too much money chasing too few goods), today the situation has changed significantly.

Inflation today is caused more by global rather than by domestic factors. Naturally, as the Indian economy undergoes structural changes, the causes of domestic inflation too have undergone tectonic changes. The main cause of rise in the rate of inflation rate in India is the pricing disparity of agricultural products between the producer and consumers in the Indian market. Moreover, the sky-rocketing of prices of food products, manufacturing products, and essential commodities have also catapulted the inflation rate in India. Furthermore, the unstable international crude oil prices have worsened the situation.

Defining Causes of Inflation

What exactly is the nature of this inflation which has the nation in its grip? The different causes of inflation which are experienced in Indian economy in a large proportion would be:

- **Demand-Pull Inflation:** This is basically when the aggregate demand in an economy exceeds the aggregate supply. It is also defined as `too much money chasing too few goods.' Bare-boned, it means that a country is capable of producing only 100 items but the demand is for 105 items. It's a very simple demand-supply issue. The more demand there is, the costlier it becomes. Much the same as the way real estate in the country is rising.
- **Cost-Push Inflation:** This is caused when there is a supply shock. This represents the condition where, even though there is no increase in Aggregate Demand, prices may still rise. I.e., non availability of a commodity would lead to increase in prices. This may happen if the costs of especially wage cost rise.
- **Imported Inflation:** This is inflation due to increases in the prices of imports. Increases in the prices of imported final products directly affect any expenditure-based measure of inflation. They play an important role in driving the rise in domestic prices. The rise in the global prices of crude oil and agricultural commodities, including food grains, and industrial products, and setbacks to global economy resulting from sub-prime mortgage disaster and US recession have contributed to India's inflation.

Other Causes:

- When the government of a country print money in excess, prices increase to keep up with the increase in currency, leading to inflation.
- Increase in production and labor costs, have a direct impact on the price of the final product, resulting in inflation.
- When countries borrow money, they have to cope with the interest burden. This interest burden results in inflation.
- High taxes on consumer products, can also lead to inflation. An increase in indirect taxes can also lead to increased production costs.
- Inflation can artificially be created through a circular increase in wage earners demands and then the subsequent increase in producer costs which will drive up the prices of their goods and services. This will then translate back into higher prices for the wage earners or consumers. As demands go higher from each side, inflation will continue to rise.
- Debt, war and other issues that cause a drastic financial blunder can also cause the inflation.

Measuring Inflation

Inflation in India is mainly estimated on the basis of fluctuations in the wholesale price index (WPI). The wholesale price index comprises of the following indices:

- Domestic Wholesale Price Index (DWPI)
- Export Price Index (EPI)
- Import Price Index (IPI)

- Overall Wholesale Price Index (OWPI)

The WPI consists of about 435 items and has three broad categories. They are:-

- Primary Articles (weight of 22.0253) — 22% Index
- Fuel, Power, Light, and Lubricants (weight of 14.2262) – 14% Index
- Manufactured Products (weight of 63.7485) — 64% Index

The base year of the WPI is 1993–94. The base year usually chosen is one where there has been fairly less volatility. The Indian WPI figure is released weekly on every Thursday. But recently the government has approved the proposal to release a wholesale price based inflation data on a monthly basis, instead of every week. The new series of WPI based inflation with 2004–05 as the base year would be launched soon. The move is aimed at improving the accuracy of the inflation data.

The monthly release of WPI is a widely-followed international practice. And, it is expected to improve the quality of data. Collection of price data of manufactured products will, accordingly, have a monthly frequency consistent with the practice of release of WPI. The new series of WPI based inflation with 2004–05 as the base year would be launched soon. However, the government will continue to release a weekly index for primary articles, and commodities in the fuel, power, light and lubricants groups. The weekly index will facilitate monitoring of prices of agricultural commodities and petroleum products, which are sensitive in nature.

Problems of Inflation

It has been reported that the manufacturing capacity in India is running around 95%, which usually means it is running at full capacity. Therefore, when the price of manufactured products is increasing, it means that demand is usually higher than supply and that is a clear case of demand-pull inflation. On the primary goods front, which consists of fruits, vegetables, food-grains etc., it is not that straight-forward. It has certainly been all over the news that the prices of fruits and vegetables are increasing and a trip to the supermarket or local grocery shop will testify to that. Although it is a clear case of demand-pull inflation, on the other, it is also a bit of a supply shock when one considers the fact that there is an abnormally high percentage of fruits and vegetables that goes to waste because of the lack of cold-storage facilities. Some estimates say 50% of produce goes to waste and that is a conservative number. The fuel price hike is a straight example of cost push inflation. When OPEC (The Organization of the Petroleum Exporting Countries) was formed, it squeezed the supply of oil and this caused oil prices to rise, contributing to higher inflation. Since oil is used in every industry, a sharp rise in the price of oil leads to an increase in the prices of all commodities.

The in depth problems due to inflation would be:

- When the balance between supply and demand goes out of control, consumers could change their buying habits, forcing manufacturers to cut down production.

- Inflation can create major problems in the economy. Price increase can worsen the poverty affecting low income household.
- Inflation creates economic uncertainty and is a dampener to the investment climate slowing growth and finally it reduce savings and thereby consumption.
- The producers would not be able to control the cost of raw material and labor and hence the price of the final product. This could result in less profit or in some extreme case no profit, forcing them out of business.
- Manufacturers would not have an incentive to invest in new equipment and new technology.
- Uncertainty would force people to withdraw money from the bank and convert it into product with long lasting value like gold, artifacts.

The imbalances inflation has created in the Indian economy:

- It has created a new rich class in social and political lives who are corrupt themselves and also corrupt the overall society.
- The increased prices reduced the capacity to save and people preferred present consumption to future consumption.
- It has provided protection and subsides to industries which bred inefficiency.
- It has lead to misallocation of resources due to distortion of relative prices and finally a redistribution of wealth from the poor to the rich.
- It disturbs balance of payments.

Curbing Inflation

There are several reasons why we should worry about the spike in the inflation rate. Inflation is a tax on the poor and long-term lenders. Inflation is already too high, though it is definitely not at economy-wrecking levels. But it's best to be serious about the threat it poses. Inflation has emerged as the biggest risk to the global outlook, having risen to very high levels across the world, levels that have not been generally seen for a couple of decades.

Currently, in India, we go through boom-and-bust cycles; sometimes GDP growth rates are very high and sometimes GDP growth rates drop sharply. This boom-and-bust cycle is unpleasant for every household. There is a powerful international consensus that stabilizing inflation reduces this boom-and-bust cycle of GDP growth.

India is facing the problem of inflationary pressure because of the increase in Aggregate Demand while Aggregate Supply is respectively constant. The inflationary pressure faced by Indian Economy is due to Demand-Pull inflation i.e., Aggregate Demand > Aggregate Supply. Thus to curb inflation need to fill the gap between Aggregate Demand and Aggregate Supply. For this either we need to increase Aggregate Supply or decrease Aggregate Demand that can hamper economic development. To increase Aggregate Supply either there is a need to increase production capacity of all current production units or to build new production plants. But as quoted in a survey done by RBI that all the production plants are running at their full production capacity thus all resources are full employed. The other way is to build new plant but to do this will take at least 18 months to 2 years. Thus meanwhile we need to decrease Money Supply, which is opted by RBI. Increasing production of useful goods and services is what India should focus on.

As in the short run it is not possible to meet the gap between Aggregate Demand and Aggregate Supply thus RBI is planning to decrease liquidity by reducing Money Supply from the market. RBI planned that Liquidity from the market can be drained by decreasing money supply and to do so it is increasing CRR, repo rate, reverse repo rate and taking other measure like that.

CRR i.e., Cash Reserve Ratio (Liquidity Ratio) is the percentage of deposit that a commercial bank needs to keep with RBI by which RBI control liquidity in the market and create Money Supply. Repo Rate is the rate at which RBI lends money to other commercial Banks.

The Reserve Bank said that such decisions had been taken to curb inflation in India. RBI is taking positive steps to reduce the inflation since inflations rates are going up week by week. By raising the reserve rate, a deflationary pressure can be put on the economy, since the money multiplier has been reduced. People will therefore save more. But in this hike, there is negative impact in terms of higher interest rates and personal loans, vehicle loans and other loans become costly. RBI may hike the rate to reduce the money circulation in the country but it also decreased the sales of all loan items and further it reduces the manufacturing activity of many industries. Now the public and private sector banks may raise the interest rate at which they lend money to borrowers. Produce more exports than imports than another country, then your money deflates with respect to that currency. Exporting becomes a problem cause buyers from outside feel that the goods are expensive so they prefer buying some other country's goods with cheaper rate. Thus money does not come in. in the same way, when public has more money they buy foreign goods, thus money goes out which is bad. There is a need to encourage people to purchase goods produced within the country.

It is important for policymakers to make credible announcements and degrade interest rates. Private agents must believe that these announcements will reflect actual future policy. If an announcement about low-level inflation targets is made but not believed by private agents, wage-setting will anticipate high-level inflation and so wages will be higher and inflation will rise. A high wage will increase a consumer's demand (demand pull inflation) and a firm's costs (cost push inflation), so inflation rises. Hence, if a policymaker's announcements regarding monetary policy are not credible, policy will not have the desired effect.

Keynesians emphasize reducing demand in general, often through fiscal policy, using increased taxation or reduced government spending to reduce demand as well as by using monetary policy. Supply-side economists advocate fighting inflation by fixing the exchange rate between the currency and some reference currency such as gold. This would be a return to the gold standard. All of these policies are achieved in practice through a process of open market operations.

As Individuals What Can We Do to Stop Inflation?

Firstly save!!! As much of your money as possible should be saved. This will reduce the demand on the economy and hopefully reduce inflation. Do not overuse daily essentials like cooking gas, electricity etc. Cut down on inessentials when buying groceries. Look for cheaper alternatives to products that you normally buy.

Keep roads, highways, sidewalks, etc., beautified to help attract tourism and bring additional monetary into a growing economy. Stop illegal immigration. Illegal activities reap the benefits of the country but don't pay taxes. Government-backed investment schemes such as Post Office Savings Schemes, Public Provident Funds (PPF) and National Savings Certificates (NSC) are best to invest in when inflation is slowly inching up and you are only looking at safety, not returns. Invest in short term deposits and funds, commodities and property. This will help you to slowly reach your financial goals while safeguarding your hard-earned money.

CLASS ACTIVITY

"GLOBAL TRADE SIMULATION: NEGOTIATING BILATERAL TRADE AGREEMENTS"

Objective: To understand the complexities and dynamics of international trade negotiations and the impact of bilateral agreements on the global economy. Facilitate a class discussion on the potential outcomes of these agreements on the global economy. Discuss concepts like comparative advantage, trade balances, and the impact on specific industries.

Conclude with a reflection session where students analyze the challenges and successes of the negotiation process. Ask them to consider how real-world factors like political considerations, domestic economic pressures, and global economic trends might influence trade negotiations.

SUMMARY

- The concept of the international economy pertains to the various economic activities and transactions that transpire across national boundaries, involving trade, investment, and financial movements among different countries. In contrast, globalization denotes the mechanism through which these interactions and integrations are hastened and intensified, fostering a more interconnected and interdependent global economy.
- International economics is concerned with the effects upon economic activity from international differences in productive resources and consumer preferences and the international institutions that affect them.
- The economic theory of international trade differs from the remainder of economic theory mainly because of the comparatively limited international mobility of the capital and labor.
- Modern trade analysis moves away from the restrictive assumptions of the H-O theorem and explores the effects upon trade of a range of factors, including technology and scale economies. It makes extensive use of econometrics to identify from the available statistics, the contribution of particular factors among the many different factors that affect trade.
- Globalization has had profound effects on human resource management. International assignments, outsourcing, coping with legal and cultural differences and managing talent from foreign countries all pose challenges as globalization continues to shrink the world.
- The economics of international finance does not differ in principle from the economics of international trade, but there are significant differences of emphasis. The practice of international finance tends to involve greater uncertainties and risks because the assets that are traded are claims to flows of returns that often extend many years into the future.
- Elementary considerations lead to a presumption that international migration results in a net gain in economic welfare. Wage differences between developed and developing countries have been found to be mainly due to productivity differences which may be assumed to arise mostly from differences in the availability of physical, social and human capital.
- International trade and economic growth are two concepts that go together, because international trade contributes to the growth of a country's economy in several ways. Some of these ways include the effects of import and export, specialization, increased productivity and improved infrastructure.
- Global growth has been accompanied by a change in the pattern of trade, which reflects ongoing changes in structure of the global economy. These changes include the rise of regional trading blocs, deindustrialization in many advanced economies, the increased participation of former communist countries, and the emergence of China and India, Invisible trade, in economics, the exchange of physically intangible items between countries. Invisible trade can be distinguished from visible trade, which involves the export, import, and re-export of physically tangible goods.

REVIEW QUESTIONS

1. What are the critical challenges faced by global companies in managing human resources across different countries?
2. How does capital mobility affect economic stability and growth in emerging markets?
3. What are the advantages and disadvantages of countries joining trading blocs versus pursuing unilateral trade policies?
4. To what extent does international trade contribute to economic development in developing countries?
5. In what ways do international trade centers contribute to enhancing trade efficiency and reducing trade barriers globally?

REFERENCES

1. Acemoglu, D. (2005). Politics and economics in weak and strong states. Journal of *Monetary Economics, 52*(6), 1199–1226. https://doi.org/10.1016/j.jmoneco.2005.05.012.
2. Acemoglu, D., & Robinson, J. A. (2008). Paths of economic and political development. In G. M. Hodgson (Ed.), The Oxford handbook of Political Economy. Oxford University Press.
3. Ahmed, A., Bouis, H., Gutner, T., & Lofgren, H. (2001). *The Egyptian Food Subsidy System: Structure, Performance and Options for Reform (Research Report 119).* International Food Policy Research Institute (IFPRI). Washington, D.C.
4. Ahmed, G., Hamrick, D., Guinn, A., Abdulsamad, A., & Gereffi, G. (2013). Wheat Value Chains and Food Security in the Middle East and North Africa Region. Duke Center on Globalization, Governance & Competitiveness.
5. Al-Shawarby, S., & El-Laithy, H. (2010). *Egypt's Food Subsidies: Benefit Incidence and Leakage (Report No. 57446).* The World Bank.
6. Alvesson, M., & Deetz, S. (2000). Doing Critical Management Research. Sage Publications.
7. Baldwin, R. (1969). The case against infant-industry tariff protection. Journal of Political Economy, 77(3), 295–305. https://doi.org/10.1086/259517.
8. Barbeay, C. (2009). Le Secteur du Blé en Egypte: Fiche de Synthèse. UBI France et les missions Economiques.
9. Blattman, C., Clemens, M. A., & Williamson, J. G. (2003). Who Protected and Why? Tariffs the World Around 1870–1938. Harvard Institute of Economic Research Discussion Paper No. 201). SSRN 431740.
10. British Cereal Exports. (2010). British Cereal Export Target Markets: Egypt. AHDB-HGCA agriculture and horticulture development bank, United Kingdom.

11. Bruton, H. J. (1998). A reconsideration of import substitution. Journal of Economic Literature, 36(2), 903–936.

12. Nordås, H. K., Miroudot, S., & Kowalski, P. (2006). *Dynamic Gains from Trade (OECD Trade Policy Working Paper No. 43).* OECD Trade Policy Papers. https://doi.org/10.1787/18166873.

CHAPTER 2

Foundations of Modern Trade Theory: Comparative Advantage

LEARNING OBJECTIVES

After studying this chapter, you will be able to:

- Learn about the international trade and development
- Discuss on international trade services
- Evaluate the barrier of international trade

KEY TERMS FROM THIS CHAPTER

Capitalism
Gross domestic product (GDP)
International marketing
Trade agreement
Transformation curve
External debt
International Chamber of Commerce
Ratification
Trade delegation
Voluntary export restraint (VER)

INTRODUCTION

With its development starting in the middle of the 20th Century, modern trade theory signifies a fundamental change in our comprehension of international economic relations. Fundamentally, this theory deviates from previous mercantilist and classical theories that placed emphasis on comparative advantage and trade balance, respectively, in favor of using rigorous economic frameworks to explain the patterns and effects of international trade. The theory of comparative advantage, which was developed and expanded upon in the 20th century after being introduced by David Ricardo in the early 19th century, is one of the fundamental ideas of contemporary trade theory. According to this theory, nations ought to focus on producing goods and services in areas where their opportunity costs are lower than those of other countries. Theoretically, nations can maximize their overall welfare and attain higher levels of consumption through specialization and trade based on comparative advantage than would be feasible in a closed economy.

Expanding upon Ricardo's observations, the Heckscher-Ohlin model, which was first presented in the early 1900s, offered an additional crucial structure for comprehending trade trends. This model highlights how comparative advantages and trade patterns are driven by variations in factor endowments—such as capital, labor, and natural resources—across nations. Countries that have an abundance of a particular production factor will typically import goods that require those factors in relatively small quantities while exporting goods that heavily rely on those factors.

Furthermore, the scope of contemporary trade theory has grown to include increasingly intricate elements like technological disparities, imperfect competition, and economies of scale. For example, Paul Krugman's New Trade Theory introduced the idea of economies of scale and product differentiation as trade drivers, emphasizing the advantages that businesses can have from producing more for both domestic and foreign markets. The emergence of the gravity model of trade, which postulates that the amount of trade between 2 nations is inversely proportional to their distance from one another and proportional to their respective economic sizes (often measured by GDP), is another significant development. This model has been a mainstay in empirical studies on patterns of international trade since it has shown to be reliable in explaining bilateral trade flows worldwide. Recent developments in trade theory have also gone deeper into comprehending how globalization, policies, and institutions influence trade dynamics. By lowering trade barriers and promoting economic integration between nations, organizations like the World Trade Organization (WTO) and regional trade agreements have further impacted patterns of international trade.

All things considered, contemporary trade theory keeps developing and adapting to the shifting conditions of the global economy. It provides understanding of the advantages and difficulties of international trade, the distributional effects within nations, and the implications for global economic growth and development. Informed discussions on trade policy, globalization, and the interdependence of national economies in the 21st century, it continues to be a fundamental component of economic analysis and policymaking.

2.1. HISTORICAL DEVELOPMENT OF MODERN TRADE THEORY

Ideas in economic theory have evolved to produce modern trade theory. The framework for contemporary trade theory has been largely provided by the writings of the mercantilists and, later, the classical economists, including Adam Smith, David Ricardo, and John Stuart Mill. In Europe between 1500 and 1800, a group of writers emerged whose work focused on the process of nation building. The main issue, according to mercantilists, was how a country could control its internal and foreign affairs in order to advance its own interests. A robust foreign trade sector held the key to the solution. A nation would realize net payments from the rest of the world in the form of gold and silver if it could attain a positive trade balance, or a surplus of exports over imports. These revenues would support higher spending as well as higher employment and domestic output. The mercantilists supported trade regulation by the government in order to foster a positive trade balance.

The mercantilists suggested using tariffs, quotas, and other commercial policies to reduce imports and safeguard a country's trading position.

The mercantilists' economic strategies were heavily contested by the 18th century. The price-specie-flow doctrine of David Hume states that a positive trade balance can only exist temporarily before eventually disappearing on its own. As an example, let's say that England experiences a trade surplus leading to an influx of gold and silver. The addition of these precious metals to England's money supply results in a rise in the total amount of money in circulation. England's price level rises as a result of this increase in comparison to its trading partners. As a result, residents of England would be encouraged to buy goods made abroad, while England's exports would decrease. Consequently, the nation's trade surplus would ultimately disappear. Hence, the price-specie-flow mechanism demonstrates that mercantilist policies could only, at most, result in temporary economic gains. Another criticism leveled at mercantilists was their static conception of the global economy. The mercantilists believed that global wealth was fixed. According to this perspective, not all countries could profit from international trade at the same time, and a nation's gains from trade came at the expense of its trading partners. The publication of Adam Smith's The Wealth of Nations in 1776 put this viewpoint to the test. Smith (1723–1790) believed that there is no set amount of wealth in the world. The division of labor and specialization are made possible by international trade, which raises national productivity levels and, ultimately, global output (wealth). According to Smith's dynamic theory of trade, increased levels of production and consumption could be experienced by both trading partners at the same time.

Despite the disprovement of its foundations, mercantilism still exists today. But these days, employment is prioritized over gold and silver holdings. Neo-mercantilists argue that imports are bad because they transfer jobs from domestic workers to foreign workers, while exports are good because they create jobs for domestic workers. Trade is therefore viewed as a zero-sum game in which a country must lose in order for another to win. It is a widely held belief that trade can yield benefits for every nation, including increased employment opportunities as global prosperity rises.

2.1.1. Why Nations Trade: Absolute Advantage

The international division of labor was promoted by free trade, or open markets, according to classical economist Adam Smith. Countries could focus their production on the goods they could produce most cheaply under free trade, reaping the benefits of this division of labor. Smith attempted to elucidate the reasons behind the variations in costs across countries, acknowledging that these variations dictate the global flow of goods. According to Smith, the primary factor influencing production costs is the productivities of the factor inputs. These productivities are predicated on both innate and learned advantages. While the latter include specialized knowledge and abilities, the former include elements related to soil, climate, and mineral wealth. Smith reasoned that a country would produce an item at a lower cost and so become more competitive than its trading partner if it had a natural or acquired advantage in it. Smith believed that the supply side of the market determines competitiveness.

Smith's theory of cost originated from the labor theory of value, which holds that the price or cost of an item is solely determined by the quantity of labor needed to produce it and that labor is the only factor of production and homogeneous (of one quality) within each nation. For instance, if the US employs less labor than the UK to produce a yard of fabric, the Production expenses will be reduced.

The absolute advantage principle was Smith's trading tenet: in a world with two nations and two products, international trade and specialization will be advantageous if one country has an absolute cost advantage (i.e., requires less labor to produce a unit of output) in one good and the other country has an absolute cost advantage in the other good. Every country needs to produce a good that it is unquestionably more efficient at producing than its trading partner in order for the world to profit from specialization. When a country has an absolute cost disadvantage, it will import those goods; when it has an absolute cost advantage, it will export those goods.

The concept of absolute advantage is demonstrated with the aid of an arithmetic example.

Assume, with reference to Table 2.1, that laborers in the United States can produce five wine bottles or 20 yards of cloth in an hour, whereas laborers in the United Kingdom can produce 15 wine bottles or 10 yards of cloth in the same amount of time.

The productivity of American cloth workers (output per worker hour) is higher than that of the United Kingdom, which results in lower costs (less labor needed to produce a yard of cloth). This gives the United States a clear competitive advantage in the cloth production industry. Similarly, when it comes to wine production, the United Kingdom is completely at an advantage.

Table 2.1. World Output Possibilities in the Absence of Specialization: A case of absolute advantage when each nation is more efficient in the production of one good

	OUTPUT PER LABOR HOUR	
Nation	**Wine**	**Cloth**
United States	5 bottles	20 yards
United Kingdom	15 bottles	10 yards

Source: https://wyamaka.wordpress.com/wp-content/uploads/2019/08/international-economics_30.pdf.

2.1.2. Why Nations Trade: Comparative Advantage

Rich London merchant David Ricardo (1772–1823) was fascinated when, while on vacation, he came across The Wealth of Nations in 1800. Although Ricardo found Smith's case for free trade to be compelling, he felt that some of Smith's analysis needed to be strengthened. Smith argues that in order for trade to be mutually beneficial, every country must produce at least one good at the lowest cost that it can export to its trading partner. Disappointed with this looseness in Smith's theory, Ricardo developed a principle to show that mutually beneficial trade can occur whether or not countries have any absolute advantage. But what if a country is more efficient than its trading partner in the production of all goods? The theory put forth by Ricardo was later named the principle of comparative advantage. Similar to Smith, Ricardo placed emphasis on the market's supply side. The cost differentials between countries, which were bolstered by their acquired and natural advantages, provided the initial foundation for trade. Ricardo placed more emphasis on comparative (relative) cost differences than did Smith, who stressed the significance of absolute cost differences among nations. It is true that nations frequently create comparative advantages, as Table 2.2 illustrates. The principle of comparative advantage states that a country may still have a foundation for profitable trade even if it faces an absolute cost disadvantage in producing both goods. The less efficient country should focus on and export the good (where its absolute disadvantage is least) in which it is comparatively less inefficient. The nation with higher efficiency should focus on and export the good in which it has a relative advantage. (where its absolute advantage is greatest).

Table 2.2 Examples of Comparative Advantages in International Trade

Country	Product
Canada	Lumber
Israel	Citrus fruit
Italy	Wine
Jamaica	Aluminum ore
Mexico	Tomatoes
Saudi Arabia	Oil
China	Textiles
Japan	Automobiles
South Korea	Steel, ships
Switzerland	Watches
United Kingdom	Financial services

Source: https://wyamaka.wordpress.com/wp-content/uploads/2019/08/international-economics_30.pdf.

To demonstrate the principle of comparative advantage, Ricardo formulated a simplified model based on the following assumptions:

1. The world consists of two nations, each using a single input to produce two commodities.
2. In each nation, labor is the only input (the labor theory of value). Each nation has a fixed endowment

of labor, and labor is fully employed and homogeneous.

3. Labor can move freely among industries within a nation but is incapable of moving between nations.
4. The level of technology is fixed for both nations. Different nations may use different technologies, but all firms within each nation utilize a common production method for each commodity.
5. Costs do not vary with the level of production and are proportional to the amount of labor used.
6. Perfect competition prevails in all markets. Because no single producer or consumer is large enough to influence the market, all are price takers. Product quality does not vary among nations, implying that all units of each product are identical.

There is free entry to and exit from an industry, and the price of each product equals the product's marginal cost of production.

7. Free trade occurs between nations; that is, no government barriers to trade exist.
8. Transportation costs are zero. Consumers will thus be indifferent between domestically produced and imported versions of a product if the domestic prices of the two products are identical.
9. Firms make production decisions in an attempt to maximize profits, whereas consumers maximize satisfaction through their consumption decisions.
10. There is no money illusion; that is, when consumers make their consumption choices and firms make their production decisions, they take into account the behavior of all prices.
11. Trade is balanced (exports must pay for imports), thus ruling out flows of money between nations.

The situation where one country has a complete advantage in producing both goods is illustrated by Table 2.3, which applies Ricardo's principle of comparative advantage. Let us assume that in an hour, U.S. Employees can make 40 yards of fabric or 40 bottles of wine, but U. K. 10 yards of fabric or 20 bottles of wine can be produced by laborers. Smith's theory of absolute advantage states that there is no foundation for trade and specialization that benefit both parties because the U.S. Employee productivity is higher when producing both items.Nonetheless, the comparative advantage principle acknowledges that U.S. Workers are only twice as efficient in producing wine (40/20 2) as they are in producing cloth (40/10). In cloth, therefore, the United States has a larger absolute advantage than in wine, whereas in wine, the United Kingdom has a smaller absolute disadvantage than in cloth. Every country focuses on and exports the good in which it has a comparative advantage, such as the UK in wine and the US in cloth.

Table 2.3. World Output Possibilities in the Absence of Specialization

	OUTPUT PER LABOR HOUR	
Nation	**Wine**	**Cloth**
United States	40 bottles	40 yards
United Kingdom	20 bottles	10 yards

Source: https://wyamaka.wordpress.com/wp-content/uploads/2019/08/international-economics_30.pdf

As a result, the two countries benefit from the output gains from specialization through trade. Like Smith, Ricardo claimed that trade benefits both countries. In other words, Ricardo's principle of comparative advantage holds that labor productivity disparities between countries are the only factor influencing international trade. The fundamental tenet of Ricardo's principle is that nations will typically export goods where labor productivity is high. The US has experienced significant trade deficits (imports exceeding exports) with nations like China and Japan in recent years. Some people who have observed the influx of imports into the US appear to be of the opinion that the US lacks a comparative advantage in any area. While it is possible for a country to be completely unopposed in all areas, it is not feasible for one country to be unopposed in all areas and the other to be unopposed in all areas. This is so because relative costs determine comparative advantage. As we've seen, it makes sense for a country that is absolutely disadvantaged in every good to focus on producing the good where its disadvantage is the least. There's no justification for the US to give up and rely solely on Chinese production. Both China and the United States would suffer as a result of the decreased global output that would result from U.S. Resources were not being used. Absolute advantage and comparative advantage are not to be confused with the notion that a country has nothing to offer.

2.1.3. Production Possibilities Schedules

According to Ricardo's law of comparative advantage, trade and specialization can benefit both countries. However, the labor theory of value's restrictive assumption—that labor is the only factor input—was the foundation of his theory. In actuality, labor is just one of many input factors. Modern trade theory offers a more comprehensive theory of comparative advantage in recognition of the limitations of the labor theory of value. A production possibilities schedule, also known as a transformation schedule, is used to illustrate the theory. This schedule illustrates the range of possible pairings of two goods that a country can produce with optimal utilization of its factor inputs (land, labor, capital, and entrepreneurship). Thus, a country's maximum output possibilities are depicted in the production possibilities schedule.

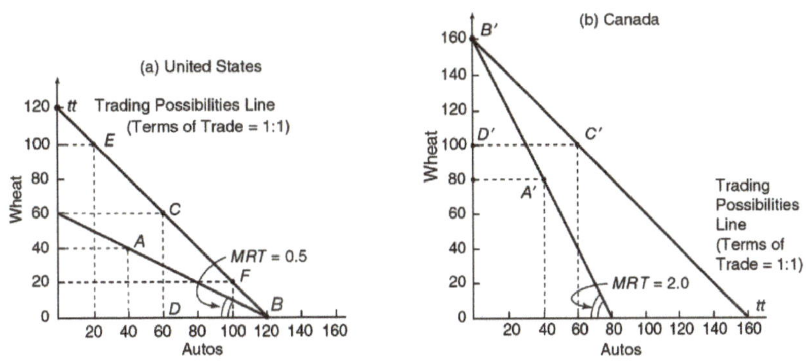

Figure 2.1. *Trading under constant opportunity costs.*

Source: https://slideplayer.com/slide/15910364/88/images/3/Trading+under+constant+opportunity+costs.jpg.

The hypothetical production schedules for the United States and Canada are shown in Figure 2.1. In a given amount of time, the United States can produce either 60 bushels of wheat or 120 autos, or specific combinations of the two products, by fully utilizing all available inputs with the best available technology. In a similar vein, Canada is capable of producing 80 cars, 160 bushels of wheat, or specific combinations of the two. What is the formula that a production possibilities schedule uses to show the idea of comparative cost? The formula is the production possibilities schedule's slope, or marginal rate of transformation (MRT). The MRT shows the amount of one product a nation must sacrifice to get one additional unit of the other product:

$$MRT = \frac{\Delta Wheat}{\Delta Autos}.$$

The opportunity cost of a product is another term for this rate of sacrifice. The MRT is equal to the absolute value of the slope of the production possibilities schedule since this formula also takes that slope into account.

The MRT of wheat into autos in Figure 2.1 indicates how much wheat needs to be sacrificed for every extra auto that is produced.

The United States' production possibilities schedule demonstrates that moving from the top endpoint to the bottom endpoint entails sacrificing 60 bushels of wheat in order to produce 120 additional autos at a relative cost.

With this sacrifice, the bushels of wheat sacrificed (60/120 0.5) represent the relative cost of each auto produced, or the MRT 0.5. In a similar vein, Canada's MRT 2.0, or the relative cost of each car produced, is equal to two bushels of wheat.

2.1.4. Trading Under Constant-Cost Conditions

The constant-cost case is a helpful teaching tool for studying international trade, despite its possible lack of real-world applicability. Two questions are the main topic of discussion. In reference to Figure 2.1, note that the production possibilities schedules for the United States and Canada are drawn as straight lines. First, what are the foundations of trade and the direction of trade? Secondly, what are the potential gains from trade, for a single nation and for the world as a whole? These schedules' linearity suggests that when the economy switches from producing only wheat to only cars, or any other combination thereof, the relative costs of the two goods remain constant. In the US, the relative cost of an automobile increases or decreases by 0 5 bushels of wheat as output grows, whereas in Canada, it increases or decreases by 2 bushels of wheat.

Costs are constant for two reasons. Initially, the production factors are ideal interchangeable parts. Secondly, every unit belonging to a specific factor has the same quality. A nation won't have to turn to resources that are insufficient for the production of the good if it shifts resources from the production of wheat to the production of automobiles, or vice versa. Therefore, regardless of how many cars the nation currently produces, it must sacrifice exactly the same amount of wheat for every extra car produced.

2.1.4.1. Basis for Trade and Direction of Trade

Now let's look at trade in a constant-cost environment. Assume, with reference to Figure 2.1, that the United States would prefer to produce and consume at point A on its production possibilities schedule, with 40 automobiles and 40 bushels of wheat, in an autarky (the absence of trade). Assume further that, with 40 cars and 80 bushels of wheat, Canada produces and consumes at point A on its production possibilities schedule. The relative cost of one product in relation to the other is indicated by the slopes of the production possibilities schedules for the two nations. For the United States, the cost of producing an extra auto is only 0.5 bushels of wheat, but for Canada, it is 2 bushels of wheat. Because of the disparities in the relative costs of the two countries, this situation offers a foundation for mutually beneficial trade and specialization, in accordance with the principle of comparative advantage. In terms of trade patterns, the US specializes in and exports cars, while Canada specializes in and exports wheat.

2.1.4.2. Production Gains from Specialization

According to the law of comparative advantage, every nation will find it advantageous to specialize in producing the good that gives it a comparative advantage through trade, and it will exchange some of this good for the good that gives it a comparative disadvantage. The United States shifts from production point A to production point B in Figure 2.1, focusing entirely on auto production. By going from production point A to production point B in the figure, Canada demonstrates its complete specialization in wheat production. Using specialization to one's advantage can increase output for both nations.

We discover that the US produces 40 cars and 40 bushels of wheat before specialization. However, despite total specialization, the US only produces 120 cars and no wheat. Regarding Canada, its production point under complete specialization is 160 bushels of wheat and no autos, whereas its production point under non-specialization is 40 autos and 80 bushels of wheat. When we combine these findings, we discover that, in the case of total specialization, both countries have gained net production of 40 cars and 40 bushels of wheat.

2.1.4.3. Dynamic Gains from Trade

The idea of "dynamic gains from trade" refers to the long-term advantages that nations that trade internationally experience beyond the "static gains" that are usually connected to quick improvements in resource allocation. Dynamic gains emphasize larger, longer-term effects on economic growth, technological advancement, and structural transformation, whereas static gains concentrate on immediate improvements in production efficiency and consumer welfare through comparative advantage and specialization.

Innovation and the spread of technology are two main sources of trade's dynamic gains. Trade facilitates the exchange of ideas, technologies, and knowledge across borders. Countries are exposed to new technologies and production techniques used by their trading partners when they trade with each other and specialize in producing goods and services in accordance with their comparative advantages. This exposure may result in technological adaptations and spillovers that boost domestic productivity and innovation. For example, trade is frequently accompanied by foreign direct investment (FDI), which provides recipient nations with advanced technologies and managerial know-how in addition to capital.

International trade can also promote efficiency gains and competition in home industries. Businesses that are exposed to foreign markets are compelled to innovate to meet global standards, lower costs, and improve product quality in order to remain competitive. This pressure from competition can boost output and create a dynamic atmosphere that is favorable to innovation and ongoing progress.

Trade also promotes production specialization and economies of scale. Businesses that specialize in creating particular products and services for export markets can benefit from economies of scale, which reduce average costs and increase production efficiency. Because of its efficiency, businesses can put the money they save back into research and development (R&D), which advances technology and contributes to long-term economic growth.

Trade additionally encourages economies to undergo structural change. As nations integrate into international markets, they frequently experience structural changes in their export and production patterns. This transition usually entails a move away from more traditional industries, like agriculture, and toward more sophisticated ones, like manufacturing and services, which are usually linked to higher income and productivity levels.

Additionally, trade can support the growth of human capital and skill development. Engaging in international markets necessitates having a workforce with the necessary skills to adjust to changing market demands and technological advancements. The need for skilled labor in increasingly globally integrated industries arises from trade and specialization between nations, prompting investments in education and training that improve the accumulation of human capital.

While dynamic gains from trade highlight the long-term benefits that result from technological advancement, productivity improvements, structural transformation, and the development of human capital, static gains from trade concentrate on short-term efficiency gains. These dynamics highlight how trade has a transformative effect on economic growth and development, emphasizing its role in influencing future prospects for prosperity as well as raising living standards today.

2.1.5. Changing Comparative Advantage

The dynamic process through which nations' patterns of trade and specialization change over time as a result of different factors affecting their economic capacities and the state of the global economy is known as "changing comparative advantage."

Although comparative advantage has historically been based on variations in the endowments of labor, capital, and natural resources, there are a number of reasons why it can change dramatically. Changes in technology have a significant impact on comparative advantage. Production technique innovations, like automation or digitalization, can lower costs and increase productivity, changing a nation's competitive environment in industries that use these technologies.

Shifting comparative advantage is also influenced by modifications in factor endowments. Changes in the population, expenditures on infrastructure and education, and the discovery or depletion of natural resources can all affect a nation's comparative advantage by affecting the relative abundance or scarcity of factors that are essential to its production. Furthermore, changes to trade laws and regulations may have an immediate impact on comparative advantage. Modifications to tariffs, subsidies, or regulations may impact production costs and market accessibility, thereby impacting an industry's competitiveness and, consequently, its comparative advantage.

Comparative advantage is further shaped by market dynamics and global economic trends. Certain industries or technologies may benefit from changes in consumer preferences, demand patterns, or the move toward sustainable products, leading nations to modify their production strategies appropriately.

All things considered, shifting comparative advantage highlights how dynamic global trade and economic growth are. It emphasizes how nations constantly adjust to changes in the global market environment, policy changes, factor availability, and technological advancements in order to preserve or improve their competitive positions.

2.1.5.1. The Impact of Trade on Jobs

Because it involves intricate relationships between labor markets, international trade dynamics, and policy responses, the effect of trade on jobs is a topic of substantial discussion and analysis in the field of economics. Trade can affect jobs in various ways, both positively and negatively, depending on the specific circumstances and context:

1. **Job Creation:** International trade can create new job opportunities by expanding markets for domestically produced goods and services. Export-oriented industries often experience growth, leading to increased demand for workers involved in production, logistics, marketing, and related services. For example, a country specializing in electronics may see growth in employment within its tech manufacturing sector due to increased export demand.
2. **Job Displacement**: On the flip side, trade can lead to job displacement in sectors that face increased competition from foreign producers. Import competition can pressure domestic industries to become more efficient or shift resources to other sectors, potentially resulting in job losses, particularly in industries where comparative disadvantages exist. For instance, textile industries in some countries have faced challenges due to cheaper imports from low-cost production countries.
3. **Structural Adjustment**: Trade can prompt structural adjustments in economies, influencing the composition of jobs and industries. As countries specialize in sectors where they have a comparative advantage, there may be shifts in employment from traditional sectors (e.g., agriculture or manufacturing) towards more advanced industries (e.g., technology or services). This structural transformation can affect the skills required in the labor force and the geographic distribution of jobs.
4. **Wage Effects**: Trade can impact wages depending on the sector and skill level of workers. Industries benefiting from export opportunities may offer higher wages to attract skilled labor, contributing to wage growth in those sectors. Conversely, import competition in labor-intensive industries may exert downward pressure on wages, especially for low-skilled workers.

5. **Job Quality and Standards**: Trade agreements and global supply chains can influence labor standards and job quality. Increased trade integration may incentivize countries to improve labor regulations and working conditions to maintain competitiveness and attract investment. Conversely, concerns exist about potential job quality reductions in sectors facing intense global competition and cost-cutting pressures.
6. **Policy Responses**: Governments often respond to trade-related job impacts through policies aimed at supporting affected workers and industries. These policies may include trade adjustment assistance programs, retraining initiatives, investment incentives, or trade barriers. These interventions seek to mitigate negative employment effects while promoting economic adaptation and resilience.

Through market expansion and specialization, international trade presents opportunities for economic growth and job creation, but it also presents challenges like job displacement and wage pressure in certain sectors. It is necessary to take into account sectoral dynamics, labor market conditions, policy responses, and broader economic trends that shape the effects of globalization on employment in order to comprehend the complex effects of trade on jobs.

2.2. INTERNATIONAL TRADE AND DEVELOPMENT

International trade and development have a complex relationship that varies greatly depending on the specific systems and structures in place in each nation. In the best-case scenario, gains from advantageous trade agreements are used to support domestic economic growth and raise the gross domestic product. International trade and development are mutually reinforcing. However, there may be other situations where trade either has no effect on development at all or even works to impede it.

Trade should ideally enable developing countries to obtain foreign capital in exchange for cheap labor or natural resources. If all goes according to plan, the foreign capital can then be used to fund infrastructure projects, social advancements, agriculture, and local industry. Success in these areas can then lead to more profits and capital inflows from trade, creating a positive feedback loop that can raise living standards and economic output steadily.

Several countries have this kind of relationship between development and international trade. China is a prime example of a development success story, having increased the size and technical caliber of its manufacturing base while simultaneously improving domestic economic conditions and living standards through the effective use of trade and foreign investment. In this instance, trade was not free trade because China used tariffs to support home manufacturing against foreign competition, which is essentially a mercantilist policy.

In certain situations, free trade can lead to similarly favorable results for economic development. Mexico has benefited immensely from the relaxation of trade restrictions with the rest of North America and is a success story in international trade and development. Trade increased employment in Mexico and raised living standards and productivity in regions where jobs related to trade with other countries were concentrated (Figure 2.2).

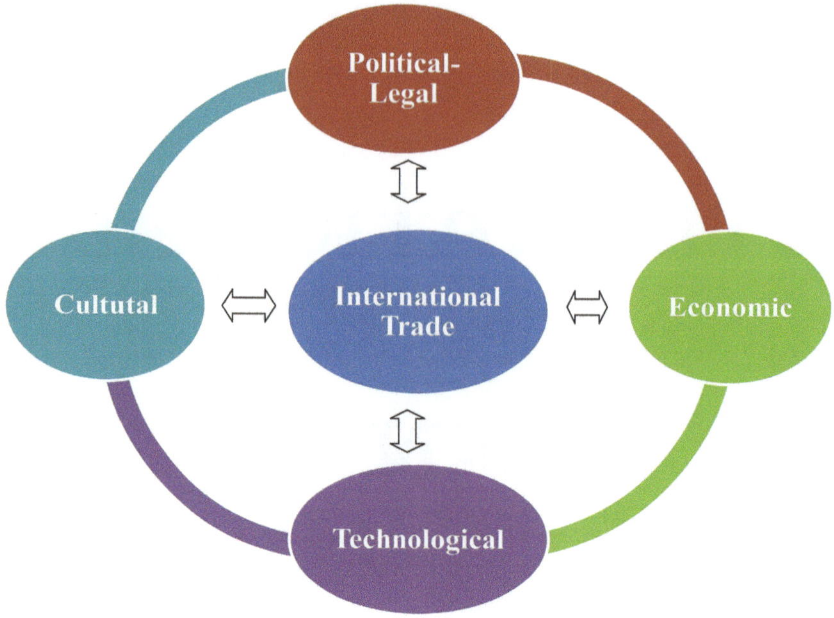

Figure 2.2. *Trading environment of international trade.*

Source: https://www.simplynotes.in/wp-content/uploads/2016/03/International-trade.jpg.

But trade is not always good for developing countries. When corruption is widespread, foreign trade profits are frequently siphoned off through graft and corruption, and no real economic development occurs. Wealth from trade, particularly that derived from extractive industries like mining and oil, can sometimes cause states to become weaker rather than stronger by igniting civil wars and other forms of criminal activity.

2.2.1. Patterns of Trade

Trade patterns have changed in tandem with global growth, reflecting ongoing shifts in the composition of the world economy. The emergence of regional trading blocs, the deindustrialization of many advanced economies, the increased involvement of former communist nations, and the rise of China and India are some of these changes.

2.2.1.1. Degrees of National Participation

Countries differ greatly in how much they trade internationally. Roughly speaking, a country's involvement in foreign trade decreases with increasing physical size and population, primarily due to the greater variety of raw materials available within its borders and the larger size of its internal market.

As a result, when expressed as a percentage of GDP, the United States' and the former Soviet Union's participation has been relatively low. The U.S. Nonetheless, the United States continues to be one of the most significant trading nations in the world due to its enormous GDP in comparison to other nations. The combined export and import amounts of a few of the smaller Western European nations, like the Netherlands, come close to matching their GDPs.

2.2.1.2. Trade Among Developed Countries

Trade between developed, capital-rich nations accounts for the majority of trade volume; these include major industrialized nations like Australia, Belgium, Canada, France, Germany, Italy, Japan, the Netherlands, Spain, Sweden, the United Kingdom, and the United States. A nation's participation in international trade typically increases faster than its GDP as it becomes more economically developed.

The benefits of increased trade between these nations are aptly demonstrated by the EU. It is highly likely that the elimination of trade barriers is responsible for a significant portion of the increases in real income in EU member states. However, since EU members impose tariffs on goods coming from outside the Union, the EU's formation cannot be seen as unqualifiedly embracing the free-trade principle.

2.2.2. Invisible Trade

In the language of economics, invisible trade is the transfer of physically intangible goods between nations. It is possible to distinguish between visible and invisible trade. Visible trade is the export, import, and reexport of tangible goods. Services (receipts and payments from operations like shipping or customer service); foreign investment income in the form of interest, profits, and dividends; private or governmental money transfers between nations; and intellectual property and patents are basic categories of invisible trade.

The great majority of invisible trade consists of services. These services include international travel, banking, insurance, and other financial services; freight and passenger transportation; and scientific and technical exchange. Foreign investment income ranks second in terms of its contribution to invisible trade, with private and public transfers making up the smallest portion.

Payments for invisibles exceed receipts for them in many developing nations. The foreign debt and interest payments that developing nations frequently make to developed nations are closely related to this deficit. A number of developed countries' invisible trade earnings from foreign investments are also in jeopardy, as a result of certain developing nations' mounting external debt and their incapacity to pay back the loans and interest. Situations like these have prompted demands that creditor nations provide debt relief to debtor nations.

2.2.3. Trade Sanctions

Trade sanctions are penalties connected to trade that a nation imposes on one or more other nations. These sanctions, which are more broadly classified as economic sanctions, can be applied to further political, military, or economic policy goals. Trade sanctions typically take the form of import tariffs, import volume quotas, licensing fees, or other administrative barriers to trade.

Trade sanctions aimed at achieving economic goals are frequently implemented by a nation that feels mistreated by a trading partner. Subsidizing a home industry, dumping inexpensive goods on the global market, or erecting tariffs or nontariff trade barriers are examples of actions that could be deemed unfair. These sanctions are frequently referred to as "trade remedies" by the US, which has a history of using them as payback for unfair trade practices. A single instance of the U.S. In order to combat unfair practices, trade sanctions were used by President George W. Bush imposed tariffs on steel imports, saying he was safeguarding the U.S. steel industry against competitors in Europe and Asia who illegally dump cheap steel. According to the World Trade Organization (WTO), the U.S. claiming that tariffs were unlawful, which led a number of European nations to threaten retaliatory tariffs. This ultimately led to the U.S. to remove its tariffs on steel.

Trade sanctions may also be employed as a military or political tactic. Sanctions have been used to pressure nations to alter their political conduct; these efforts have focused on issues like the defense of human rights, civil liberties, and the prevention of aggression and the development of WMDs. Sanctions in these situations are typically a component of an all-encompassing military and diplomatic strategy. In other instances, sanctions have been applied to stop providing financial support to nations and groups deemed to pose a risk to international law or to peace and security.

For nations that are members of the WTO, trade sanctions are a crucial tool for policy. Enshrined in its bylaws is a binding dispute resolution procedure that enables member countries to approach the WTO as an unbiased third party to resolve any disputes pertaining to trade. When a nation receives a favorable ruling from the WTO, it is frequently granted permission to impose sanctions on the offending nation. Trade sanctions have been applied occasionally, but they are infamously hard to carry out and rarely work as intended. This is primarily due to the fact that most goods and services are traded internationally. If a trade partner imposes tariffs on a specific import, the country of destination can still export the item to other trading partners. Because of this, trade sanctions that are imposed by a group of nations collectively are typically more effective than those that are imposed individually.

2.2.4. Trade Between Developed and Developing Countries

Trade between developed and developing nations often gives rise to challenging issues. The economies of the majority of less developed nations are based on agriculture, and many of them are tropical, so they are largely dependent on the export of one or two commodities, like sugar, coffee, or cacao. These products are subject to fierce competition on the market, as defined by economists, meaning that price changes are highly responsive to shifts in supply or demand. On the other hand, the costs of manufactured goods, which are developed nations' usual exports, are typically far more stable. As a result, the tropical nation's "terms of trade," or the ratio of export prices to import prices, fluctuate greatly in tandem with the price of its export commodity, frequently having detrimental effects on the home economy. Price stabilization and output control have been attempted for almost all significant primary commodities. The results of these efforts have been mixed.

There has been much debate over trade between developed and developing nations. The exploitation of foreign labor, the environment, and the needs for domestic labor are cited by critics as multinational corporations from developed nations shift their operations to less developed nations with cheaper labor pools and less political or economic clout. The work of the WTO came under increasing scrutiny from its critics, particularly after 1999, when trade talks were interrupted by anti-globalization protestors during the WTO ministerial conference in Seattle. The most serious criticisms focused on issues like the rights of domestic workers, the democratic nature of the WTO, national sovereignty, the impact on the environment, health and safety, and the wisdom of supporting free trade and commercialism at the expense of other values. These critics raised a variety of concerns about the authority and reach of the WTO.

2.2.5. International Trade Law

The set of rules and agreements that control how nations conduct business with one another is known as international trade law. Many nations rely, at least in part, on their ability to import and export goods for their economies to remain strong. The rules governing these trades are outlined by international trade laws. The majority of the time, laws are made to guarantee justice for all parties involved and to establish a kind of globally consistent and predictable set of norms. International trade law is primarily divided into three categories. First, there is the national level: any nation that establishes its own internal guidelines for conducting international trade or sets export limits for specific resources has established an international trade law. Bilateral comes in second. Bilateral trade agreements, also known as trade laws, are created when two nations come to an agreement to open trade freely across their borders or to conduct trade in a particular manner. Lastly, nations frequently participate in multilateral agreement-making, which establishes uniform guidelines and standards that various international actors must adhere to. When most people think about trade law, they usually think of multilateral trade agreements. The two main institutions engaged in the formation of multilateral agreements are the United Nations (UN) and the World Trade Organization (WTO). Representatives from all over the world comprise each group, and together they attend meetings, exchange ideas, and draft laws and regulations that have the power to influence global trade policies. The foundation for the majority of international trade laws is established during these meetings.

Most of the most well-known traders in the world are members of UNCITRAL, the UN Commission on International Trade Law, and the World Trade Organization. Among the most involved nations are the US, Canada, China, Japan, and the majority of the EU. The goal of the WTO and UNCITRAL is to enable wide-ranging dialog between nations. While not every conversation ends with agreement, many do.

National representatives typically pledge that their own national laws will comply with the terms of the agreement when they consent to specific international trade standards or conditions. These agreements can occasionally be implemented fairly easily. A pledge to allow trade with nearby nations is one instance. It may take more time and legal weight to implement agreements to limit trade with nations known to deal in nuclear weapons, for example, or pledges to establish trade regulations prohibiting the export of specific goods to specific locations. An international trade agreement needs to be ratified at the national level before it can become trade law. This implies that each nation must ensure that the terms and conditions of the agreement are reflected in its own national laws. Ratification can take years to complete and frequently necessitates extensive legal drafting and revisions.

As a result, the development of international trade law can be a slow but ongoing process. Trade laws have no set completion date, largely due to the fact that trade customs are subject to change over time. International economic law plays a significant role in trade law, necessitating close attention to changes in currency exchange rates and the balance of power among global leaders. International trade law must change in order to remain relevant as global trade dynamics shift, new leaders take office, and international markets shift.

2.2.6. State Interference in International Trade

2.2.6.1. Methods of Interference

All countries obstruct international trade to some extent, regardless of what the comparative advantage theory may say about the benefits of free trade. Tariffs can be applied to imports; in certain cases, these can be so high as to prevent the good in question from entering at all. A quota may restrict the amount of imports that are allowed. The state may provide subsidies in an effort to promote exports. Exports of money and capital may be limited or outlawed. Foreign investment in domestic machinery and plants may also be restricted.

Certain groups may be negatively impacted by import competition, leading to special-interest pleading, which could be the cause of these interferences. Alternatively, limitations may be imposed by a government that feels compelled to consider factors that comparative advantage ignores. It is interesting to note that, with regard to goods and services, the general pattern of interference adheres to the antiquated mercantilist maxim that encourages exports and discourages imports.

If tariffs or quotas prevent a company from entering a lucrative foreign market, they may be able to get around the obstacle by setting up a manufacturing facility in that nation. Following World War II, this foreign plant investment policy significantly expanded, with U.S. businesses assuming the lead by making investments, especially in South America, Asia, Western Europe, and Canada. Similar trends were seen in other developed nations' industries, with numerous foreign businesses setting up operations both domestically and abroad. The governments of the nations affected by this new investment are not entirely sure how they feel about it. More than just more jobs and increased production capacity could result from the opening of new foreign-owned plants; new technologies and improved business-control strategies could also be introduced. However, the government that embraces these advantages must also be prepared for accusations of "foreign control," a defense that will unavoidably be made by domestic plant owners who are afraid of new competitors that tariffs cannot stop. This has been a pressing problem for many governments, particularly insofar as investment by U.S. firms is involved, and it is a chief complaint of critics who view globalization as a form of economic exploitation. Some countries, such as the United Kingdom and Canada, have been liberal in their admissions policy; others, notably Japan, have imposed tight restrictions on foreign-owned plants.

2.2.6.2. Tariffs

A tax imposed on goods upon their entry into a customs area is known as a tariff or duty. A country or a group of nations that have decided to levy a single tax on goods entering their borders may define the boundary. Tariffs are frequently categorized as either revenue-generating or protective. Protective tariffs work by increasing the cost of the imported good to shield home producers from overseas competition. Tariffs on revenue are not intended to limit imports; rather, they are meant to raise revenue. Naturally, the two sets of goals are not exclusive of one another. Revenue tariffs provide some protection to any domestic producer of the duty-bearing goods, whereas protective tariffs yield revenue unless they are so high as to keep out imports. A transit duty, also known as a transit tax, is a levy imposed on goods traveling through a customs area on their way to another nation. Similar to this, a tax levied on goods leaving a customs area is known as an export duty or export tax. Finally, while import subsidies are rarely used, some nations offer export subsidies. The operation of tariffs. Import taxes can be imposed in a number of ways. Should they be enforced based on the actual amount of an import (e.g., the amount per ton, per yard, per item, etc.), they are known as particular tariffs. Ad valorem tariffs are applied when the amount of the tax is determined by the import's value. Different imports from different countries may be subject to different tariffs. For example, they might be lower between nations that have special agreements, like the trade preferences that EU members grant to one another. Tariffs can be applied in a variety of ways, and each one will impact the economy of the nation applying it differently. Tariffs may stimulate domestic production by driving up the cost of imported goods. Domestic employment typically increases in tandem with rising domestic product expenditures. For this reason, industries under pressure from overseas rivals tend to favor tariffs. Insofar as it reduces foreign competition, the tariff may also foster tendencies toward a monopolistic market structure, which would diminish incentives for innovation and modernization. Tariffs raise the cost of an imported good, which may lead to a decrease in consumption. The price of the import may be forced lower if the decline in demand is significant enough in comparison to the global market.

2.2.6.3. Measuring the Effects of Tariffs

Evaluating the impact of tariff barriers between nations is a challenging task. Needless to say, a number of factors will influence how import demand reacts to tariff changes. These include how producers and consumers respond to changes in prices, how much of imports are used in domestic production and consumption, whether imports can be substituted for native goods, and more. The way different countries and commodities respond to different tariff levels will also vary. Therefore, a tariff's level does not always indicate how restrictive it is. These kinds of comparisons usually only cover goods for which tariffs serve as the primary safeguard. This is usually the case for non-agricultural goods in developed nations (agricultural commodities are typically protected by other means, such as import quotas). Tariffs imposed on imported raw materials will shield domestic producers of those goods from foreign competition, but they will also drive-up costs for domestic manufacturers that rely on those raw materials. It is necessary to distinguish between nominal and effective rates of protection in light of these circumstances.

The percentage tariff a product faces upon entering the nation is known as the nominal rate of protection. For instance, if apparel is subject to a 20% value-based tariff upon entry, the corresponding 20% nominal rate of protection would apply. The idea of the effective rate of protection is more intricate when you take into account that the same product—clothing—costs $100 on foreign markets. The $60 material inputs that are imported are used to make the clothing. If there is free trade, a company cannot charge more than $100 (not including shipping) for an identical item of apparel. The clothing manufacturer can add up to $40 for labor, profit markup, rent, and other expenses after importing the fabric for $60. The term "value added" refers to the $40 that separates the product's price from the $60 cost of material inputs.

Tariffs, such as 20% on apparel and 10% on fabric, could be used to simulate the same scenario. A 10% tariff on fabrics would result in an increase in material costs of $6 to $66 for the domestic producer, while a 20% tariff on clothing would raise the domestic price by $20 to $120. With protection, the company would be able to operate with a $54 value-added margin, which is the difference between the $120 domestic price and the $66 material cost. A $14 margin is provided by the difference between the value added of $40 with tariff protection and $54 with it. Accordingly, the ratio of $14 to $40, or the effective rate of protection of the domestic processing activity, would be 35%. The nominal rate of protection, which is only 20%, is less than the effective rate of protection, which is 35%. This will always be the case when the final product's tariff rate is higher than the input tariff rate. Effective rates of protection are typically higher than nominal rates—often significantly higher—because countries typically impose higher tariffs on final goods than on inputs.

The percentage of value added in the product price that determines the effective rate of protection is another factor. Effective rates may be extremely low if value added to the imported good makes up a large portion of the total cost, or extremely high if value added accounts for a small portion of the price. Therefore, even though a country's nominal tariffs may be lower, its effective protection may be significantly higher than that of another if the latter tends to import goods with low ratios of value added to product price and high levels of fabrication.

2.2.6.4. Nontariff Barriers

Trade restrictions may also come from other laws and policies. Certain commodities may not be allowed to be imported at all or in limited quantities due to quotas or quantitative restrictions. These quotas are typically enforced by requiring importers to obtain licenses in order to import specific goods. Similar to tariffs, quotas also cause price increases, but because they are physical limits on quantity, they have a direct effect on imports. Raising prices isn't going to attract more merchandise. Additionally, the way tariffs and quotas affect revenue is different. Under quotas, import license holders receive a windfall in the form of the difference between the high domestic price and the low international price of the import. With tariffs, the government receives revenue.

The voluntary export restraint (VER), which is recognized for having a less detrimental impact on international relations, is another obstacle. It is also not too difficult to remove. This strategy was used in the early 1980s when Japanese automakers, pushed by U.S. rivals "voluntarily" reduced the amount of cars they exported to the U.S. market. Similar to quotas, VERs restrict trade volume, which drives up the cost of imported goods. In this instance, the VER increased the cost of Japanese cars and reduced their availability in the U.S. Because they were more expensive for consumers, cars made domestically became more appealing. Japanese exporters were also able to raise their prices thanks to this strategy. Consequently, Japanese exporters, as opposed to U.S. importers, who gained the most from the VER. VERs are typically not meaningfully voluntary. To avoid a U.S. in this instance, the Japanese automakers consented to a VER. U.S. import cap. State trading organizations and potentially biased government procurement procedures are still additional obstacles. Government procurement agencies in the U.S are required by "buy American" legislation to give preference to domestic products. Trade restrictions may also come from health laws, marking requirements, and customs classification and valuation processes. For instance, Japan has limited U.S. imports. U.S. citing the possibility that the apples may be tainted with the fire blight virus. Finally, if excise taxes are applied to imports more heavily than to domestic products, they may operate as a trade barrier.

2.2.6.5. Protectionism in the Less-Developed Countries

A significant portion of the late 20th-century industrialization witnessed in certain developing nations was typified by the growth of industries that faced import competition and were shielded by high tariff barriers. Tariffs and other quantitative restrictions on manufactured goods were common in many of those nations, but because the goods were frequently highly fabricated and the amount of value added in production after importation was low, the effective rates of protection were frequently even higher. Though they were usually the exception, nations like South Korea, Taiwan, and Hong Kong focused their manufacturing sectors primarily on exports. More often than not, developing countries have made the mistake of trying to compete on the home market with goods made abroad. High levels of protection in these nations have frequently caused production to slow down, and the export of primary commodities has deterred the growth of exports of more valuable manufactured goods. While producing nondurable consumer goods domestically can lead to rapid economic growth in the early stages of development, producing more sophisticated, value-added commodities has proven to be a significant challenge for less developed nations. They experience all the drawbacks of small home markets plus a dearth of incentives for advancement in technology.

2.2.7. Methods of International Trade Regulation

Regulation of international trade is complicated because different laws apply to different goods and can occasionally conflict with one another. Within the U.S. the government sets the laws and regulations governing trade and commerce across the nation, while individual states also have some authority. The World Trade Organization (WTO) aims to shield trading nations from any dishonest or unfair trade practices by implementing regulations on a global scale. In order to protect nations from receiving dangerous goods or products that may have been made illegally, specific strategies could involve enforcing regulations while maintaining market competition.

Prior to implementing any international trade regulation strategies, regulators need to be aware of emerging potentially harmful behaviors. Regulatory organizations recognize potential and real risks to global trade and establish regulations in response. These laws exist to safeguard not only the final consumer who may use or consume imported goods, but also the participating countries and businesses in trade.

Enforcing regulations pertaining to international trade involves taking steps to prevent monopolies while maintaining the promotion of fair competition. This may entail prohibiting any one organization in a closed-economy setting from engaging in trade with only one country. The main goal of regulation is to support an open economy that allows for greater freedom in importing and exporting goods. Any economy can be seriously harmed by protectionism, but a nation that depends significantly on foreign trade is particularly vulnerable.

Protectionism is more likely to occur in recessionary economic times when a nation tries to lessen international competition by imposing tariffs, quotas, and high taxes on traded goods. Attempting to enact and uphold legislation intended to stop protectionist actions could be one way of regulating international trade.

International trade regulations are frequently set up in a way that does not hinder trade activity. Additionally, regulations are in place to stop traders from engaging in dishonest or compromising behavior. This can be challenging given the conflicting national standards. On the other hand, voluntary agreements between participating trading nations may support common goals amongst them. A document may list specific behaviors that are considered appropriate and inappropriate for use in global trade. These themes could include, for example, an agreement to import and export goods made in an environmentally friendly manner and goods that will also benefit consumers' quality of life in terms of the environment.

2.3. INTERNATIONAL TRADE SERVICES

Companies that trade internationally can profit from a variety of services, such as those that provide guidance on export planning so the company can capitalize on its experience and distinctive selling propositions in foreign markets. Assistance may also be provided with regard to export license requirements, product standards, and regulations in foreign markets. Considerations such as product pricing, payment options, and freight contract terms need to be made; professional services can assist with this. Providers of international trade services can assist a company in finding freight forwarders and in drafting international contracts. Among the services offered for international trade are help organizing trade delegations, participating in trade shows, and locating agents or partners in overseas markets. Businesses looking to enter a new international market are probably going to require the assistance of a market research firm, which can provide an analysis of the foreign market, the rivals operating in that market, the most effective methods of entering the market, and the best marketing plan. In order to determine public preference trends in the international market and to offer an analysis of business opportunities, the market research company may conduct social research. Research on a company's brand's influence in foreign markets, its advantages and disadvantages, and the strength and weakness of rival brands can be beneficial. There are organizations that provide services related to trade shows and promotions, which businesses can use to showcase their goods and services abroad. In addition to assisting with space reservations and exhibition setup, intermediaries can also aid with business promotion abroad. Other organizations focus on planning business executive group tours to explore conditions in their industry abroad; the intermediary organization can set up meetings between the executives and government and industry representatives. These groups might also offer interpreters and translation services.

Seeking possible local partners abroad is a component of other international trade services. Companies may be searching for a partner in another nation due to local regulations, the need to collaborate with a business that has local expertise, or the need to establish a local distribution network. The business might require assistance in locating a fit local company to join in a partnership or joint venture on a contractual or equity basis. Other kinds of intermediaries might locate agents to represent a company abroad or provide international trade services that match buyers and sellers in a specific international market.

2.3.1. Methods to Measure the Gain from International Trade

Economists have adopted various methods to measure the gains from international trade which are explained as under:

2.3.1.1. The Classical Method

Jacob Viner points out that the classical economists followed three different methods or criteria for measuring the gains from international trade: (1) differences in comparative costs; (2) increase in the level of national income; and (3) the terms of trade.

But they often intermixed these methods without specifying them clearly. We discuss them as under.

2.3.1.1.1. Ricardo's Approach

In accordance with Ricardo's method, a nation will import goods with high comparative production costs and export those with lower comparative production costs. As a result, the nation uses its resources more efficiently, earning more money overall for a given quantity of them than it would if it tried to produce everything on its own.

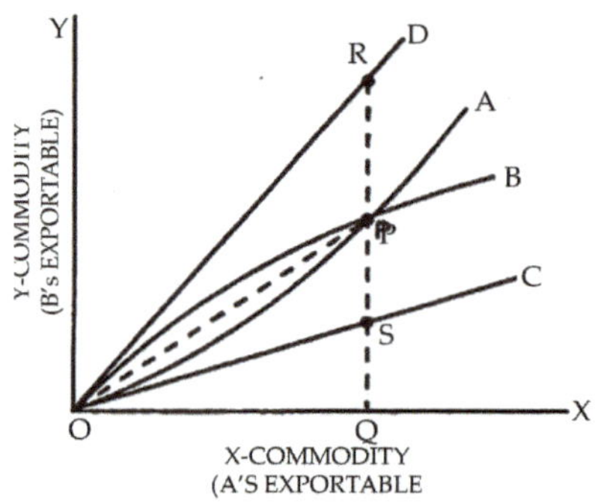

Figure 2.3. *Ricardo's approach.*

Source: https://www.economicsdiscussion.net/wp-content/uploads/2018/03/clip_image002_thumb-10.jpg.

Prof. Ronald Findlay in his Trade and Specialization has explained Ricardo's approach to the gains from international trade in terms of Figure 2.3. In the pre-trade situation, AB is the production possibility curve of a country which produces two commodities X and Y, given the quantity of labor input. On AS, the country is in equilibrium at point E.

After it enters into trade, its international price ratio is given by the slope of the line CB. Suppose that it is in equilibrium at point F on the line CB. If the quantities of X and Y represented by the combination at F are to be produced domestically, the quantity of labor input will have to increase sufficiently to shift the domestic production possibility curve up from AB to A_1B_1 The gains from trade will thus be measured by BB_1/OB.

But Malthus criticized Ricardo for greatly over-estimating the gains from trade. In terms of Fig 2.3, Malthus's view is that with the shifting of the domestic production possibility curve to A_1B_1 F would not be the equilibrium point. Relative prices along A_1B_1 would not be more favorable to the exported commodity X than along CB, so that consumer will prefer a point to the right of F on A_1B_1, rather than F itself. Hence the gains from trading along CB cannot be measured by an increase of labor input in the ratio BB_1/OB. This is because the change to the right of F on A_1B_1 is preferable to that on CB. Prof. Ronald Findlay has modified the Ricardo measure of the gains from trade using the community indifference curve Cl. If the labor input is increased sufficiently to push the production possibility curve to A_0B_0 instead of to A_1B_1 the point G on the CI curve will make each individual as better as he is at the free trade point F. The gains from trade would, therefore, be equal to BBJOB instead of the larger BB_1IOB. This measure satisfies Malthus's criticism of Ricardo.

2.3.1.1.2. Mill's Approach

J.S. Mill analyzed the gains as well as the distribution of the gains from international trade in terms of his theory of reciprocal demand. According to Mill, it is reciprocal demand that determines terms of trade which, in turn, determine the distribution of gains from trade of each country. The term 'terms of trade' refers to the barter terms of trade between the two countries i.e., the ratio of the quantity of imports for a given quantity of exports of a country.

To take an example, in country A, 2 units of labor produce 10 units of X and 10 units of Y, while in country B the same labor produces 6X and 8K. The domestic exchange ratio (or domestic terms of trade) in country A is IX = 1 Y, and in country B, IX = 1.33У. This means that one unit of X can be exchanged with one unit of Y in country A or 1.33 units of Y in country B. Thus the terms of trade between the two countries will lie between 1X or 1Y or 1.33 Y.

However, the actual exchange ratio will depend upon reciprocal demand, i.e., "the relative strength and elasticity of demand of the two trading countries for each other's product in terms of their own product." If A's demand for commodity Y is more intense (inelastic), then the terms of trade will be nearer IX = IK. The terms of trade will move in favor of B and against country A. B will gain more and A less. On the other hand, if A's demand for commodity Y is less intense (more elastic), then the terms of trade will be nearer IX = 1.33K. The terms of trade will move in favor of A and against B. A will gain more and B less.

The distribution of gains from trade is explained in terms of the Marshall-Edge worth offer curves in 2.4. OA is the offer curve of country A, and OB of country B. OP and OQ are the domestic constant cost ratios of producing O X and Y in country A and B respectively. These rays are, in fact, the limits within which the terms of trade between the two countries lie. However, the actual terms of trade are settled at E the point of inter-section of OA and OB.

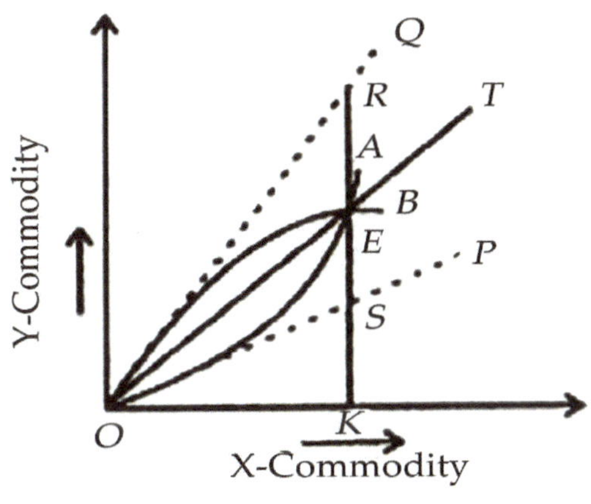

Figure 2.4. *Mill's approach.*

Source: https://www.economicsdiscussion.net/wp-content/uploads/2018/03/clip_image004_thumb-6.jpg.

The line OT represents equilibrium terms of trade at E. The cost ratio within country A is KS units of Y: OK units of X. But it gets KE units of Y through trade. SE units of Y is, therefore, its gain. The cost ratio within country B is KR units of Y: OK units of X. But it imports OK units of X from country A in exchange for only KE units of Y. EP units of Y is its gain. Thus both countries gain by entering into trade.

2.3.1.2. The Modern Approach

The benefits of international trade are distinguished in modern trade theory between the benefits of exchange and specialization. By considering demand and supply, the analysis is explained in terms of the general equilibrium of a closed economy. It is identified by the equality of the marginal rates of substitution between commodities in production and consumption with the domestic terms of trade or commodity price ratio, as well as the tangency of a community indifference curve with the transformation curve. Gains from specialization and exchange are realized thanks to the advent of international trade. The new marginal rates of substitution in consumption and transformation in production are equal to the terms of trade or international price ratio when equilibrium is reached and these gains are maximized. As a result, by producing and consuming more than before trade, both producers and consumers benefit from international trade. Figure 2.4 explains the gains from inter-national trade. AB is the transformation curve representing the supply side and CI_0 is the community indifference curve representing the demand side of an economy. The closed economy (no trade) equilibrium is shown by point E where the AB and CI_0 curves are tangent to each other and both equal the domestic terms of trade or commodity price ratio (line) P.

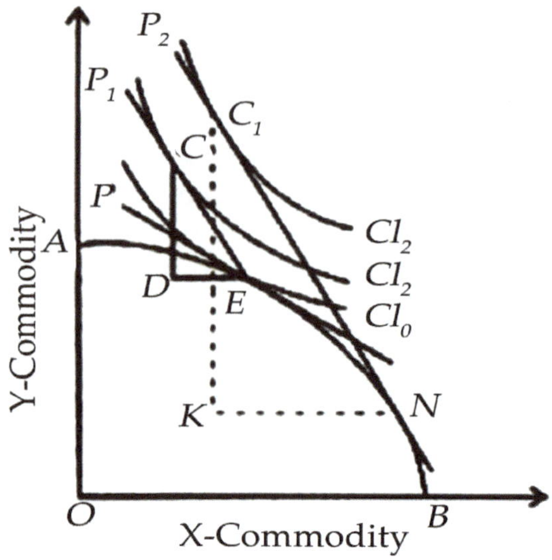

Figure 2.5. *The modern approach.*

Source: https://www.economicsdiscussion.net/wp-content/uploads/2018/03/clip_image005_thumb-3.jpg.

With the introduction of international (or free) trade, the international price ratio (terms of trade) will be different from the domestic price ratio (terms of trade). It is shown as P_1 and is steeper than the domestic price ratio P. It means that the price of commodity X has increased in relation to commodity Y in the world market. At the X-Commodity international price line P_1 the consumers move to point C on a higher Figure 2.5 community indifference curve CI_0 from point E on the CI_0 curve. This movement from E to C measures the gain from exchange or consumption gain with no change in production.

Since the price of X has increased in the world market, producers increase its production and decrease that of Y. This leads to movement along the transformation curve from point E to N where a new international price line P, is tangent to the AB curve. In other words, at N the marginal rate of transformation in production equals the international price ratio. The new world terms of trade ratio P_2 is the same as P_1 because it is parallel to P_1. At N the country exports KN of X in exchange for KC_X imports of Y.

As a result of increased specialization in the production of X, there is a shift in consumption from point C on the CI_1 curve to point C_1 on the CI_1 curve, where consumers consume larger quantities of both X and Y. This movement from C to C_1 measures the gain from specialization in production or production gain. At C, the marginal rate of substitution and the international price ratio are equal. Hence the gains from international trade are maximized at points N and C, because the marginal rate of transformation in production and the marginal rate of substitution in consumption are equal to the international price ratio P_2. The total gain from free trade is the sum of the consumption and production gains and is shown as improvement in welfare from CI_0 to CI_2.

Increase in National Income. This analysis also explains the increase in the real income and hence the gains from trade. Point N on the price line P_2 corresponds to a higher real income than the pre-trade point E at the price line P. This is because at the new price line P_2 there are production and consumption gains to the country after trade.

2.3.2. Role of International Trade

Every nation's economy depends heavily on international trade. The amount of imports relative to exports, or the balance of trade, determines how a nation's GDP is calculated and, in turn, affects how the general public views the state of the economy. More significantly, since workers are hired to produce the goods that are sold abroad, trade opens up previously unreachable markets for sellers and boosts productivity in the home nation. 95% of a company's potential market is overseas, according to a common business axiom. A business loses out on enormous growth opportunities if it restricts itself to sales made within its own borders. From an economic standpoint, the primary goal of international trade for corporations and many other kinds of enterprises is to maximize profits for owners.

Governments take a broader view of the impact of global trade on the state of the economy. Because the business sector can produce goods for export, more people are employed nationwide, which increases the amount of inventory produced. Additionally, since the nation is practically exporting its values and way of life along with its goods, it indicates that the nation is in a stronger position internationally. Every successful domestic product in a foreign nation makes it more difficult for the government of that nation to take a chance on deteriorating trade relations in international negotiations on unrelated issues.

International trade has an impact on the gross domestic product, an economic indicator that tracks a nation's level of production. A nation's GDP will probably decline over time if it imports more goods than it exports because it will become dependent on imports and be unable to use its own workforce to produce the goods that the public wants to purchase. The goal of international trade in the economy is to maintain a balance between imports and exports that supports a high standard of living and a robust national economy.

Maintaining the health and happiness of a nation's population may be the primary function of international trade. Trade with other countries supplies all the resources and goods that a nation is unable to efficiently produce on its own. Many would be dissatisfied if they could only purchase goods produced in their own nation, from supplying wood products to desert nations to making coffee available in Alaska. Governments are finding it more difficult to persuade the public that it is okay to live without the modern conveniences that citizens of other nations take for granted as global communication improves. Over time, the absence of contemporary goods has played a role in inciting citizen uprisings in nations where the government has attempted to isolate the nation from the outside world.

2.3.3. International Trade Strategies

Businesses that are thinking about expanding internationally need to plan out their operations and create international trade strategies. It is imperative to gather comprehensive data regarding international markets, contemplate forthcoming advancements in the sector, and implement a strategic marketing plan. A company needs to determine if its goal in the other country is to establish a presence or just trade with importers. If so, the company needs to determine whether to open a sales office or conduct business via a subsidiary or branch. The creation of a regional holding company could be part of an international trade strategy for companies that trade across borders in a given region. This would allow them to take advantage of the best possible regional knowledge and coordination, which could lead to favorable tax and regulatory treatment.

All possible business risks must be considered when analyzing the potential overseas market. International trade strategies need to consider the possibility of revenue loss due to a decline in demand brought on by shifts in consumer preferences and fashion. Risks like increases in interest rates or the value of real estate in the other nation must be taken into account. If the foreign nation uses a different currency, exchange rate risk must also be taken into account. When creating international trade strategies, it is important to take political risk into consideration. Examples of political risk include the potential for a foreign government to expropriate assets or the effects of political instability. The best legal structure to use must be taken into consideration if the business is to create a presence in the other nation through which it can conduct business. While it might not be too difficult to establish a branch, some nations demand that foreign businesses establish a subsidiary company. In addition to registering with the foreign government, a branch or subsidiary may also need to register with the tax authorities. In certain nations, the company might have to accept involvement from a local business in the form of a joint venture or equity. The company must also determine whether foreign investor activities in the industry it plans to trade in are subject to any restrictions. When determining where to locate manufacturing facilities abroad, businesses creating international trade plans ought to search for free zones or special economic zones.

These zones might have benefits like lower rent, better infrastructure, or tax breaks. It is crucial to confirm that a business is eligible for the concessions provided by the zone, as certain business categories may be excluded from these zones. Strategies for international trade should consider the potential need to pay customs charges when importing goods and raw materials into another nation. When creating the plan, it's important to take into account the tax situation in the foreign nation and how it affects the tax situation in the nation of origin.

2.3.4. Advantages of International Trade

Even in the 21st century, the idea of international trade is still debatable. International trade in products, services, and labor can have many advantages for all parties involved, but it can also have many drawbacks. The market's consistency and diversity, freedom from regional monopolies, technological and cultural exchange, and the potential for higher environmental and human rights standards are some benefits of global trade. Many of the benefits of global trade can only be realized with the aid of social activism and governmental regulations; these benefits are not always intrinsic.

The number of customers who can reasonably access the goods that are available is a common indicator of market size. In earlier times, only people who lived nearby could visit a market by foot or by bicycle. People were consequently restricted to the products and services generated nearby. The enormous technological developments in preservation and transportation contributed to the "globalization" of markets. Globalization has made a wider range of goods available to consumers, which is one of the main benefits of international trade.

Consistent availability is one of the agricultural market's most beneficial outcomes of international trade. Certain fruits and vegetables can only be grown in certain places during specific seasons due to differences in climate; for example, in a temperate climate, strawberries can only be locally harvested in the late spring. However, international trade has made it possible for strawberries and many other types of produce to be available year-round due to warmer climates and quick transportation.

The variety of products available on global marketplaces also shields consumers from the negative consequences of monopolies. Prices typically decrease in an environment of healthy global competition because buyers will seek out the best offers. Lack of competition can cause the market to stagnate or, worse, to be cornered by one company. Prices usually soar when a single local supplier controls the whole market. The ability of global trade to increase consumer choice and prevent suppliers from establishing monopolies is one of its main benefits.

Some people believe that the exchange of technology and culture that results from free trade is one of the most important benefits of international trade. Sociologists usually contend that fear of the unknown is the root cause of cultural mistrust and hatred; xenophobia can be eliminated and relationships can be strengthened by providing opportunities for trade between various nations. When it comes to technology, developing countries often gain from new technology imported from developed countries, which can expedite the development of business and infrastructure. Even though it's not always given priority, some social and environmental activists think that one of the main advantages of global trade is the chance to raise labor and environmental standards everywhere. Industrialized nations can contribute to reducing ecological damage and improving human rights by forming partnerships with countries that promise to use environmentally safe practices and give workers fair wages and hours.

2.3.5. Terms of Trade

The relationship that exists between a nation's export and import prices is known as the terms of trade. A nation's terms of trade are said to have improved if the prices of its exports increase in relation to the prices of its imports.

This is because the nation now effectively receives more imports for every unit of goods exported.

The terms of trade specify how the profits from international trade will be divided among trading nations and are based on the global supply and demand for the goods involved. Additionally, the idea is applied to various economic sectors (e.g., the manufacturing and agricultural sectors).

A sudden modification to a nation's trade terms (e.g., a significant decline in the price of a primary product that is a nation's principal export) can result in major balance-of-payments issues if the nation depends on the foreign exchange received from its exports to pay for the import of its capital equipment and manufactured goods. A thorough analysis of trade statistics has not revealed any evidence to support any of the numerous theories that have been proposed to explain changes in the terms of trade.

A long-held misconception was that less developed nations' exports were mostly primary goods (like coffee or rubber), while their imports were mostly manufactured and, thus, more expensive goods from developed nations. This led to the idea that the terms of trade tended to move against less developed nations. More recent research has looked at the potential effects on a nation's terms of trade of labor inflows (via immigration) and capital inflows (through foreign investment).

2.3.6. Facets of International Trade

Businesses that are efficient enough to compete on the global market conduct international trade. Businesses in different nations typically focus on distinct industries; for instance, developed nations may have firms that are experts in financial services or high-tech manufacturing, while developing nations may export primarily agricultural goods. In order to shield specific domestic industries from foreign imports, governments impose tariffs or quotas, which hinder international trade. Reducing tariff barriers and offering dispute resolution procedures are two ways that international agreements and organizations have sought to increase trade. Improved transportation methods, containerization, and uniform terms for international contracts have all benefited world trade. International agreements and organizations like the World Trade Organization (WTO) have made it easier to trade internationally. Tariffs and quotas that had been impeding international trade have been lowered as a result of negotiations. In the event that disagreements emerge regarding the application of tariffs, a dispute resolution process exists that involves penalizing nations that violate regulations. WTO negotiations guarantee that international trade issues are carefully considered, despite the fact that international agreements are frequently difficult to reach. Reducing farmer subsidies in developed nations and taking into account the need for protection for agriculture and other sectors in less developed nations are among the issues pertaining to global trade that still need to be resolved as of 2011. The advent of containerization has greatly simplified the logistics of shipping goods internationally. International trade has been boosted by the growth of sizable container seaports, inland dry ports, and quick docking, loading, and unloading procedures. Larger ships can carry heavier loads and are guided to port by radar. The ports have grown in size to handle the cargo and have built the necessary infrastructure to move it quickly. Organizations like the International Chamber of Commerce (ICC) have worked to harmonize terms used in international contracts. Standard contracts lessen the chance of miscommunication regarding the division of freight and insurance expenses between buyers and sellers. In order to ensure that financial matters are completed as quickly and smoothly as possible, letters of credit have been modified in response to the decrease in payment concerns brought about by the increased use of electronic means of payment. The implementation of dispute resolution mechanisms by organizations like the United Nations Commission on International Trade Law (UNCITRAL) may facilitate the resolution of disputes pertaining to international trade. By establishing bilateral investment protection agreements that offer specific guarantees to investors and provide for dispute resolution, nations have made it easier for businesses to conduct business internationally. In a similar vein, bilateral agreements aimed at preventing double taxation of companies engaged in international trade also serve as a means of resolving tax disputes between nations.

2.4. BARRIER OF INTERNATIONAL TRADE

The global economy depends heavily on international trade because it makes cross-border exchanges of goods and services possible. Trade barriers are the most significant challenge to this exchange, though it is not without its difficulties. These obstacles can be in the form of many different things, affecting importers and exporters alike and having an effect on market access, economic growth, and general welfare.

Tariffs are a common form of barrier to global trade. Tariffs are levied by governments to increase the cost of imported goods relative to those made domestically. Customers pay more as a result, and overseas producers are less competitive. Tariffs may also set off countermeasures from trading partners, leading to trade disputes that destabilize international markets and threaten economic stability.

Non-tariff barriers (NTBs) are a class of restrictions that extend beyond tariffs and constitute another barrier. Quotas, import permits, product standards, and sanitary and phytosanitary laws are examples of non-trade barriers (NTBs). Even though the goal of these regulations may be to safeguard homegrown businesses, they may also effectively restrict foreign producers' access to the market, which would inhibit innovation and competition. NTBs place a heavy burden on both importers and exporters because they frequently necessitate adherence to intricate and expensive regulatory frameworks.

Variations in exchange rates are another thing that hinders trade internationally. Unpredictable currency fluctuations put businesses involved in cross-border transactions at risk and create uncertainty. A weak currency can raise the cost of imported goods, which will impact domestic consumers, while a strong domestic currency can increase the cost of exports and make them less competitive in overseas markets. Businesses must manage currency risk if they want to stay profitable and competitive in international markets.

International trade can also be hampered by legal and political obstacles. Foreign investment can be discouraged and business environments made unpredictable by political instability, corruption, and policy changes. The ease of conducting international trade operations is impacted by legal barriers that differ greatly between countries, including those pertaining to intellectual property rights protection, dispute resolution procedures, and regulatory transparency. International trade patterns are influenced by social and cultural barriers as well. Language barriers, cultural norms, and customer preferences can all affect market demand, necessitating adjustments to a company's offerings and advertising plans. International trade partnerships require the development of relationships and trust across cultural divides. Moreover, trade efficiency and cost-effectiveness are affected by infrastructure and logistical obstacles. Transaction costs can rise due to insufficient ports, transportation networks, and customs procedures. To increase trade facilitation and lower entry barriers into markets, infrastructure improvements and logistics optimization are essential.

Despite these difficulties, numerous strategies have been used in an effort to lower trade barriers internationally. The goal of trade agreements, such as regional trade blocs and free trade agreements (FTAs), is to harmonize regulations and reduce tariffs among participating nations. A more transparent and stable international trading system is promoted by international organizations such as the World Trade Organization (WTO), which offer frameworks for trade agreement negotiations and dispute resolution. Although there are many prospects for economic growth and development in international trade, there are also many difficult challenges to overcome.

These include tariffs, non-tariff measures, exchange rate fluctuations, political and legal unpredictabilities, cultural differences, and logistical difficulties. In order to create a more inclusive and sustainable global trading environment, governments, corporations, and international organizations must work together to address these barriers.

Countries can fully utilize the potential of international trade to improve their economies and societies by lowering trade barriers and fostering honest and open trade practices.

2.4.1. Dispute the Trade Barriers

Even though they are sometimes seen negatively, trade barriers are essential for maintaining national interests, ensuring regulatory compliance, and defending home industries. For example, tariffs serve as a way for governments to recoup costs while simultaneously providing a level playing field for domestic producers facing off against imports that are cheaper. Governments can counteract unfair trade practices like dumping, in which overseas manufacturers sell their goods below cost in order to gain unfair market share, by imposing tariffs.

The goals of non-tariff barriers (NTBs), such as regulatory standards and quotas, are the same: maintaining environmental protection, consumer safety, and quality standards. By ensuring that imported goods adhere to domestic regulatory standards, these precautions stop the entry of inferior goods that might harm the environment or public health. Quotas and licenses for imports aid in controlling the amount of goods that enter the nation, avoiding market saturation and preserving the viability of regional industries.

Changes in exchange rates can be advantageous as well as challenging. Lower import costs translate into cheaper prices for customers purchasing foreign goods when their home currency appreciates. On the other hand, a depreciating currency makes exports more competitive and increases the demand for domestically made goods in foreign markets. Exchange rate mechanisms and prudent monetary policies can effectively manage these fluctuations, enabling nations to adapt to global economic conditions. Although perceived as obstacles at times, political and legal barriers play a crucial role in upholding stability and implementing regulatory frameworks.

Stable political environments encourage long-term investments and business operations, and strong legal frameworks safeguard intellectual property rights and offer effective channels for settling disputes. These frameworks guarantee that companies can conduct business in overseas markets with assurance and predictability.

Although social and cultural differences are frequently mentioned as obstacles, they also offer chances for market adaptation and diversification. Businesses can effectively tailor their products and marketing strategies to local customs and preferences, increasing consumer acceptance and brand loyalty in a variety of markets. Establishing partnerships based on respect and understanding as well as developing cultural competency are key components of long-lasting and mutually beneficial trade partnerships.

Notwithstanding their importance, logistical and infrastructural issues are increasingly being resolved by investments in cutting-edge transit systems, digital infrastructure, and expedited customs processes. These upgrades lower transaction costs, cut down on delays, and boost supply chain effectiveness, enabling more seamless trade flows and greater access to international markets for companies.

Trade barriers are necessary for maintaining regulatory standards, safeguarding home industries, and promoting fair competition, even though they can present difficulties. Governments can encourage a more robust and sustainable international trading system by finding a balance between advancing free markets and defending national interests. To maximize the advantages of international trade for all parties involved and navigate through its complexities, countries must work together with the support of international organizations and trade agreements.

2.4.2. Tariff Barriers of International Trade

Tariff barriers are levies applied to goods that, although not always the intention behind their establishment, effectively obstruct trade. Because they restrict the quantity of goods that can be imported into a nation, these obstacles are also occasionally referred to as import restraints. Both tariff and non-tariff trade barriers are a source of concern for many pro-trade organizations, and several countries have made the decision to drastically lower their trade barriers in order to encourage the flow of goods across national borders.

Goods that cross international borders may be subject to a variety of duties. For instance, in the case of an ad valorem duty, the importer is required to pay a fee that is determined by a percentage of the value of the goods being imported. Environmental tariffs penalize countries with bad environmental records, while specific tariffs are fixed amounts imposed on imported goods, regardless of value. Tariff barriers can make it more difficult for importers to enter a nation.

The importer might have to charge more for the goods in order to justify importing, or it might be forced to import less because the tariff barriers are too expensive. In order to level the playing field between importers and domestic producers and enable expensive domestic producers to compete with importers who might be able to bring in goods at a lower cost, tariffs are intended to force importers to take this action.

Protectionism is widespread in many countries, but it is also disliked, especially by those that wish to be able to export goods for trade with other nations. Protectionism advances the interests of domestic producers by placing restrictions on importers. To lessen the burden on importers, organizations like the World Trade Organization have advocated for the removal of tariff barriers. Organizations that support free trade also work to remove non-tariff barriers like import quotas. Even in countries that are highly open to free trade, certain tariff barriers are probably going to be in place for a long time. Restructuring the tax, tariff, and related expenditure structures is an ongoing endeavor, and countries sometimes retaliate by drastically changing their trade barriers and tariffs.

Trade barriers are another tool that nations can use to make political statements intended to exert pressure on other nations to change their ways. For instance, until Country B can provide proof that its meat supply is free of bovine spongiform encephalitis (BSE), commonly known as mad cow disease, Country A may refuse to import beef from Country B. Tariffs, also known as customs duties, are levied by the government of the importing nation typically as a tax on goods as they cross national borders. It is acceptable to use the terms tariff, duty, and customs interchangeably.

2.4.3. Objectives of Tariffs

Tariffs can be applied to protect or to raise revenue, but a tariff intended primarily for protection may also have a significant protective effect. On the other hand, a tariff intended primarily for revenue raising may result in revenue.

In The Theory of International Trade (1937), Gottfried von Haberler proposed that comparing the impact of revenue duties and protective duties on domestic versus foreign producers is the most effective method of differentiating between them, regardless of the legislators' intentions.

The duty is not protective if domestically produced goods are taxed equally with similar imported goods, if the foreign goods subject to the duty are not produced domestically, and if there are no domestically produced substitutes that the tariff directs demand toward. A purely protective duty has the tendency to cause production to move from export-oriented industries to domestic industries that are protected or to other industries that produce substitutes that are in higher demand. A purely revenue duty, on the other hand, will direct resources toward the production of those goods and services upon which the additional government receipts are spent, rather than encouraging investment in industries producing the taxed goods or close substitutes for such goods.

From the perspective of revenue alone, a nation can choose to import a relatively small number of general-purpose goods at low duty or levy an equivalent tax on domestic production (to avoid protecting it) to prevent the tendency of resources to be diverted into industries that produce such taxed goods (or substitutes for them). However, a nation's list of protected goods will be extensive and its tariff rates high if it wants to safeguard its domestic industries. Tariffs are frequently imposed or removed in order to achieve political objectives. Three categories of tariffs exist: import duties, export duties, and transit duties.

2.4.3.1. Transit Duties

This kind of tax is applied to goods that are shipped from one nation to another after passing through another. As the name suggests, the nation through which the goods pass imposes transit duties. Although these tariffs are no longer significant tools for determining trade policy, they were useful in controlling trade routes and directing trade during the mercantilist era (16th–18th century) and even into the middle of the 19th century in some nations. Prussia's use of its authority to impose transit duties contributed to the creation of the German Zollverein, or customs union, in the first part of the 1800s. The most obvious and direct result of transit duties is a decrease in the volume of commodities traded globally and an increase in the cost of those goods for the country that imports them.

2.4.3.2. Export Duties

The burden of an export duty will probably fall on the domestic producer, who will receive the world price less the duty and other charges, if the nation imposing the duty supplies a small portion of the global exports and if competitive conditions prevail. However, output will decline if the nation produces a sizable share of the global output and if domestic supply is sensitive to lower net prices; as a result, world prices will likely rise, and the export tax will be borne by both domestic producers and foreign consumers. The extent to which a nation can utilize export duties to capitalize on its exclusive status as a supplier of specific raw materials is contingent upon the degree to which rival nations are able to identify alternatives or alternative sources of supply.

2.4.3.3. Import Duties

The most significant and prevalent kind of customs charges are import duties. Tariffs are an unsatisfactory way to raise money because they tend to encourage economically inefficient domestic production of the dutied item. They may be imposed for protection, revenue, or both. To avoid uneconomical protection, it is preferable to tax all consumption rather than just the consumption of imports, even if imports make up the majority of the available revenue base. In developed nations, import taxes are no longer a significant source of income. For instance, in the United States, import duty income in 1808 was twice as much as all government spending, but by 1837 it was less than one-third of that amount. Prior to the close of the 1800s, the customs receipts of the U.S. Approximately half of its revenue came from the government. Prior to the start of World War II, this percentage had dropped to roughly 6% of total receipts, and it has since continued to decline.

A tariff can be compound, ad valorem, or specific i.e., or a mix of the two. A specific duty is a charge of a certain amount of money, like $1 per yard or per pound, per unit of the import. In contrast, an ad valorem duty is determined as a percentage of the import's value. While the real burden of specific rates varies inversely with changes in the prices of the imports, ad valorem rates provide a constant degree of protection at all price levels (assuming prices change at the same rate at home and abroad). On the other hand, a specific duty penalizes lower grades of imported goods more severely. This problem can be partially avoided by carefully and thoroughly classifying imports according to the level of finishing (e.g., finished goods, or raw materials), but this process results in incredibly drawn-out and intricate tariff schedules.

A tariff schedule is essentially a list of all import duties. Regardless of the country of origin, all imports are subject to the same tariff schedule. This means that the column that appears next to the listed commodities only has one duty listed. Different rates are applied to commodities based on their country of origin under a double-column or multicolumn tariff, with lower rates applied to goods originating from nations with which tariff agreements have been negotiated. The most-favored-nation clause, which applies to all parties to the agreement regardless of the concessions made to the most-favored nation, is the foundation of the majority of trade agreements. Every nation has a free list of goods that are admitted duty-free; however, little information regarding the effect of tariffs on trade can be gleaned from the free list and the value of the goods that are imported into a nation.

Furthermore, estimating the height of a tariff wall and comparing the level of protection between nations using the ratio of tariff receipts to the total value of imports is practically hard. By using this method, one could mistakenly conclude that a nation that exempts more than half of its imports from duties has very little tariff protection. However, such a conclusion is untrue because certain goods are subject to extremely high tariffs, and the volume of dutied imports declines as those tariff levels rise. Converting all duties into ad valorem figures (based on the value of the goods) and then estimating the weighted-average rate is a better way to measure the height of a tariff wall. A tariff on food, for example, may have a far greater impact than a tariff on luxuries that are favored by a select few. The weighting of the imports should take this into account. Furthermore, a deeper comprehension of protectionism can be attained by examining the effective rate of protection.

It acknowledges that the level of protection granted to a specific domestic industry is contingent upon the tariffs imposed not only on the final product (output) but also on the inputs used to make it. Assume, for instance, that 100% of the import duties apply to half of the inputs used in an industry. There is no real protection if the imports that the industry competes with have duties that are lower than 50%. In a real-world scenario, figuring out how effective protection is requires intricate economic analysis.

2.4.4. Tariff Reduction and the Growth of International Trade

International trade increased significantly in the second half of the 20th century for both goods and services. The total amount of trade in the world increased by 22 times between 1950 and 2000. Simultaneously with the global reduction or even elimination of trade barriers, particularly tariffs, there was an upsurge in multilateral international trade. The General Agreement on Tariffs and Trade (GATT), a set of trade agreements enacted in 1948, was a primary catalyst for the expansion of trade globally. A number of trade talks centered on tariff reductions were facilitated by the GATT system. The majority of the early trade agreements focused on tangible goods like steel, cars, processed foods, and agricultural products. The World Trade Organization (WTO) was established in 1995 as a result of the Uruguay Round of negotiations.

The 1990s saw significant progress in information technology, which changed the focus of many trade agreements. The WTO's Basic Telecommunications Agreement (BTA) and Information Technology Agreement (ITA) reduced tariffs on computer and telecommunications products as well as some intangible goods that are thought to be key components of the emerging knowledge-based economy in 1997. In part because many nations were slow to adopt bilateral free-trade agreements that included provisions covering e-commerce, the Internet's and e-commerce's rapid growth represented some of the most difficult new issues in the field of international trade. Both the ITA and the BTA marked a significant shift from previous national economic policies, particularly in instances where nations employed excessively high tariffs and subsidies to shield their technology sectors from foreign rivals. WTO-sponsored agreements, according to proponents of free trade and the WTO, present the most effective way to lower consumer prices for a variety of goods while fostering more equitable competitive conditions for foreign suppliers.

Opponents of globalization disrupted trade talks during the 1999 WTO ministerial conference in Seattle, Washington, bringing the organization's work under closer scrutiny. The most severe criticisms focused on topics like the rights of domestic workers, the rights of the environment, health and safety, the democratic nature of the WTO, and the long-term wisdom of supporting free trade and commercialism at the expense of other values. These critics raised a variety of concerns about the authority and reach of the WTO. Nonetheless, there is no denying that tariff reduction has a significant positive economic impact. WTO supporters have highlighted the organization's benefits by highlighting income growth, efficiency gains, and lower living expenses. Despite acknowledging the contentious nature of the WTO's principles and regulations, which advocate for reduced tariffs among participating countries, these proponents maintain that the organization offers a democratic platform for settling disputes in a transparent, fair, and open manner.

2.4.5. Nontariff Barrier

Any measure or policy that limits imports but does not constitute a tariff is known as a nontariff barrier. Tariffs are levied by the government on goods imported and exported with the intention of regulating the balance of trade between two nations. National quality standards and onerous customs procedures are just two examples of the many policies and practices that can have the effect of limiting imports. Nontariff barriers can be broadly classified into three groups: indirect barriers, regulatory barriers that also have the effect of restricting imports, and barriers that directly seek to limit imports in order to protect a national interest.

International trade organizations work to advance unrestricted access to markets and global free trade. A Chinese company should have unrestricted access to the US market and vice versa from the standpoint of free trade. Demand for goods ought to be the ultimate leveler, and consumers ought to be free to choose products according to their own needs rather than those of the federal government. Free trade appears to be the perfect embodiment of market capitalism, but in practice, nations seek to safeguard their own sectors of the economy, maintain employment for their workforce, and expand their industries. The balance of trade between a nation and other nations determines that nation's economic standing. Stated differently, the goal of governments is to attain a balance or, at the very least, export more than they require. A country's industry can be completely destroyed and economic output can be adversely affected if imports from abroad surpass exports. A higher volume of imports indicates that fewer workers were needed to produce goods domestically.

Governments have historically imposed tariffs to control imports. Import taxes increase the cost of foreign countries' access to the domestic market. International trade organizations oppose the imposition of tariffs because they are an extremely blunt method of attempting to restrict imports. In contrast, a nontariff barrier can accomplish the same goal as a tariff without requiring the government to establish an import strategy. Nontariff barriers typically fall into one of three categories. In order to safeguard a significant national interest—like the survival of a specific industry or the advancement of a public interest like reducing unemployment—the first category explicitly seeks to restrict imports.

A customs surcharge on imports or an export subsidy are two instances of nontariff barriers. Imports are restricted by regulatory barriers, which fall under the second category. Both domestic and foreign businesses must overcome these obstacles, but due to the state of their respective industries, it is typically more difficult for the foreign business to do so. An illustration of this kind of nontariff barrier is a safety requirement for kid's toys that is common in one nation but challenging for the importer to carry out.

The third type of nontariff barriers are indirect ones. It covers any policy that has the effect of a trade restriction even though it is not meant to be one. Local laws, customs, and traditions that inadvertently discourage the purchase of foreign goods are a few examples.

CASE STUDY

THE TRADE RELATIONSHIP BETWEEN THE UNITED STATES AND CHINA

1. Background

United States:

- **Economy Type:** Mixed economy with a focus on services, technology, and manufacturing.
- **Key Exports:** Machinery, aircraft, electrical machinery, vehicles, and agricultural products.
- **Key Imports:** Electronics, machinery, furniture, toys, and clothing.

China:

- **Economy Type:** Socialist market economy with a significant role of state-owned enterprises and a growing private sector.
- **Key Exports:** Electronics, machinery, furniture, toys, clothing, and vehicles.
- **Key Imports:** Integrated circuits, crude oil, iron ore, and copper.

2. Trade Relationship

Volume of Trade:

- The United States and China have been among each other's largest trading partners. The trade relationship is characterized by a significant trade deficit for the U.S., meaning the U.S. imports more from China than it exports.

Key Trade Issues:

- **Trade Deficit:** The U.S. has consistently run a trade deficit with China. This imbalance has been a point of contention in trade discussions.
- **Intellectual Property Rights:** The U.S. has raised concerns about intellectual property theft and forced technology transfers in China.
- **Tariffs and Trade Wars:** In recent years, the trade relationship has been strained by tariffs and trade wars. For example, during the U.S.-China trade war (2018-2020), both countries imposed tariffs on each other's goods, impacting global supply chains and trade flows.

3. Trade Policies and Agreements

China's Policies:

- **Made in China 2025:** An initiative aimed at advancing technology and reducing reliance on foreign technology, which has been a point of contention with the U.S.

- **Belt and Road Initiative (BRI):** A global development strategy adopted by China to invest in infrastructure projects around the world, potentially affecting trade routes and relationships.

U.S. Policies:

- **Tariffs and Trade Barriers:** The U.S. has imposed tariffs on a range of Chinese products to address trade imbalances and intellectual property concerns.
- **Phase One Trade Deal (2020):** A trade agreement aimed at easing tensions, where China agreed to increase purchases of U.S. goods and strengthen intellectual property protections.

4. Economic Impact

For the U.S.:

- **Job Creation and Losses:** While U.S. companies benefit from cheap imports, certain industries, like manufacturing, have faced job losses due to competition with Chinese products.
- **Consumer Prices:** Tariffs and trade barriers can lead to higher consumer prices for goods imported from China.

For China:

- **Export Growth:** The U.S. is a major market for Chinese goods, and trade restrictions can impact Chinese export growth.
- **Economic Diversification:** China has been working to diversify its economy and reduce reliance on exports.

5. Broader Implications

Global Supply Chains:

- The trade relationship between the U.S. and China has significant implications for global supply chains. Disruptions can affect industries worldwide, from electronics to automotive parts.

Geopolitical Tensions:

- Trade tensions are often intertwined with broader geopolitical issues. Trade policies and disputes can impact diplomatic relations and regional stability.

Economic Integration:

- Despite trade tensions, the U.S. and China remain economically integrated. Both countries are crucial players in the global economy, and their trade interactions have ripple effects worldwide.

6. Future Outlook

Potential for Cooperation:

- There is potential for further cooperation through trade agreements that address the concerns of both nations while fostering mutual economic benefits.

Ongoing Challenges:

- Addressing issues such as intellectual property rights, market access, and tariffs will be crucial for improving the trade relationship and reducing economic friction.

CONCLUSION

The trade relationship between the United States and China is complex and multifaceted, reflecting both economic opportunities and challenges. While trade tensions have posed significant obstacles, ongoing negotiations and agreements aim to address these issues and foster a more balanced and cooperative trade environment. The global impact of this relationship highlights the interconnected nature of international trade and its broader implications for the global economy.

CLASS ACTIVITY

In our class activity on trade, we explored the fundamental principles and impacts of international trade. Students engaged in discussions on comparative advantage, examining how countries specialize to maximize efficiency and welfare. We also analyzed the effects of trade on jobs, considering both the opportunities created through export growth and the challenges posed by import competition. Through case studies and simulations, we deepened our understanding of how trade influences economic growth, industry dynamics, and global interdependence, preparing us to critically assess trade policies and their implications for future economic development.

SUMMARY

- Modern trade theory, as developed from the mid-20th Century onwards, represents a fundamental shift in understanding global economic interactions.
- Although the constant-cost case may be of limited relevance to the real world, it serves as a useful pedagogical tool for analyzing international trade.
- The law of comparative advantage asserts that with trade each country will find it favorable to specialize in the production of the good of its comparative advantage and will trade part of this for the good of its comparative disadvantage.
- The concept of dynamic gains from trade refers to the long-term benefits that accrue to countries engaging in international trade beyond the static gains typically associated with immediate efficiencies in resource allocation.
- Changing comparative advantage refers to the phenomenon where a country's pattern of specialization and trade shifts over time due to various factors influencing its production capabilities and global market conditions.
- Invisible trade, in economics, the exchange of physically intangible items between countries. Invisible trade can be distinguished from visible trade, which involves the export, import, and re-export of physically tangible goods.
- Trade sanctions are trade-related penalties levied by one country against one or more other countries. These sanctions fall into the broader category of economic sanctions, and they might be used to achieve economic policy objectives, political objectives or military objectives.
- International trade law is the body of laws and agreements that governs how countries do business with each other.
- These interferences may be simply the result of special-interest pleading, because particular groups suffer as a consequence of import competition.
- Businesses engaging in international trade can benefit from a range of services, including those that offer advice on export planning so the business can exploit its expertise and unique selling points in overseas markets.
- International trade plays an important role in every country's economy. The balance of trade, or the amount of imports versus exports, drives a country's evaluation of its gross domestic product (GDP) and ultimately impacts the public's perception of the health of the economy.

REVIEW QUESTIONS

1. What are the patterns of trade?
2. Write a short note on international trade law.
3. Evaluate the effect of state interference in international trade.
4. Explain the methods of international trade regulation.
5. Focus on tariff barriers of international trade.
6. Discuss on tariff reduction and growth of international trade.

REFERENCES

1. Abd El Aziz, S. (2012). *Manufacture of Flour and Bread in Egypt.* General Authority for Supply Commodities. (In Arabic).
2. Abed, G. T., & Gupta, S. (2002). *The Economics of Corruption: An Overview.* International Monetary Fund.
3. Acemoglu, D. (2005). Politics and economics in weak and strong states. *Journal of Monetary Economics, 52*(6), 1199–1226. https://doi.org/10.1016/j.jmoneco.2005.05.012.
4. Acemoglu, D., & Robinson, J. A. (2008). Paths of economic and political development. In G. M. Hodgson (Ed.), *The Oxford Handbook of Political Economy*. Oxford University Press.
5. Ahmed, A., Bouis, H., Gutner, T., & Lofgren, H. (2001). *The Egyptian Food Subsidy System: Structure, Performance and Options for Reform (Research Report 119).* International Food Policy Research Institute (IFPRI). Washington, D.C.
6. Ahmed, G., Hamrick, D., Guinn, A., Abdulsamad, A., & Gereffi, G. (2013). *Wheat Value Chains and Food Security in the Middle East and North Africa Region.* Duke Center on Globalization, Governance & Competitiveness.
7. Al-Shawarby, S., & El-Laithy, H. (2010). *Egypt's Food Subsidies: Benefit Incidence and Leakage (Report No. 57446*). The World Bank.
8. Barbeay, C. (2009). *Le Secteur du blé en EGYPTE: Fiche de Synthèse.* UBI France et les missions Economiques.
9. British Cereal Exports. (2010). *British Cereal Export Target Markets: Egypt.* AHDB-HGCA Agriculture and Horticulture Development Bank, United Kingdom.
10. Croppenstedt, A. (2005). *Measuring Technical Efficiency of Wheat Farmers in Egypt (ESA Working Paper No.05-06).* Agriculture and Development Economics Division, The Food and Agriculture Organization of the United Nations.
11. Croppenstedt, A., Saade, M., & Siam, G. (2006). *Food Security and wheat Policy in Egypt.* Role of Agriculture Project, Policy Brief.
12. Dubois, A., & Gadde, L. E. (2002). Systematic combining: An abductive approach to case research. *Journal of Business Research, 55*(7), 553–560. https://doi.org/10.1016/S0148-2963(00)00195-8.
13. Egyptian Cabinet Information and Decision Support Center. (2008). *Current Status Quo for Bread Production in Egypt.* Egyptian Cabinet Information and Decision Support Center. (In Arabic).
14. Kemp, M. C. (2008). Gottfried Haberler's principle of comparative advantage. In *International Trade Theory: A Critical Review.* Routledge.
15. Raye, P., & Siam, G. (2013). *Les Stocks Alimentaires et la Régulation de la Volatilité des Marchés en Afrique.* A Savoir 23, Agence Française de Development.

CHAPTER

3 Tariffs

LEARNING OBJECTIVES

After studying this chapter, you will be able to:

- Understand the concept of tariffs
- Define tariff escalation
- Explain the postponing import tariffs
- Describe tariff effects
- Discuss arguments for trade restrictions

KEY TERMS FROM THIS CHAPTER

Ad valorem tariffs
Optimum tariff
Scientific tariff
Tariff escalation
Tariff rates
Export taxes
Protectionism
Specific tariff
Tariff evasion
Trade war
Import duties
Revenue effect
Tariff avoidance
Tariff liberalization

INTRODUCTION

Tariffs are taxes or duties imposed by a government on imported or exported goods. They serve multiple purposes, primarily economic and political. Economically, tariffs are often used to protect domestic industries by making foreign goods more expensive compared to locally produced ones. This protectionist approach aims to shield domestic producers from foreign competition, thereby supporting local employment and economic stability.

Politically, tariffs can also be leveraged as a tool for diplomacy and negotiation. Governments may impose tariffs strategically to address trade imbalances, encourage fairer trade practices, or retaliate against perceived unfair trade policies of other nations. This dual role of tariffs as both economic shields and diplomatic tools underscores their significance in international trade relations.

Historically, tariffs have been central to shaping global trade dynamics. They can influence the competitiveness of industries, impact consumer prices, and even spark broader economic repercussions such as trade wars or retaliatory measures. Therefore, understanding tariffs involves examining not only their immediate economic implications but also their broader political and social ramifications on a global scale.

3.1. CONCEPT OF TARIFFS

Tariffs are barriers to trade that limit the flow of goods and services across international borders. Taxes are levied by the local government on the total amount or value of goods imported from other countries. Although the tax is paid by the importer, the final consumers bear the final cost. The categories of import barriers include import duties, import quotas, standardization, and licenses.

Economists support free-trade agreements and emphasize how crucial cross-border trade in goods and services is to a country's ability to grow economically. Conversely, import barriers are essential for protecting homegrown manufacturers. Import taxes are typically deliberate policies that have the potential to boost employment rates, strengthen national security, spark retaliation, or deter specific foreign countries.

A government's taxation of imported goods results in an increase in the product's price on the domestic market. Consequently, there will be a decrease in the import of that specific product. In other words, import barriers discourage the import of foreign goods while favoring domestic producers. Import barriers are a source of income for the government, just like all taxes (Krugman Paul, 1993).

3.1.1. Types of Tariffs

Tariffs can be specific, ad valorem, or compound. A specific tariff is expressed in terms of a fixed amount of money per physical unit of the imported product. For example, a U.S. importer of a German computer may be required to pay a duty to the U.S. government of $100 per computer, regardless of the computer's price. Therefore, if 100 computers are imported, the tariff revenue of the government equals $10,000 (100 × 100 = 10,000).

Similar to a sales tax, an ad valorem (of value) tariff is expressed as a fixed percentage of the imported product's value. Assume that imported cars are subject to a 2 percent ad valorem duty. Thus, in the event that automobiles valued at $100,000 are imported, the government receives $2,500 in tariff revenue (100,000 × 2.5 percent = 2,500). Regardless of whether ten $10,000 Nissans or five $20,000 Toyotas are imported, this $2,500 is still collected.

A compound tariff is a combination of specific and ad valorem tariffs. For example, a U.S. importer of a television might be required to pay a duty of $20 plus 5 percent of the value of the television. Table 3.1 lists U.S. tariffs on certain items.

Table 3.1. Selected U.S. Tariffs

Product	Duty Rate
Brooms	32 cents each
Fishing reels	24 cents each
Wrist watches (without jewels)	29 cents each
Ball bearings	2.4% ad valorem
Electrical motors	6.7% ad valorem
Bicycles	5.5% ad valorem
Wool blankets	1.8 cents/kg + 6% ad valorem
Electricity meters	16 cents each + 1.5% ad valorem
Auto transmission shafts	25 cents each + 3.9% ad valorem

Source: Robert J. Carbaugh; International Economics; ISBN 13: 978-1-4390-4076-8.

3.1.1.1. Specific Tariff

Particularly for standardized commodities and staples where the value of the dutiable goods cannot be easily observed, a specific tariff—a fixed monetary duty per unit of the imported product—is relatively simple to apply and administer. One of the primary drawbacks of a particular tariff is that the level of protection it offers to home producers fluctuates in direct proportion to changes in import costs. For instance, imports of cars costing $20,000 each will be more deterred than those costing $25,000 by a specific $1,000 tariff. The protective effect of a particular tariff is somewhat diminished in periods of rising import prices. Because of this, domestic producers are incentivized to produce goods at a lower cost, which in turn enjoys a higher level of protection against imports. But, in a downturn in the economy, when consumers are buying less expensive goods, a specific tariff offers the benefit of giving home producers additional protection. Decreased prices from overseas rivals are thus gradually offset by specific tariffs for domestic producers.

3.1.1.2. Ad Valorem Tariff

Since ad valorem tariffs can be applied to products with a wide range of grade variations, they typically work better for manufactured goods. An ad valorem tariff can identify minor variations in product quality to the extent that they are reflected in the price of the product by applying a percentage to the product's value. A person importing a $20,000 Honda would be required to pay a higher duty than someone importing a $19,900 Toyota under an ad valorem tariff system. In the event of a system of distinct tariffs, the duty would remain constant. An additional benefit of an ad valorem tariff is its propensity to keep domestic producers protected to a consistent level even in times of fluctuating prices. The duty is $40 if the imported product costs $200 and the tariff rate is 20% ad valorem. The duty collected increases to $60 if the product price rises to $300, for example, and decreases to $20 if the product price drops to $100. Revenues from an ad valorem tariff are proportionate to values, ensuring a consistent level of relative protection across all price points. The real proportionate tax burden or protection remains constant despite changes in the tax base, a feature that sets an ad valorem tariff apart from proportional taxes. Ad valorem duties, as opposed to specific duties, have been used more frequently in recent decades in response to global inflation and the growing significance of international trade in manufactured goods.

Ad valorem principle duty determination seems straightforward at first, but in reality, administrative complications have made it difficult. The primary challenge has been attempting to value an imported good—a process known as customs valuation. Customs appraisers estimate import prices; their estimates may differ regarding the value of the products. Furthermore, import prices frequently change over time, which adds difficulty to the valuation process.

Differences in the approaches taken to ascertain the value of a commodity give rise to another issue with customs valuation. For instance, the United States has long utilized free-on-board (FOB) valuation, in which the value of the product is subject to a tariff as soon as it is exported. However, the cost-insurance-freight (CIF) valuation method has been used by European nations historically. Under this method, ad valorem tariffs are applied as a percentage of the imported commodity's total value upon arrival at its destination. Thus, transportation expenses like freight and insurance are included in the CIF price.

3.1.1.3. Compound Tariff

When manufactured goods contain tariffed raw materials, compound duties are frequently imposed. In this instance, the duty's specific component offsets the cost disadvantage faced by domestic manufacturers as a result of tariff protection for domestic raw material suppliers, and the duty's ad valorem component safeguards the finished-goods sector. For instance, woven fabrics are subject to a compound duty of 48.51 cents per kilogram plus 38% in the United States. The precise amount of the duty (48.05 cents) reimburses the U.S. cloth producers for the tariff immunity provided to the U.S. Cotton growers receive protection for their own woven fabrics from the 38% ad valorem portion of the duty (Kluge Friedrich, 1989). How high are import tariffs around the world? Table 3.2 provides examples of tariffs of selected industrial and developing countries.

Table 3.2. Examples of Tariffs for Selected Countries (in Percentages)

	United States	Canada	Japan	China	European Union
Textiles and clothing	9.6	11.7	7.4	17.5	7.9
Footwear	4.3	5.7	6.4	14.6	4.2
Metals	2.1	1.9	1.3	7.3	1.9
Chemicals	3.4	3.0	2.5	7.5	4.5
Nonelectrical machinery	1.2	1.5	0.0	9.9	1.7
Electrical machinery	1.9	2.4	0.2	10.4	2.5
Petroleum	1.9	3.0	1.7	5.0	3.1
Sugar	13.0	4.3	10.2	33.6	11.4
Dairy products	19.0	7.4	28.0	24.5	7.7
Average	3.9	4.1	3.2	12.4	4.2

Source: Robert J. Carbaugh; International Economics; ISBN 13: 978-1-4390-4076-8.

3.1.2. Effective Rate of Protection

We took for granted that a certain product is made fully in a single nation. One such example is a desktop PC made by Dell, a U.S. the product of employing solely American labor and materials, could be the firm. But this doesn't account for the possibility that Dell imports some of the components used to make desktop computers, like microprocessors, memory chips, and hard drives.

The level of protection afforded to Dell in cases where some inputs used to produce finished desktops are imported is contingent upon the presence of tariffs on the inputs utilized in their production as well as the tariff rate applied to desktops. The main argument is that the tariff rate on desktops might not fairly reflect the protection afforded to Dell when it imports some of the inputs needed to make desktops.

Economists distinguish between the nominal and effective tariff rates when examining tariffs. The tariff rate listed in the nation's tariff schedule is known as the nominal tariff rate. It refers to the cost of an imported finished good into a nation. Any tariff rate applied to import inputs used in the production of a finished product is also taken into account when calculating the effective tariff rate, in addition to the nominal tariff rate on the finished product.

It is clear that Dell is taxed rather than protected if a completed desktop is imported into the US at a zero tariff rate while imported components used to produce desktops are subject to taxes. While a tariff on imported components taxes Dell by raising its costs, a nominal tariff on desktops protects Dell's production. These two effects are balanced by the effective tariff rate.

The protection Dell receives from a nominal tariff on desktops and a tariff on inputs used in desktop production is referred to as the effective tariff rate. It calculates the percentage increase in value added (or domestic production activities) per unit of output that tariffs on imported inputs and finished goods make possible. Put simply, a desktop tariff that is combined with a low tariff on imported inputs will provide more protection than a high tariff on components. Assume that Dell adds value by assembling computer components that are made overseas in order to demonstrate this idea. Assume the imported parts are allowed entry into the US duty-free (zero tariff). Assume further that domestic assembly activities account for 20% of a desktop's final value (value added). The value of the imported components is represented in the remaining 80%. Furthermore, let Dell and its overseas rival, Sony Inc., to pay the same price for the desktop's components of Japan. Assume next that Sony is able to manufacture and market a desktop computer for $500. Assuming that the United States applies a 10% nominal tariff on desktop computers, Table 3.3 illustrates how the domestic import price increases from $500 to $550 per unit. Certainly not! The imported components enter the nation duty-free (at a nominal tariff rate lower than that of the finished desktop), so the effective rate of protection is 50%. Does this mean that Dell realizes an effective rate of protection equal to 10%? In comparison with a free trade scenario, Dell can increase its production activities by 50% and maintain its competitiveness.

Table 3.3. The Effective Rate of Protection

Sony's Desktop Computer	Cost	Dell's Desktop Computer	Cost
Component parts	$400	Imported component parts	$400
Assembly activity (value added)	100	Assembly activity (value added)	150
Nominal tariff	50	Domestic price	$550
Import price	$550		

Source: Robert J. Carbaugh; International Economics; ISBN 13: 978–1-4390–4076–8.

The detailed figures are displayed in Table 3.3. A $500 import would be possible for a Sony desktop under free trade (zero tariff). Dell would need to keep its assembly costs below $100 in order to meet this price. However, Dell can pay up to $150 for assembly under the tariff's protective cover and still match the $550 price of imported desktops. As a result, Dell's assembly costs could increase to $50 million above what they would be in a free-trade environment ($150 – $100)/$100 = 0.5).

In general, the effective tariff rate is given by the following formula:

$$e = \frac{(n - ab)}{(1 - a)},$$

Where;

e is the effective rate of protection; n is the nominal tariff rate on the final product; a is the ratio of the value of the imported input to the value of the finished product; and b is the nominal tariff rate on the imported input.

When the values from the desktop example are plugged into this formula, we obtain the following:

$$e = \frac{0.1 - 0.8(0)}{1 - 0.8} = 0.5, \text{or 50 percent.}$$

Thus, a 50% increase in domestic production activities—five times the nominal rate—is permitted by the nominal tariff rate of 10% levied on the finished desktop.

On the other hand, a tariff on imported desktop parts lessens Dell's actual protection. Due to this reduction, the effective protection rate for any given nominal tariff on the finished desktop decreases with increasing value of b in the formula above. Assume, for instance, that a 5 percent tariff applies to imported desktop components. The effective rate of protection would equal 30%:

$$e = \frac{0.1 - 0.8(0.05)}{1 - 0.8} = 0.3, \text{or 30 percent.}$$

This is less than the 50% effective protection rate that arises from the absence of import component tariffs.

These examples allow us to make a number of inferences. The effective rate of protection is higher than the nominal tariff when the tariff on the final product is higher than the tariff on the imported input. The effective rate of protection, however, is lower than the nominal tariff and may even be negative if the tariff on the final product is lower than the tariff on the imported input. Such a scenario might arise if the national government decided to give greater protection to domestic raw material suppliers than to domestic manufacturers. Effective tariff rates are typically higher than nominal rates because national governments typically admit raw materials and other inputs either duty-free or at a lower rate than finished goods. Examples of nominal and effective tariff rates for China in 2001 are shown in Table 3.4.

Table 3.4. China's Nominal and Effective Tariff Rates in Forestry Products, 2001

Product	Nominal Rate (%)	Effective Rate (%)
Mouldings	9.4	26.6
Furniture	11.0	21.8
Veneers	4.0	9.4
Plywood	8.4	11.7
Fiberboard	7.5	9.2
Particleboard	9.6	10.6

Source: Manatu Aorere, Tariff Escalation in the Forestry Sector, New Zealand Ministry of Foreign Affairs and Trade, Wellington, New Zealand, August 2002.

3.2. TARIFF ESCALATION

It is common to observe when examining national tariff structures that import tariffs on processed goods are higher than those on basic raw materials. For instance, import tariffs may not apply to logs, but they do to processed goods like plywood, veneers, and furniture. By allowing the import of logs, which are used to make plywood, duty-free or at a reduced rate, and by imposing higher tariffs on imported plywood that competes with domestic plywood, this tariff strategy aims to safeguard, for example, the domestic plywood industry (Michell, 2014). Tariff escalation is the name given to this policy, in which nominal and effective protection rises at each stage of production, despite the fact that raw materials are frequently imported at zero or low tariff rates. In many industrialized nations, tariffs frequently increase dramatically in proportion to the degree of processing, as shown in Figure 3.1. This is particularly valid for goods derived from agriculture. In fact, the industrialized countries' tariff structures may deter processing expansion, making it more difficult for less developed countries to diversify into higher value-added exports. While the high protective rates imposed on manufactured goods provide a significant barrier to entry for any developing nation hoping to compete in this space, the low tariffs imposed by industrialized nations on primary commodities encourage developing nations to expand their operations in these sectors.

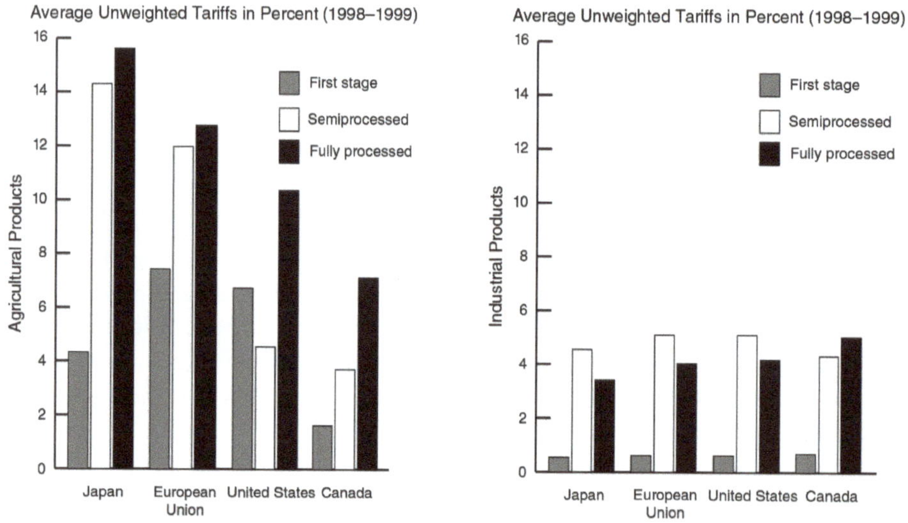

Figure 3.1. *Tariff escalation on industrial countries' imports from developing countries.*

Source: The World Bank, Global Economic Prospects and the Developing Countries, 2002 and World Trade Organization, Market Access: Unfinished Business, 2001, available at http://www.wto.org/.

It might be in the best interests of less developed countries to oppose disproportionate tariff reductions on raw materials. These tariff reductions have the effect of enlarging the gap between the industrialized countries' effective and nominal tariffs, thereby deteriorating the less developed countries' potential competitive position in the manufacturing and processing industries.

3.2.1. Outsourcing and Offshore-Assembly Provision

A vital component of the global economy is outsourcing. It could happen if some steps in the manufacturing process of a product are carried out in multiple nations. For instance,

American-made electronic parts are shipped to Singapore, or another easily accessible nation with cheap labor costs, to be assembled into television sets. After assembly, the sets are shipped back to the US for additional packaging, distribution, and processing. Production sharing in the form of foreign assembly has developed into a crucial competitive tactic for numerous U.S. manufacturers of labor-intensive, low-cost goods.

Improvements in cost competitiveness through foreign assembly often allow businesses to maintain higher production and employment levels in the United States than might otherwise be feasible, preserving market share both domestically and internationally.

Outsourcing operations may be planned to enter foreign markets where high tariffs or other trade barriers prevent the direct export of finished goods, in addition to using overseas assembly plants to save labor costs. Certain exclusive foreign production technologies, labor skills, raw materials, or specialized components may also be leveraged through outsourcing. U.S. trade policy includes an offshore-assembly provision (OAP) that provides favorable treatment to products assembled abroad from U.S.-manufactured components. Under OAP, when a finished component originating in the United States (such as a semiconductor) is sent overseas and assembled there with one or more other components to become a finished good (such as a television set), the cost of the U.S.

component is not included in the dutiable value of the imported assembled article into which it has been incorporated. American import duties thus apply only to the value added in the foreign assembly process, provided that U.S.-manufactured components are used by overseas companies in their assembly operations. Manufactured goods entering the United States under OAP have included motor vehicles, office machines, television sets, aluminum cans, and semiconductors.

The U.S. OAP is not limited to U.S. businesses, as well as to international ones. For instance. U.S.

A computer company could manufacture parts in the US, ship them to Taiwan for assembly, and then import computers back to the US with a positive OAP. As an alternative, a Japanese photocopier company that wants to sell to the US could buy U.S. produced parts, put them together in Malaysia, and then export photocopiers to the US with a good OAP.

Assume that television sets costing $300 each are imported into the United States from South Korea. Each television that enters the United States would be subject to a $30 duty if the tariff rate on these devices is 10%. The cost to the U.S. $330 would be the consumer. Let's now assume that U.S. components, which have a \$200 value, are utilized in the television sets put together by Koreans. In accordance with OAP, the 10% U.S. tariff rate is applied to the difference between the import set's value and the U.S. parts that went into making the set. The set's dutiable value upon entering the US is therefore \$300 – \$200 = \$100, and the duty is 0.1 × \$100 = \$10. What it costs the U.S.S. After the tariff is applied, the customer will receive \$300 + \$10 = \$310. The consumer benefits from the OAP system since the effective tariff rate is only 3.3 percent (\$10/\$300) as opposed to the 10% indicated in the tariff schedule.

Potential benefits for the US are offered by the OAP. By lowering import taxes on sets that are assembled abroad and bear U.S. component purchases from U.S. suppliers, OAP offers incentives to Korean manufacturers who wish to export to the United States sources; as a result, sales and jobs are created in the U.S. component sectors. On the other hand, American television assembly workers oppose OAP, arguing that it exports jobs that are legitimately theirs. As such, they should advocate for the elimination of OAP.

3.2.2. Dodging Import Tariffs: Tariff Avoidance and Tariff Evasion

There are financial incentives to avoid an import tariff when one country imposes one. Tariff avoidance, or the lawful manipulation of the tariff system to one's own benefit in order to lower the amount of tariff that is payable through legal means, is one method of getting around a tariff. Tariff evasion, on the other hand, is the illegal practice of people or businesses avoiding tariffs through the smuggling of imported goods into a nation. Let's examine each of these approaches.

3.2.2.1. Ford Strips Its Wagons to Avoid High Tariff

Ford Motor Company ships its Transit Connect five-passenger wagons from its Turkey-based factory to Baltimore, Maryland, several times a month. Most of the passenger wagons are taken to a warehouse in Baltimore after they arrive, where workers blaring rock music remove the rear windows, seats, and seat belts. Why?

Ford is attempting to manage a protracted trade dispute in part by acting in this way. High tariffs on imported chicken were imposed by Europe in the 1960s, mainly to deter US sales to West Germany. In retaliation, President Lyndon Johnson imposed a 25% tariff on trucks and commercial vans (automobiles used for the transportation of goods) built in other countries. Even if trucks and commercial vans are made abroad by an American company, they are still subject to this tariff as of right now. But the U.S. Import taxes for automobiles classified as "wagons" and "cars"—that is, motor vehicles used for passenger transportation—are substantially lower, at 2.5 percent.

Ford launched a program in 2009 to avoid the 25% tariff after realizing that it would drastically raise the cost of its cargo vans sold in the US and reduce their competitiveness. This is how it operates. The Transit Connects wagons that Ford ships to the US are subject to a 2.5 percent tariff. The wagons are then converted into cargo vans at a processing facility in Baltimore. The rear seats and seat belts are taken out, and a new floorboard is screwed into place in their stead. The rear windows are taken out and replaced with a sheet of metal. Ford transforms the wagons, which have 5 seats at first, into two-seat cargo vans. The steel components are disassembled, the fabric is shredded, and everything is sent to be recycled with the glass. As stated by U.S. Customs officers, this procedure conforms to the text of the legislation. Transforming wagons into cargo vans costs Ford hundreds of dollars per vehicle, but the process saves the company thousands in terms of tariff duties. For example, on a $25,000 passenger wagon a 2.5 percent tariff would result in a duty of only $625 (25,000 × 0.025 = 625). This compares to a duty of $6,250 that would result from a 25% tariff imposed on a cargo van (25,000 × 0.25 = 6,250). The avoidance of the higher tariff on cargo vans would save Ford $5,625 on each vehicle (6,250 – 625 = 5,625), minus the cost of transforming the passenger wagon into a cargo van. Smart, huh? One method of avoiding tariffs is through Ford's transformation process. Some automakers have steered clear of the U.S. tariffs utilizing various methods. As an illustration, Toyota Motor Corp. Nissan Motor Company as well as Honda Motor Co. chose the easy route and established plants in the US rather than bringing cars liable to import tariffs from Japan into the US market (Adlung & Roy, 2005).

3.2.2.2. Smuggled Steel Evades U.S. Tariffs

The United States imports approximately 38 million tons of steel worth $12 billion annually. Tariffs ranging from pennies to hundreds of dollars per ton are applied to about half of this steel. The type of steel product—of which there are roughly 1,000—and the country of origin—of which there are roughly 100—determine the tariff's amount. The selling price of steel in the US is subject to these tariffs. American customs inspectors examine shipments coming into the country carefully to ensure that tariffs are applied correctly. However, with the small customs service staff, monitoring shipments is challenging. Because of this, there is a small chance of getting caught for smuggling and facing consequences, but there is a large chance of making money illegally. For instance, in the first 10 years of the new millennium, Ivan Dubrinski smuggled 20,000 tons of steel into the US. It was simple. All he did was alter the shipping paperwork for a product known as "reinforcing steel bar" to make it seem as though it was included in a shipment of "flat-rolled" steel, a different variety of steel. By lying, he avoided paying about $38,000 in import taxes. If you multiply this instance of tariff evasion several times, you will have smuggled steel and avoided paying millions of dollars in duties. Steel smuggling worries the U.S. government, which incurs losses from tariffs, as well as the U.S. the steel sector, which insists it cannot afford to compete with goods produced at a lower cost through tariff evasion. Although larger U.S. importers of steel generally pay correct duties, it is the smaller, often fly-by-night importers that are more likely to try to slip illegal steel into the country.

These traders use one of three methods to evade tariffs. One method is to falsely reclassify steel that would be subject to a tariff as a duty-free product. Another is to detach markings which indicate that the steel came from a country subject to tariffs and make it appear to have come from one that is exempt. A third method involves altering the chemical composition of a steel product enough so that it can be labeled duty-free. Despite their best efforts, customs inspectors are powerless to stop steel imports once it passes through their hands. The steel that has been smuggled cannot be seized because it is frequently already sold and in use. In the meantime, American steel companies that compete with smuggled steel find that their sales and profits are declining, while the people purchasing the steel benefit from a nice price break.

3.3. POSTPONING IMPORT TARIFFS

In addition to making it possible to avoid tariffs, U.S. Tariff law permits tariff postponement. Let's examine how a foreign trade zone and bonded warehouse can help delay tariffs.

3.3.1. Bonded Warehouse

As stated by U.S. duty-free imports are permitted under tariff law to enter the U.S. and placed, duty-free, in a bonded warehouse for a short time. Importers may request permission from the U.S. Customs Service to operate a bonded warehouse on their property, or they may choose to employ a public warehouse that has been granted permission to do so. Storage facility owners are required to post a bond as collateral to guarantee they will fulfill their customs duty obligations. This clause states that in the event that the importing company is unable to pay the customs duties, the bonding company will guarantee payment of those duties.

For a maximum of five years, imported goods may be kept, repackaged, or subjected to additional processing in the bonded warehouse. Goods made in the country are not permitted to enter a bonded warehouse. No customs duties are due if the item is warehoused at the point of initial entry. Duties must be paid on the value of the imported goods at the time of withdrawal rather than at the time of entry into the bonded warehouse when the time comes to remove them from the warehouse. There is no duty to pay if the goods are withdrawn for export.

The owner may put the goods through any necessary procedures while they are in the warehouse in order to get them ready for market sale. These procedures could involve the roasting of coffee, the bottling of wines, and the repackaging and mixing of tea. However, neither product manufacturing nor the assembly of imported components into finished goods are permitted in bonded warehouses. The fact that duties are not paid until the goods are removed for domestic consumption is one of the main benefits of a bonded warehouse entry. When the goods are withdrawn from the bonded warehouse, the importer is allowed to keep control of the duty money until it is paid. The benefit of selling goods for exportation is that the importer can avoid paying duties if it is unable to find a domestic buyer for the goods or if it cannot sell the goods domestically at a profit. Additionally, it can be costly to pay duties when goods are first brought into the nation. By using a bonded warehouse, importers can defer paying duties until after the goods are sold and can access funds from sales before paying duties upfront.

3.3.2. Foreign-Trade Zone

Created in the 1930s, the foreign-trade zone (FTZ) program of the United States broadens the concept of a bonded warehouse. A FTZ is an area within the United States where business can operate without the responsibility of paying customs duties on imported products or materials for as long as they remain within this area and do not enter the U.S. marketplace. Customs duties are due only when goods are transferred from the FTZ for U.S. consumption. If the goods never enter the U.S. marketplace, then no duties are paid on those items. For example, if imported components enter a FTZ, are assembled into a final product, and re-exported abroad, no customs duty is paid. Moreover, both foreign and domestic goods can be stored inside a FTZ and there is no time limit on how long goods can be stored.

Numerous FTZs are located at U.S. some are situated at inland distribution points, but others are situated at seaports, like the Port of Seattle. Over 230 FTZs are in existence in the US at the moment. Exxon, Caterpillar, General Electric, and International Business Machines (IBM) are a few companies that benefit from FTZ status. You can pretty much do anything you want to an item once it has entered an FTZ. Repackaging, destroying or repairing damaged goods, assembling component parts into completed products, and exporting both the parts and the finished products are all possible. In FTZs, manufacturing of goods is also permitted. Because bonded warehouses only allow for the storage of imported goods and a restricted amount of repackaging and processing, importers using FTZs are able to engage in a wider range of business activities.

Subzones and general-purpose zones make up FTZs. General-purpose zones are public areas utilized by multiple companies; these are usually ports or industrial parks where small and medium-sized enterprises assemble, process, store, and distribute their products. Additionally, there are subzones that include a single company's location used for larger-scale assembly or manufacturing, which is difficult to do in a general-purpose zone.

The FTZ initiative promotes U.S. based corporate operations by eliminating some of the obstacles related to American manufacturing. When a product is imported into the US from overseas, the duty is paid on the entire product instead of the parts, materials, or components that make up the product. An U.S. Therefore, if an American-based company had to pay a higher rate on parts, materials, or components imported for use in the manufacturing process—a practice known as "inverted tariffs"—it would be at a disadvantage compared to its foreign competitor. The FTZ program makes up for this imbalance by treating goods produced there as though they were made overseas when determining tariffs.

Let's take an example where an FTZ user imports a motor that is subject to a 5 percent duty rate and uses it to make a free-of-duty lawn mower. When the lawnmower travels from the FTZ into the U.S. marketplace, the motor's duty rate decreases from 5% to 0%, making lawn mowers free. The lawn mower manufacturer has reduced the cost of this component by 5 percent by taking part in the FTZ program, which removes the duty on it.

Additionally, a FTZ can assist a business in removing import taxes on product waste and scrap. Consider the case of a U.S. To make a specific chemical that also has a 10% duty, a chemical company imports raw materials, which are subject to a 10% duty. Raising the imported raw material to extremely high temperatures is a necessary step in the production process. 20% of the raw material is lost as heat during this process. The chemical company will pay \$100,000 (1 million × 0.1 = 100,000) in duties when the raw material enters the country if it imports \$1 million worth of raw materials annually. But because it is a part of the FTZ program, duty-free raw materials are not charged until they are exported from the zone and brought into the U.S. market. The raw material is currently only worth \$800,000 because 20% of it is lost as heat during the manufacturing process. In the event that the entire finished chemical is sold in the US, the \$80,000 customs duty would only amount to 10% of the total. This results in a \$20,000 savings. Although it might seem that the FTZ program exclusively helps the U.S. chemical company, it is crucial to keep in mind that its rivals who manufacture the same product overseas already enjoy the benefit of not being liable for waste loss incurred during the chemical's production.

3.3.3. FTZ's Benefit Motor Vehicle Importers

Toyota Corporation is one business that profited from the U.S. Program FTZ. As an illustration, Toyota maintains car processing facilities inside US FTZs. The processing centers clean and install accessories like CD players and radios on imported Toyotas before shipping them to American dealers. The principal advantage of having the processing center situated within a Free Trade Zone (FTZ) is the ability to defer paying customs duties until after the vehicle has been processed and delivered to the dealer.

Toyota also maintains parts distribution centers inside FTZ sites for parts imported into the United States.

Toyota has to keep a sizable inventory of parts in the US for an extended amount of time due to extended warranties, which is why the FTZ program is appealing from a duty deferral standpoint. Furthermore, a lot of parts might have to be destroyed because they are no longer functional. Toyota can avoid paying customs duties on parts that are destroyed or become outdated by designating its parts distribution center as an FTZ.

The potential decrease in the import vehicle's dutiable value based on the inverted duty principle is another advantage of a free trade zone (FTZ) for Toyota.

Assume that a Toyota processing center located within an FTZ site has a CD player installed that was imported from Japan. In 2009, the final Toyota car incurred a 2 percent duty, while the imported CD player incurred a 4 percent duty. Therefore, by installing the CD player at its processing center within the FTZ site, Toyota can lower the duty on the cost of the player by 1.9 percent (4.4–2.5 = 1.9).

3.4. TARIFF EFFECTS

Import taxes are known as tariffs. They raise the cost of the product for buyers, which lowers demand. As an example, let's say there is a U.S. company as well as a foreign supplier of computers. How much the U.S. -made computer costs $1,000, while a computer made abroad costs $750. The U.S. In this case, the computer company is unable to remain competitive.

Assume that $300 import duties are applied to each computer by the US. The $300 tariff raises the price of imported computers above the price they would have paid abroad. Computer suppliers in the United States who now compete with import computer suppliers may charge $1,050 (750 + 300 = 1,050) for their computers in addition to the foreign price. The domestic demand for imported computers declines as their price rises. Simultaneously, the increased cost has prompted US suppliers to increase production, resulting in a decrease in imports. Take note that the American computer industry can thrive without a tariff raising the cost of imported computers above that of their domestic counterparts. It ought to be set at a level that minimizes the price difference between the computer manufactured in the United States and the one that is imported.

If no tariff were imposed, as under free trade, Americans would have saved money by buying the cheaper foreign computer. The U.S. computer industry would either have to become more efficient in order to compete with the less expensive imported product or face extinction. Although the tariff benefits producers in the U.S. computer industry, it imposes costs to the U.S. economy:

- Computer buyers will have to pay more for their protected U.S.-made computers than they would have for the imported computers under free trade.
- Jobs will be lost at retail and shipping companies that import foreign-made computers.
- Jobs will be lost in any domestic industries that suffer from retaliatory tariffs.
- The extra cost of the computers gets passed on to whatever products and services that use these computers in the production process.

3.4.1. Tariff Welfare Effects: Consumer Surplus and Producer Surplus

It is helpful to distinguish between the effects of trade policies on producers and consumers in order to assess how they affect national welfare. A welfare metric, known as consumer surplus and producer surplus, is required for each group.

The gap between what consumers actually pay and what they would be willing and able to pay for a good is known as the "consumer surplus.." As an example, let's say that a Pepsi costs $0.50. Assume, if you were particularly thirsty, that you could afford to spend up to $0.75 on a Pepsi. For this purchase, your consumer surplus comes to $0.25 ($0.75 – $0.50 = $0.25). Consumer surplus is just the total of the surplus for each unit of Pepsi that is purchased.

Another visual representation of consumer surplus is possible. First, keep in mind that in a competitive market, buyers pay a single price (the equilibrium price) for every unit they purchase. Secondly, the height of the market demand curve represents the maximum price that buyers are willing and able to pay for each subsequent unit of the good. Now, assuming the market price of gasoline is $2 per gallon, let's look at Figure 3.2(a). Customers will spend $8, or area ACED, if they buy four gallons at this price. According to area ABCED, buyers would be willing and able to pay $12 for those four gallons. Consumer surplus, shown by area ABC and equal to $4 in this instance, is the difference between what consumers actually spend and what they are willing and able to spend.

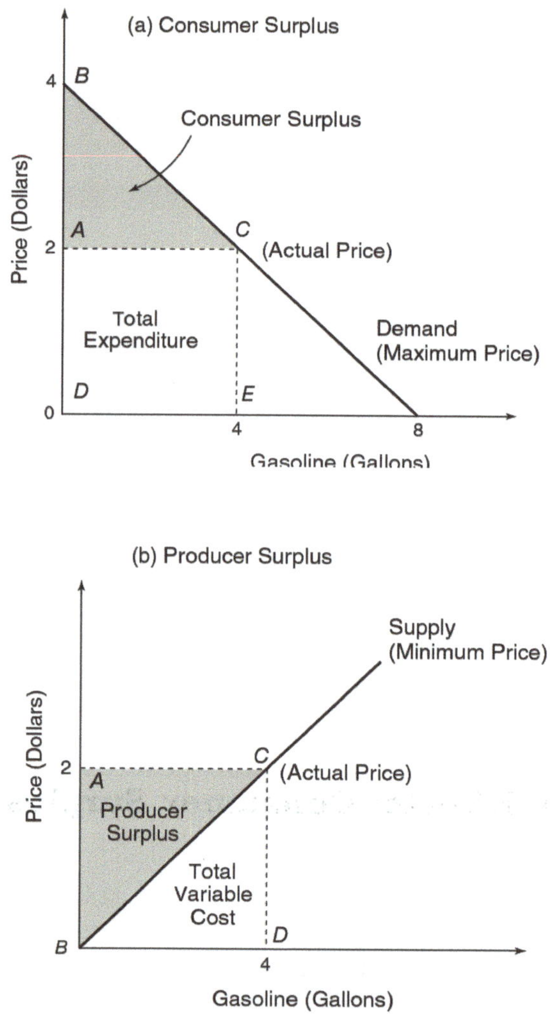

Figure 3.2. *Consumer surplus and producer surplus.*

Source: Robert J. Carbaugh; International Economics; ISBN 13: 978–1-4390–4076–8.

The region above the gasoline supply curve and below the market price of the good in Figure 3.2(b) represents the producer surplus. Remember that the lowest price at which producers will supply gasoline is indicated by the height of the market supply curve; due to rising marginal costs, this minimum price rises as output levels. Assume that four gallons of gasoline are supplied and that the market price is $2 per gallon. $8 in revenue is distributed to producers, as shown by the area ACDB. Area BCD shows that the minimum revenue required to produce four gallons is equal to the total variable cost of $4. Area ABC represents the producer surplus, which is the difference of $4 ($8 – $4 = $4).

If the market price of gasoline rises, more gasoline will be supplied, and the producer surplus will rise. It is equally true that if the market price of gasoline falls, the producer surplus will fall.

3.4.2. Tariff Welfare Effects: Small-Nation Model

Take into consideration the scenario of a country whose imports make up a very small percentage of the global market supply in order to gauge the impact of a tariff on the welfare of that country. This tiny country would be a price taker because the global price of the commodity it imports would always be the same. This is not an isolated instance; many countries are too small to have an impact on the conditions under which they trade (Eaton & Grossman, 1985).

Figure 3.3 shows how the intersection of a small country's domestic supply and demand schedules determines the market equilibrium point E, where cars are produced prior to trade. There are 50 vehicles supplied and 50 vehicles demanded at the equilibrium price of $9,500.

Assume for the moment that the global auto price is $8,000 and that the economy is open to foreign trade. Since there will always be an infinite supply of cars available on the global market for $8,000, the world supply schedule will seem like a perfectly elastic horizontal line. Line S_{d+w} displays the total amount of cars from both domestic and foreign sources that are available to small-nation consumers. Under free trade, this overall supply schedule would be in place.

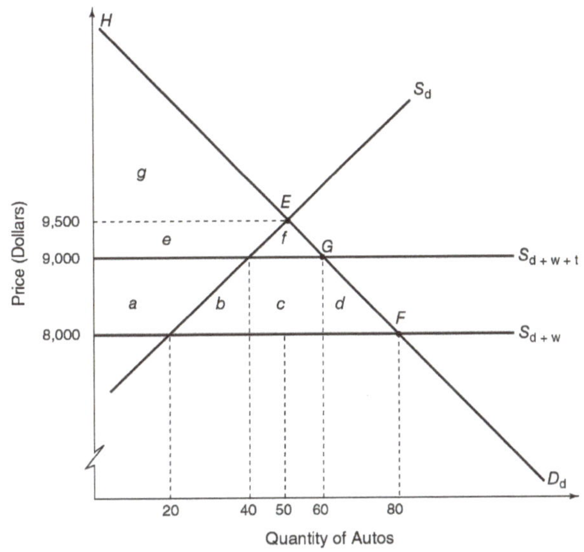

Figure 3.3. *Tariff trade and welfare effects: small nation model.*

Source: Robert J. Carbaugh; International Economics; ISBN 13: 978–1-4390–4076–8.

Free-trade equilibrium is located at point F in the figure. Here the number of autos demanded is 80, whereas the number produced domestically is 20. The import of 60 autos fulfills the excess domestic demand. Compared with the situation before trade occurred, free trade results in a fall in the domestic auto price from $9,500 to $8,000. Consumers are better off because they can import more autos at a lower price. However, domestic producers now sell fewer autos at a lower price than they did before trade.

Foreign competition is hurting the home auto industry under free trade. Sales and earnings in the industry are declining, and employment is being lost. Let's say labor and management band together to persuade the government to impose a protective tariff on imports of automobiles. Let's say the tiny country puts a $1,000 import tax on cars. The global supply price of automobiles is not impacted by the tariff since this small country is not significant enough to change the dynamics of the global market. The small country's terms of trade have not changed as a result of this lack of price change. The imposition of the tariff results in an increase in the home price of imports equal to the whole duty, which is entirely borne by domestic consumers. The total supply changes from S_{d+w} to S_{d+w+t}, increasing by the tariff amount.

Point G, where the domestic auto price is $9,000, is the new equilibrium quantity created by the protective tariff. While domestic consumption decreases by 20 units, domestic production rises by 20 units. Imports drop from 60 units at the pretariff level to 20 units. The decrease in domestic consumption and the increase in domestic production are the reasons for this reduction. The tariff's effects are to protect home producers and obstruct imports. What impact does the tariff have on the welfare of the country, though?

Figure 3.3 illustrates how consumer surplus equated to areas a + b + c + d + e + f + g prior to the tariff's imposition. The tariff reduces consumer surplus to areas e + f + g, resulting in a total loss of consumer surplus equal to areas a + b + c + d. Many factors impact the welfare of the country as a result of this change. A tariff's revenue, redistribution, protective, and consumption effects are among its welfare influences. The tariff, as might be expected, helps domestic automakers and gives the government more tax revenue, but it also wastes resources and hurts domestic consumers. The government's revenue-generating effect from the tariff is the collection of duties. Government revenue is equal to area c, or $20,000. This can be found by multiplying the number of imports (20 units) by the tariff ($1,000). This revenue is the monetary amount that the government receives as a portion of the loss in consumer surplus. The revenue effect simply shifts the consumer surplus from the private to the public sector, not causing a loss in overall welfare for the country.

The redistributive effect is the financial transfer of the consumer surplus to the domestic manufacturers of the product that is competing with imports. Area a stands for this, and it is $30,000. Domestic home buyers will purchase 40 cars at a cost of $9,000 from domestic companies under the tariff, for a total of $360,000. The same 40 cars would have brought in $320,000 at the free-trade price of $8,000. Home producers thus receive additional revenue from the tariff, equal to areas a + b, or $40,000 (the difference between $360,000 and $320,000). However, producers must pay a portion of the increased revenue as higher production costs, represented by area b, or $10,000, as the tariff encourages domestic production to increase from 20 to 40 units. The $30,000 in remaining revenue is a net gain for the producer. Therefore, a transfer of income from consumers to producers is the redistributive effect. It does not cause an overall loss of economic welfare, similar to the revenue effect.

The $10,000 in area b is known as the tariff's protective effect. It demonstrates the harm done to the national economy by squandering resources that could have been used to create more cars at higher cost per unit. Unit production costs rise as resources less suited to auto production are eventually used as a result of the tariff-induced expansion of domestic output. Because of this increase, resources are being used less effectively than they would have under free trade, when cars would have been bought from low-cost foreign manufacturers. Thus, the protective effect of a tariff results from the substitution of more efficient foreign production for less efficient domestic production. With reference to Figure 3.3, supply schedule Sd illustrates how the domestic cost of producing automobiles rises as domestic output rises from 20 to 40 units. However, prior to the tariff, the same increase in automobiles could have been had for $8,000 per unit. The protective effect is shown in Area b, which shows a $10,000 loss to the economy. It is evident that determining the protection effect only entails figuring out triangle b's area. Recall from your geometry classes that a triangle's area is equal to (base × height)/2. Triangle B's height ($1,000) represents the price increase brought on by the tariff, and Triangle B's base (20 cars) represents the rise in domestic auto production brought on by the tariff. Thus, $20 × $1,000)/2 = $10,000 is the protection effect. The government received c as revenue, home producers received a as income, and the economy lost b due to inefficient domestic production, accounting for the majority of the consumer surplus lost as a result of the tariff. Area d, or $10,000, represents the consumption effect, which is the remaining amount not taken into consideration elsewhere. It results from the artificial increase in auto prices from $8,000 to $9,000 caused by the tariff, which reduces consumption. Because of the higher price and decreased consumption, there is a loss of welfare. You'll notice that in order to calculate the consumption effect, the area of the triangle must be calculated. The base (20 autos) represents the decrease in domestic consumption caused by the tariff, while the height of the triangle ($1,000) represents the price increase in autos as a result of the tariff. The result is (20 × $1,000)/2 = $10,000 for the consumption effect. Similar to the protective effect, the consumption effect is not a transfer to other economic sectors but rather a true cost to society. The deadweight loss of the tariff (areas b + d in the figure) is equal to the sum of these two effects.

Levying an import tariff inevitably reduces a country's national welfare, so long as it is assumed that the country represents a negligible portion of global trade. This is because the tariff does not have a positive welfare effect that would counteract the deadweight loss of the consumer surplus. A country would benefit more from trade if it could impose a tariff that would enhance its terms of trade with its trading partners. By increasing national welfare, this higher share would help to offset the deadweight loss of the consumer surplus. However, a small country cannot affect the terms of trade because it is so small in comparison to the global market. Therefore, imposing an import tariff lowers the welfare of a small country.

3.4.3. Tariff Welfare Effects: Large-Nation Model

Economists may seem to support free trade so strongly that it would seem impossible for a tariff to ever be advantageous. But this isn't always the case. When imposed by an importing country large enough to affect the global price of the good when changes in the volume of its imports are made possible through tariff policy, a tariff may improve national welfare. This large-nation status extends to other economic giants like Japan and the European Union, as well as to the United States, which imports a lot of consumer electronics, steel, oil, and autos. American consumers will pay more if the US imposes a tariff on automobile imports. As a result, there is less demand, which could be substantial enough to compel Japanese companies to lower the price at which they export their goods.

Japanese companies are likely to choose to lower their price to the United States in order to limit the decline in their sales because they can produce and export smaller quantities at a lower marginal cost. Thus, the impact of the tariff is divided between U.S.

Japanese companies realize a lower price for each auto exported than under free trade, while consumers pay a higher price for each auto imported than under free trade.

The tariff duty accounts for the difference in these two prices. When the US can transfer a portion of the tariff to Japanese companies through lower export prices, the welfare of the US increases. Japan loses out on improved trade terms for the United States.

In Table 3.5, the degree to which U.S. Tariffs on imports have the potential to lower global import prices. As an illustration, an 11% rise in the U.S. Tariffs on imports of ball bearings are projected to raise costs for American consumers by 10.2%. The quantity of ball bearings demanded in the US declines as a result of this price increase, and the global price drops by 0.8 percent. Using Figure 3.4, the domestic supply schedule is shown by line Sd, and the domestic demand schedule is shown by line D_d. What are the economic effects of an import tariff for a large country?

At point E, autarky equilibrium takes place. The importing country is subject to a S_{d+w} total supply schedule under free trade. The quantity of cars that both domestic and foreign manufacturers jointly provide to domestic consumers is displayed in this schedule. The foreign supply price is not a fixed constant, so the overall supply schedule slopes upward rather than horizontally. The cost is determined by the quantity that a major importer of the good—a country—purchases.

Table 3.5. Effects of Increases in U.S. Tariffs on the World Price of Imported Goods

Product	Tariff (or Equivalent)	Increase in U.S. Price	Decrease in World Price
Ball bearings	11.0%	10.2%	0.8%
Chemicals	9.0	6.5	2.5
Jewelry	9.0	5.4	3.6
Orange juice	30.0	21.7	8.3
Glassware	11.0	7.3	3.7
Luggage	16.5	11.0	5.5
Resins	12.0	5.4	6.6
Footwear	20.0	16.1	3.9
Lumber	6.5	4.1	2.4

Source: Hufbauer & Elliot, K. (1994). Measuring the Costs of Protection in the United States (pp. 28, 29). Washington, DC: Institute for International Economics.

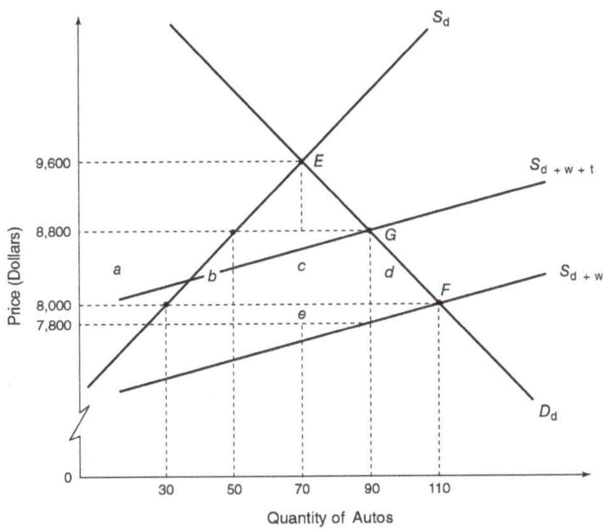

Figure 3.4. *Tariff trade and welfare effects: large nation model.*

Source: Robert J. Carbaugh; International Economics; ISBN 13: 978–1-4390–4076–8.

Our nation reaches market equilibrium at point F through free trade. Car prices drop to $8,000, domestic production drops to 30 units, and domestic consumption increases to 110 units. 80 auto imports cover the excess domestic demand.

Assume that a $1,000 specific tariff is applied to imported cars by the country of import. The tariff causes a change in the total supply schedule from S_{d+w} to S_{d+w+t} by raising the selling cost. The product price increases from $8,000 to $8,800 as the market equilibrium moves from point F to point G. The redistributive effect is represented by the reduction in the tariff-levying nation's consumer surplus of areas a + b + c + d. Area a, or $32,000. This amount is transferred from domestic consumers to domestic producers. The deadweight loss from the tariff, the decline in national welfare as a result of lower consumption (consumption effect = $8,000), and the wasteful use of resources (protective effect = $8,000) are shown in Areas d and b.

The revenue effect of a tariff is the import tariff times the volume of autos imported, just like in the small nation example. As a result, areas c + e, or $40,000, are produced. But note that in addition to domestic consumers, foreign producers are now providing the government with tariff revenue. This outcome is not the same as the small nation case, where domestic consumers bear the full burden of the tariff and the supply schedule is horizontal.

The $8,000 free-trade import price is increased by $1,000 in tariff. The price in the protected market will be higher than the foreign supply price by the duty, but it won't be higher than the price in the free-trade foreign supply market by the same amount. In comparison to the $8,000 foreign supply price set for free trade, domestic consumers only pay an extra $800 for each imported vehicle. This is the tariff portion that has been passed on to the customer. The price of cars supplied overseas drops by $200 concurrently. This implies that for every car exported, foreign manufacturers make $7,800 less in revenue. Because foreign production occurs in an environment of rising costs, a decrease in foreign production is brought about by a decrease in foreign imports, which in turn results in a decrease in unit costs. The $200 decrease in the foreign supply price is the amount of tariff that the foreign producer is responsible for paying. In an effort to keep sales in the country that imposes tariffs, foreign producers lower their prices, which results in a rise in the domestic price of the import of only a portion of the duty. If the price the importing country pays for auto imports falls while the price it charges for its exports stays the same, it will discover that its terms of trade have improved.

Therefore, there are two parts to the revenue impact of an import tariff in a large country. First, the amount of tariff revenue that is transferred from domestic consumers to the government that imposes tariffs is shown in Figure 3.4, where it is equal to the quantity of imports (40 units) times the amount of import tariff that domestic consumers bear ($800). The domestic revenue effect, which comes to $32,000, is shown in Area C. The second component consists of the tariff income that is obtained by lowering the supply price from overseas manufacturers. The terms-of-trade effect is represented by area e, which is equal to $8,000, and is found by multiplying auto imports (40 units) by the portion of the tariff that falls on foreign producers ($200). Be aware that the new terms of trade result in a redistribution of income from the foreign country to the country that levies tariffs. This is known as the terms-of-trade effect. Thus, the terms-of-trade and domestic revenue effects are included in the tariff's revenue effect.

A country that imports a significant amount of a good is in a favorable trade position. It can enhance trade conditions and, consequently, national welfare by using its tariff policy. But keep in mind that the deadweight loss of the consumer surplus resulting from the effects of consumption and protection is what constitutes a tariff's negative welfare effect. With reference to Figure 3.4, we must weigh the advantages of better trade terms (area e) against the effects of deadweight loss (areas b + d) in order to determine whether a tariff-levying country can increase national welfare. he conclusions regarding the welfare effects of a tariff are as follows:

1. If e > (b + d), national welfare is increased.
2. If e > (b + d), national welfare remains constant.
3. If e ? (b + d), national welfare is diminished.

The welfare of the domestic economy would decrease by $8,000 in the example above. This is due to the fact that the $8,000 welfare gain attributable to the terms-of-trade effect was more than offset by the $16,000 in deadweight welfare losses.

3.4.3.1. The Optimum Tariff and Retaliation

As we've seen, putting a tariff on imports can help a big country's terms of trade. A tariff, on the other hand, lowers the volume of imports, which lowers the welfare of the country by decreasing its consumption of inexpensive imports. As a result, there is a gain from better terms of trade and a loss from lower import volume (Feinberg & Kaplan, 1993).

With reference to Figure 3.4, a country seeks to maximize its economic welfare by enacting a tariff rate at which the net benefit of better terms of trade (area e) is equal to the net loss of economic efficiency resulting from the protective effect (area b) and the consumption effect (area d). Such a tariff rate is known as the optimum tariff. It makes sense that a large country can persuade its trading partners to accept lower prices for its imports the lower the foreign elasticity of supply.

The United States is a likely candidate to impose the best tariff because, in comparison to global demand, it imports a significant amount of goods, including electronics and cars. But keep in mind that the importing country is the only one who benefits from an optimal tariff. Imitating an optimal tariff is a beggar-thy-neighbor policy that may provoke retaliation because any gain accruing to the importing nation through a lower import price implies a loss to the foreign exporting nation. If all countries impose optimal tariffs, it is likely that everyone's economic welfare will decrease as the volume of trade declines. After all, if the United States imposes an optimal tariff of 25% on its imports, why should Japan and the European Union not levy tariffs of 40 or 50% on their imports? For any country debating whether to raise tariffs, the threat of foreign retaliation might be enough of a deterrent.

A classic case of a tariff-induced trade war was the implementation of the Smoot-Hawley Tariff Act by the U.S. government in 1930. This tariff was initially intended to provide relief to U.S. farmers. However, senators and members of Congress from industrial states used the technique of vote trading to obtain increased tariffs on manufactured goods. The result was a policy that increased tariffs on more than 1,000 products, with an average nominal duty on protected goods of 53%! Viewing the Smoot-Hawley tariff as an attempt to force unemployment on its workers, 12 nations promptly increased their duties against the United States. American farm exports fell to one-third of their former level, and between 1930 and 1933 total U.S. exports fell by almost 60%. Although the Great Depression accounted for much of that decline, the adverse psychological impact of the Smoot-Hawley tariff on business activity cannot be ignored.

3.5. ARGUMENTS FOR TRADE RESTRICTIONS

In theory, the free-trade argument makes sense. It says that in the long run, everyone will benefit from lower prices and higher levels of output, income, and consumption than could be attained in isolation if each country produces what it does best and allows trade. In a dynamic world, changes in technology, input productivities, wages, and demand cause comparative advantage to fluctuate constantly. A free market demands that changes be made. Resources will either shift from low-productivity to high-productivity uses, or an industry's efficiency must increase. Trade barriers such as tariffs are perceived as instruments that impede economic adjustment, leading to a state of economic stagnation.

Almost all countries have placed limits on the movement of capital, goods, and services across international borders, despite the free-trade argument frequently taking center stage in classroom discussions. Proponents of protectionism frequently claim that while free trade makes sense in theory, it is inapplicable in practice. Current trade theory operates under the assumption of perfectly competitive markets, which do not correspond to actual market conditions. Furthermore, protectionists frequently contend that noneconomic benefits like national security outweigh the economic losses, even though they may acknowledge that tariffs and other restrictions cause economic losses. Labor unions and domestic industries seek protection against imports in an effort to safeguard their financial well-being. Numerous arguments have been made over the years to persuade Congress and the president to pass restrictive legislation.

3.5.1. Job Protection

Trade restrictions on imported goods have been imposed by government officials primarily due to the employment issue. In times of economic downturn, employees are particularly keen to highlight how low-cost imports undermine domestic manufacturing, forcing domestic jobs to be replaced by foreign labor. Alleged job losses to foreign competition historically have been a major force behind the desire of most U.S. labor leaders to reject free-trade policies.

But this viewpoint is seriously lacking in one important area: it ignores the dual character of international trade. A country's exports and imports of products and services are directly correlated. Countries export goods in order to import goods from other countries. Foreigners gain purchasing power from U.S. imports of goods, which they will eventually spend on U.S. products, services, or monetary resources. Then, American export sectors experience increases in employment and sales, while the reverse is true for U.S. competitors with imports. As part of the process by which they reduce employment in other industries, imports tend to create job opportunities in some industries rather than increasing overall unemployment. On the other hand, the public typically notices job losses resulting from foreign competition more visibly than job gains brought about by free trade policies. The more noticeable defeats have prompted numerous U.S. Leaders in business and labor should band together to oppose free trade.

Trade restrictions increase jobs in the protected industry (steel, for example) by driving up the cost (or lowering the supply) of rival import goods. Employment is created in industries that are the protected industry's main suppliers of inputs. Nevertheless, sectors like the auto industry that buy the protected product have to pay more.

Lower sales are the consequence of passing these costs on to the customer through higher prices. As a result, employment in these associated industries declines. The Federal Reserve Bank of Dallas's economists have looked at the impacts on U.S. application of trade restrictions on steel, autos, and textiles and clothing. They come to the conclusion that, over time, trade protection has little to no beneficial impact on employment levels. Trade restrictions typically result in job losses dispersed across numerous industries, while they also tend to create jobs for a select few.

One startling reality about job preservation initiatives is that, frequently, the costs to domestic consumers incurred by each job kept in the specialty steel industry in the United States amount to $1 million annually, far more than the wages paid to production workers in that sector. This was the case in 1986.

The argument that an alternative strategy should be used to assist workers and that workers leaving an industry facing foreign competition should be liberally compensated (subsidized) for moving to new industries or taking early retirement is supported by the fact that costs to consumers for each production job saved are so high.

3.5.2. Protection Against Cheap Foreign Labor

One of the most common arguments used to justify the protectionist umbrella of trade restrictions is that tariffs are needed to defend domestic jobs against cheap foreign labor. As indicated in Table 3.6, production workers in Canada and the United States have been paid much higher wages, in terms of the U.S. dollar, than workers in countries such as Brazil and Mexico. So it could be argued that low wages abroad make it difficult for U.S. producers to compete with producers using cheap foreign labor and that unless U.S. producers are protected from imports, domestic output and employment levels will decrease.

Table 3.6. Hourly Compensation Costs in U.S. Dollars for Production Workers in Manufacturing, 2007

Country	Hourly Compensation (dollars per hour)
Canada	31.91
United States	30.56
Japan	23.95
South Korea	18.30
Czech Republic	9.67
Taiwan	8.15
Brazil	7.13
Mexico	3.91

Source: U.S. Department of Labor, Bureau of Labor Statistics, International Comparisons of Hourly Compensation Costs in Manufacturing, 2007 available at http://www.bls.gov.

In fact, it's commonly held that American workers suffer unfairly and negatively from competition from goods made in low-wage nations. Furthermore, it is believed that businesses that manufacture goods abroad in order to benefit from cheap labor should not be able to set the wages that are paid to American workers. A solution: Impose a tariff or tax on goods brought into the United States equal to the wage differential between foreign and U.S. workers in the same industry. That way, competition would be confined to who makes the best product, not who works for the least amount of money. Therefore, if Calvin Klein wants to manufacture sweatshirts in Pakistan, his firm would be charged a tariff or tax equal to the difference between the earnings of a Pakistani worker and a U.S. apparel worker.

This is a widely held opinion, but it ignores the connections between productivity, wages, and costs of production. Should domestic labor prove to be more productive than foreign labor, domestic labor costs could remain competitive, despite the higher wages. The total labor costs are a function of both the output per labor hour and the wage rate. The cost of labor will be lower at home than abroad if the superior productivity of domestic labor more than makes up for the higher wage rate.

Table 3.7 lists the 2002 manufacturing labor productivity (output per worker), wages, and unit labor costs for a number of countries in comparison to the U.S. It is evident that these countries' wages were tiny portions of U.S. wages, but these countries' labor productivity levels were also only a small portion of the U.S. productivity of labor. A foreign nation would have greater unit labor costs even if its wages are lower than those in the U.S. if its labor productivity is significantly lower than the U.S. productivity of labor. The aforementioned countries—Hong Kong, Poland, the United Kingdom, Norway, Hungary, and Denmark—had unit labor cost ratios (which are calculated by multiplying the wage ratio by the labor productivity ratio) greater than 1.0. Because workers in these countries were more productive than their wages, the unit labor costs of labor in these countries were higher than in the U.S. In other words, low wages do not automatically translate into low production costs.

Table 3.7. Productivity, Wages, and Unit Labor Costs, Relative to the United States: Total Manufacturing, 2002 (United States = 1.0)

Country	Labor Productivity Relative to United States	Wages Relative to United States*	Unit Labor Cost Relative to United States	
Hong Kong	0.25	0.57	2.28	
Poland	0.08	0.13	1.63	
United Kingdom	0.56	0.82	1.46	
Norway	0.57	0.82	1.44	
Hungary	0.07	0.10	1.43	U.S. More Competitive
Denmark	0.60	0.69	1.15	
Japan	0.89	0.79	0.89	U.S. Less Competitive
Mexico	0.27	0.21	0.78	
India	0.05	0.03	0.60	
South Korea	0.66	0.39	0.59	
China	0.09	0.03	0.33	

Source: Robert J. Carbaugh; International Economics; ISBN 13: 978–1-4390–4076–8.

The cheap-foreign-labor argument is further limited by the fact that low-wage countries typically only have a competitive advantage when producing goods that require a large amount of labor and little in the way of other factor inputs, or when wages account for the majority of production costs. It is true that when producing labor-intensive commodities, a high-wage country may face relative cost disadvantages in comparison to its low-wage trading partner. However, this does not imply that foreign manufacturers can undercut the nation in every sector of the economy, lowering the standard of living there as a whole. International countries ought to use the money they make from exporting goods to buy goods in which their own country has a competitive edge—i.e., goods that need a significant portion of the abundant domestic production inputs.

Remember that the factor-endowment theory contends that, in the presence of competitive markets, resource payments tend to equilibrate across countries as economies grow more interdependent through trade. A country with high labor costs will typically import goods made with a lot of labor. The decrease in demand for domestic labor resulting from rising imports and declining domestic output will drive domestic wages down to levels seen abroad.

3.5.3. Fairness in Trade: A Level Playing Field

Another argument for protectionism is the need for trade fairness. Workers and business organizations frequently contend that unfair competitive advantages are granted to foreign firms by governments that operate under different regulations from those of their home country. Import restrictions, according to domestic producers, should be implemented to counteract these foreign advantages and level the playing field so that all producers can compete fairly.

American businesses frequently claim that foreign companies are exempt from the same government regulations pertaining to worker safety and pollution control; this is particularly true in many developing countries (like South Korea and Mexico), where environmental laws and enforcement have been slack. Furthermore, foreign companies might not be subject to employment laws like affirmative action, minimum wages, and overtime pay, nor might they have to pay as much in corporate taxes. Additionally, foreign governments may subsidize their producers to increase their competitiveness in global markets or they may erect high trade barriers that effectively close their markets to imports.

Foreign competitors are gaining market share from organized lobbyists, who frequently make fair-trade arguments. Because they are presented in terms of equality and fair play, voters may find them appealing. There are, however, a number of arguments opposing the imposition of restrictions on imports from countries with high trade barriers or that impose less onerous regulations on their producers. First, trade boosts the national economy regardless of trade barriers imposed by other countries. Our welfare may be lowered by export-related foreign restrictions, but it is further reduced when we impose retaliatory import barriers that shield ineffective domestic producers.

Secondly, the argument fails to acknowledge the possible influence on international trade. A global escalation in trade restrictions would result from every country imposing greater trade restrictions whenever foreign restrictions surpassed domestic ones. This would lead to a reduction in trade volume, a drop in employment and production levels, and a decline in welfare. There might be a case for threatening to impose trade restrictions unless other countries ease their own; however, it would not be ideal if talks break down and national restrictions are implemented. Trade policies of other nations are rarely a sufficient defense for trade restrictions imposed domestically.

3.5.4. Maintenance of the Domestic Standard of Living

Trade barrier proponents frequently argue that tariffs help the home country's economy remain robust and create jobs. One argument for tariffs is that they boost domestic economic activity by lowering the amount of imports. The level of employment and income in the home country will rise as a result. This argument is worth qualifying in a few ways, even though it seems reasonable at first. Tariffs cannot be imposed by all nations combined to raise living standards at home. This is due to the fact that tariffs cause the benefits of trade to be redistributed among countries. The standard of living of a trading partner is jeopardized when a country imposes tariffs that increase its own revenue and employment. Countries that suffer from trade barriers are likely to respond with retaliatory tariffs, which will lower global welfare. It should come as no surprise that tariffs intended to raise a country's standard of living at the expense of a trading partner are known as "beggar-thy-neighbor" policies.

3.5.5. Equalization of Production Costs

The goal of those who support a scientific tariff is to stop foreign competition that they perceive to be unfair. Foreign sellers may have cost advantages over domestic companies due to things like lower wage costs, tax breaks, or government subsidies. Tariffs equal to the cost difference should be applied to offset any such benefit. In actuality, these clauses were included in the U.S. The 1930 and 1922 Tariff Acts.

In practice, the scientific tariff suffers from a number of problems. Because costs differ from business to business within a given industry, how can costs actually be compared? Suppose that all U.S. steelmakers were extended protection from all foreign steelmakers. This protection would require the costs of the most efficient foreign producer to be set equal to the highest costs of the least efficient U.S. company. Given today's cost conditions, prices would certainly rise in the United States. This rise would benefit the more efficient U.S. companies, which would enjoy economic profits, but the U.S. consumer would be subsidizing inefficient production. Because the scientific tariff approximates a prohibitive tariff, it completely contradicts the notion of comparative advantage and wipes out the basis for trade and gains from trade.

3.5.6. Infant-Industry Argument

An argument for tariff protection that is more widely accepted is the infant industry argument. The case for free trade is not refuted by this argument. It does, however, argue that trading nations must temporarily protect their emerging industries from foreign competition in order for free trade to have any real meaning. If not, established foreign companies that are more efficient at the moment could force upstart domestic companies out of the market. Free trade should only occur once the young businesses have had time to mature into capable manufacturers and the tariff barriers have been removed.

The infant industry argument has some validity, but it needs to be qualified in a few ways. First off, even after an industry reaches industrial maturity, it is exceedingly difficult to remove a protective tariff once it is put in place. Policy makers are frequently persuaded by special interest groups that more protection is warranted. Second, predicting which industries will be able to realize their potential for comparative advantage and, consequently, deserve protection, is extremely difficult. Third, for developed, industrialized countries like the US, Germany, and Japan, the infant-industry argument is usually invalid. Fourth, there might be additional strategies for shielding a nascent sector from fierce rivalry. The government might choose to provide the industry with a subsidy rather than enact a protective tariff. The benefit of a subsidy is that it does not affect relative prices or domestic consumption; the disadvantage is that, unlike import tariffs, subsidies spend money rather than earning it.

3.5.7. Noneconomic Arguments

The justifications for protectionism also take into account noneconomic factors. National security is one such factor. According to the national-security argument, a nation that depends significantly on foreign suppliers could find itself in danger in the event of a global crisis or war.

Tariff protection should be given to domestic producers despite the fact that they are less productive. This will guarantee their survival. An effective way to use this argument is with the major oil-importing countries. In the 1973 Middle East conflict, several Arab countries forced oil boycotts on the West in an effort to gain support for their position against Israel. Determining what defines an essential industry is the issue, though. Should the term be interpreted widely, numerous industries could be granted import protection, which would render the argument meaningless.

The national security argument for protectionism also has implications for foreign investments, such as foreign acquisitions of American companies and assets. Although the United States has traditionally welcomed foreign investment, it provides authority to the president to suspend or prohibit any foreign acquisition, merger, or takeover of a U.S. corporation determined to threaten the national security of the United States. Examples of actions generally considered harmful to the security of the United States include the denial of critical technology or key products to the U.S. government or U.S. industry, moving critical technology or key products offshore that are important for national defense or homeland security, and shutting down or sabotaging a critical facility in the United States. Therefore, the U.S. government reviews foreign investment transactions beyond the defense industrial base, including energy and natural resources, technology, telecommunications, transportation, and manufacturing. Such reviews have become more stringent since the September 11, 2001, terrorist attack against the United States.

Cultural and sociological factors serve as the foundation for yet another noneconomic argument. Small-scale fishing in New England might be protected, while West Virginia might support tariffs on hand-blown glassware because these crafts enhance society; some goods, like drugs, might be deemed socially undesirable and their importation might be restricted or outright banned. These are valid arguments that should not be disregarded. The economist's only role is to highlight the costs and consequences of protection from the economy and suggest other means of achieving the same goal.

In Canada, many nationalists maintain that Canadian culture is too fragile to survive without government protection. The big threat: U.S. cultural imperialism. By the 1990s, the envelope of Canada's cultural protectionism was expanding. The most blatant example was a 1994 law that levied an 80% tax on Canadian ads in Canadian editions of U.S. magazines— in effect, an effort to kill off the U.S. intruders. Without protections for the Canadian media, the cultural nationalists feared that U.S. magazines such as Sports Illustrated, Time, and Business Week could soon deprive Canadians of the ability to read about themselves in Maclean's and Canadian Business. Although U.S. protests of the tax ultimately led to its abolishment, the Canadian government continued to examine other methods of preserving the culture of its people.

It is significant to highlight that the majority of arguments in favor of tariffs are predicated on the notion that both individual and societal welfare will increase. One of the primary reasons reciprocal tariff liberalization has happened so gradually is the strategic significance of tariffs for the welfare of import-competing producers. It makes sense that producers facing import competition would present such compelling and persuasive political cases that greater foreign competition will be detrimental to both their own and the country's overall welfare. While some groups may suffer from the removal of tariff barriers, it is important to distinguish between the welfare of the individual and the welfare of the country. The overall welfare of the country will rise if tariff reductions lead to higher welfare gains from trade and if the party that is negatively impacted can be made whole for the losses it has suffered. It is very challenging to demonstrate that in reality the gains outweigh the losses.

3.5.8. A Supply and Demand View of Protectionism

An analysis of import protection's political economy can be done using supply and demand. The domestic government provides protectionism, while domestic businesses and laborers provide the demand. The availability of protection is influenced by four factors: (1) societal costs; (2) political significance of producers who compete with imports; (3) adjustment costs; and (4) public support.

Government officials with a conscience understand that while protectionism helps domestic producers, society as a whole bears the price. These expenses include lost economies of scale as opportunities for further trade are passed up, the loss of the incentive that import competition provided for technological development, and the losses of consumer surplus due to higher prices and the ensuing deadweight losses as import volume is reduced. It is less likely that government officials will protect an industry from import competition the higher the costs of protection to society.

The political significance of the industry that competes with imports has an impact on the supply of protectionism as well. An industry has a better chance of winning import protection if it has strong legislative representation. Politicians find it more difficult to disagree with one million autoworkers than with 20,000 copper workers. An industry's political significance is taken into account in the national security case for protection. For instance, the U.S. The coal and oil sectors were able to secure a national-security clause in the U.S. trade legislation allowing for protection in cases where imports pose a risk to national security. When domestic producers and workers must bear the heavy burden of adapting to increased import competition, such as through wage concessions or unemployment, the supply of protection also tends to increase. This protection is thought to be a means of postponing the entire adjustment burden.

Additionally, more protection against goods made abroad tends to be provided when public sympathy for a group of domestic producers or workers grows (for instance, if workers receive low wages and have few alternative work skills). The domestic industry's demand for protectionism is driven by four factors on the demand side: (1) comparative disadvantage; (2) import penetration; (3) concentration; and (4) export dependence.

As the comparative disadvantage of the domestic industry grows, so does the demand for protection. It is observed in the U.S. steel industry, which in recent decades has aggressively fought for defense against low-cost steel producers in South Korea and Japan. Demands for protection rise in tandem with higher import penetration rates, which indicate greater competitive pressures on home producers. When the AFL-CIO began to support protectionism in the late 1960s, it marked a significant shift in the organization's support for the policy from its long-standing belief in the benefits of free markets. The fast increase in import-penetration ratios that took place in the 1960s in sectors like footwear and electrical consumer goods was the main cause of this change in the union's stance.

The concentration of domestic production is another factor that could influence the demand for protection. The U.S. The Big Three, for instance, control the auto industry. These companies can fund support for import protection without worrying that a significant portion of the advantages of protectionism will go to non-participating companies. On the other hand, an industry like meat packing, which consists of a lot of small producers, understands that producers who don't pay their fair share of the expenses associated with passing protectionist laws could end up with a large portion of the benefits that come with protectionism. Therefore, the more concentrated the domestic industry, the greater the need for protection.

Lastly, the level of export dependence may have an impact on the need for protection. Companies like Boeing, whose sales to foreign customers account for a sizable amount of their overall revenue, should not be overly concerned about import protection, one would think. Their principal concern is that if trade barriers are imposed domestically, there may be international retaliation, which would destroy their export markets.

CASE STUDY

THE IMPACT OF INTERNATIONAL TARIFFS ON GLOBAL TRADE

Background

In 2020, two major economies, Country A and Country B, engaged in a trade dispute that escalated into a series of tariff impositions. Country A, a leading producer of agricultural goods, accused Country B of subsidizing its domestic agricultural sector unfairly, leading to a flood of cheap imports that undercut local producers in Country A. In response, Country A decided to impose tariffs on all agricultural products imported from Country B.

Timeline of Events

1. **Initial Tariff Implementation (2020):**
    - Country A imposes a 25% tariff on all agricultural imports from Country B, covering products such as wheat, corn, and soybeans.
2. **Immediate Economic Effects:**
    - **Country B's Exporters:** Exporters in Country B immediately face higher costs when selling their products to Country A. This reduces their competitiveness in Country A's market, leading to a decline in export volumes and revenue.
    - **Consumers in Country A:** Consumers in Country A experience higher prices for agricultural products due to reduced supply and increased costs from tariffs. This could lead to inflationary pressures on food prices.
3. **Political and Diplomatic Responses:**
    - **Country B's Government:** Responds with diplomatic protests and retaliatory tariffs on select goods imported from Country A, such as electronics and automobiles. This escalates the trade dispute further.
    - **International Community:** Other trading partners and international organizations express concerns about the escalating tariffs, urging both countries to resolve their differences through negotiation rather than tariff escalation.
4. **Long-Term Economic Impact:**
    - **Supply Chain Adjustments:** Companies in both countries begin to reconsider their supply chain strategies, potentially shifting production locations or seeking alternative markets to avoid tariffs.
    - **Global Market Confidence:** Uncertainty caused by the trade dispute impacts global market confidence, leading to volatility in financial markets and affecting investment decisions.

5. **Negotiation and Resolution (2021):**
   - After several rounds of negotiations facilitated by international mediators, both countries reach a temporary agreement. Country A agrees to reduce tariffs gradually in exchange for Country B scaling back its subsidies to its agricultural sector.
6. **Post-Resolution Effects:**
   - **Market Reactions:** Investors and businesses react positively to the resolution, leading to stabilization in affected markets and a gradual return to normal trade patterns.
   - **Lessons Learned:** Both countries and the international community reflect on the importance of dispute resolution mechanisms and the potential pitfalls of using tariffs as a tool for economic policy.

CONCLUSION

The case study of Country A and Country B illustrates the complexities and consequences of international tariffs. While tariffs can be used as a tool to protect domestic industries and correct trade imbalances, they also carry significant economic and diplomatic risks. Ultimately, resolving trade disputes through negotiation and international cooperation is crucial for maintaining stable global trade relations and fostering economic growth.

CLASS ACTIVITY

Objective:

To illustrate the impact of tariffs on international trade and economic interactions between countries.

Materials Needed:

- Index cards or slips of paper
- Markers or pens
- Printouts or access to information about real-world tariffs (optional)

Activity Steps:

Discuss why countries might impose tariffs (protecting domestic jobs, addressing trade imbalances, etc.). Divide the class into small groups (3–4 students per group). Assign each group a different country (or let them choose from a list) and provide basic information about that country's economy and industries.

Assessment:

- Evaluate student understanding through their presentations and participation in the discussion.
- Assess critical thinking skills in how well students justify their proposed tariffs and articulate their understanding of the economic impacts.

SUMMARY

- Tariffs act as obstacles to international trade, impeding the smooth movement of goods and services between countries. Local governments impose taxes on the imported goods' total value, with importers bearing the initial cost but passing it on to the final consumers. Import barriers encompass import duties, quotas, standardization, and licensing requirements.
- There are several types of tariffs. A specific tariff represents a fixed amount of money per unit of the imported commodity. An ad valorem tariff is stated as a fixed percentage of the value of an imported commodity. A compound tariff combines a specific tariff with an ad valorem tariff.
- Concerning ad valorem tariffs, several procedures exist for the valuation of imports. The free-on-board (FOB) measure indicates a commodity's price as it leaves the exporting nation. The cost-insurance-freight (CIF) measure shows the product's value as it arrives at the port of entry.
- The effective tariff rate tends to differ from the nominal tariff rate when the domestic import competing industry uses imported resources whose tariffs

differ from those on the final commodity. Developing nations have traditionally argued that many advanced nations escalate the tariff structures on industrial commodities to yield an effective rate of protection several times the nominal rate.

- American trade laws mitigate the effects of import duties by allowing U.S. importers to postpone and prorate over time their duty obligations by means of bonded warehouses and foreign trade zones.
- The welfare effects of a tariff can be measured by its protective effect, consumption effect, redistributive effect, revenue effect, and terms of-trade effect.
- If a nation is small compared with the rest of the world, its welfare necessarily falls by the total amount of the protective effect plus the consumption effect if it levies a tariff on imports. If the importing nation is large relative to the world, the imposition of an import tariff may improve its international terms of trade by an amount that more than offsets the welfare losses associated with the consumption effect and the protective effect.
- Because a tariff is a tax on imports, the burden of a tariff falls initially on importers, who must pay duties to the domestic government. However, importers generally try to shift increased costs to buyers through price increases. Domestic exporters, who purchase imported inputs subject to tariffs, thus face higher costs and a reduction in competitiveness.
- Although tariffs may improve one nation's economic position, any gains generally come at the expense of other nations. Should tariff retaliations occur, the volume of international trade decreases, and world welfare suffers. Tariff liberalization is intended to promote freer markets so that the world can benefit from expanded trade volumes and the international specialization of inputs.
- Tariffs are sometimes justified on the grounds that they protect domestic employment and wages, help create a level playing field for international trade, equate the cost of imported products with the cost of domestic import competing products, allow domestic industries to be insulated temporarily from foreign competition until they can grow and develop, or protect industries necessary for national security.

REVIEW QUESTIONS

1. What is the concept of tariffs in international trade?
2. Explain tariff escalation and provide examples of how it affects international trade.
3. How do postponing import tariffs influence a country's economy and trade dynamics?
4. Discuss the effects of tariffs on consumer prices and the domestic economy.
5. What are the main arguments in favor of imposing trade restrictions such as tariffs?

6. Contrast the economic impacts of tariffs on exporting and importing countries.
7. How do tariffs impact global supply chains and international investment flows?
8. Examine the relationship between tariffs and the balance of trade in a country.

REFERENCES

1. Adlung, R., & Molinuevo, M. (2008). Bilateralism in services trade: Is there fire behind the (BIT-) smoke? *Journal of International Economic Law, 11*(2), 365–409.
2. Adlung, R., & Roy, M. (2005). Turning hills into mountains? Current commitments under the General Agreement on Trade in Services and prospects for change. *Journal of World Trade, 39*(6), 1161–1194.
3. Belderbos, R. A., & Sleuwaegen, L. (1998). Tariff jumping DFI and export substitution: Japanese electronics firms in Europe. *International Journal of Industrial Organization, 16*(5), 601–638.
4. Burke, S., & Bairoch, P. (1989). Chapter I–European trade policy, 1815–1914. In P. Mathias & S. Pollard (Eds.), *The Cambridge Economic History of Europe from the Decline of the Roman Empire, Vol. 8: The Industrial Economies: The Development of Economic and Social Policies* (pp. 1–160). Cambridge University Press.
5. Carter, C., & Gunning-Trant, C. (2007). U.S. trade remedy law and agriculture: Trade diversion and investigation effects. Mimeo, University of California Davis.
6. Chang, H.-J. (2012). Africa needs an active industrial policy to sustain its growth. *The Guardian*. Retrieved from: https://www.theguardian.com (accessed on 3 July 2024).
7. Curtis, T. B. (1971). *The Kennedy Round and the Future of American Trade*. H. G. Johnson, *Aspects of the theory of tariffs* (1971); H. R. Nau (Ed.), *Domestic trade politics and the Uruguay Round* (1989).
8. Eaton, J., & Grossman, S. (1985). Tariffs as insurance: Optimal commercial policy when domestic markets are incomplete. *Canadian Journal of Economics, 18*(2), 258–272.
9. Falvey, R. E., & Lloyd, P. J. (1991). Uncertainty and the choice of protective instrument. *Oxford Economic Papers, 43*(3), 463–478.
10. Feinberg, R. M., & Kaplan, S. (1993). Fishing downstream: The political economy of effective administrated protection. *Canadian Journal of Economics / Revue canadienne d'Économique, 26*(1), 150–158.
11. Kluge, F. (1989). *Etymologisches Wörterbuch der deutschen Sprache* (22. Aufl.). Berlin: De Gruyter.
12. Krugman, P. R. (1993). The narrow and broad arguments for free trade. *American Economic Review: Papers and Proceedings, 83*(3), 362–366.
13. Martina, M. (2017). *U.S. Tech Group Urges Global Action Against Chinese 'Mercantilism.'* Reuters. Retrieved from: https://www.reuters.com (accessed on 3 July 2024).
14. Michell, H. (2014). *The Economics of Ancient Greece*. Cambridge University Press.

CHAPTER

4 Nontariff Trade Barriers

LEARNING OBJECTIVES

After studying this chapter, you will be able to:

- Define non-tariff barriers
- Explain about import quota
- Discuss about tariff-rate quota: a two-tier tariff
- Explain export quotas
- List the domestic content requirements
- Define subsidies
- Explain about dumping
- Elaborate antidumping regulations
- Discuss about antidumping law unfair
- Describe other nontariff trade barriers

KEY TERMS FROM THIS CHAPTER

Antidumping duty	Demand allocation	Domestic production subsidy
Dumping	Export quotas	Export subsidy
Global quota	Import license	Import quota
Nontariff trade barriers	Persistent dumping	Predatory dumping
Selective quota	Social regulation	Sporadic dumping
Tariff-rate quota		

INTRODUCTION

Nontariff trade barriers (NTBs) encompass a range of regulatory and procedural constraints imposed by countries to control the import and export of goods without resorting to tariffs. Unlike tariffs, which are straightforward taxes on imports, NTBs are often more subtle and diverse, including quotas, import licensing, technical barriers to trade (TBTs), sanitary and phytosanitary measures (SPS), administrative hurdles, subsidies, and voluntary export restraints (VERs). Quotas limit the quantity of goods that can be imported, protecting domestic industries from foreign competition. Import licensing adds another layer of control by requiring importers to obtain permission to bring goods into a country. TBTs and SPS measures ensure that products meet specific health, safety, and environmental standards, which, while protecting consumers and ecosystems, can also act as barriers by making compliance costly and complex for foreign producers. Administrative barriers such as intricate customs procedures and excessive paperwork increase the time and cost associated with importing goods, deterring foreign trade. Subsidies and domestic support distort trade by giving local industries a competitive edge, while VERs are agreements that limit the export quantity to a particular country, reducing market saturation. NTBs significantly impact global trade dynamics by creating additional challenges for exporters, leading to higher prices and reduced choice for consumers, and can contribute to international trade disputes. Despite their complexity, understanding and managing NTBs is crucial for fostering a fair and open global trading system, ensuring that protectionist measures do not unduly hinder the free flow of goods and services. Thus, NTBs play a pivotal role in shaping international trade policies and practices, balancing protectionism with the need for economic cooperation and market access.

4.1. NON-TARIFF BARRIERS

Trade barriers that impose restrictions on the import or export of goods without using tariffs are known as non-tariff barriers. Non-tariff trade barriers include import licensing, pre-shipment inspections, rules of origin, custom delayers, and other trade-prevention or trade-restricting measures, according to the World Trade Organization (WTO).

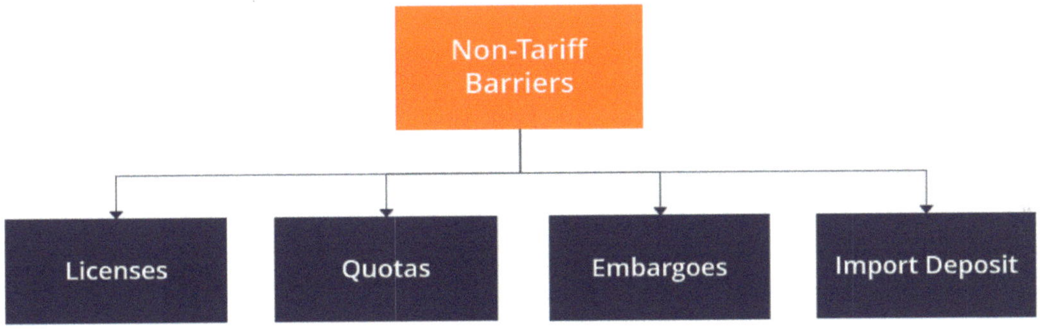

Figure 4.1. *Non-tariff barriers.*

Source: https://cdn.corporatefinanceinstitute.com/assets/non-tariff-barriers.png.

Non-tariff barriers are an economic tactic used by developed nations to limit the volume of trade they engage in with other nations. Countries consider the availability of goods and services for import and export, as well as their current political alliances with other trading partners, when deciding which non-tariff trade barriers to impose. Developed nations may decide to eschew imposing additional taxes on goods imported or exported from other nations in favor of establishing alternative non-tariff trade barriers that have a distinct financial impact.

4.1.1. Origin of Non-Tariff Barriers

Countries had to come up with strategies for raising capital during the establishment of nation-states in order to fund ongoing expenses and local projects. Introducing tariffs, which imposed limitations on the import and export of goods and services, was one of these strategies. However, because they had established alternative funding sources, industrialized nations made the switch from tariff barriers to non-tariff barriers. The majority of developing nations still rely on tariff barriers to control international trade with other nations and raise funds for domestic projects.

For a variety of reasons, the industrialized nations later shifted from tariff to non-tariff barriers. One justification was to control global trade even in the absence of tariffs. It has produced other significant non-traffic barriers in place of exempting certain nations from paying additional taxes on goods. Supporting vulnerable industries impacted by the removal or reduction of tariff barriers is a second justification for the introduction of non-tariff barriers. The last justification is that, in the absence of trade tariffs, interest groups can still influence trade regulation through non-tariff barriers.

4.1.2. Types of Non-Tariff Barriers

Non-tariff barriers may take the following forms:

1. **Protectionist Barriers:** Protectionist trade barriers aim to safeguard specific domestic industry sectors at the cost of other nations. Other nations find it challenging to compete favorably with locally produced goods and services due to the restrictions. The obstacles could be in the form of import deposits, antidumping duties, quota allocation, licensing requirements, etc.
2. **Assistive Policies:** While assistive policies implement measures that can obstruct free trade with other countries, they do not directly restrict trade with other countries, even though they are intended to protect domestic businesses and enterprises. Customs procedures, packaging and labeling regulations, technical standards and norms, sanitary standards, etc., are a few examples of assistive barriers.

   For international companies to be permitted to export or import specific goods into the market, they have to fulfill the necessary requirements. In order to make domestic businesses competitive in both domestic and foreign markets, governments also assist domestic businesses by giving them bailouts and subsidies.
3. **Non-Protectionist Policies:** Although the overall effects of non-protectionist policies may result in limitations on free trade, they are not intended to directly restrict the import or export of goods and services. The main goals of the policies are to preserve the environment's integrity while safeguarding human and animal health and safety.

Licensing, packaging and labeling regulations, plant and animal inspections, import prohibitions for particular fishing or harvesting techniques, sanitary regulations, etc., are a few examples of non-protectionist policies.

4.1.3. Examples of Non-Tariff Barriers

1. **Licenses:** One of the most popular tools used by nations to control the import of goods is the license. A license system permits approved businesses to import particular commodities that are on the licensed goods list.

   There are two types of product licenses: one-time and general. For a limited time, the general license permits the import and export of approved items. A one-time license that details the product's cost, country of origin, and customs point of entry permits an importer of that particular product to import a certain quantity of that product.
2. **Quotas:** Quotas are quantitative limitations placed for a predetermined amount of time

on the import and export of a particular good. Quotas limit the number of nations in which businesses are permitted to trade specific commodities and are used by governments as direct administrative controls over foreign trade. The quantity of goods that can be imported or exported at any given time is limited by it.

3. **Embargoes:** Embargoes, which can be applied to the import or export of specific goods that are supplied to or from specific countries, are complete prohibitions on trade in particular commodities. These are regarded as legal trade barriers, and governments may impose them in order to accomplish particular political and economic objectives.

4. **Import Deposit:** A type of foreign trade regulation known as an import deposit mandates that importers give the nation's central bank a certain amount of money for a predetermined amount of time. The payment amount must match the price of the imported goods.

4.2. IMPORT QUOTA

A physical limit on the amount of goods that can be imported within a designated time frame is known as an import quota. Generally speaking, the quota keeps imports below what they would be under free-trade conditions. A quota might, for instance, prohibit the import of more than 1 million kilograms of cheese or 20 million kilograms of wheat during a given time frame. Examples of import quotas implemented by the US government are provided in Table 4.1.

Obtaining an import license is a standard procedure used by the government to manage an import quota. The license details the maximum amount of imports that are permitted. The license necessitates that the importer invest time in completing paperwork and awaiting formal approval. Licenses can be provided to importers for a flat fee or at a competitive price. Alternatively, a government might simply award licenses to importers who it deems worthy. Nevertheless, this allocation scheme encourages bribery and political lobbying.

Table 4.1. Examples of U.S. Import Quotas

Imported Article	Quota Quantity (yearly)
Condensed milk (Australia)	91,625 kg*
Condensed milk (Denmark)	605,092 kg
Evaporated milk (Germany)	9,997 kg
Evaporated milk (Netherlands)	548,393 kg
Blue-mold cheese (Argentina)	2,000 kg
Blue-mold cheese (Chile)	80,000 kg
Cheddar cheese (New Zealand)	8,200,000 kg
Italian cheese (Poland)	1,325,000 kg
Italian cheese (Romania)	500,000 kg
Swiss cheese (Switzerland)	1,850,000 kg

Source: From U.S. International Trade Commission, Tariff Schedules of the United States, Washington, DC, Government Printing Office, 2000.

World Trade Organization import quotas on manufactured goods are prohibited. To safeguard farmers, developed nations like the US and Japan have implemented import quotas. Recent trade talks, however, have demanded that nations convert their quotas to comparable tariffs.

An effective means of managing import restrictions is by means of a global quota. This method allows a certain amount of goods to be imported annually, but it doesn't say where the product is shipped from or who can import it. Restocking of the product is prohibited for the balance of the year after the quota has been reached (maximum amount imported).

In reality, the rush by foreign and domestic exporters to get their goods into the country before the quota is filled makes the global quota unmanageable. Early-year importers receive their goods, while late-year importers might not. Furthermore, because shipping products from far-off places takes longer, there is often discrimination against them. In comparison to larger merchants, smaller retailers who lack strong trade relationships might potentially be at a disadvantage. Allegations of partiality against merchants who have the good fortune to be the first to secure a substantial share of the market afflict global quotas.

Import quotas are typically assigned to particular nations in order to circumvent the issues associated with a global quota system; this kind of quota is referred to as a selective quota. A nation may set a global apple quota of 30 million per year, of which 14 million must come from the US, 10 million from Mexico, and 6 million from Canada. The amount of a specific good that enters the country from each source is tracked by customs officials in the importing country; once the quota for that source is reached, no more goods are allowed to be imported.

Global quotas and selective quotas have many of the same issues. Take Kmart as an example. In the 1980s, Kmart placed an order for wool sweaters from China valued at over a million dollars. The Chinese quota for the year was reached before the sweaters arrived in the US, so Kmart was unable to import them until the next year. The sweaters had to be sold for less at that point because they were out of style. Based on its estimation, the company only made up 60 cents of every dollar sold of sweaters.

Quotas also have the potential to result in a domestic production monopoly and higher prices. When a domestic company understands that foreign producers are unable to exceed their quotas, it may decide to increase its prices. Tariffs do not always result in monopoly power because there is no cap on the quantity of goods that can be brought into the country.

4.2.1. Trade and Welfare Effects

Like tariffs, import quotas have an impact on the health of an economy. Figure 4.2 illustrates the cheese case, wherein U.S. commerce with the EU, the European Union.

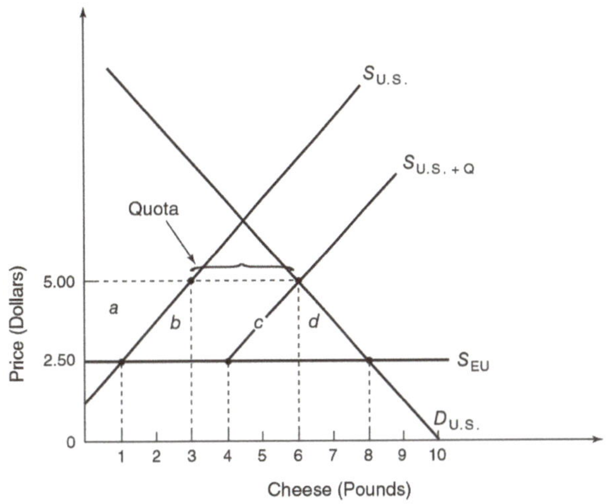

Figure 4.2. Import quota: trade and welfare effects.

Source: https://wyamaka.wordpress.com/wp-content/uploads/2019/08/international-economics_30.pdf.

A quota raises import prices by limiting the amount of an imported good that can be imported. The import-competing good's domestic producers are able to increase prices thanks to this price umbrella. The consumer surplus declines as a result. The protective effect, the consumption effect, and the portion of the revenue effect that is retained by the foreign exporter make up the welfare loss to the importing country of this amount.

In the context of the global cheese market, the United States is a "small" nation. Let us assume that SU. S. as well as DU. S. indicate the cheese supply and demand schedules in the US. The EU's supply schedule is represented by the SEU. The cost of cheese from the EU and the U.S. The price of cheese is $2.50 per pound. For this amount, U.S. businesses create one pound, U.S. Eight pounds are bought by consumers, and seven pounds are imported from the EU.

Let's say the US imposes an import quota, capping the amount of cheese it imports at three pounds. Over the price of free trade, the entire U.S. cheese supply currently equals U.S. output in addition to the quota. This is shown by a shift in the supply curve from Figure 4.2. S. to $S_{U.\ S.\ Q}$. The equilibrium price rises to $5.00 upon the reduction of imports from seven to three pounds, which prompts an increase in the quantity supplied by U.S. from one to three pounds, as well as a decline in the U.S. Requested amount decreased from eight pounds to six.

The welfare effects of import quotas can be examined using the same framework as tariffs in the chapter before. Given that our example's quota raises the price per pound to $5,001, the U.S. The reduction in consumer surplus is equal to area a + b + c + d ($17.50). The redistributive effect is represented by area a ($5.00), the protective effect by area b ($2.50), and the consumption effect by area d ($2.50). The protective effect plus the consumption effect show the deadweight loss of welfare to the economy as a result of the quota. However, what about the revenue effect of the quota, which is represented by area c ($7.50)? This amount results from the fact that U.S. Because of the quota-induced scarcity of cheese, consumers are required to pay an additional $2.50 for each of the three pounds of cheese imported under the quota. The term "quota rent" or "windfall profit" refers to the revenue effect. It belongs to the person who is allowed to import goods into the nation and sell them on the protected market. What happens to this unexpected profit?

It is helpful to consider a sequence of exchanges similar to the one in the following example in order to ascertain the distribution of the quota's revenue effect. Assume that grocery stores (importing companies) in the United States purchase cheese from European exporting companies, which then sells it to U.S. consumers:

European exporting companies	→	U.S. grocery stores (importing companies)	→	U.S. consumers

The prices that are common in the exchanges between these groups will decide how the quota's revenue effect is distributed. Who benefits from this unexpected profit will rely on how competitively the involved exporting and importing businesses are able to operate.

One result is when exporting businesses in Europe are able to band together and effectively turn into monopoly sellers. American grocery stores will compete with one another to purchase European cheese if they act as buyers. The cost of cheese delivery will increase from $2.50 to $5.00 per pound. Thus, European exporting businesses profit handsomely from the quota's windfall. The unexpected profit that European exporters make turns into a loss for American welfare. S. economy, aside from the deadweight losses brought on by the effects of consumption and protection.

Rather, let's say that U.S. Grocers unite as a single importing firm (like Safeway grocery stores) and develop into monopoly purchasers. Assume also that exporting businesses in Europe are sellers in a competitive market. Right now, U.S. Cheese can be bought by importing businesses at the going global price of $2.50 per pound and sold to U.S. customers for the cost of $5.00 per pound. In this instance, the importing companies benefit financially from the quota. This accrual does not represent a welfare loss for the United States because these companies are American. S. economy.

As an alternative, the U.S. The government may recoup the revenue impact of the quota from the importing businesses. Assume import permits are sold by the government to U.S. supermarkets. The government keeps all or a portion of the windfall profit from the quota by charging to import. All of the windfall profit that importing companies would have made under the quota would go to the government if import licenses are auctioned off to the highest bidder in a competitive market. Due to the fact that the quota's revenue effect benefits the U.S. government, this accrual doesn't indicate a reduction in welfare for the U.S. economy (presuming the government reinvests the money it receives).

4.2.2. Allocating Quota Licenses

Not all domestic importers can obtain the same quantity of imports as they could under free trade because an import quota restricts the amount of imports, typically below the freetrade quantity. As a result, governments distribute the limited supply of imports among their own citizens.

When it comes to dairy and oil, the U.S. Based on their historical share of the import market, the government has granted import licenses. However, importers looking to import goods for the first time are discriminated against by this method. Other times, the U.S. Pro rata import quotas have been distributed by the government, meaning that U.S. Importers get a portion of their demand that is equal to the import quota divided by the total amount that U.S. importers have collectively demanded. S. importers.

The U.S The government has also thought of auctioning import licenses to the highest bidder in a competitive market as an additional means of distributing licenses among domestic importers. Australia and New Zealand have also employed this method.

Think of a fictitious U.S. quota textile imports. Because of the quota, American textile prices are higher than those around the globe, creating an exceptionally lucrative market. Windfall gains may be obtained by U.S. importers (like Wal-Mart and Sears) if they purchase textiles at a lower global price and resell them to U.S. purchasers at the increased cost made feasible by the quota.

In light of these unexpected gains, U.S. The right to import textiles would probably be paid for by importers. The government could profit from windfall profits by auctioning import licenses to the highest bidder in a competitive market (the revenue effect shown as area c in Figure 4.2).

The government would receive the full revenue effect from the auction price rising to a point where no windfall profits remained due to importers competing to obtain licenses. A quota would become more like a tariff through the auctioning off import licenses, which brings in money for the government's coffers. Few countries have actually used auctions to distribute import rights under quotas.

4.2.3. Quotas Versus Tariffs

According to earlier research, import tariffs and import quotas have different revenue effects. Additionally, there may be differences between these two commercial policies' effects on trade volume. An import quota restricts the volume of imports more than an equivalent import tariff does during times of growing demand, as the following example shows.

A fictitious auto trade scenario for the United States is shown in Figure 4.3. The U.S. Auto supply and demand schedules are provided by $S_{U.S.0}$ and $D_{U.S.0}$ and S_{J0} stand for the Japanese auto supply schedule, respectively. Assume that the U.S. To safeguard American automakers, the government may choose to impose a tariff or quota on imports businesses from overseas rivals.

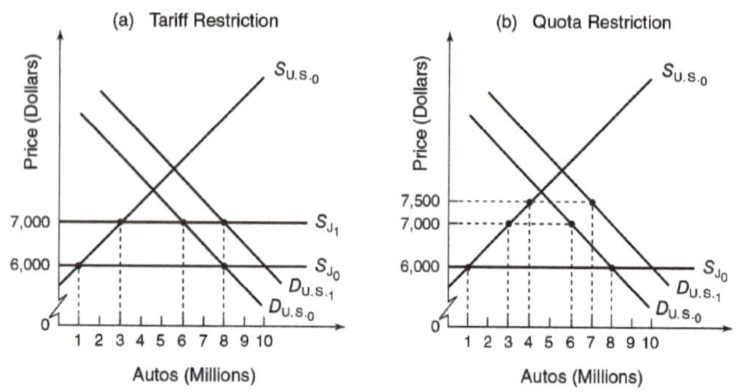

Figure 4.3. Trade effects of tariffs versus quotas.

Source: https://wyamaka.wordpress.com/wp-content/uploads/2019/08/international-economics_30.pdf.

As shown in Figure 4.3(a), a $1,000 tariff would result in a $7,000 price increase for Japanese cars, bringing the total number of imports down from 7 million to 3 million. According to Figure 4.3(b), a 3 million unit import quota would place the US in a similar trading position to that of the tariff: the quota-induced scarcity of cars drives up their price from $6,000 to $7,000. As of right now, it seems that the quota and the tariff have similar restrictive effects on trade volume.

An import tariff is a less onerous trade restriction than an equivalent import quota in a market that is expanding. When there is an import tariff in place, the amount of the product that is imported rises in response to an increase in domestic demand. A rise in demand causes a rise in product price when there is an import quota. While imports stay the same, the price increase causes production of the good that is competing with imports to increase and consumption to decrease.

Let's now assume the U.S. Auto demand increases from $D_{U.S.0}$ to $D_{U.S.1}$. Figure 4.3(a) illustrates that the cost of imported cars stays at $7,000 despite rising demand. This is a result of the U.S. price cannot deviate more than the tariff duty from the Japanese price. The number of imported cars increases from 3 million to 5 million. Therefore, domestic adjustment under an import tariff takes the form of higher auto import volumes rather than higher auto prices.

The same increase in demand causes a rise in domestic auto prices in Figure 4.3(b). There is no cap on the amount that the U.S. can import under the quota. S. price may increase over that of Japan. In light of rising domestic auto costs, U.S. Businesses are able to increase their output. Until increased production and a fixed level of imports are equal to domestic demand, domestic prices will rise. Figure 4.3(b) illustrates the rise in $D_{U.S.0}$ demand to $D_{U.S.1}$ drives up the cost of cars from $7,000 to $7,500. 4 million units are produced domestically and 7 million units are consumed domestically at the new price. 3 million units are imported, which is the same quantity as allowed by the quota prior to the rise in domestic demand.

Therefore, adjustments are made to local prices as opposed to the volume of imported cars.

Therefore, an import quota is a more restrictive trade barrier than an equivalent import tariff during times of rising demand. The government arbitrarily caps the amount of imports under a quota. If domestic consumers are willing and able to pay the tariff, they can purchase an unlimited quantity of the import; otherwise, the domestic price can only rise above the world price by the tariff amount. The quota keeps consumers from moving to the imported good, even if the comparative disadvantage of the domestic industry gets worse. Therefore, regardless of shifting market conditions, a quota guarantees the home industry a ceiling on imports.

In short, a quota is a more stringent import barrier than a tariff. Tariffs raise domestic prices, but they don't always restrict the amount of goods that can be brought into a nation. Successful importers who can afford the tariff duty still receive the goods. Furthermore, a foreign producer that can lower prices and reduce profit margins may be able to offset a tariff. Tariffs therefore permit a certain level of competition.

However, a quota is more restrictive than a tariff because it places an absolute limit on the imported good, which stifles competition. Put simply, the market mechanism determines the level of protection afforded by a tariff, whereas a quota prevents the market mechanism from functioning. Consequently, the World Trade Organization's member nations have chosen to gradually phase out import quotas in favor of tariffs, a move known as tariffication.

4.3. TARIFF-RATE QUOTA: A TWO-TIER TARIFF

The tariff-rate quota is another measure used to shield a home industry from overseas competition. The U.S. This restriction on imports of steel, brooms, cattle, fish, sugar, milk, and other agricultural products has been put in place by the government. A tariff-rate quota exhibits both quota-like and tariff-like traits, as the name would imply. With the help of this device, a certain quantity of goods may be imported at a single tariff rate (the within-quota rate); imports beyond this amount are subject to an increased tariff rate (the over-quota rate). The over-quota tariff rate is frequently set so high that it prevents the product from being imported into the country. Thus, a tariff-rate quota consists of two parts: an over-quota tariff and a quota that sets the maximum volume of imports and applies the within-quota tariff. A tariff-rate quota is essentially a two-tier tariff. Tariff-rate quotas are implemented for every trade year; if they are not met in a given year, market access under the quota is forfeited. Examples of tariff-rate quotas applied to U.S. goods are shown in Table 4.2 imports. The import quota covered earlier in this chapter and the tariff-rate quota seem to be very similar. The difference is that, legally speaking, an import quota prohibits importing more than a predetermined quantity. Imports may, however, surpass this cap under a tariff-rate quota; however, the excess is subject to a higher, over-quota tariff. In theory, imports are granted greater access under a tariff-rate quota than under an import quota. Many over-quota tariffs are actually unreasonably high and effectively bar imports that exceed the quota. It is feasible to create a tariff-rate quota that replicates the import quota's trade-volume cap. The most popular method of enforcing tariff-rate quotas in terms of administration is license on demand allocation. Licenses are needed under this system in order to import at the within-quota tariff. Prospective importers are encouraged to apply for import licenses prior to the start of the quota period.

The system functions similarly to a first-come, first-served system if there is less demand for licenses than there is quota. Generally, the requested import volume is lowered proportionately across all applicants if demand surpasses the quota. Auctions and historical market share are two other methods of quota license allocation. Following the establishment of the World Trade Organization (WTO) in 1995, member nations modified their import protection policies for agricultural products aided by government farm initiatives. All nontariff trade barriers (such as import quotas, variable levies, discretionary licensing, outright import bans, etc.) must be converted to tariffs by WTO members.) relevant to imports from other participants. Put differently, it reduced all nontariff barriers to a single, easily measurable standard—tariffs—that any exporter could grasp. During this conversion period, tariff-rate quotas may be adopted by members as a transitional measure. The length of this conversion period was not specified at the time this text was written. Tariff-rate quotas will therefore probably remain in place for a while. Tariff-rate quotas have also been employed as a short-term safeguard against the surge in non-agricultural product imports into the US. Steel, brooms, fish, and stainless steel flatware are a few of these products.

Table 4.2. Examples of U.S. Tariff-Rate Quotas

Product	Within-Quota Tariff Rate	Import-Quota Threshold	Over-Quota Tariff Rate
Peanuts	9.35 cents/kg	30,393 tons	187.9 percent ad valorem
Beef	4.4 cents/kg	634,621 tons	31.1 percent ad valorem
Milk	3.2 cents/L	5.7 million L	88.5 cents/L
Blue cheese	10 cents/kg	2.6 million kg	$2.60/kg
Cotton	4.4 cents/kg	2.1 million kg	36 cents/kg

Source: From U.S. International Trade Commission, Harmonized Tariff Schedule of the United States, (Washington, DC, U.S. Government Printing Office, 2006).

4.3.1. Sugar Tariff-Rate Quota Bittersweet for Consumers

The U.S An illustration of the results of a tariff-rate quota is given by the sugar industry. Historically, the U.S. Government price supports, which result in a price higher than the free market price, have been given to sugar growers. This artificially high price may draw in cheaper import sugar, bringing the price down. In order to avert this result, the U.S. Tariff-rate quotas are the second way that the government enters the market. Tariff-rate quotas for refined sugar are distributed globally on a first-come, first-served basis; those for raw cane sugar are distributed among 41 countries on a country-by-country basis. For sugar coming into the U.S. A reduced tariff is imposed within the tariff-rate quota. A substantially higher tariff rate is set for sugar imports that exceed the tariff-rate quota, thereby making these imports all but impossible. The trade-volume limit of an import quota, which was covered earlier in this chapter, is roughly equivalent to the tariff-rate quota in this way. But the U.S. When the government feels that there may not be enough sugar produced domestically to meet domestic demand at fair prices, it may choose to set higher tariff-rate quota amounts. The tariff-rate quota has the effect of preventing foreign sugar supplies from entering the US, which raises the price of sugar significantly on the domestic market. The U.S. Because of the tariff-rate quota, the price of sugar has frequently been twice as high as the global market price. For instance, in 2006, the disparity between the U.S. The difference between the market price of 20.94 cents per pound and the raw cane sugar price of 10.42 cents per pound was 101%. Due to this disparity, American consumers now spend an additional $2 billion on sugar annually. A well-known illustration of concentrated benefits and distributed costs is the sugar tariff-rate quota. For a relatively small number of sugar growers and refiners in the United States, it generates enormous revenues. But the expenses associated with offering these benefits are dispersed throughout the U.S. economy, particularly to American families who consume sugar and manufacturers of sugar-filled products like soft drink companies. To put it simply, the U.S. The way the government handles sugar trade is "bittersweet" for consumers in the US.

4.4. EXPORT QUOTAS

Countries have used export quotas in addition to import quotas to limit trade. When they do this, they usually negotiate an orderly marketing agreement, which is another name for a voluntary export restraint agreement, which is a market sharing agreement. Its primary goal is to temper the ferocity of global competition by permitting less productive domestic producers to enter markets that they otherwise would not have been able to enter due to competition from overseas producers offering cheaper, better products. For instance, Taiwan might consent to reduce textile exports to the US, or Japan might put limits on its steel exports to Europe. In the sense that they provide an alternative to more restrictive trade restrictions that an importing country might impose, the export quotas are voluntary. During the 1980s, trade in television sets, steel, textiles, cars, and ships was regulated by voluntary export quotas; however, new trade agreements have made it impossible to utilize this trade restriction going forward.

The economic effects of voluntary export quotas are typically the same as those of equivalent import quotas, with the exception that exporting countries implement them. Therefore, the foreign exporting company or its government is the one who receives the revenue effect of an export quota.

An examination of the three main U.S. In the 1980s, voluntary export restraint agreements pertaining to automobiles, steel, textiles, and apparel were concluded to have resulted in foreign exporters capturing approximately 67% of the costs incurred by American consumers as profit. As seen through the eyes of the U.S. Generally speaking, voluntary export restrictions are more expensive than tariffs for the economy. Let's look at a voluntary export limitation pact from the 1980s.

4.4.1. Japanese Auto Restraints Put Brakes on U.S. Motorists

As domestic auto sales declined in 1981, protectionist sentiment increased in the U.S. Congress, and bills requesting import quotas were presented. The Reagan administration's desire to negotiate a voluntary restraint agreement with the Japanese was greatly influenced by this momentum. Japan reportedly believed that voluntary restrictions on its auto shipments would sabotage any protectionist momentum in Congress for more restrictive measures, which is why it accepted this agreement. Under the restraint program, Japanese auto exports to the US were subject to self-imposed export quotas for a three-year period starting in 1981. It was planned to limit first-year shipments to 1.68 million units, which would be 7.7 percent less than the 1.82 million units exported in 1980. Up until 1984, the quotas were renewed yearly with a small increase in the volume figures. The export agreement's goal was to support U.S. carmakers by rerouting U.S. clients from Japan to the U.S. showrooms. American autoworkers would find more jobs as domestic sales grew. The assumption was that Japan's export quota would help the U.S. the auto industry during a phase of transition wherein production was redirected toward smaller, more fuel-efficient vehicles and production was modified to become more cost-competitive. The export quota did not equally impact all Japanese automakers. By mandating that Japanese automakers organize an export cartel to compete with the U.S. consumer, the quota permitted the big, well-known companies (Toyota, Nissan, and Honda) to raise the price of cars sold in the US. Japanese automakers exported cars to the US with more luxurious trim, larger engines, and extra amenities like air conditioning and premium stereos as standard equipment in order to profit more from a small number of vehicles. Enhancement of products was another way the Japanese expanded their influence in the U.S. promote and improve the perception of their vehicles. The big Japanese manufacturers made record profits in the US as a result. Smaller Japanese automakers like Suzuki and Isuzu, however, were against the export quota because they believed that the allocation of quotas favored large producers over small producers. The U.S. was the biggest loser. S. customer who, in 1984, was required to pay an additional $660 for each Japanese car they bought and an additional $1,300 for each American-made vehicle. In 1981–1984 U.S. Due to the quota, consumers had to pay an extra $15.07 billion for automobile purchases. The consumer cost per job saved was estimated to be more than $100,000, despite the fact that the quota saved about 44,000 jobs for American autoworkers.

By 1985, American manufacturing facilities had been established by Nissan, Honda, and Toyota. United Auto Workers (UAW) and the U.S. had requested this outcome. vehicle manufacturers. They believed that by doing this, the Japanese would have to hire Americans and deal with the same intense competition in the manufacturing sector as the U.S.S. vehicle manufacturers. But, events did not transpire as the American auto industry had hoped. When producing goods in the U.S. Japanese automakers modified their manufacturing processes and created new automobiles especially for this market. Vehicles made at the Japanese transplant factories more than filled the market gap, even though their exports did decline, meaning that the U.S. The market share held by producers decreased. Furthermore, the Japanese were able to maintain low labor costs because the UAW was unable to organize workers at the majority of transplant factories.

4.5. DOMESTIC CONTENT REQUIREMENTS

A lot of products these days, like cars and airplanes, are made all over the world. Production sharing, also referred to as outsourcing, occurs when domestic producers of these goods acquire materials or carry out assembly tasks abroad. For instance, Ford buys cylinder heads from European suppliers, General Motors gets engines from its Mexican subsidiaries, and Chrysler buys ball joints from Japanese manufacturers. Businesses have utilized outsourcing to benefit from lower production costs—including lower wage rates—in other countries. Workers in the country frequently object to this practice, arguing that outsourcing results in the loss of their jobs due to low-cost foreign labor and pressure on the wages of those who are able to retain their jobs.

Domestic content requirements have been pushed for by organized labor in an effort to curtail the practice of outsourcing. These specifications outline the minimal proportion of a product's total value that needs to be made in the country of origin in order for the product to be eligible for zero tariff rates. Requirements regarding content have the effect of pressuring foreign and domestic companies that sell goods in the nation of origin to use domestic labor as an input in the production of those goods. As a result, there is a greater demand for domestic inputs, which drives up input costs. Manufacturers typically oppose domestic content laws because they make it more difficult for them to get inputs at the best price, which drives up costs and reduces their ability to compete. In the automotive industry globally, local content requirements have drawn the most attention. As Table 4.3 demonstrates, developing nations have frequently employed content requirements to promote domestic auto production.

Table 4.3. Domestic Content Requirements Applied to Automobiles in Selected Countries

Country	Minimum Domestic Content Required (percent) to Qualify for Zero Duty Rates
Argentina	76
Mexico	62
Brazil	60
Uruguay	60
Chinese Taipei	40
Ecuador	35
Venezuela	30
Colombia	30

Source: From U.S. Department of Commerce, International Trade Administration, Office of Automotive Affairs, Compilation of Foreign Motor Vehicle Import Requirements, July 2008, at http://www.ita.doc.gov/.

The potential welfare effects of requiring Australian content in cars are depicted in Figure 4.4. Assume that SJ represents the $24,000 supply price of Toyota vehicles exported to Australia, and DA represents the Australian demand schedule for Toyota cars. Australia imports 500 Toyotas thanks to free trade. The manufacturers of this vehicle, who are Japanese resource owners, earn a total of $12 million, as indicated by area c + d.

Let's say the Australian government requires cars to have a certain amount of domestic content. Because of this policy, Toyota has had to build a factory in Australia to make cars that will replace the Toyotas that Australia used to import. Assume that the transplant factory uses Australian labor and materials along with Japanese management to produce vehicles.

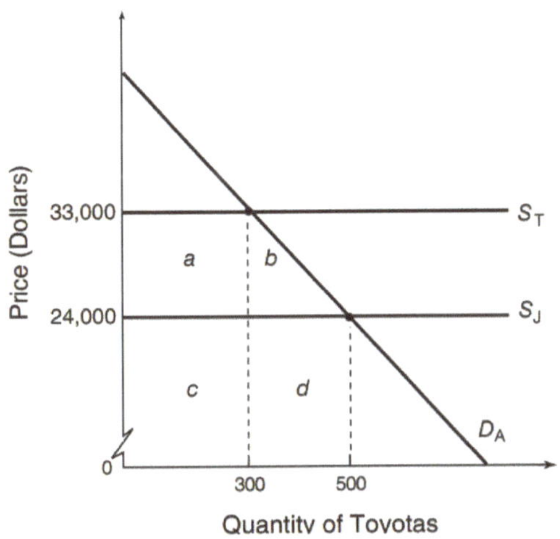

Figure 4.4. Welfare effects of a domestic content requirement.

Source: https://wyamaka.wordpress.com/wp-content/uploads/2019/08/international-economics_30.pdf.

Assume further that the transplant's supply price, indicated by ST, is $33,000 due to high Australian resource prices (wages). Australian consumers require 300 vehicles in order to meet the content requirement. The production shift from Japan to Australia has resulted in a $12 million income loss for Japanese resource owners. After deducting the income paid to Japanese managers and the return on Toyota's capital investment (factory) in Australia, Australian resource owners earn $9.9 million (area a + c).

Manufacturers are "forced" to locate production facilities in high-cost countries as a result of rising production costs and prices caused by domestic content requirements. Domestic consumers suffer welfare losses as a result of the content requirement, even though it helps maintain domestic jobs.

But Australian consumers pay a price for the wealth gains of resource owners in Australia. The content requirement raises the cost of Toyotas by $9,000, which results in a decrease in the Australian consumer surplus of area a + b ($3.6 million). Area B ($900,000) represents a deadweight welfare loss for Australia out of this total.

The consumer cost of using more expensive Australian resources rather than less expensive Japanese resources is represented by Area a ($20.7 million); this sum signifies a redistribution of welfare from Australian consumers to Australian resource owners. Content requirements result in domestic consumers subsidizing the domestic producer, much like other import restrictions.

4.6. SUBSIDIES

Occasionally, national governments provide subsidies to their producers in an effort to strengthen their position in the market. A subsidy gives domestic companies a cost advantage, enabling them to advertise their goods at prices below what their true costs and profits would dictate. Governmental subsidies can take many different forms, such as direct cash payments, tax breaks, insurance policies, and loans with interest rates below market rates. In the context of our conversation, it is possible to distinguish between two different kinds of subsidies: export subsidies, which are given to companies that produce goods intended for international markets, and domestic production subsidies, which are given to companies that produce goods that rival imports. In both situations, the government does not deduct from the buyer's price; instead, it adds a certain amount. The price paid by the buyer plus the subsidy is the net price that the producer actually receives. So, at this price, the subsidized producer can provide a larger quantity. Let's examine the impacts of these two kinds of subsidies using Figure 4.5.

4.6.1. Domestic Production Subsidy

The idea behind a domestic production subsidy is to encourage the output and thus vitality of import-competing producers; so if a nation decides that the maintenance of an aircraft industry, or semiconductor industry, is necessary for the good of the public, would it not be better just to subsidize it directly instead of forbidding imports of that product? The trade and welfare effects of a production subsidy given to producers who compete with imports are depicted in Figure 4.5(a). Let us assume that curves $S_{U\ S.\ 0}$ represent the initial supply and demand schedules for steel in the United States and $D_{U.\ S.\ 0}$; consequently, $430 per ton represents the market equilibrium price. Furthermore, assume that because of the United.

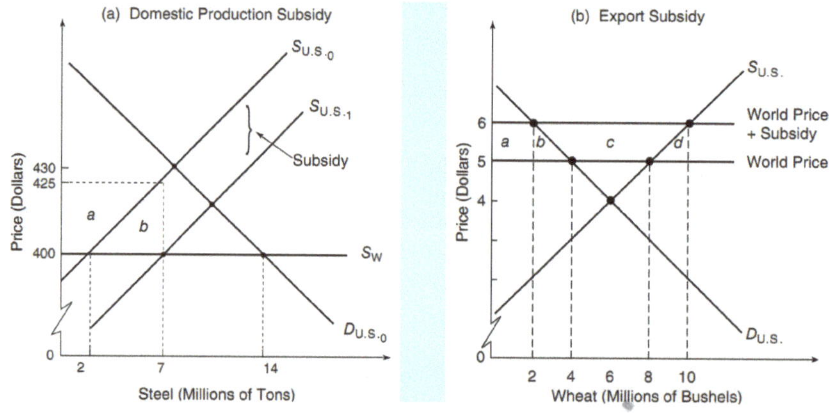

Figure 4.5. Trade and welfare effects of subsidies.

Source: https://wyamaka.wordpress.com/wp-content/uploads/2019/08/international-economics_30.pdf.

Increased domestic production and decreased imports result from government subsidies given to producers who compete with imports. Producer surplus and high-cost production absorb the subsidy revenue that the producer receives (protective effect). Exporters can sell their goods overseas for less than what it costs them thanks to a subsidy that is provided to them. However, in terms of the consumption and protective effects, it results in a deadweight welfare loss to the home country.

States is a small buyer of steel; variations in its purchases have no impact on the $400 per ton global price. The United States imports 12 million tons of steel, produces 2 million tons, and uses 14 million tons at a free-trade price of $400 per ton.

Assume that in order to shield domestic producers from overseas competition, the U.S. They receive a $25 production subsidy per ton of steel from the government. The subsidy's ability to provide a cost advantage causes a change in the U.S. $S_{U.S.0}$ supply schedule. for $S_{U.S.1}$. Imports decrease from 12 to 7 million tons, while domestic production rises from 2 to 7 million tons. These adjustments reflect the trade impact of the subsidy.

The United States' national welfare is impacted by the subsidy as well. Figure 4.5(a) indicates that the subsidy allows U.S. Up to 7 million tons will be produced. Observe that the net price to the steelmaker at this output is $425, which is the product of the consumer price ($400) and the subsidy ($25). Regarding the U.S. government, the entire cost of safeguarding its steelmakers comes to $175 million, which is the product of the subsidy ($25) multiplied by the volume of production (7 million tons).

A portion of this subsidy revenue is redistributed to the more efficient U.S producers as an excess of producers. Area a ($112.5 million) in the figure represents this sum. Additionally, the subsidy has a protective effect, allowing more expensive domestic output to be sold on the market. In the figure, area b ($62.5 million) represents this effect. For the United States as a whole, the welfare benefit is offset by the protective effect.

Table 4.4. North American Content of Automobiles Sold in the United States, 2007 (Sales Weighted)

Automaker	North American Content
Chrysler (domestic brands)	78%
Ford (domestic brands)	78
GM (domestic brands)	74
Honda, Acura	59
Nissan/Infiniti	46
Toyota/Lexus	47
Mitsubishi	36
Subaru	26
Isuzu	17
BMW	10
Foreign automaker average	40

Source: From Level Field Institute at http://www.levelfieldinstitute.org.

A government may apply import tariffs or quotas to boost output by its producers who compete with imports. However, the national welfare is sacrificed more as a result of tariffs and quotas than it is under an equivalent subsidy. Tariffs and quotas, in contrast to subsidies, allow for less efficient domestic production while also distorting domestic consumer choices and lowering domestic demand for imports. As a result, the home country bears a deadweight loss of the consumer surplus, which is the well-known consumption effect of protection. The subsidy case does not include this welfare loss. As a result, subsidies typically have the same effect on home producers as comparable tariffs or quotas, but at a lesser expense to the welfare of the country.

Subsidies, however, are not free goods because someone has to pay for them. The public's tax money is required to cover the direct cost of the subsidy, which is a burden. Furthermore, when an industry receives a subsidy, it frequently happens in exchange for agreeing to government demands on important issues (like wage and salary levels). As a result, this analysis may not support the notion that subsidies are better than other forms of commercial policies.

4.6.2. Export Subsidy

A government could pay a subsidy on exports only instead of providing import-competing producers with a production subsidy. Dairy and agricultural products are the most often subsidized export product categories.

Figure 4.5(b) illustrates how an export subsidy works. Assume that curves represent the supply and demand curves for wheat in the United States. $S_{U\,S}$. as well as $D_{U.\,S}$., resulting in a $4 bushel autarky equilibrium price. Additionally, assume that variations in wheat production in the US have no impact on global wheat prices because the US is a very small producer. At a global price per bushel of, let's say, $5, the US produces 8 million bushels, buys 4 million, and exports 4 million bushels.

Assume that the U.S. To promote export sales, the government pays $1 for every bushel of wheat exported. The grant enables U.S. exporting companies to make $6 per bushel in revenue, which is the same as the $5 world price plus the $1 subsidy. These companies are willing to sell to domestic consumers only at the higher price of $6 per bushel, even though the subsidy is not available on domestic sales. This is because the companies could always make that much on sales to the rest of the world, so they would never sell wheat in the US for less than $6 per bushel. When the price increases from $5 to $6 per bushel, the amount that is purchased in the US decreases to 2 million bushels, the amount that is supplied increases to 10 million bushels, and the amount that is exported rises from 4 million bushels to 8 million bushels.

The welfare effects of the export subsidy on the U.S. It is possible to analyze the economy in terms of producer and consumer surpluses.

The export subsidy causes the producer surplus of area a + b + c ($9 million) to increase and the consumer surplus of area a b to decrease in the figure ($3 million). The export subsidy's taxpayer cost is equal to the amount of wheat exported (8 million bushels) times the per-unit subsidy of $1, meaning that the total cost is equal to area b + c + d ($8 million). Consequently, U.S. The U.S. loses out to wheat producers. S. both a taxpayer and a consumer.

Additionally, the export subsidy results in a welfare loss that is deadweight to the U.S. economy.

This includes area d ($1 million), which represents a deadweight loss as a result of rising domestic wheat production costs, and area b ($1 million), which represents a loss of consumer surplus as a result of rising prices.

In this instance, we've assumed that the exporting nation is a tiny one. But in reality, the exporting nation may be a sizable producer on the global market; as a result, when it imposes an export subsidy, its terms of trade will decline.

Why would this happen? Its firms would have to lower the price in order to export more product. The terms of trade for the exporting nation would deteriorate if the price of the exported good dropped. One instance of how the US uses export subsidies is through the Export Enhancement Program. This program, which was started in 1985, aims to counteract the negative effects on U.S. agricultural exports as a result of unfair trade policies or subsidies from rival exporters, especially the European Union. This application enables U.S. By offering cash bonuses, exporters can encourage their products to be sold in targeted markets at prices lower than their costs. It has been crucial to the export of numerous agricultural goods, including dairy, wheat, and barley.

4.7. DUMPING

The antidumping argument strengthens the case for shielding producers facing import competition from overseas competition. It is acknowledged that international price discrimination takes the form of dumping. It happens when, after deducting tariff duties and transportation expenses, domestic consumers pay higher prices for the same product than do foreign consumers. Dumping also includes selling in overseas markets at a price lower than the cost of production.

4.7.1. Forms of Dumping

Most people consider commercial dumping to be intermittent, predatory, or persistent in nature. Every kind is applied in a distinct setting.

A company engages in sporadic dumping, also known as distress dumping, when it sells excess inventory on overseas markets for less than it would charge domestically. This type of dumping could be the outcome of foreign producers' misfortune or ill-preparedness. Unexpected shifts in the dynamics of supply and demand may lead to excess inventory and subsequent dumping. For import-competing producers, who face declining sales and immediate losses, intermittent dumping can be highly disruptive, even though it may be advantageous for importing consumers. Temporary tariff duties can be imposed to safeguard domestic producers, but governments are hesitant to provide tariff protection in these situations because intermittent dumping has little impact on global trade.

When a producer temporarily lowers the prices it charges overseas in an attempt to force foreign competitors out of business, this is known as predatory dumping. Prices are increased in proportion to the producer's market power once it has managed to establish a monopoly.

The new price level needs to be high enough to make up for any losses sustained during the period of aggressive pricing. Presumably, the company would have faith in its ability to keep out prospective rivals long enough for it to make a profit. For predatory dumping to be effective, it must be carried out extensively in order to give customers enough chances to shop for deals. Home governments may respond with antidumping duties that close the price gap because they are typically worried about predatory pricing used for monopolizing purposes. Although it is theoretically possible, economists have not discovered any empirical evidence to support the existence of predatory dumping. The likelihood of actually realizing full monopoly profits appears remote given the prospect of a protracted and expensive period of predation and the likelihood of a limited ability to deter subsequent entry by new rivals. As the name implies, persistent dumping doesn't end. A manufacturer may regularly sell their goods overseas for less money than they do domestically in an attempt to maximize economic profits.

4.7.2. International Price Discrimination

Think about a domestic seller who benefits from barriers that limit domestic competition and thus has market power. Let's say this company sells in fiercely competitive international markets. In this case, domestic demand is less elastic than foreign demand, which implies that domestic consumers will react to a price change less quickly than their overseas counterparts. International price discrimination would help a profit-maximizing company charge a higher price in domestic markets where demand is less elastic and competition is weak and a lower price in overseas markets to compete. In comparison to what would happen in the absence of price discrimination, the practice of identifying distinct groups of product buyers and charging different prices to these groups results in increased revenues and profits for the company.

The demand and cost conditions of South Korean Steel Inc. are depicted in Figure 4.6. (SKS), which supplies steel to consumers in Canada (a more elastic market) and South Korea (a less elastic market); these two submarkets make up the entire steel market. Let DSK represent the steel demand from South Korea and DC the demand from Canada. MRSK and MRC, respectively, stand in for the corresponding marginal revenue schedules. The market demand schedule is shown by the DSK C, which is obtained by adding the demand schedules of the two submarkets horizontally. The market marginal revenue schedule is shown by the MRSK C. MC and ATC stand for the marginal cost and average total cost schedules, respectively, of SKS. By manufacturing and selling 45 tons of steel at a marginal revenue equal to marginal cost, South Korea Steel maximizes total profits. ATC is \$300 per ton at this output level, meaning that the total cost is \$13,500 (\$300 × 45 tons). The company must decide how to divide its 45-ton total output between its two selling submarkets and set a price for each. Should the company offer a uniform (single) price for steel to buyers in South Korea and Canada, or should it engage in discriminatory pricing?

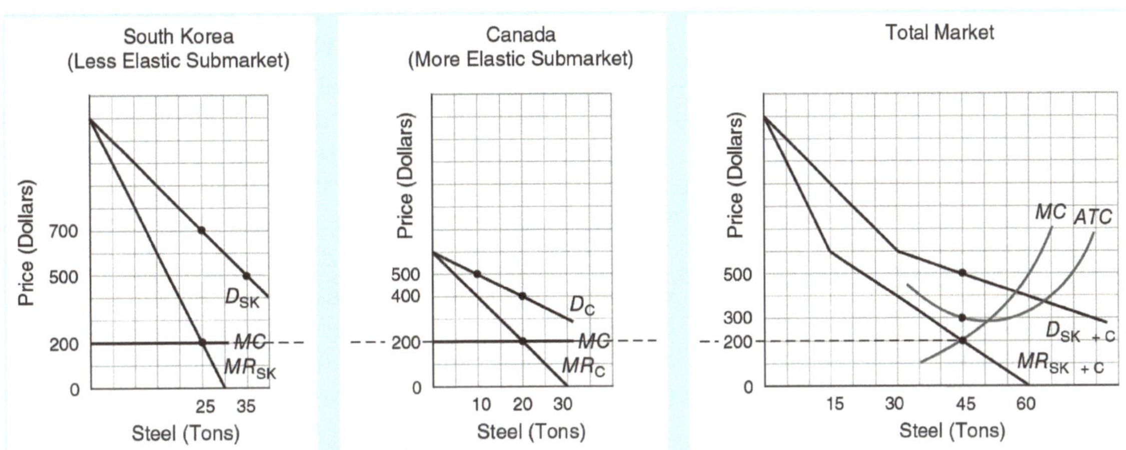

Figure 4.6. International price discrimination.

Source: https://wyamaka.wordpress.com/wp-content/uploads/2019/08/international-economics_30.pdf.

A price-differentiating company that sets prices based on marginal revenue in each submarket equals profits. When there is less elastic demand and less competition, the company will charge a higher price; when there is more elastic demand and more competition, the price will be lower. When dumping is done successfully, the company makes more money than it would have in the absence of dumping. SKS, acting as a non-discriminating seller, sells 45 tons of steel to buyers in South Korea and Canada for $500 per ton, which is the highest price allowed by demand schedule $D_{SK + C}$ at the output level MR = MC. To determine the number of tons of steel sold in each submarket, draw a horizontal line at the $500 price point in Figure 4.6. Where the horizontal line crosses the demand schedules of the two countries is where the optimal output in each submarket is found. As a result, SKS makes $17,500 in revenue from selling 35 tons of steel to South Korean buyers at a price of $500 per ton. The company makes $5,000 when it sells 10 tons of steel to Canadian buyers for $500 a ton. The total sales revenue for both submarkets is $22,500. SKS makes a profit of $9,000 on a total cost of $13,500. As a non-discriminating seller, SKS makes a profit, but it is not the best profit. Price discrimination allows the business to raise overall revenue without raising costs, which boosts profit. The company does this by charging Canadian customers, whose demand schedules are more elastic, lower prices, and South Korean customers, whose demand schedules are less elastic, higher prices.SKS, a price-discriminating seller, must once more figure out how to split its 45 tons of steel production between the two submarkets it serves and determine a set price for each. The company uses the well-known MR = MC principle—which states that each submarket's marginal revenue equals its marginal cost at the output that maximizes profits—to achieve this. By first drawing a horizontal line from $200, the point where MC = $MR_{SK + C}$, Figure 4.6 illustrates this idea. The point at which this horizontal line crosses the submarkets' MR schedules is the optimal output and price for each submarket. As a result, SKS makes $17,500 in revenue from selling 25 tons of steel to South Korean buyers at a price of $700 per ton. The company makes $8,000 by selling 20 tons of steel to Canadian buyers for $400 per ton. The two submarkets' combined revenues come to $25,500, which is $3,000 more than they would have if there had been no price discrimination. The company makes a profit of $12,000 with a total cost of $13,500 as opposed to $9,000 with a single pricing policy. As a result, SKS makes more money as a price-differentiating seller. It is evident that the company used price discrimination to its advantage, charging different prices in the two submarkets: $400 per ton to Canadian buyers and $700 per ton to South Korean steel buyers. There are requirements that must be met for international price discrimination to be successful. First, the demand conditions in the two submarkets must differ in order to guarantee that, at any price, the demand schedules in the two submarkets have different demand elasticities. For instance, domestic purchasers might have different income brackets or tastes and preferences from overseas buyers. In order to prevent any significant resale of commodities from the lower-priced market to the higher-priced market, the firm must be able to divide the two submarkets. This is due to the fact that consumer resale will typically counteract the impact of price differentials and reduce the discriminatory price structure until it resembles a single price for all customers. International market separation is frequently simpler than national market separation due to high transportation costs and trade restrictions imposed by governments.

4.8. ANTIDUMPING REGULATIONS

Governments have often imposed penalty duties on commodities they believe are being dumped into their markets from overseas, even though dumping may benefit importing consumers. U.S. Antidumping laws are intended to stop price discrimination and sales below cost that harm Americans sectors. In the U.S. law, a charge against dumping is applied when the U.S. When the Department of Commerce finds that a particular category or type of foreign goods is being sold for less than fair value (LTFV), the U.S. The International Trade Commission (ITC) concludes that LTFV imports are harming or posing a risk of material harm to a U.S. party, including joblessness and lost revenue and earnings sector. These antidumping duties are applied in addition to the standard tariff to counteract the effects of sales that are made below cost or price discrimination.

The amount by which the foreign market value surpasses the U.S. is the margin of dumping cost. There are two ways to define foreign market value. The priced-based definition states that dumping happens anytime a foreign business sells a product in the U.S. market at a lower cost than what the identical product sells for in the domestic market. An attempt is made to ascertain the price of the good in a third market when a home-nation price is unavailable (for instance, if the good is produced exclusively for export and is not sold domestically).

If the definition of foreign market value that is based on price cannot be applied, then a definition based on cost may be used. Using this method, the cost of manufacturing the product, general expenses, profit from sales in the home market, and packaging costs for shipping to the US are added together to determine the foreign market value, which is then "constructed" by the Commerce Department. At least 10% of the manufacturing cost must go toward general expenses, and at least 8 percent of the manufacturing cost plus general expenses must go toward profit.

A complaint filed concurrently with the International Trade Commission and the Commerce Department is the first step in an antidumping case. The complaint, which includes data demonstrating material injury or threat of injury and evidence of dumping, originates from within an industry that competes with imports, such as a company or labor union.

First, the Commerce Department estimates the size of the dumping margin and makes a preliminary determination about whether or not dumping has occurred. Should the initial inquiry uncover proof of dumping, U.S. On all imports of the contested product, importers are required to pay an immediate special tariff equal to the estimated dumping margin. The final decision regarding the existence of dumping and the extent of the dumping margin is then made by the Commerce Department. The Commerce Department will return any special tariffs that were previously collected to the U.S. if it determines that no dumping occurred importers. In the absence of such circumstances, the International Trade Commission decides whether or not the dumping caused material harm.

The special tariffs are returned to the United States if the International Trade Commission determines that import-competing businesses were not harmed by the dumping importers. However, a permanent tariff equal to the amount of the dumping margin determined by the Commerce Department in its final investigation is imposed if both the International Trade Commission and the Department of Commerce find that the dumping petition is justified.

The average antidumping duty levied by the US in recent years has been roughly 45%, with some duties reaching 100%. Targeted imports have generally decreased by 50 to 70% during the first three years of protection, demonstrating the significant impact of these duties on trade. Let's look at a few instances of dumping.

4.8.1. Smith Corona Finds Antidumping Victories Are Hollow

Antidumping duties can be a blunt instrument, even though their goal is to shield home producers from imports that are priced unfairly. Examine the Smith Corona, Inc. case, which from the 1970s to the 1990s won multiple antidumping cases but produced little in return. In the 1970s, Smith Corona faced fierce competition from Brother Industries Ltd., which led to problems. of Japan, inundating the U.S. its portable typewriters to the market. In 1980, in response to Smith Corona's allegation of dumping, the U.S. Brother portables are subject to 49% antidumping duties from the government. Brother discovered that the antidumping ruling only applied to typewriters lacking a memory or calculation function, so Smith Corona's antidumping victory turned out to be hollow. Brother avoided responsibility by using the strategy of product evolution to upgrade its typewriter and add a small computer memory. Smith Corona had to wait until 1990 for the federal court of appeals in Washington, DC, to close this loophole. By then, Brother had discovered a more reliable way to get around antidumping duties: it started putting together portable typewriters in the US using parts made in Malaysia and Japan. Since these typewriters were no longer "imported," the tariffs from the 1980s were not applicable.

Then, the personal word processor became the focus of competition. Smith Corona began to complain in 1990 that word processors were being dumped in the US by Brother and other Japanese manufacturers. This grievance prompted the U.S. In 1991, the government levied import duties on Japanese word processors that were nearly 60%. However, that triumph was also vacuous, as it was limited to word processors made in Japan; the Japanese companies assembled their word processors in the US. Smith Corona was unfazed and continued to file complaints, citing a clause in U.S. trade law that was intended to prevent foreign companies from bringing in components and assembling them in the US in order to avoid paying antidumping duties. However, the clause did not cover components made in third countries because it was assumed that imported parts would originate from domestic (Japanese) factories. Identifying this loophole, Brother proved that its word processors were exempt from antidumping duties by proving that their imported components originated from third countries. All things considered, Smith Corona found it challenging to receive relief from foreign dumping goods!

4.8.2. Canadians Press Washington Apple Producers for Level Playing Field

Not only have overseas manufacturers flooded the US market with goods, but U.S. Businesses have occasionally dumped goods overseas. The Canadian government declared in 1989 that U.S. About 4,500 commercial apple growers were harmed when delicious apples, mostly from Washington, were thrown onto the Canadian market.

Table 4.5. Normal Value and the Margin of Dumping: Delicious Apples, Regular Storage, 1987–1988

U.S. FOB per Packed Box (42 pounds)	Normal Value (in dollars)
Growing and harvesting costs	5.50
Packing, marketing, and storing costs	5.49
Total costs	10.99
Profit (8% margin)	0.88
Total normal value	11.87
Margin of Dumping	**Percentage**
Range	0–63.44
Weighted-average margin	32.53

Source: From statement of reasons: Final determination of dumping respecting delicious apples originating in or exported from the United States of America, Revenue Canada, Customs and Excise Division, December 1988.

The decision prohibited the sale of a 42-pound box of Washington apples in Canada for less than $11.87 (in USD), which is considered the "normal value" (equivalent to the U.S. the Canadian government's "fair value" concept for apples kept in regular storage. Importers from Canada buying U.S. Apples that were below average in value were required to pay the Canadian government an antidumping duty in order to bring the total cost of purchase up to the set amount. The antidumping order covered the period of 1989 to 1994, or five years. According to the Canadian apple growers' complaint, the United States' massive tree planting efforts in the late 1970s and early 1980s led to an overabundance of apples produced. Growers in Washington saw record harvests in 1987 and 1988, with inventories exceeding storage capacity. The price of Delicious apples collapsed in North America as a result of the growers' drastic price cuts to market their crop. The Canadian government calculated the typical value of a box of U.S. apples when Washington apple growers neglected to submit timely information. S. apples utilizing the most up-to-date data available. As can be observed in Table 4.5, a box of apples typically cost $11.87 (in USD) during the 1987–1988 crop year. In this time frame, the U.S. The cost of exporting a box to Canada was approximately $9 USD. The weighted-average dumping margin was calculated to be 32.53% by comparing the export price to the average apple value. The Canadian government concluded that during the 1987–1988 growing season, Canadian apple growers lost between $1 and $6.40 (in Canadian dollars) per box due to the displacement of low-cost Washington apples from the Canadian market. Washington apples were subject to antidumping duties by the Canadian government, which determined that the dumping of apples had hurt Canadian growers.

4.9. ANTIDUMPING LAW UNFAIR

The argument put out by proponents of antidumping laws is that unfair import competition must be eliminated in order to provide "level playing fields" for domestic producers. A level playing field is ensured by antidumping laws, which neutralize artificial sources of competitive advantage. An antidumping duty restores parity with the domestic producer by covering the difference between the dumped price and fair market value. Critics point out that while antidumping duties may benefit protected industries, they usually hurt consumers of the protected good and the overall economy more. Therefore, it is not unexpected that antidumping laws are criticized, as will be covered in more detail below.

4.9.1. Average Variable Cost Be the Yardstick for Defining Dumping

When a foreign producer sells goods in the United States for less than fair value, it is considered dumping under current regulations. The average total cost plus an 8 percent profit allowance is considered fair value. Many economists contend, however, that average variable cost—rather than average total cost—should serve as the basis for fair value, particularly in situations where the domestic economy experiences a brief decline in demand. Assume the following for the case of a radio producer: (1) The producer's physical capacity is 150 units of output over the specified time period; and (2) The demand for radios in the domestic market is price-inelastic, while the demand for radios abroad is price-elastic. Check out Table 4.6. Assume the producer charges both domestic and foreign consumers $300 per unit at a uniform price (no dumping). Domestic sales total 100 units with inelastic domestic demand.

Table 4.6. Dumping and Excess Capacity

	No Dumping	Dumping
Home sales	100 units @ $300	100 units @ $300
Export sales	0 units @ $300	50 units @ $250
Sales revenue	$30,000	$42,500
Less variable costs of $200 per unit	–20,000	–30,000
	$10,000	$12,500
Less total fixed costs of $10,000	–10,000	–10,000
Profit	$ 0	$ 2,500

Source: https://wyamaka.wordpress.com/wp-content/uploads/2019/08/international-economics_30.pdf.

Let us assume, however, that the producer is unable to sell any radios at the going rate due to elastic demand conditions overseas. Sales income would be $30,000, and fixed and variable costs would add up to $30,000. The company would have 50 radios in excess of its capacity if it didn't dump. Furthermore, the company's domestic market operations would only break even.

Assume that this producer chooses to sell radios for less money overseas than they do domestically. Any price that goes toward fixed costs will allow for higher profits (less losses) than what would be possible with idle plant capacity on hand, provided all variable costs are paid. As per Table 4.6, the company can sell 100 units if it charges $300 to residential customers. Let's say the company is able to sell an extra 50 units overseas by setting a $250 price per unit. $42,500 in total sales revenue would allow for a $2,500 profit in addition to covering fixed and variable costs.

Even though it is selling overseas at a lower price than its average total cost (average total cost = $40,000/150 = $267), the company is still able to increase profits through dumping.

Businesses that have excess capacity for production may therefore be motivated to increase sales by lowering the prices they charge to foreign customers—possibly to levels that barely cover average variable costs. Naturally, domestic prices need to be high enough to maintain the company's profitability over the relevant time frame.

To put it simply, a lot of economists contend that antidumping laws are unfair because they determine fair value by utilizing the average total cost as a benchmark. They point out that economic theory predicts that businesses price their goods at average variable costs—which are lower than average total costs—when there is competition. As a result, companies that are just acting in a way that is typical of markets that are competitive are penalized by the antidumping laws. Additionally, the law is unjust because U.S. Businesses that sell online are not bound by the same regulations. It is possible, in fact, for a foreign company selling at a loss both domestically and in the US to be found guilty of dumping when U.S. Businesses are also accepting losses and selling at the exact same price on the home market.

4.9.2. Antidumping Law Reflect Currency Fluctuations

The fact that the antidumping law does not take currency fluctuations into account is another point of criticism. Examine the definition of dumping that is based on price: selling in a foreign market at a reduced price.

Foreign producers may "dump" in accordance with the legal definition if exchange rate fluctuations occur because they frequently have to set their prices in terms of a foreign currency for overseas customers. Say, for instance, that the value of the Japanese yen rises relative to the U.S. dollar, indicating that a dollar can be purchased with fewer yen.

However, if Japanese steel exporters are competing in the US market and setting their prices in US dollars, the yen's appreciation will result in a decline in the price of their exports in US dollars, giving the impression that they are dumping. In line with the U.S. under the antidumping law, American businesses are exempt from the requirements placed on foreign businesses that sell in the country. Does unfairness get corrected or is it made worse by the antidumping law?

4.9.3. Antidumping Duties Overused

Antidumping actions were primarily employed as a protectionist tactic by a small group of wealthy nations, namely the United States, Canada, Australia, and Europe, until the 1990s. Since then, the number of antidumping cases brought by developing countries like Turkey, Mexico, and India has skyrocketed. The United States has become an increasingly frequent target of antidumping measures due to rising use by other countries.

Given the significant degree of trade liberalization that has occurred throughout the global economy, the use of antidumping duties has expanded, which is not surprising. Economists, however, generally see the rise in antidumping duties as a concerning development—a kind of backdoor protectionism that contradicts the post-World War II trend of lower trade barriers. Despite the fact that antidumping measures are permitted by WTO regulations, there is worry about a vicious cycle in which one country's antidumping actions prompt retaliatory actions by other nations.

Regarding U.S. Producers, you now have a much easier time obtaining antidumping duties as a means of protecting yourself from import competition. One explanation for this is the expansion of the scope for filing an antidumping action, which now covers any type of international price discrimination in addition to predatory pricing. The application of antidumping duties has increased as a result of stricter criteria for determining how imports affect home industries.

Opponents of the U.S. antidumping laws assert that the U.S. The Department of Commerce virtually invariably concludes that dumping has taken place, despite favorable conclusions of material harm by the U.S. There are fewer International Trade Commissions. Critics also point out that under the antitrust laws of the same countries, imports that were found to be dumped under the current regulations would not have been questioned as posing a threat to anticompetitiveness. Put differently, if the importers' actions had been taken by a domestic company, they would not have raised concerns about anticompetitiveness or other negative effects.

4.10. OTHER NONTARIFF TRADE BARRIERS

Government codes of conduct that are applicable to imports make up other NTBs. Even though these clauses are frequently well hidden, they nevertheless contribute significantly to commercial policy. Let's look at three of these barriers: social rules, sea transport and freight regulations, and government procurement policies.

4.10.1. Government Procurement Policies

Governmental organizations are appealing clients for overseas suppliers since they are significant consumers of goods and services. The pattern of trade would not be very different from what happens in a competitive market if governments only bought goods and services from the lowest-cost vendors. Nonetheless, while purchasing goods and materials, the majority of governments give preference to domestic vendors over foreign ones. This is demonstrated by the fact that compared to the private sector, the public sector's import to total purchase ratio is substantially lower.

Governments frequently use buy national policies as a means of giving preference to domestic suppliers. The U.S. The government openly discriminates against foreign suppliers when making procurement decisions by enacting explicit laws. Even though the majority of other governments do not formally have preferences for domestic suppliers in law, they frequently use covert administrative procedures and rules to discriminate against foreign suppliers. These governments may publicize government contracts in a way that discourages foreign suppliers from submitting a bid, or they may use closed bidding systems that limit the number of businesses permitted to bid on sales.

In an effort to boost jobs at home during the Great Depression, the U.S. The Buy American Act was passed by government. This law mandates that federal agencies buy supplies and goods from U.S. suppliers if their costs do not exceed those of their overseas rivals in a "reasonable" manner.

A product must be manufactured in the United States and contain at least 50% domestic components in order to be considered domestic. As of right now, U.S. A 6 percent preference margin is granted to vendors serving civilian agencies. By this margin, a U.S. The government contract goes to the supplier, provided that the U.S.

The low bid is not more than 6% more than the foreign competitor's offer. This preference margin increases to 50% if the purchase is made by the Department of Defense and to 12% if the low domestic bidder is located in a labor-surplus area. These preferences are not applied in cases where it is found that the U.S. -produced good is either not readily available in large enough quantities or is of inadequate quality.

Buy-national policies impede free trade because they favor domestic suppliers over low-cost foreign suppliers. It is allowed for domestic suppliers to pay resource prices above free trade limits and to employ less productive production techniques. Due to the protective and consumption effects, this latitude results in deadweight welfare losses for the country and increased project costs for the government.

The Buy American mandate under U.S. With the 1979 adoption of the Tokyo Round of Multilateral Trade Negotiations, government has become more liberal. The agreement does not, however, cover the procurement of goods and materials by regional and local government organizations. Currently, there are more than 30 states with Buy American laws, which range from clear bans on buying foreign goods to ambiguous policy directives supporting U.S. goods.

For instance, the San Francisco–Oakland Bay Bridge was partially rebuilt by the California Transit Authority between 2001 and 2004 after an earthquake. But the project ended up costing almost $4 billion—three times more than the agency had anticipated. One reason was the Buy American laws in California, which stipulated that foreign steel could only be utilized on the bridge if the price of the steel was at least 25% lower than that of domestic steel. Since there was only a 23% difference in this instance, the state was forced to buy domestic steel. The price increase of $400 million was due to this discrepancy. It was hard to see how this requirement helped California taxpayers, even though it benefited domestic steel producers.

4.10.2. Social Regulations

Since the 1950s, countries have taken on a more and more significant role in controlling the standard of living for their citizens. Social regulation aims to address a range of unfavorable side effects of an economy that are related to the environment, safety, and health—effects that markets, left to their own devices, frequently overlook. Social regulation pertains to specific issues, like environmental quality, and influences the actions of businesses in numerous industries, including steel, chemicals, and automobiles.

4.10.3. CAFÉ Standards

While social regulations have the potential to promote health, safety, and environmental objectives, they may also act as obstacles to global trade. Take the example of the U.S.-imposed fuel economy standards. S. government regulations on automakers.

The corporate average fuel economy standards, or CAFE, were first implemented in 1975 and serve as the cornerstone of U.S. policies for energy conservation. The standards, which are applicable to all passenger cars sold in the US, are based on the average fuel economy of all cars offered by all automakers. The CAFÉ standard for passenger cars has been 27.5% miles per gallon since 1990. Manufacturers will incur fines if their average fuel efficiency is not up to par.

In the 1980s, CAFÉ regulations served to safeguard American jobs while simultaneously encouraging fuel efficiency. S. autoworkers. The quickest route for U.S. Car manufacturers could have increased the fleet average fuel efficiency by importing smaller, more fuel-efficient vehicles from their European and Asian subsidiaries. Still, this would have reduced employment in a sector that was already in decline. The U.S. As a result, the government established uniform but distinct regulations for both domestic and foreign passenger cars. Hence, in order to meet CAFÉ targets for both types of vehicles, General Motors, Ford, and Chrysler—who produced automobiles in the United States in addition to selling imported vehicles—would have to comply. Consequently, U.S. By averaging the fuel efficiency of their imports with their less fuel-efficient, domestically produced vehicles, businesses could not meet CAFÉ standards. Through the separate computation of import and domestic fleets, the U.S. Government regulations sometimes impose effective import barriers on foreign commodities, whether they are intended to do so or not, which aggravates foreign competitors. In other words, government attempted to force domestic firms to not only manufacture more efficient vehicles, but to produce them in the United States!"

4.10.3.1. Europe Has a Cow Over Hormone-Treated U.S. Beef

Another example of how social regulations can cause issues is the EU's ban on hormone-treated meat. Livestock producers use growth-promoting hormones extensively to accelerate growth rates and produce leaner livestock that better conforms to consumer preferences for lower-fat and lower-cholesterol diets. On the other hand, detractors of hormones assert that eating meat can result in cancer. The production and importation of beef from animals given growth-promoting hormone treatments were outlawed by the EU in 1989. The EU defended the ban by stating that it was required to safeguard consumers' health and safety.

The United States immediately challenged the ban. s. producers, who produced 90% of their beef with the use of hormones. The United States claimed that the restriction on beef imports due to health concerns lacked a scientific foundation. The prohibition, on the other hand, was only an effort to shield the comparatively expensive European beef sector from outside competition. European producers had amassed sizable, expensive-to-store beef surpluses at the time the ban was implemented, according to American producers, which put tremendous political pressure on lawmakers to restrict beef imports. According to the United States, the EU's focus on health issues was essentially a smokescreen for shielding a sector of the economy that was at a slight disadvantage.

After a long legal battle, the trade dispute was taken to the WTO, which declared that the EU's ban on hormone-treated beef was unlawful and cost the U.S. beef exports worth $117 million to the European Union. However, the EU declined to remove its prohibition, citing consumer preference. As a result, the WTO gave the US permission to apply tariffs to the tune of $117 million, banning European exports to the US. As it was entitled to do, the US imposed 100% tariffs on a range of European goods, which included hams, pasta, citrus fruit, tomatoes, prepared mustard, Roquefort cheese, and other items. The U.S. Products from Denmark, France, Germany, and Italy—the countries that support the EU's ban on hormone-treated beef—dominated the hit list. The 100% tariffs forced the Europeans to liberalize their imports of American beef products by essentially doubling the prices of the targeted goods. By negotiating a four-year agreement in 2009, the EU and the US took a first step toward settling their trade dispute. The EU will triple import quotas for hormone-free U.S. products during this time. S. beef, but it won't import American beef that has been hormone-treated. In exchange, while maintaining current sanctions, the US will refrain from imposing new ones on more EU goods. By the end of the fourth year, the two parties aim to reach a longer-term trade agreement whereby the U.S. Sanctions against the European Union will end. If this initial step leads to a long-term trade agreement for beef, that is yet to be determined.

4.10.4. Sea Transport and Freight Regulations

In the 1990s, the U.S. Shipping firms using Japanese ports have voiced complaints about an extremely restrictive port services system. They claimed that in order to manage competition, divide up harbor work amongst themselves, and thwart shipping companies' attempts to reduce costs, the Japanese association of stevedore companies—companies that unload cargo from ships—used a system of prior consultations.

Shipping companies specifically claimed that they were compelled to bargain with the Japanese stevedore-company association over a wide range of issues, including arrival times and warehouse and stevedore selection. Foreign carriers were unable to bargain with specific stevedore companies regarding rates and schedules because port services were governed by the stevedore-company association. Additionally, U.S. Carriers contended that by rejecting licenses for new players in the port services industry and by endorsing the mandate that international carriers hold talks with Japan's stevedore-company association, the Japanese government sanctioned these punitive measures.

A midnight trip to Tokyo Bay illustrates the frustration of U.S. shipping companies. Despite the Sealand Commerce having just docked, the lights are low and the wharf is quiet. At one in the morning lights come on, cranes begin to move, and trucks start to unload the ship's containers, which are loaded with American-made pet food, paper plates, and computers. But at 4:00 a.m. The work stops and the lights go out. The longshoremen won't be back until 8:30 a.m. and will take a further three hours off in the afternoon. Just 169 of the 488 containers that need to be handled have been unloaded before the ship departs for Oakland. The task will take until after noon at this rate, but at least it's not Sunday, when docks are closed completely.

But by the time the Sealand Commerce gets to Oakland, U.S. Dockworkers will load and unload cargo around the clock, saving 30% of the time and cost. The ship had to clear every aspect of its visit with the Japanese stevedore-company association in order to enter Tokyo Bay; in order to enter the U.S. It will only alert the Coast Guard and port authorities. As stated by U.S. Exporters, because it creates a barrier to trade, this unfair treatment on waterfronts makes U.S. In Japan, exports are more expensive.

The United States and Japan were on the verge of a trade war in 1997 following the U.S. government made the decision to order the Coast Guard and customs service to prevent ships flying the flag of Japan from unloading at U.S. ports. The U.S. In order to get around the stringent policies of Japan's stevedore-company association, the government insisted that international shipping companies be permitted to negotiate directly with Japanese stevedore companies for the unloading of their ships. Following discussions between the two administrations, a decision was made to liberalize port services in Japan. Consequently, the US lifted its embargo on Japanese ships.

CASE STUDY

SWIMMING UPSTREAM: THE CASE OF VIETNAMESE CATFISH

In 2003, the U.S. government was strongly criticized for assaulting catfish imports from Vietnam. According to Senator John McCain and other critics, this policy was an example of how wealthy countries preach the gospel of free trade when it comes to finding markets for their manufactured goods, but become highly protectionist when their farmers face competition. Let us consider this trade dispute.

After pursuing pro-capitalistic reforms, Vietnam became one of globalization's success stories in the 1990s. The nation transformed itself from being a rice importer to the world's second largest rice exporter and also an exporter of coffee. Vietnam's rural poverty rate declined from 70 to 30%. The normalization of communication between the governments of Vietnam and the United States resulted in American trade missions intended on increasing free enterprise in Vietnam.

On one of these trade missions, delegates saw much promise in Vietnamese catfish, with the country's Mekong Delta and cheap labor providing a competitive advantage. Within several years, some half-million Vietnamese were earning income from the catfish trade. Vietnam captured 20% of the frozen catfish-filet market in the United States, forcing down prices. To the alarm of catfish farmers in Mississippi, the hub of the U.S. catfish industry, even local restaurants were serving Vietnamese catfish.

Before long, Vietnamese farmers faced a nasty trade war waged by Mississippi's catfish farmers involving product labeling and antidumping tariffs. Although these farmers are usually not large agribusinesses, they were strong enough to persuade the U.S. government to close the catfish market to the very Vietnamese farmers whose enterprise it had originally encouraged. The government declared that out of 2,000 types of catfish, only the American-born family could be called "catfish." So the Vietnamese could market their fish in America only by using Vietnamese words such as "tra" and "Basa." Mississippi catfish farmers issued warnings of a "slippery catfish wannabe," saying such fish were "probably not even sporting real whiskers" and "floating around in Third World rivers nibbling on who knows what." This disinformation campaign resulted in decreased sales of Vietnamese catfish in the United States.

Not satisfied with its labeling success, the Mississippi catfish farmers initiated an antidumping case against Vietnamese catfish. In this case, the U.S. Department of Commerce did not have strong evidence that the imported fish were being sold in America more cheaply than in Vietnam, or below their cost of production. But rather than leaving Mississippi catfish farmers to the forces of international competition, the department declared Vietnam a "nonmarket" economy. This designation implied that Vietnamese farmers must not be covering all the costs they would in a market economy such as the United States, and thus were dumping catfish into the American market. Thus, tariffs ranging from 37 to 64% were imposed by the department on Vietnamese catfish. The U.S. International Trade Commission made the tariffs permanent by stating that the American catfish industry was injured by unfair competition due to dumping by Vietnam. According to critics, this nonmarket designation should not have been used because the U.S. government was encouraging Vietnam to become a market economy.

CLASS ACTIVITY

Assign students to write a report on a recent trade dispute involving nontariff barriers and propose potential resolutions, focusing on how international trade agreements could address these issues.

SUMMARY

- Nontariff trade barriers (NTBs) encompass a range of regulatory and procedural constraints imposed by countries to control the import and export of goods without resorting to tariffs.
- The World Trade Organization (WTO) identifies various non-tariff barriers to trade, including import licensing, pre-shipment inspections, rules of origin, custom delayers, and other mechanisms that prevent or restrict trade.
- During the formation of nation-states, countries had to devise ways of raising money to finance local projects and pay recurrent expenditures.
- Protectionist barriers are designed to protect certain sectors of domestic industries at the expense of other countries.
- Although assistive policies are designed to protect domestic companies and enterprises, they do not directly restrict trade with other countries, but they implement actions that can impede free trade with other countries.
- Non-protectionist policies are not designed to directly restrict the import or export of goods and services, but the overall outcomes may lead to free trade restrictions.
- Licenses are one of the most common instruments that countries use to regulate the importation of goods.
- Quotas are quantitative restrictions that are imposed on imports and exports of a specific product for a specified period.
- Embargoes are total bans of trade on specific commodities and may be imposed on imports or exports of specific goods that are supplied to or from specific countries.
- Import deposit is a form of foreign trade regulation that requires importers to pay the central bank of the country a specified sum of money for a definite period.
- An import quota is a physical restriction on the quantity of goods that can be imported during a specific time period; the quota generally limits imports to a level below what would occur under free-trade conditions.

REVIEW QUESTIONS

1. Explain non-tariff barriers. What are the types of non-tariff barriers?
2. How does the revenue effect of an import quota differ from that of a tariff?
3. What are the major forms of subsidies that governments grant to domestic producers?
4. What is meant by voluntary export restraints, and how do they differ from other protective barriers?
5. What do you understand by international price discrimination?

REFERENCES

1. Agreement on Technical Barriers to Trade. (1994). Retrieved from: https://www.wto.org/english/docs_e/legal_e/17-tbt_e.htm (accessed on 3 July 2024).
2. Beghin, J. C. (2006). Nontariff barriers. Retrieved from: https://ageconsearch.umn.edu/record/18436/ (accessed on 3 July 2024).
3. Benz, S., & Jaax, A. (2019). Quantifying the costs of regulatory barriers to trade in services: New estimates of ad valorem equivalents based on the OECD STRI. Conference paper presented at the 22nd annual conference on global economic analysis, Warsaw, Poland. Retrieved from: https://www.gtap.agecon.purdue.edu/resources/res_display.asp?RecordID=5842 (accessed on 3 July 2024).
4. Borchert, I., Gootiiz, B., Magdeleine, J., Marchetti, J., & Mattoo, A. (2014). Barriers to international trade in services–New evidence from the World Bank-WTO database. Conference paper.
5. Bown, C. P., & Crowley, M. A. (2016). The empirical landscape of trade policy. In Handbook of commercial policy (Chapter 1). Retrieved from: https://meredithcrowley.weebly.com/uploads/2/1/7/6/21768054/bown-crowley-handbook-february-2016.pdf.
6. Carrere, C., & De Melo, J. (2019). WTO rules and their enforcement are threatened by unilateral trade policies and the general rise of protectionism. FERDI. Retrieved from: https://ferdi.fr/en/programs/reducing-trade-barriers (accessed on 3 July 2024).
7. Cohen, R. B. (2019). Nontariff barriers to high-technology trade. Retrieved from: https://books.google.com.ua/books?hl=en&lr=&id=5KqbDwAAQBAJ&oi=fnd&pg=PT8&dq=nontariff+trade+barriers&ots=zSfd3UIpYr&sig=h2DkW9FLtwaDNXpM1Sc3ar7OF5w&redir_esc=y#v=onepage&q=nontariff%20trade%20barriers&f=false (accessed on 3 July 2024).
8. Dal Bianco, A., Boatto, V., Caracciolo, F., & Santeramo, F. (2016). Tariffs and non-tariff frictions in the world wine trade. *European Review of Agricultural Economics, 43*(1), 31–57.
9. Deardorff, A. V., & Stern, R. M. (1997). Measurement of nontariff barriers (A1.159 WP 395). Retrieved from: https://ssrn.com/abstract=54045 or http://dx.doi.org/10.2139/ssrn.54045 (accessed on 3 July 2024).
10. Economic and Social Commission for Asia and the Pacific. (2015). Trade and non-tariff measures impacts in the Asia-Pacific region. *Emerging Issues in Trade and Investment: Volume No. 1*. 70 pages.
11. Essays, UK. (2018). Examples of non-tariff barriers to trade. Retrieved from: https://www.ukessays.com/essays/economics/examples-of-non-tariff-barriers-to-trade-economics-essay.php?vref=1 (accessed on 3 July 2024).
12. Gallagher, P. (1998). International marketing margins for agricultural products: Effects of some nontariff trade barriers. *American Journal of Agricultural Economics, 80*(2), 325–336.
13. Grübler, J., Ghodsi, M., & Stehrer, R. (2016). Assessing the impact of non-tariff measures on imports. The Vienna institute for international economic studies. Retrieved

from: https://pdfs.semanticscholar.org/994a/fcdb38d293b7bbfafcaf95b2e6341f591916.pdf (accessed on 3 July 2024).

14. Grundke, R. (2019). Hidden protectionism? Evidence from non-tariff barriers to trade in the United States. *Journal of International Economics, 117*, 143–157.

15. Imbruno, M. (2016). China and WTO liberalization: Imports, tariffs and non-tariff barriers. *China Economic Review, 38*, 222–237.

16. International Trade Centre (ITC). (2015). The invisible barriers to trade–How businesses experience non-tariff measures. Geneva: ITC.

17. Kinzius, L., Sandkamp, A., & Yalcin, E. (2019). Global trade protection and the role of non-tariff barriers. VOX, CEPR Policy Portal. Retrieved from: https://voxeu.org (accessed on 3 July 2024).

18. Kinzius, L., Sandkamp, A., & Yalcin, E. (2019). Trade protection and the role of non-tariff barriers. *The Review of World Economics, 155*(4), 603.

19. Krishnan, V. (2016). Impact of non-tariff barriers on Indian exports: An econometric analysis. *Journal of Tropical Agriculture, 54*(2). Retrieved from: http://jtropag.kau.in/index.php/ojs2/article/view/452 (accessed on 3 July 2024).

20. Lawson, C., Dietrich, C., Cavan, D., & Murray, T. (2019). The effect of trade barriers and governmental regulation on overall economic well-being. *Econometric Analysis Undergraduate Research Papers*. Retrieved from: https://smartech.gatech.edu/handle/1853/62052 (accessed on 3 July 2024).

21. Lee, B. H. (2017). The effects of non-tariff barriers on export of fresh strawberry of South Korea. *Korean Journal of Food Marketing Economics, 34*(3), 45–70.

22. Lupan, R. (2018). Non-tariff barriers and deepening economic integration within the European Union. In *Simpozion Ştiinţific Internaţional al Tinerilor Cercetători*, 16th Edition, April 27–28, 2018, Chișinău (pp. 18–21). Chișinău, Republica Moldova: Departamentul Editorial-Poligrafic al ASEM.

23. McEwen, J. (n.d.). Addressing non-tariff trade barriers. Department of Foreign Affairs and Trade. R.G. Casey Building, Crescent Barton ACT 0221 Australia. Retrieved from: https://dfat.gov.au/trade/exporters-and-importers/Pages/addressing-non-tariff-trade-barriers.aspx (accessed on 3 July 2024).

24. Medin, H. (2019). Trade barriers or trade facilitators? The heterogeneous impact of food standards in international trade. *The World Economy, 42*(4), 1057–1076.

25. Reporting, Monitoring and Eliminating Mechanism. (2019). Non-tariff barriers. Presented at the 22nd annual conference on global economic analysis, Warsaw, Poland. Retrieved from: https://www.gtap.agecon.purdue.edu/resources/res_display.asp?RecordID=5753 (accessed on 3 July 2024).

26. Schuenemann, F., & Kerr, W. (2019). European Union non-tariff barriers to imports of African biofuels. *Agricultural Economics Research, Policy and Practice in Southern Africa, 58*(4), Agri-food trade and non-tariff measures.

27. Shepotylo, O. (2016). Effect of non-tariff measures on extensive and intensive margins of exports in seafood trade. *Marine Policy, 68*, 47–54.

28. United Nations Conference on Trade and Development. (2012). Classification of non-tariff measures. Retrieved from: http://unctad.org/en/PublicationsLibrary/ditctab20122_en.pdf (accessed on 3 July 2024).

29. USAID. (2013). Non-tariff barriers to trade regional agricultural trade environment. Summary USAID maximizing agricultural revenue through knowledge, enterprise development and trade (Market) project. Retrieved from: https://2012-2017.usaid.gov/sites/default/files/documents/1861/Nontariff_barriers.pdf.

30. Vakulchuk, R., & Knobel, A. (2018). Impact of non-tariff barriers on trade within the Eurasian Economic Union. *Post-Communist Economies, 30*(4), 459–481.

31. Yalcin, E., Felbermayr, G., & Kinzius, L. (2017). Hidden protectionism: Non-tariff barriers and implications for international trade. IFO Center for International Economics, Munich.

CHAPTER

5

Trade Regulations and Industrial Policies

LEARNING OBJECTIVES

After studying this chapter, you will be able to:

- Discuss the basics of international trade
- Learn about U.S. tariff policies before 1930
- Discuss the Smoot-Hawley act and reciprocal trade agreements act
- Understand about general agreement on tariffs and trade
- Describe the world trade organization
- Explain the failed trade negotiations from Doha to Hong Kong
- Understand the trade promotion authority (fast-track authority)
- Explain the industrial policy
- Discuss the industrial policies of the United States and Japan

KEY TERMS FROM THIS CHAPTER

Commodity Credit	Consumer protection	Disinvestment
Foreign Exchange Regulation Act	Globalization	Government regulation
Industrial licensing	Industrial policy	Intellectual property rights
International Trade	Macroeconomic policies	Mixed economy
Smoot-Hawley Act	Trade	Trade regulation

INTRODUCTION

Trade regulation is a branch of law that is frequently combined with antitrust (hence the term "antitrust and trade regulation law"). It deals with the regulation by the government of unfair business practices and unfair methods of competition. Trade regulation law is frequently regarded as a subset of antitrust law. Trade regulation law can occasionally include franchise and distribution law, consumer protection law, and advertising law.

Government policies aimed at promoting the expansion and growth of the economy, either fully or partially, in order to achieve a public objective are known as industrial policies (Juhász Réka & Steinwender Claudia, 2024). In the past, it has frequently concentrated on developing a competitive advantage in new technologies, the manufacturing sector, or strategically significant industries. The goal of government actions is to support structural transformation while enhancing the capabilities and competitiveness of domestic businesses. Industrial policy is greatly aided by a nation's infrastructure, which includes its telecommunications, energy, and transportation sectors.

Industrial policies are interventionist tactics that are common in nations with mixed economies. Trade policy and other interventionist practices share many characteristics with industrial policies. Generally speaking, industrial policy is considered distinct from more general macroeconomic measures like capital gains taxation and credit tightening. Subsidizing export industries and import-substitution-industrialization (ISI), which imposes temporary trade barriers on certain important sectors, like manufacturing, are two classic examples of industrial policy. Certain industries are given time to learn (by doing) and improve when they are given selective protection. These limitations are removed once the chosen industries are sufficiently competitive to enter foreign markets. Modern industrial policies include things like encouraging cross-firm links and supporting upstream technologies (Wear Andrew, 2017).

The contribution of industrial policy to economic development and industrialization has been discussed by economists (Juhász Réka et al., 2024). They have also discussed worries that free trade and international cooperation are threatened by industrial policy (Bown Chad, 2024).

5.1. BASICS OF INTERNATIONAL TRADE

The textile industry, which has been around for centuries, is thought to be the most vibrant, varied, and job-rich sector. As a result of nations colonizing one another, trade began to develop as a means for nations to expand their markets. Countries rely on one another for trade; in the past, the most developed nations dominated the market, but in the present, the majority of skilled nations control the textile and clothing sector (Hayashi, 2017).

5.1.1. Trade

One of the most important ideas in the study of economics is trade. Ricardo noted that comparative cost, as opposed to the total cost of production, drives trade. For instance, a nation may be more productive than others in producing goods if it can do so with fewer labor and capital inputs than other nations need to produce an equivalent amount of goods.

As a result, trade based on comparative advantage benefits nations.

Tariffs and import quotas are the two key concepts in trade. An excise levied on the sale of imported goods is known as a tariff. Tariffs were imposed on imported goods in order to protect domestic producers and deter imports, which also served as a source of income for the government.

Tariffs are, to put it simply, the price increase that domestic producers receive and that domestic consumers in the importing countries must pay. In addition to tariffs, import quotas were imposed, suggesting or legally limiting the amount of goods that can be imported into the respective countries. These quotas are typically managed through licensing agreements.

5.1.2. History of Trade

Bartering, or the exchange of goods and services between individuals, is a custom from earlier times. New theories have surfaced as political theorists have begun to investigate the nature and purpose of trade with other nations. The exquisite cotton textiles from India served as an inspiration for British capitalists in the late 1600s as they looked for ways to produce goods outside of the domestic market. Consequently, Indian textiles were prohibited by English laws from creating automated spinning and weaving processes, leading to the Industrial Revolution. The foundation for turning the western world into an international economy has been laid by this revolution.

However, in the years that followed, the development of numerous mill towns, factories, work opportunities for women outside the home, and industrial reforms, along with Eli Whitney's cotton gin and Samuel Slater's inventions, revolutionized the industry. The British imposed restrictions as soon as the industry started to develop in the states, which was one of the major turns in the process. In order to safeguard Native American cotton production, Congress established tariffs and embargoes on foreign cotton products by the 1700s. The trade regulations for fair trade were subsequently influenced by these import restrictions on textiles.

Before the American Civil War, the cotton industry became one of the nation's major producers, making the 19th century a pivotal time for the US. The deals were larger and more comprehensive. The interdependence of the global economy has grown in many ways. By establishing the international textile and clothing markets that will thrive in the 21st century, the 20th century helped to close the gaps between the continents.

5.1.3. Globalization and Contemporary Trade

Globalization can be considered the market expansion or exchange at a scale beyond regions of the nations. Some forms of globalization included are as follows:

- **Mercantilism:** In this kind of trading system, a country seeks to enforce a positive trade balance, or more exports than imports in terms of value, in order to promote the growth of the national economy. Trade monopolization results from this kind of trading system. A trading system that favors one party at the expense of the others is known as mercantilism. However, this kind of mercantilism has been recognized as the cornerstone of the international trading system.
- **Neomercantilism:** Trade in more recent times has demonstrated this type of mercantilism. Through developmental goals, this trading system seeks to create a positive trade balance in order to meet the economically structured cost system. Under neomercantilism, export-oriented strategies are encouraged by the government's provision of subsidy systems like free trade zones. These trading systems lead to the regulation of tariffs and non-tariff measures, which safeguards the domestic business sectors. As such, this kind of tactic may be deemed debatable.
- **Absolute Advantages:** The mechanism behind this trade mostly depends on the resources of the country, i.e., when a nation can successfully manufacture goods with less capital and labor than other possible rivals. The country primarily exploits its advantage in this trade by exporting the goods it lacks and trading its excess. A primary disadvantage of this viewpoint is that trade is prohibited with countries that do not have a comparative advantage; as a result, their trade is not very profitable. Absolute advantage is typically a persistent feature; trade can go on as long as the resources are accessible or there is a market for them, or else it becomes inefficient and exposes countries to danger.
- **Comparative Advantage:** In situations where a country enjoys a comparative advantage, it can concentrate on this advantage across a broad range of economic sectors (difference between the competitors and their production cost). Productivity is increased under this kind of trading system because countries without a definite advantage can achieve notable productivity gains. The transient nature of the competitive

advantage, which is vulnerable to shifts in labor costs and technology breakthroughs, is one of its disadvantages.

- **Factor Endowments:** It is a broader interpretation of comparative advantage, emphasizing that trade is a related factor that begins with basic resources such as labor, capital, and land. Goods with notable factor endowments will be exported from the country, while goods with scarce factor endowments will be imported. For instance, whereas nations with high capital endowments concentrate on capital-intensive activities, low labor cost countries concentrate on labor-intensive tasks. Improvements to this kind of endowment are made possible by financial and human resource investments.

5.1.4. International Trade

The exchange of capital, goods, and services across international borders or between territories due to a specific need for particular goods or services is referred to as international trade. Stated differently, international trades are business dealings that take place between nations. Through trade, nations can access goods and services that would be difficult to obtain on their own markets and grow their current markets. Among the consumer goods that are frequently traded are raw materials, machinery, apparel, and so forth. As a result of increased pricing competition brought about by globalization, consumers can now purchase cheaper goods at home. Throughout history, there has been international trade via the Silk Road, Uttarapatha, Amber Road, Salt Roads, Scramble for Africa, and other routes.

The terms "import" and "export" refer to the global market; an import is something that is brought from the global market, and an export is a product that is sold there. Nations possess natural resources (land, labor, capital, technology, etc.) and foreign assets. Countries can produce goods faster, cheaper, and more effectively thanks to international trade. Trade contributes significantly to GDP (gross domestic product) in the majority of nations (Figure 5.1).

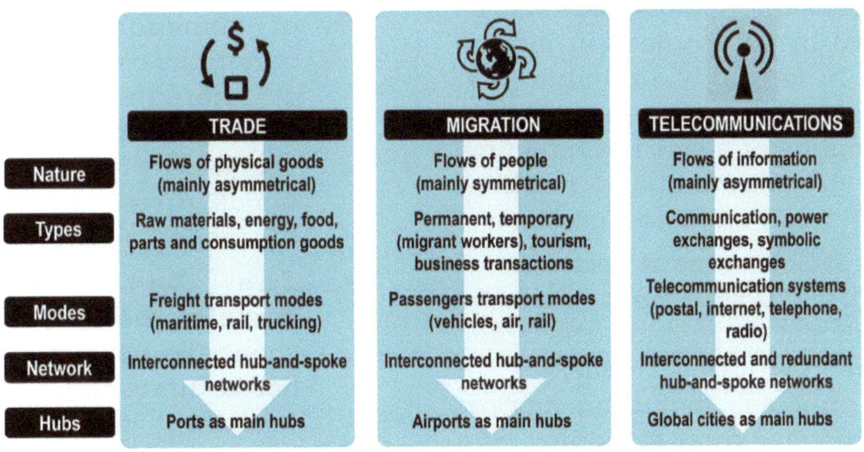

Figure 5.1. *The flows of globalization.*

Source: https://egyankosh.ac.in/bitstream/123456789/100420/1/Unit-6.pdf.

5.1.5. Factors Affecting International Trade

Comparatively speaking to the trade process, understanding international trade can be more difficult because it has a greater impact on a country's economy. For this reason, it's critical to identify the factors that will affect trade.

- **Impact of Inflation:** The general increase in the cost of goods or services, which results in a decline in the purchasing power of currency, is known as inflation. For instance, the countries with which trade is conducted are anticipated to decline or fall when the country's relative inflation rate rises. Inflationary nations' consumers and businesses will probably buy goods and services abroad, lowering their exports.
- **Impact of National Income:** National income is the total amount of money earned by the nation's economic activities over the course of a year. This amount includes wages, interest, rent, and profits. The rise in the consumption of goods will be matched by an increase in income levels. It is highly probable that any percentage increase in the consumption of goods is a reflection of the growing demand for both domestic and imported goods.
- **Impact of Government Restrictions:** A country's government can have a significant impact on the trade balance through a variety of trade policies, including import prohibitions, export subsidies, and measures to combat piracy. Three main trade restrictions—tariffs, subsidies, and quotas—are in place to safeguard home producers. When an imported good crosses an international border, the importing nation imposes a tax, which is known as a tariff. A payment made by the government to domestic producers in accordance with their capacity for production is known as a subsidy. A quota is a constraint that sets a maximum amount of goods that can be imported or exported.
- **Impact of Exchange Rates:** The value of one country's currency relative to another is known as the currency exchange rate, and it is one of the important variables. Direct or indirect quotes of local or foreign currency are possible in exchange rates. The price per unit of foreign currency is expressed in domestic currency rates under the direct system. The cost per unit of domestic currency is expressed in foreign currency in the indirect system, though.
- **Geographical Location:** Geographical factors such as a nation's proximity to coasts, ease of transportation, and climatic variations can all have a big impact on international trade. The cost of transportation increases with the complexity of the travel routes, which drives up the total cost of the goods or services.
- **The Level of Economic Development:** The level of economic development in a nation has a direct impact on its relative standing in international trade as well as its foreign trade. For instance, developing nations are less likely to become major players in the global trade market due to

their comparatively undeveloped trade and resource management systems.

- **Lack of Restrictions on Piracy:** The word "piracy" refers to manufactured goods that bear striking similarities to their original designs. Because many governments do not impose restrictions on piracy, piracy will have a major impact on international trade, which will lower demand for imported or exported goods. Stated differently, the costlier products were those that were imported or exported and compared to products that were pirated.
- **Competitiveness:** The degree of interdependence between markets is multiplying several times over as competition grows. The relative capacity of various nations to offer more services or goods at a level that is generally embraced by the populace is known as competitiveness. Global trade is heavily influenced by competitiveness because the most competitive nations achieve the highest levels, which makes life challenging for less developed nations.
- **Globalization:** Globalization is the overall trend of national economies integrating for mutual advantage. Over the past few decades, international trade has increased due to globalization. Technology, transportation, and the ability for businesses to conduct cross-border business have all contributed to its facilitation.

5.1.6. Benefits of International Trade

A company that trades internationally can benefit from increased profits and revenues due to a wider pool of potential customers, reduced competition in untapped foreign markets, diversification, and potential gains from fluctuations in foreign exchange rates.

5.1.7. Need for International Trade

The main reason international trade was created was to give nations access to new products and services that they would not otherwise have access to or be difficult to find on the domestic market, as well as to expand their potential markets. Education, government regulations, the availability of natural resources, labor laws, and financial opportunities are some common factors that promote international trade.

5.1.8. Common Barriers to International Trade

Trade barriers are one thing that could prevent goods from being traded between nations. Trade barriers are put in place to increase exports, decrease imports, and support domestic products. Common trade restrictions imposed by the nations include non-tariff trade barriers, tariffs, quotas, and subsidies.

A subsidy is a type of incentive that governments give to their local producers or industrial workers to encourage them to produce more goods at a lower cost and thereby become more competitive in the global market.

Taxes on imports are known as tariffs. The primary purpose of a tariff is to increase the cost of imports so that consumers feel compelled to purchase them, which eventually leads to a decrease in imports. To put it another way, tariffs can be explained as follows: as prices rise, consumers become less interested in those products. Consequently, they choose local products and services.

Trade restrictions known as quotas limit the amount of goods and services that can be imported into a given nation. These kinds of quotas typically have an inbuilt licensing system that requires documentation of particular restrictions and guidelines.

The other restrictions on trade that exist outside of tariffs are known as non-tariff barriers. It consists of rules, permits, and penalties. This is a common tactic used by some nations to restrict trade with other nations. Non-tariff barriers include rules governing the quality or content of products. A license under the non-tariff barrier permits restricted businesses to import products from overseas. Sanctions are a type of non-tariff barrier whereby the government forbids companies from engaging in business dealings with specific nations.

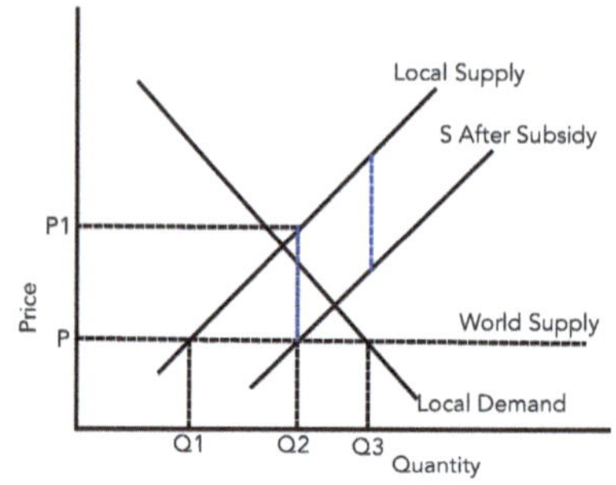

Figure 5.2. *Example of the effects of trade barriers.*

Source: https://egyankosh.ac.in/bitstream/123456789/100420/1/Unit-6.pdf.

Figure 5.2 can be further explained as follows: Q1 represents production from the home industry, Q2 represents local demand, and Q3 represents imported goods. P stands for the world price.

5.2. U.S. TARIFF POLICIES BEFORE 1930

Table 5.1 illustrates how the history of US tariffs has been characterized by volatility. The primary goal of the early American tariff laws was to give the government a significant stream of tax income. The primary motivation behind Congress's adoption of the first tariff law in 1789 and the subsequent 12 tariff laws by 1812 was this revenue target. However, as the US economy expanded and produced substitute tax revenue streams, the case for revenue became less compelling. The federal government's current tariff collection represents a negligible 1 percent of total federal revenues.

Table 5.1. US Tariff History: Average Tariff Rates

Tariff Laws and Dates	Average Tariff Rate (%)
McKinley Law, 1890	48.4
Wilson Law, 1894	41.3
Dingley Law, 1897	46.5
Payne-Aldrich Law, 1909	40.8
Underwood Law, 1913	27.0
Fordney-McCumber Law, 1922	38.5
Smoot-Hawley Law, 1930	53.0
1930–1949	33.9
1950–1969	11.9
1970–1989	6.4
1990–1999	5.2
2008	3.5

Source: Robert J. Carbaugh. International Economics, 13th Edition. South-Western Cengage Learning. https://wyamaka.wordpress.com/wp-content/uploads/2019/08/international-economics_30.pdf.

The defense of tariffs got stronger as the case for revenue grew weaker. The infant industry argument, put forth by Alexander Hamilton in his renowned "Report on Manufacturers" to Congress in 1791, suggested that import protection be extended to the nation's fledgling industries until they could develop and thrive. Protectionist sentiments were well-established in the US by the 1820s, despite the fact that Hamilton's writings had no immediate legislative effect. The average rate of tariffs on US imports in the 1920s was three to four times higher than the 8 percent rates in 1789.

The enactment of the so-called Tariff of Abominations in 1828 marked the pinnacle of the burgeoning protectionist movement. The South, which desired low duties for its imported manufactured goods, was incensed by this measure, which raised duties to an average of 45%, the highest level in the years preceding the American Civil War. Due to the South's resistance to this tariff, the Compromise Tariff of 1833 was passed, resulting in a reduction in the level of tariff protection for American manufacturers. The United States government discovered in the 1840s and 1850s that its tax revenue exceeded its outlays. To end the budget deficit, the government enacted the Walker tariffs, which reduced duties to an average of 23%. In 1857, additional tariff reductions were implemented, resulting in average tariff levels reaching their lowest point since 1816, approximately 16%.

The Morill Tariffs of 1861, 1862, and 1864 were passed during the Civil War era, raising tariffs once more.

The main goal of these actions was to raise money for the Civil War. Protection reached its peak again in the 1840s by 1870, but this time there would be no decrease in tariff levels. American labor and business leaders claimed that cheap labor from abroad was driving goods into the country, and their arguments were persuasive to US policy makers in the late 1800s. This argument served as a major justification for the McKinley and Dingley Tariffs' implementation. Tariffs on imports that were protected averaged 46% by 1897.

The Payne-Aldrich Tariff of 1909 was a turning point in the fight against rising protectionism, but the Underwood Tariff of 1913 was the legislation that actually lowered duties to an average of 27%. If not for the start of World War I, trade liberalization might have continued more permanently. Pressures toward protectionism intensified during the war and persisted after it was over. Influential in the early 1920s, the scientific tariff idea resulted in the Fordney-McCumber Tariff in 1922, which included a provision allowing the president to raise tariff levels in the event that foreign production costs were lower than American ones. Under the Fordney-McCumber law, average tariff rates increased to 38%.

5.3. SMOOT-HAWLEY ACT

Following the Smoot-Hawley Act's enactment in 1930, which increased average US tariffs on protected imports to 53%, US protectionism reached its pinnacle. Formal protests from overseas countries descended upon Washington as the Smoot-Hawley bill made its way through the US Congress; these eventually accumulated into a document that was roughly 200 pages long. Nevertheless, the bill was approved by the Senate and the House of Representatives. President Herbert Hoover was urged by roughly 1,000 US economists to veto the legislation, but he refused, and on June 17, 1930, the tariff became operative. In short, the goal of the Smoot-Hawley Act was to shift the country's demand from imports to products made in the country.

25th of the US's trading partners retaliated against the bill. The US tariffs on cork, oranges, and grapes prompted Spain to impose the Wais Tariff. In opposition to new taxes on shoes and watches, Switzerland boycotted US exports. In response to US tariffs on lumber, logs, and numerous food items, Canada raised its tariffs threefold. Italy retaliated with tariffs on US cars against hats and olive oil tariffs. The following countries took part in the tariff wars: Mexico, Cuba, Australia, and New Zealand. In addition, other beggarly-neighbor measures like currency depreciation and foreign exchange controls were put into place.

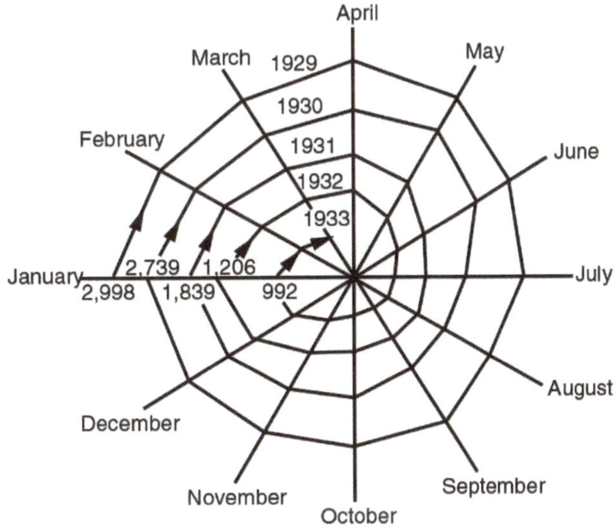

Figure 5.3. *Smoot-Hawley protectionism and world trade, 1929–1933 (millions of dollars).*

Source: Robert J. Carbaugh. International Economics, 13th Edition. South-Western Cengage Learning. https://wyamaka.wordpress.com/wp-content/uploads/2019/08/international-economics_30.pdf.

The international trading system collapsed as a result of multiple countries' attempts to run a trade surplus by cutting imports. US exports fell by almost two-thirds in the two years following the Smoot-Hawley Act. The decline in international trade during the Great Depression is depicted in Figure 5.3. President Hoover felt obligated to follow the 1928 Republican platform that called for tariffs to support the faltering farm economy, but how did he fall into such a protectionist trap? The 1929 stock market crash and the impending Great Depression contributed to the climate of crisis. For many years, Republicans had supported protectionism. They now saw import tariffs as a way to satisfy demands that the government take proactive measures to address unemployment at home.

President Hoover felt constrained by convention and the Republican Party platform. During their evening together, Henry Ford asked President Hoover to veto what he called "economic stupidity." Other auto industry executives supported Ford. Nevertheless, President Hoover was not going to create a precedent by vetoing tariff legislation, as this had never happened before. "Our foreign trade will continue to expand with returning normal conditions," stated President Hoover."

US trade with other countries had collapsed by 1932. Franklin Roosevelt, a presidential contender, criticized the trade laws as disastrous. In response, Hoover said that Roosevelt would put US laborers up against foreign peasant labor. The Democrats repealed the Smoot-Hawley Act after Herbert Hoover lost the 1932 presidential contest. However, they exercised caution and relied on reciprocal trade agreements rather than the US granting general tariff concessions. The speaker of the House of Representatives, Sam Rayburn, insisted that members of his party must embrace trade reciprocity rather than protectionism in order to be considered for appointment to the House Ways and Means Committee. After the Smoot-Hawley strategy was exposed as flawed, the US pursued trade liberalization through reciprocal trade agreements.

5.4. RECIPROCAL TRADE AGREEMENTS ACT

US trade policy was reversed as a result of the Great Depression's combined effects on US exports and the foreign retaliatory tariffs imposed in response to the Smoot-Hawley Act. The Reciprocal Trade Agreements Act, passed by Congress in 1934, altered US trade policy by giving the president, who tended to take the national interest into consideration when forming trade policy, authority over the Congress, which typically favored domestic producers that competed with imports. This shift created the conditions for a wave of trade liberalization by tipping the scales in favor of lower tariffs. The act included two features that were specifically intended to reduce tariffs: generalized reductions and negotiation authority.

The president was granted unparalleled power to negotiate bilateral tariff-reduction agreements with foreign governments (like the United States and Sweden) under this law. The president may reduce tariffs by up to 50% of the current level without the consent of Congress. Any tariff reductions could only be implemented if other countries agreed to likewise cut their own tariffs on US goods. The United States entered into 32 bilateral tariff agreements between 1934 and 1947, and during this time, the average level of tariffs on protected products decreased to roughly half of the levels in 1934.

The Reciprocal Trade Agreements Act additionally facilitated broad tariff reductions via the utilization of the most favored nation (MFN) provision. This clause is an agreement between two countries to impose tariffs on one another at the same rates as they would any other country with MFN status.

For instance, the United States is required to apply the same low-tariff treatment to machinery imports from Brazil if it grants Brazil MFN treatment and then imposes a low tariff on machinery imports from France. As a result, Brazil is treated in the same way as France, the country that was initially given preference. Brazil benefits from MFN status because it can look into all US tariff policies regarding imported machinery and determine whether any country is treated better than Brazil. If better terms are found, Brazil can demand equal treatment. In other words, tariff reductions were made non-discriminatorily as a result of the MFN clause: if a nation reduced a tariff to one nation, it would reduce them to all nations. The phrase "most favored nation" was replaced with "normal trade relations" by the US government in 1998.

The United States' attempts to liberalize trade were hampered by the Reciprocal Trade Agreements Act's piecemeal, bilateral approach, even though it shifted the political tide in favor of lower tariffs. The US realized that multilateral trade liberalization required a more all-encompassing strategy.

5.5. GENERAL AGREEMENT ON TARIFFS AND TRADE

The United States and some of its allies attempted to impose order on trade flows following World War II, in part as a reaction to trade disruptions during the Great Depression. The 1947 signing of the General Agreement on Tariffs and Trade (GATT) marked the first significant postwar step toward multilateral trade liberalization. GATT was designed as a contract between contracting parties, or member countries, with the goal of lowering trade barriers and putting every country on an equal footing in trade relations. GATT is a collection of agreements among nations worldwide to lower trade barriers and create broad guidelines for commercial policy; it was never meant to become an organization.

GATT was renamed the World Trade Organization (WTO) in 1995. The main ideas of GATT are embodied in the WTO, but it also serves as a mechanism to enhance GATT's dispute resolution process for member countries' trade disputes. Let's start by going over the main tenets of the original GATT framework.

5.5.1. Trade Without Discrimination

A member nation of the GATT is prohibited from treating its trading partners differently. The national treatment principle and the MFN principle (normal trade relations) served as the two cornerstones of the nondiscrimination principle.

The MFN principle stated that a GATT member had to provide all other GATT members with the same tariff rate if it granted another member a lower tariff rate for one of its products. Therefore, "favor one, favor all" was the MFN. GATT members were free to apply the most-favored nation (MFN) principle to non-member nations, but they were required to limit its application to other GATT members. Equal treatment was not always guaranteed by MFN status, though. Bilateral trade agreements established exclusive clubs among a nation's MFN partners before the GATT. The MFN club was abolished under GATT since each nation was required to treat all other GATT members equally under the principle.

In accordance with GATT, the MFN clause had two exceptions: first, industrialized countries could offer preferential tariffs to developing countries that they could not offer to other industrialized countries; second, countries that were part of a regional trading agreement, like the North American Free Trade Agreement, could remove tariffs on goods imported from other members of the agreement while keeping tariffs on imports from non-members.

Differential tariffs and MFN status grants have both been employed as foreign policy tools. For instance, a country may impose high import tariffs on the goods of its enemies and low tariffs on its allies. Most of the countries that the US trades with have been granted MFN status. North Korea and Cuba were not granted MFN status by the US as of 2010. Tariffs on comparable imports from countries granted MFN status are frequently three, four, or even more times lower than those on imports from these countries (Table 5.2). Additionally, the US granted temporary MFN status to a number of nations, including Vietnam and Russia.

Table 5.2. US Tariffs on Imports from Nations Granted, and Not Granted, Normal Trade Relation Status: Selected Examples

	TARIFF (PERCENT)	
Product	**With Normal Trade Relation Status**	**Without Normal Trade Relation Status**
Hams	1.2 cents/kg	7.2 cents/kg
Sour cream	3.2 cents/liter	15 cents/liter
Butter	12.3 cents/liter	30.9 cents/liter
Fish	3% ad valorem	25% ad valorem
Saws	4% ad valorem	30% ad valorem
Cauliflower	10% ad valorem	50% ad valorem
Coffee	10% ad valorem	20% ad valorem
Woven fabrics	15.7% ad valorem	81% ad valorem
Babies' shirts	20.2% ad valorem	90% ad valorem
Gold necklaces	5% ad valorem	80% ad valorem

Source: Robert J. Carbaugh. International Economics, 13th Edition. South-Western Cengage Learning. https://wyamaka.wordpress.com/wp-content/uploads/2019/08/international-economics_30.pdf.

Treating locals and visitors equally, or applying national treatment, was the second component of trade without discrimination. Members of the GATT were required to treat the industries of other members equally to how they treat their own domestic industries under the national treatment principle. Therefore, once foreign goods have entered the domestic market, domestic laws and internal taxes cannot be biased against them. But when foreign goods are imported into a nation, tariffs may be imposed. The use of discriminatory taxes to place a heavier burden on a foreign product than on a domestic one is exemplified by the Canadian periodicals industry. For instance, the government of Canada has long maintained that the magazine industry serves as a vehicle for Canadian ideas and interests and as a means of advancing Canadian culture. The Canadian government imposed a high tax in the 1990s on American magazines that were distributed to Canadians, including Sports Illustrated. The tax was designed to protect Canadian publications' advertising revenue by making it unprofitable for US companies to publish special edition periodicals targeted at the Canadian market. Due to their discriminatory nature against foreign magazines, these taxes were found to be in violation of the GATT's national treatment guidelines.

5.5.2. Promoting Freer Trade

Promoting freer trade through its involvement in the resolution of trade disputes was one of GATT's other objectives. Traditionally, trade disputes were limited to the parties involved and did not involve a third party to whom they could seek a favorable resolution. Because of this, disputes frequently went unsolved for years. In most cases, the stronger nation prevailed over the weaker nation when they were settled. By creating complaint procedures and a conciliation panel that a victimized nation could address its concerns, GATT enhanced the dispute-resolution process. The World Trade Organization was inspired to form by the fact that the GATT's dispute-settlement process lacked the power to impose the conciliation panel's recommendations.

Members of GATT are also required to protect their home industries through tariffs rather than quotas. Because quotas imposed a maximum ceiling on imports, allowed the user to discriminate between suppliers, and were unpredictable and opaque to exporters, GATT assumed that quotas were intrinsically more trade distorting than tariffs. There were also exclusions from the GATT's ban on quotas in this case. Quotas could be used by members to protect their balance of payments, encourage economic growth, and enable the continuation of domestic agricultural support initiatives. Because they were voluntary, quota-based agreements governing export restrictions also did not fall under the GATT's quota restrictions.

5.5.3. Predictability: Through Binding and Transparency

Reducing trade barriers is not always as important as promising not to raise them, as the former gives businesses a better idea of what opportunities they may have in the future. Under the GATT, nations would "bind" their agreements to open their markets to the trade of goods and services. These bindings essentially served as caps on the rates at which developed countries could impose import tariffs; typically, the bound rates corresponded to the actual rates charged. The bound rates act as a ceiling because most developing nations have bound their rates slightly higher than the actual rates charged. A nation may alter its trade agreements, but only after consulting and making up for any lost trade with its trading partners. As a result, traders and investors enjoyed a far higher level of market security.

Additionally, the GATT system aimed to increase predictability and stability by maximizing the clarity and transparency of each country's trade regulations. It was mandatory for nations to notify the GATT secretariat or the public about their trade policies and practices.

5.5.4. Multilateral Trade Negotiations

Before the GATT, trade agreements were negotiated bilaterally, for example, between the US and one other nation. Trade talks were conducted on a multilateral scale with participation from all GATT members following the establishment of the GATT. Over time, GATT expanded to encompass nearly all major trading nations, despite certain countries not being members. Thus, rather than using the terms "global" or "world," the GATT system was referred to as "multilateral." Table 5.3 summarizes the GATT-sponsored rounds of negotiations that aimed to lower trade barriers other than tariffs in order to advance freer trade.

Table 5.3. GATT Negotiating Rounds

Negotiating Round and Coverage	Dates	Number of Participants	Tariff Cut Achieved (percent)
Addressed tariffs			
Geneva	1947	23	21
Annecy	1949	13	2
Torquay	1951	38	3
Geneva	1956	26	4
Dillon Round	1960–1961	26	2
Kennedy Round	1964–1967	62	35
Addressed tariff and nontariff barriers			
Tokyo Round	1973–79	99	33
Uruguay Round	1986–93	125	34
Doha Round	2002–	149	—

Source: Robert J. Carbaugh. International Economics, 13th Edition. South-Western Cengage Learning. https://wyamaka.wordpress.com/wp-content/uploads/2019/08/international-economics_30.pdf.

Tariff reductions of an average of 21% were achieved during the first round of GATT negotiations, which concluded in 1947. In contrast, much less was reduced in tariffs during the GATT rounds in the late 1940s and early 1950s. As the war-torn industries of Europe and Japan were rebuilt, protectionist pressures in the US grew during this time. The negotiation process was laborious and slow, and many countries were unwilling to consider lowering their tariffs on a wide range of goods.

GATT members took part in the trade negotiations known as the Kennedy Round, which was named after US President John F. Kennedy, from 1964 to 1967. Kennedy, who published a proposal requesting the talks. Participants in the GATT held a multilateral meeting where the format of the negotiations changed from being product-by-product to being all-encompassing. A more streamlined method was used when negotiating tariffs on large categories of goods, with a given rate reduction applying to the entire group. The Kennedy Round lowered the average rate of tariffs on manufactured goods to 10.3% ad valorem, an average reduction of 35%.

From the 1940s through the 1960s, tariff reduction was the primary focus of the GATT rounds. Nontariff barriers became more significant during the postwar era as average tariff rates in industrialized nations declined. Negotiators turned their focus to the problem of nontariff distortions in international trade in reaction to these developments.

Signatory nations to the Tokyo Round of 1973–1979 agreed to tariff cuts in the same universal form as those started in the Kennedy Round. The average tariff for manufactured goods across the 9 major industrialized nations was reduced by 39%, from 7.0% to 4.7 percent. The amount of tariff escalation was tended to be lessened because tariff reductions on finished goods were more substantial than those on raw materials. Tariffs were so low following the Tokyo Round that they posed little obstacle to trade among industrialized nations. The agreement to eliminate or reduce numerous nontariff barriers was the second achievement of the Tokyo Round. Six domains saw the establishment of codes of conduct: government procurement, import licensing, countervailing duties, antidumping procedures, and technical trade barriers like product standards.

Despite the Tokyo Round's attempts to liberalize trade, world leaders believed that the GATT system was deteriorating in the 1980s. GATT members have been using voluntary export restraints and other bilateral agreements, as well as trade-distorting measures like subsidies resulting from protectionist domestic policies, more frequently. Leaders around the world also believed that GATT should cover more ground, including trade in services, intellectual property, and agriculture. Additionally, they felt that developing nations were overlooked in earlier GATT trade negotiations and that GATT should focus more on them.

The Uruguay Round (1986–1993) was a result of these worries. The Uruguay Round resulted in general tariff reductions for industrialized nations of an average of 40%, as Table 5.4 illustrates. In a number of industries, including steel, paper, pharmaceuticals, medical equipment, and construction equipment, tariffs were completely removed.

Table 5.4. Uruguay Round Tariff Reductions on Industrial Products by Selected Countries

	AVERAGE TARIFF RATE (PERCENT)	
Country	**Pre-Uruguay Round**	**Post-Uruguay Round**
Industrial countries		
Australia	20.1	12.2
Canada	9.0	4.8
European Union	5.7	3.6
Japan	3.9	1.7
United States	5.4	3.5
Developing countries		
Argentina	38.2	30.9
Brazil	40.7	27.0
Chile	34.9	24.9
Colombia	44.3	35.3
India	71.4	32.4

Source: Robert J. Carbaugh. International Economics, 13th Edition. South-Western Cengage Learning. https://wyamaka.wordpress.com/wp-content/uploads/2019/08/international-economics_30.pdf.

Furthermore, a number of countries decided to bind, or cap, a sizeable amount of their tariffs for the first time, forfeiting the chance of rate increases in the future above the bound levels. The Uruguay Round also succeeded in lowering or getting rid of nontariff barriers. For signatory countries, the government-procurement code opened up new markets. The Uruguay Round put a lot of effort into getting rid of agricultural product quotas and forcing countries to rely solely on tariffs. By 2005, a number of bilateral quotas in the clothing and textile industry had been phased out. The application of voluntary export restrictions was forbidden by the safeguards agreement.

5.6. WORLD TRADE ORGANIZATION

The Uruguay Round officially began on January 1, 1995, and GATT was renamed the World Trade Organization. GATT was transformed from a trade agreement into a membership organization that was in charge of overseeing how its members conducted trade relations. The foundation of the WTO continues to be the GATT obligations. But the WTO agreement mandates that its members abide by the many trade agreements that have been negotiated under GATT's auspices in recent decades, in addition to GATT regulations. With this initiative, many GATT members—particularly developing nations—who have profited from new agreements negotiated in the GATT since the 1970s will no longer be able to participate in them freely. Currently, 153 countries make up the WTO, representing more than 97% of global trade.

What distinguishes the WTO from the former GATT? The former was essentially a temporary agreement administered by an ad hoc secretariat, whereas the latter is a fully fledged international organization with its headquarters located in Geneva, Switzerland. Compared to the former GATT, the WTO has a far larger purview and is the first multilateral trading system to include investment, trade in services, and intellectual property. In addition, all members of the WTO oversee a single set of agreements, whereas only a small number of countries were allowed to join the GATT framework, which contained numerous side agreements (like subsidies and antidumping laws). Furthermore, the WTO undoes protectionist policies that were largely accepted by the previous GATT in a number of "sensitive" industries, such as textiles and agriculture. Since the WTO is not a government, each country is still free to determine what standards of labor, safety, health, and the environment are appropriate.

The Uruguay Round includes numerous agreements on government procurement and civil aircraft, which are administered by the WTO through a number of councils and committees. It is responsible for supervising the application of the tariff reductions and nontariff measure reductions reached during the negotiations. It also acts as a watchdog over global trade, routinely assessing each member's trade policies. Members of these bodies flag proposed or draft measures by other parties that may lead to trade disputes. Updating a variety of trade measures and statistics—which the WTO keeps track of in a sizable database—is another requirement for members.

According to the WTO, members "bind" their promises when they open their markets by removing trade barriers. As such, when they negotiate a reduction in their tariffs, they agree to bind the tariff reduction at a specific level that they have agreed upon with their trading partners, beyond which tariffs may not be raised. One of the main tenets of the WTO's functioning is the binding of tariffs, which offers a steady and predictable foundation for trade. A clause for the renegotiation of bound tariffs is present, though.

This clause permits a nation to raise a tariff with the consent of other nations, although doing so usually necessitates lowering other tariffs as payment. Nearly all tariff rates in developed nations and roughly 75% of rates in developing nations are currently bound.

5.6.1. Settling Trade Disputes

Enhancing the GATT's trade dispute resolution mechanism is one of the WTO's main goals. The previous GATT dispute resolution process had several drawbacks, including protracted delays, the capacity of accused parties to overturn panel decisions that disagreed with them, and insufficient enforcement. Each of these shortcomings is addressed by the WTO's dispute resolution process. It establishes deadlines for every phase of the procedure and ensures that a dispute panel will be formed as soon as a case is filed. The accused party can no longer overturn the panel's decision; however, it may be appealed to a recently established appellate body. The United States was the country that used the GATT dispute mechanism the most, so the dispute-settlement issue was particularly significant to this country.

A dispute involving the United States and several other nations was resolved in the WTO's first case. The United States government enacted a regulation in 1994 that placed restrictions on the quality of gasoline that could be sold in the country. Reducing pollution from gasoline emissions was the goal of this resolution, which was created by the Environmental Protection Agency (EPA) in accordance with the Clean Air Act. For domestic and imported gasolines, the regulation established distinct pollution standards. Brazil and Venezuela both contested it before the WTO. The WTO's principle of national treatment, which states that once imported gasoline is on the US market, it cannot receive treatment less favorable than domestically produced gasoline, was allegedly broken, according to Venezuelan officials. Venezuela contended that regulations and standards governing its gasoline were far stricter than those governing gasoline made in the US.

According to WTO regulations, the United States contended, this discrimination was acceptable. The US insisted that WTO regulations allowed for the preservation of clean air because it is a finite resource. It also asserted—and the WTO approved of this—that its pollution controls were required to safeguard public health. The primary requirement is that these clauses cannot be covert acts of protectionism.

Venezuela disputed that assertion. Venezuela was not challenging the United States' authority to enforce strict environmental regulations. It did state, however, that the US should have held both domestic and imported gasoline to the same strict standards if it wanted clean gasoline.

Venezuela and its gasoline producers were significantly impacted by the new regulations imposed by the United States. Venezuela argued that it would have been far more expensive to produce gasoline in accordance with the EPA's double standard than it would have been had it adhered to the same standards as American producers. Furthermore, since the US accounted for two thirds of Venezuela's gasoline exports, the US market was vitally important to the country.

Venezuela filed a complaint with the WTO after realizing that the US would not change the discriminatory provisions of the US gasoline regime. Brazil also voiced complaints regarding the biased nature of US regulations. A WTO panel considered the two complaints and concluded in 1996 that the US was unfairly discriminating against gasoline imports. A WTO appellate board upheld the panel's conclusions after the United States filed an appeal of this decision. By amending its environmental laws, the United States committed to stop its discriminatory practices against imported gasoline. Venezuela and Brazil expressed satisfaction with the United States' action.

5.6.2. Does the WTO Reduce National Sovereignty?

The United States benefits from WTO dispute settlement by having a set of rules to which it can hold other countries accountable for their trade actions. Do WTO rules or dispute settlements reduce the sovereignty of the United States or other countries? In order to protect American rights, the US government took great care when drafting the WTO dispute settlement procedures. However, detractors from both the left and the right, like Ralph Nader and Patrick Buchanan, argue that the United States has gravely compromised its sovereignty by joining the WTO.

Supporters point out that the United States cannot be forced to amend its laws by the decisions of a WTO dispute-settlement panel. If at all, how the United States reacts to a WTO panel's recommendations is entirely up to it. If a US measure is determined to be in violation of a WTO provision, the US may choose to amend the legislation on its own, compensate a foreign nation by lowering trade barriers by the same amount in another industry, or take no action and potentially face retaliation from the affected nation in the form of increased trade barriers to US exports. However, America is free to decide whether or not to carry out a panel's recommendation. Put simply, the United States is free to create and enforce its own laws and to set its own standards for labor, health, safety, and the environment at any level it deems suitable, without being restricted by WTO agreements. However, when trade restrictions have discriminatory or selective effects on foreign producers, the WTO forbids a country from using trade restrictions to enforce its own labor, environmental, health, and safety standards.

Retaliatory trade barriers are rarely used in the amicable resolution of trade disputes before the WTO. Retaliation, however, is occasionally employed. For instance, the United States prevailed in the 1999 WTO decision that the EU had unjustly imposed import restrictions on hormone-treated beef and bananas. Thus, the US government was given permission by the WTO to increase tariffs on European exports to the US. The conflict over bananas was settled after much effort, but the EU has adamantly refused to change its stance on hormone-treated beef. It doesn't seem likely that the EU will accept US hormone-treated beef.

Most economists concur that the real question the WTO raises is not whether it reduces national sovereignty but rather whether the particular obligations it places on a country are greater or less than the advantages that country gains from imposing the same requirements on others (as well as on itself). By this measure, the advantages of US membership in the WTO far outweigh the disadvantages. The agreement increases US access to international markets by giving the US the status of normal trade relations with all 153 members. It also lessens the power of other countries to set limits on who can access their markets. The US exporting companies and their employees would suffer if the US withdrew from the WTO because it would no longer be able to use the WTO mechanism to persuade other countries to lower their own trade barriers. To put it simply, most economists argue that the WTO imposes certain restrictions on private and public sector decision-making. But the financial advantages that residents receive from more open trade exceed the costs of these restrictions.

5.6.3. Should Retaliatory Tariffs Be Used for WTO Enforcement?

The WTO's tariff-retaliation-based dispute-settlement mechanism, according to critics, disadvantages smaller nations with less market power. Assume that the small nation of Ecuador is granted permission by the World Trade Organization to take revenge for the large nation of the United States' unfair trade practices. Ecuador's national welfare will decline under competitive conditions if it imposes a higher tariff on imports from the United States. Ecuador may therefore be hesitant to apply a retaliatory tariff, even if the WTO has given its approval.

Nonetheless, the matter is less evident for nations with sufficient population to influence global market prices. This is because a retaliatory tariff has the potential to boost the terms of trade and, consequently, the welfare of a large country. The demand for the product on international markets declines if the US imposes a tariff barrier. The United States can export less to cover the cost of imports due to the lower demand, which lowers the price of imports for the country. For the US, this means an improvement in the terms of trade (export to import price ratio). The welfare reductions brought about by decreased efficiency as a result of the higher tariff are at least partially offset by this improvement.

To put it simply, a small country cannot obtain favorable movements in its terms of trade, so even if it decides to impose retaliatory tariffs to teach a larger trading partner a lesson, it will find that initiating such behavior is relatively more costly than it would be for its larger trading partner. Small countries are therefore less likely to use retaliation to force compliance with WTO rulings due to their limited market power. Smaller countries benefit from special treatment when negotiating WTO tariff concessions without having to reciprocate, but the difficulties they encounter in retaliating are the opposite.

Some argue that changes should be made to the current dispute-settlement mechanism of the WTO. For instance, free traders argue that the WTO's goal is to lower trade barriers, so they are against retaliatory tariffs. Rather, they suggest that nations that violate laws ought to pay financial penalties. One benefit of a fine system is that it does not create an unfair advantage for smaller countries and does not add to trade protection. The issue with this system, though, is determining how to assign a monetary value to infractions. Furthermore, because the government of the offending nation would need to request special budgetary authorization, it might be challenging to collect fines. Furthermore, it would probably be argued that the WTO is undermining national sovereignty and that it is taxation without representation to accept that foreigners have the right to impose financial fines on a country like the United States.

One example of retaliatory tariffs approved by the WTO are US export subsidies. American exporters were able to deduct 15–30% of their export revenue from US taxes between 1984 and 2004 thanks to a tax benefit offered by the US tax code. The US tax benefit, according to the EU's 1998 complaint to the WTO, was an export subsidy that went against WTO agreements. The WTO ruled in 2003 that the tax benefit was unlawful as a result of this complaint, allowing the EU to immediately impose $4 billion in punitive duties on US exports to Europe. Inertia caused the US government to continue its export subsidy program even though the EU gave it time to do so. As a result, in 2004, Europe started to impose retaliatory tariffs. Toys, paper, jewelry, refrigerators, and other US exports were subject to a 5 percent penalty tariff. For every month that US lawmakers did not bring US tax laws into compliance with the WTO ruling, the penalty increased by 1%. With the imposition of this tariff, the United States was subject to WTO penalties for the first time for disobeying its decisions. Congress repealed the export subsidies under pressure from the tariffs, despite the resistance of some members to give up any control to the WTO.

5.6.4. Does the WTO Harm the Environment?

The relationship between trade and the environment and the role that the WTO should play in promoting environmentally friendly trade have become hot topics of discussion in recent years. The possibility that trade and the pursuit of trade liberalization could have negative environmental effects is a major worry of those who have brought this issue to the attention of the WTO. These worries were expressed, in fact, when thousands of environmentalists showed up at the 1999 World Trade Organization summit in Seattle. They objected to the WTO's impact on issues ranging from global warming to marine devastation. Let's examine the divergent opinions regarding the connections between trade and the environment.

5.6.4.1. Harming the Environment

There are two primary defenses of trade liberalization's potential negative environmental effects. First, a "race to the bottom" in environmental standards results from trade liberalization. Industry is likely to relocate production of highly polluting or environmentally intensive products to pollution havens in certain countries if those countries have lax environmental regulations. The movement of smokestack industries across borders to pollution havens may become even more alluring with trade liberalization. Trade liberalization may indirectly contribute to environmental degradation if these industries produce pollution that has negative effects on the environment worldwide. Even worse, nations may be forced to relax their environmental regulations as a result of trade-induced competitive pressure, which would promote the sale of goods that contribute to global pollution.

Poorer countries may prioritize the benefits of production (more jobs and income) over the benefits of environmental quality, which would explain why they would adopt less stringent environmental policies than industrialized nations. Furthermore, developing countries might be better equipped than industrialized countries that still bear the consequences of previous pollution to reduce pollutants through natural processes (e.g., the rainforests of Latin America can reduce carbon dioxide in the air). Therefore, developing countries can withstand increased emissions without seeing an increase in pollution. Furthermore, the ability of the environment to reduce pollution through natural processes will probably be less affected by the introduction of a polluting industry in a developing country with a sparse population than it would be in an industrialized country with a dense population.

Social preferences are the subject of environmentalists' second concern regarding trade's role. Some people or societies may simply find certain practices intolerable, in which case they oppose trade in goods that support those practices. Leghold traps are used to catch animals for their furs, and dolphins may be killed in the process of catching tuna. Environmentalists and the World Trade Organization (WTO) clashed during the 1990s when the WTO overturned a US ban on shrimp imports from nations that use turtle-trapping nets, following complaints from Thailand, Malaysia, India, and Pakistan. The United States was also found to have violated international trade law when it prohibited the importation of Mexican tuna that was caught in a manner that drowns dolphins. Indeed, detractors contended that the WTO's free-trade policies ran counter to the objective of environmental quality.

The majority of economists believe that trade liberalization increases growth and productivity, increases competition, which lowers inflation, and creates jobs. Because of the exorbitant tariffs on imported finished wood products, US companies find it difficult to compete in Japan. In Japan, domestic demand is restricted by high local prices. However, the demand for American lumber products might soar if tariffs were lifted, resulting in an increase in logging jobs in the US and more import-related jobs in Japan. However, the removal of tariffs is seen differently by environmentalists. Their main worry is that if prices were to drop due to a nontariff market, there would be so much demand that logging would increase in the world's surviving ancient forests. These forests, according to them, provide habitat for complex ecosystems that would otherwise not be able to survive intact in forests that have been divided into fragments. Much of Alaska, Canada, and the Siberian region of Russia still have these ancient forests. Environmentalists point out that in Pennsylvania, New York, and other Northeastern states, the forests have been so severely cleared that a great number of large predators have been driven off the land, leaving almost no natural control over the deer population. Consequently, there is an overpopulation of deer.

Proponents of trade liberalization, however, downplay the negative effects, contending that lower tariffs would improve forest conditions while also boosting global economies by lowering the cost of housing, paper, and other wood-based products. For instance, US timber officials claim they could travel to Indonesia and convince local businesses to use more environmentally friendly practices.

5.6.4.2. Improving the Environment

However, some contend that trade liberalization might actually enhance environmental quality as opposed to worsening it. First, trade promotes economic expansion, and rising affluence is a major contributing factor to societal demands for environmental cleanliness. People who are wealthier have a greater desire for and ability to pay for a cleaner environment. It is true that trade can make unsound environmental policies more expensive. Increased agricultural exports will result in increased pollution, for example, if farmers freely pollute rivers. However, the answer to this problem is not to stop exports, but rather to enact stricter environmental regulations that hold polluters accountable.

Second, as markets expand and consumer demand for cleaner products rises, trade and growth can spur the creation and adoption of environmentally friendly production methods. International businesses can help create a cleaner environment by implementing the newest, greenest technology possible throughout their whole operations. This helps businesses keep a positive reputation and is less expensive than employing differentiating technology depending on the production location.

While it is undeniable that increased competition in theory could lead to pollution havens, the empirical data indicates that this has not occurred on a large scale. The primary explanation for this is that relocation decisions are unlikely to be based primarily on environmental regulations because their costs are negligible in comparison to other costs. Even the most polluting industries only devote 2 percent or less of their revenue to reducing pollution, according to data from the US Census Bureau. Much more significant variables include the cost of labor, the cost of transportation, and the quality of the infrastructure. There is no proof that environmental standards are being lowered in a competitive manner, despite all the talk of a race to the bottom.

5.7. FROM DOHA TO HONG KONG: FAILED TRADE NEGOTIATIONS

Despite the WTO's best efforts, trade liberalization can be challenging to achieve. Let's investigate why.

WTO members began a new round of trade talks for the 2000s in Seattle, Washington, in 1999. The participants devised an agenda that covered labor and environmental issues, intellectual property rights, trade in agriculture, and assistance for less developed countries. Developing countries were adamant about preventing themselves from being taken advantage of in future trade negotiations, as they felt they had been in the past. Conflicts between industrialized and developing countries contributed significantly to the meetings' breakdown. Due to the rioting and disturbances that occurred in the streets during the meeting, it became known as "The Battle in Seattle."

Despite being disheartened by the outcome of the Seattle meeting, advocates of trade liberalization persisted in calling for additional trade negotiations. The Doha Round was the outcome, and it was introduced in Doha, Qatar. The Doha Round was marketed as a way to reduce trade-distorting subsidies on farm goods, lower manufacturing tariffs imposed by developing nations, lower tariffs on textile and apparel products that were particularly important to developing nations, increase trade in services, and negotiate international regulations in four new areas: competition, investment, government procurement, and trade facilitation.

Since most WTO members are medium- to low-income developing nations, this round was officially dubbed the "Doha development agenda." These countries face the highest trade barriers and the greatest challenges in fulfilling their current WTO obligations. Liberalizing the last remaining trade barriers in the US, Japan, and Europe as well as reforming domestic trade barriers would be extremely beneficial to the developing nations. Despite having lofty goals, the Doha Round didn't accomplish much. Major portions of the agenda were rejected by countries right from the start. For instance, the EU denied having ever made a pledge to eliminate export subsidies. Many developing nations, led by India, denied ever having agreed to participate in discussions on new intellectual property and competition laws. Other developing nations were less interested in negotiating the current trade round and more interested in airing their grievances from previous ones. Many wealthy nations demonstrated little desire to make concessions. For instance, Japan seemed satisfied to merely object to any reduction in rice tariffs. Posturing of this kind led to the missing of self-imposed deadlines and the postponement of all difficult political decisions, including opening economies to trade. The goal of the December 2005 meetings in Hong Kong was for the trade ministers to conclude the Doha Round. However, the only agreement that could be signed was a significantly weaker one that only contained a promise to end farm subsidies by 2013 and small tariff reductions. All of this was well short of the initial goals set forth in the Doha Round of trade talks. Skeptics pointed out that, should the Doha negotiations falter, it would be wise to reevaluate the scope of these massive multilateral rounds and, as a last resort, turn to bilateral trade agreements between a relatively small numbers of nations.

Members of the WTO (GATT) have been able to negotiate both easy and many difficult issues over the course of the last 50 years. But at the time of the Doha Round, only the most challenging issues remained, like political power-wielding farmers receiving subsidies. These outstanding concerns might prove to be too challenging to resolve through negotiation. The trade liberalization provisions of earlier rounds will still apply in the event that the Doha Round fails, and by historical standards, trade is remarkably open.

5.8. TRADE PROMOTION AUTHORITY (FAST-TRACK AUTHORITY)

Achieving such agreements would be difficult, if not impossible, if congressional amendments were allowed for international trade agreements. A barrage of congressional amendments would soon alter the terms that the president had negotiated, much to the chagrin of the trading partner or partners who had accepted the original terms. Fast-track authority, another name for the trade promotion mechanism, was created in 1974 to avert this situation. This clause requires the president to formally inform Congress of his or her intention to start trade talks with a foreign nation. Congress has 60 legislative days from the date of this notification to approve or reject "fast-track" authority. The president has a set amount of time to finish the trade negotiations if fast-track authority is approved; extensions of this time frame are allowed with congressional approval. The conclusion of the negotiations is only subject to a simple up-or-down vote (without amendment) in each of the two houses of Congress within 90 legislative days of the agreement being made. In exchange, the president consents to actively consult with the business community and Congress during the trade agreement's negotiation. Major trade agreements like the North American Free Trade Agreement of 1993 and the Uruguay Round Agreements Act of 1994 were negotiated and implemented in large part thanks to fast-track authority. The majority of analysts argue that the president will need expedited authority in order to implement future trade agreements. Renewing fasttrack authority has encountered strong resistance, partly because of congressional apprehensions about giving the president excessive discretionary power and differences regarding the objectives of U.S.S. trade discussions. Environmentalists and labor unions in particular have worked to guarantee that trade agreements will take their concerns into account. They contend that American producers are at a competitive disadvantage due to the country's strict labor and environmental laws, and that greater trade with nations with less stringent regulations may put pressure on the US to slash its own standards. Should other nations have comparable labor and environmental standards if they are to engage in trade with the United States? Generally speaking, proponents of fast-track authority have maintained that while labor and environmental standards are significant, they have no place in a trade agreement. Rather, these matters ought to be discussed in secondary agreements that go hand in hand with trade agreements. Labor leaders and environmentalists, on the other hand, argue that previous secondary agreements have not improved the quality of life overseas because they have not included enforcement provisions.

5.9. INDUSTRIAL POLICY

The Industrial Revolution, which started in Europe and eventually extended to every continent, is considered one of the greatest human endeavors in history. The industrial revolution brought about rapid mass production. Through financial incentives and policy support, the industrialized states encouraged the export of manufactured goods. States and governments were compelled to support innovation as a result of the competitive industrialization that occurred first in various regions of Europe and then in other parts of the world. Educational institutions were established, and science and technology were encouraged. These advancements made it easier for them to provide the nation with trained labor and infrastructure. They were able to accumulate enormous wealth and make technological advancements thanks to the Industrial Revolution, which also helped them become the world's first world nations or industrially advanced economies.

5.9.1. Industrial Policy Resolutions

Indian raw materials were mostly exported to England during the colonial era, where they were processed in factories and mills and then sold back to India as finished goods. India inherited inefficient industries that were not creating any exportable surplus when the British left. Following independence, the government saw a pressing need to alter the nation's industrial structure. Jawaharlal Nehru, India's first prime minister, believed that industrialization was the key to the country's success and recognized the fundamental issues with the country's industrial sector. Although his strategy for achieving economic self-sufficiency involved large-scale industrialization rather than village industries, Nehru shared the view that India should be economically self-sufficient. In India, there has long been agreement on the role of the state in maintaining stable macroeconomic policies and providing infrastructure. Because of the policy initiatives implemented during the initial planning years, especially the second and third five-year plans, India now has a robust and diverse industrial base and is a significant global industrial power. However, South Korea, Thailand, and China have highly developed manufacturing capacities.

The deliberate state effort to promote economic transformation is known as industrial policy, i.e., the change in activities from lower to higher productivity. Any form of targeted government intervention or policy that seeks to restructure the production structure in favor of industries thought to present the best opportunities for economic growth is referred to as industrial policy. Thus, the government's standards and metrics for assessing the manufacturing sector's advancement—which eventually contributes to the nation's economic growth and development—are known as Industrial Policy. It is a vision document that gives the government instructions on how to accomplish specific goals ahead of schedule.

An industrial policy has its pre-decided aims and objective that are to be achieved in the given time frame. Following can be some of the common objectives of an Industrial Policy;

- To maintain steady growth in productivity
- To create more employment opportunities
- Utilize the available human resources effectively
- To accelerate GDP growth rate

5.9.1.1. Industrial Policy Resolution, 1948

In a resolution dated April 6, 1948, the Indian government outlined the industrial policy it intended to pursue. The Resolution placed a strong emphasis on how crucial it is to the economy to maintain both a steady rise in production and its fair distribution. It made clear that the government needed to become more actively involved in the growth of the industrial sector. It established the Central Government's monopoly on railroad transportation, atomic energy, and weapons and ammunition. The creation of new businesses in the six fundamental industries would be the sole responsibility of the State. The state may take such action if it determines that obtaining private industry's cooperation is essential for the good of the country. The remainder of the industrial sector was left to the hands of private industry, with the understanding that the state would gradually become involved as well. Some of the important take away points this resolution were as follows;

- **Mixed Economy:** In order to establish the groundwork for a mixed economy, the Industrial Policy Resolution of 1948 was India's first significant policy after independence. Private and public businesses would work together in a mixed economy to quicken the rate of industrial development. The coexistence of the public and private sectors is implied. The government will decide how much to charge, how to distribute resources, and how to allocate them in the public sector. The public sector includes companies like Tata Steel, Hero Motors, and Hindustan Unilever. For the private sector, on the other hand, all economic decisions will be made by the market. The private sector includes companies like Hinduja, Tata, and Birla.
- **Priority to Small Scale and Cottage Industries:** Small scale and cottage industries were given the importance due to their wide spread, labor intensive nature and low capital and low skill requirements.
- **Restrictions on Foreign Investments:** The government restricted foreign investments to protect domestic industries from global competition.
- Industries were divided into 4 categories:
  - o **State Monopolies:** Exclusive monopoly of central government in arms and ammunitions, production of atomic energy and management of railways. According to Cambridge Dictionary, "State monopoly is a situation wherein an organization owned by a government supplies of all particular product or service, with no competitors." For example, LIC, Air India and BSNL used to be state monopoly in India.
  - o New undertaking undertaken only by state (coal, iron and steel, aircraft manufacturing,

ship building, telegraph, telephone etc.).

- o Industries to be regulated by the government (Industries of basic importance): The entire secondary sector was by and large regulated by the government.
- o Remaining sectors were open to private enterprise, individuals and cooperatives. Although, there was not much important left behind for the private sector to perform outstandingly well.

Early on after independence, the government established policies that promoted industrialization by limiting the role of the private sector and intervening on behalf of the public sector. The private sector lacked the means and the will to take on nation-building projects, which was the reason. In contrast to the government, the private sector lacked the ability to raise money for large-scale projects anywhere. India needed to grow its basic and heavy industries—heavy engineering, power generation, and iron and steel, to mention a few. The 1948 Industrial Policy Resolution, a historically significant policy declaration designating India as a mixed economy, was a positive step toward the development of industries through state involvement. It demonstrated the socialist leanings of the Indian government. While it granted certain asset ownership rights, it also allowed the private sector some leeway to engage in the 1948–1956 industrialization process.

5.9.1.2. Industrial Policy Resolution, 1956

The 1948 Industrial Policy Resolution and the 1956 Industrial Policy Resolution came after each other. The goal was to achieve a socialist pattern of society by quickening the pace of industrialization and economic growth. It was referred to as "The Bible of State Capitalism" or the "Economic Constitution of India.." In 1956, there was a lack of capital and an inadequate foundation for entrepreneurship. Therefore, the State's role to take on a predominant and direct responsibility for industrial development was given primacy by the 1956 Industrial Policy Resolution. The 1956 Policy placed a strong emphasis on the need to develop a sizable and expanding cooperative sector, increase the size of the public sector, support the division of ownership and management in private enterprises, and, most importantly, stop the emergence of private monopolies.

The Mahalanobis Model of growth influenced the contents of the Industrial Policy Resolution 1951. According to this model, industrial investment patterns should change to focus more on developing the domestic consumer goods sector. This necessitated spending money to increase production capacity in heavy industries or capital goods, which would have resulted in an economy with a longer growth trajectory. Up until June 1991, it offered the fundamental framework for the government's industrial policy.

The Industrial Policy Resolution – 1956 classified industries into three categories;

a. **Schedule A:** The first category comprised 17 industries (included in Schedule A of the Resolution). These industries were exclusively under the domain of the Government. These included inter alia, railways, air transport, arms and ammunition, iron and steel and atomic energy.

b. **Schedule B:** The second category comprised 12 industries (included in Schedule B of the Resolution). These industries were envisaged to be progressively State owned but private sector was expected to supplement the efforts of the State.

c. **Third Category:** The third category contained all the remaining industries and it was expected that private sector would initiate development of these industries. The industries would remain open for the State as well.

The Resolution did not so much expand the public sector's purview as it solidified its dominance over the majority of important economic sectors. A number of public sector businesses expanded too quickly. According to the plans developed under the Five Year Plans, it was intended that the State would support and encourage the growth of these industries in the private sector. Adequate infrastructure and suitable fiscal measures would be guaranteed. The Resolution was sufficiently adaptable to permit the necessary alterations and modifications in the interest of the country, even though the industries were divided into distinct categories. The domestic industry was shielded from international competition by import quotas, import licensing, and other import trade barriers in accordance with the Theory of Infant Industry Argument. But because this Resolution drastically curtailed the potential for the private sector to grow, the private sector sharply criticized the IPR 1956. An important policy statement that served as the foundation for later policy announcements was the IPR, 1956.

5.9.1.3. Industrial Policy Statement, 1977

The significance of small-scale, cottage, and tiny industries, as well as decentralization, were emphasized in the 1977 Industrial Policy Statement. This policy, which was an expansion of the 1956 policy, prioritized home-based businesses and small-scale industries in an effort to disperse economic power throughout India. Its important focus was on;

- Employment to the poor and reduction in the concentration of wealth.
- Decentralization of industries
- Priority to small scale Industries
- Created a new unit called "Tiny Unit"
- Imposed restrictions on Multinational Companies (MNC)

This statement placed a strong emphasis on the decentralization of the industrial sector, giving small, cottage, and tiny businesses a bigger voice. It also made it possible for the agricultural and industrial sectors to work closely together. Power transmission and generation were given top priority. It increased the number of goods designated for small-scale industry-only production from 180 to over 500. A tiny unit was created for the first time in the small scale sector.

A tiny unit is described as one that has invested up to Rs. 0 point 1 million in machinery and equipment and is located in a town or village with fewer than 50,000 residents (as of the 1971 census). For the large-scale sector, basic goods, capital goods, high-tech industries crucial to the growth of small- and large-scale agriculture sectors were clearly defined.

Additionally, it was mentioned that foreign businesses would be treated equally with Indian businesses if they diluted their foreign equity by up to 40% in accordance with the Foreign Exchange Regulation Act (FERA) of 1973. Only highly export-oriented industries or fields involving advanced technology were permitted to have foreign companies that were fully owned. Companies were free to repatriate capital and remit profits, dividends, royalties, and other income for all authorized foreign investments. Furthermore, it was decided not to grant new licenses for the establishment of new industrial units within specific boundaries of large metropolitan cities (more than 1 million population) and urban areas (more than 0.5 million population) in order to ensure balanced regional development.

5.9.1.4. Industrial Policy Statement, 1980

The 1980 Industrial Policy Statement prioritized industry modernization, technological advancement, and fostering domestic market competition. Some of the socio-economic objectives spelt out in the Statement were as follows;

i. optimum utilization of installed capacity,
ii. higher productivity,
iii. higher employment levels,
iv. removal of regional disparities,
v. strengthening of agricultural base,
vi. promotion of export oriented industries and
vii. consumer protection against high prices and poor quality.

Public sector undertakings (PSUs) were to be made more efficient through the development of management cadres in the functional areas of operations, finance, marketing, and information systems. Up to 5% annual automatic capacity expansion was permitted, with the exception of the core sector and sectors with long-term export potential. Industrial units engaged in processes and technologies aimed at optimizing energy utilization and exploring alternative energy sources were bestowed with exclusive incentives.

5.9.2. New Industrial Policy, 1991

Different methods were used in India to enforce regulatory mechanisms. For example, industrial licensing required all entrepreneurs to obtain permission from government officials before opening a business, closing one, or determining the maximum quantity of goods that could be produced. Private enterprise was prohibited in numerous industries. Certain products were limited to production in small-scale industries, and there were restrictions on the distribution and setting of prices for specific industrial products. India experienced a Balance of Payment (BOP) crisis, double-digit inflation, slow GDP growth, and a high debt load in the late 1980s and early 1990s. The government's finances were unstable and in danger of collapsing. Experts offered a number of arguments, including high tax rates, industrial licensing, the MRTP Act, and FERA.

The International Monetary Fund (IMF) strongly recommended that we implement the economic reforms known as the New Industrial Policy, 1991, or LPG reforms. Regarding the policies pertaining to the following areas, the government made the decision to launch a number of initiatives. Public sector policy, foreign technology agreements, foreign investment, industrial licensing, and the MRTP Act. Many of these limitations were lifted by the reform measures that were implemented in and after 1991. Almost all product categories—including alcohol, cigarettes, industrial explosives, hazardous chemicals, electronics, aerospace, and pharmaceuticals—were exempt from the elimination of industrial licensing. The only sectors currently kept for the public sector are those involved in the production of atomic energy and a few essential railway transportation operations. Nowadays, a lot of the products made by small-scale businesses are underutilized. The market has been permitted to set prices in the majority of industries. Therefore, the New Industrial Policy, 1991 had the following important features;

i. Creation of a positive business environment by simplifying procedures, reducing documentation and offering fiscal incentives.
ii. Allowing foreign investment by lowering controls and regulations.
iii. Privatization of public sector enterprises, particularly sick units.
iv. Exit policy for the sick units in private sector for a smooth exit without affecting welfare of labor.
v. Financial sector reforms to deregulate interest rates, improve credit availability and to create a conducive environment for banking and finance sector.
vi. Reducing tariff and non-tariff barriers on imports and simplifying procedure for import of goods and services.
vii. Industry friendly approach of the government to promote business.
viii. Devaluation of Indian rupee by 21% and convertibility of Indian rupee on current account.

The New Industrial Policy, 1991 had the main objective of providing facilities to market forces and to increase efficiency.

5.9.2.1. L – Liberalization

It alludes to a lessening of governmental authority. There are fewer different kinds of government rules and restrictions on enterprises and other economic activity in the nation. It is said that the government is more liberal because it places far fewer restrictions than it did previously. All industries were exempt from the repeal of industrial licensing. The MRTP Act was proposed as a monopoly check. In 1991, the MRTP Act was loosened. The Competition Act of 2002, which encouraged industry expansion, mergers and acquisitions, and the adoption of best practices in business, superseded the MRTP Act.

5.9.2.2. P – Privatization

It alludes to the expansion of the private sector's influence and role. The removal of the government's initial reserve from certain sectors. In order to improve management, make more effective use of resources, and gain competitiveness, this encouraged the private sector to engage in a variety of economic activities.

5.9.2.3. G – Globalization

It alludes to India's economic integration with the global economy. The goal of globalization was to integrate the Indian economy into the world's transportation, communication, and trade networks. Trade in products and services, capital, and technology is expanding between nations. Most places on Earth are closer together. One possible approach to achieve this would be to eliminate various types of obstacles, including those related to the import and export of goods and services, labor and capital machinery, and manpower. It gave Indian businesses the chance to investigate markets throughout the globe. But this also meant that Indian markets that were officially shielded from international competition were made available to foreign corporations. They're able to sell their products and services now.

The government implemented a number of measures regarding the policies pertaining to the following areas: public sector policy, foreign technology agreements, foreign investment, industrial licensing, and the MRTP Act in an effort to achieve the goals of economic reforms.

5.9.2.4. Industrial Licensing

Industrial licensing was a method of establishing an industry that required a government license that required a difficult process, a lot of paperwork, and dishonest behavior. It hindered the nation's industrialization by discouraging business owners from opening industrial facilities. The Industries (Development and Regulation) Act, 1951 governs industrial licensing. The industries that would be reserved for development in the public sector, those that would be allowed for development through private enterprise with or without State participation, and those in which investment initiatives would typically come from private entrepreneurs were all identified by the Industrial Policy Resolution of 1956. Formerly, the License Raj, also known as the Permit Raj, was an oppressive law that discouraged industrial activity in India. It had brought about a gloomy business climate throughout the nation.

Under the general heading of economic reforms, industrial licensing was eliminated for all industries, with the exception of those listed, regardless of investment levels. In other words, anyone can open an industrial facility without a license—barring a few circumstances. The aforementioned industries will remain subject to mandatory licensing due to various reasons such as security and strategic considerations, social concerns, safety-related issues, pressing environmental concerns, production of hazardous goods, and luxury goods. The goal of the license exemption was to assist numerous vibrant small and medium-sized business owners who have been unduly hindered by the licensing process. The Indian economy as a whole will gain from becoming more efficient, competitive, and modern, and it will finally establish itself as a legitimate member of the global industrial revolution.

5.9.2.5. Foreign Investment

An economy can benefit from foreign investments in a number of ways, such as technology transfer, marketing know-how, the introduction of contemporary management practices, and new avenues for export promotion. The government had used a variety of controls, regulations, tariffs, and non-tariff barriers to limit the entry of foreign capital prior to the LPG reforms, which were started in 1991. Opportunities for boosting foreign investments in India after 1991 were a positive step toward releasing Indian industry from official controls. This opened up the Indian industry to foreign investment as well as cutting-edge technologies, expert knowledge, and the ability to realize its full potential for swift industrial growth.

It has been determined to approve direct foreign investment up to 51% foreign equity in high priority industries that demand significant investments and cutting edge technology in order to attract foreign investment in these sectors. Generally referred to as the "Appendix I industries," these sectors of the economy were already granted FERA companies discretionary investment rights. In order to promote Indian product exports, a thorough investigation of global markets must be conducted, which can only be done through extensive and extremely skilled marketing efforts. To the extent that India has not yet developed this kind of expertise.

Interacting with some of the biggest global manufacturing and marketing companies in the world is necessary to draw in significant investment and gain access to cutting edge technology. FERA was replaced with the Foreign Exchange Management Act (FEMA), which was another significant policy change. In contrast to FERA, the FEMA has less regulations. At the moment, the RBI solely oversees the nation's foreign exchange. It indicates that spending on foreign exchange is unrestricted. This has promoted the import of cutting-edge machinery and technologies, which will eventually help India's domestic industries.

5.9.2.6. Foreign Technology Agreements

Encouraging an industrial environment where acquiring technological capability is prioritized is highly necessary. The relationship between technology suppliers and users needs to be ongoing in the rapidly evolving field of technology. Achieving a relationship of this kind becomes challenging when the approval process involves needless government intervention on an individual basis, leading to persistent delays and creating uncertainty. The Indian businessman has now reached adulthood and is no longer in need of obtaining the same formal approvals for his business technology partnerships with overseas technology providers. If Indian industry is to function in such a regulatory environment, it will be extremely difficult for it to compete globally.

In order to infuse Indian industry with the appropriate degree of technological dynamism, the government automatically approves technology agreements pertaining to high priority industries that fall within predetermined bounds. Indian businesses are free to use their own commercial judgment when negotiating technology transfer terms with their international competitors. This measure is encouraging Indian industry to develop indigenous competence for the effective absorption of foreign technology by giving them predictability and independence of action. Our industry is under greater pressure to invest in research and development than it has in the past due to increased competition.

5.9.2.7. Public Sector Policy

A fundamental component of our development philosophy has been the public sector. Public ownership and control over vital economic sectors has been crucial in averting the concentration of economic power while we work toward our development goals. It guarantees that planned development serves the common good and lessens regional disparities. A strategic role in economic development was granted to the public sector by the Industrial Policy Resolution of 1956. Following independence, significant investments were made to create a public sector that now dominates the economy. Mature public enterprises that have successfully increased production, opened up new technological avenues, and accumulated a reserve of technical competence in multiple areas now control key sectors of the economy.

Following the initial success of the public sector's entry into previously untapped industrial and technological domains, several issues have started to surface in numerous public enterprises. Inadequate productivity growth, subpar project management, overstaffing, a lack of ongoing technological advancement, and a lack of focus on research and development as well as human resource development are all considered serious issues. Furthermore, public businesses have demonstrated an extremely low rate of return on capital. This has made it more difficult for them to reinvent themselves through fresh investments and technological advancements. As a result, instead of serving the government as an asset, many public enterprises now serve as a burden.

The process of moving ownership rights from the public sector to the private sector is known as privatization or disinvestment of public sector enterprises (PSEs). Disinvestment can be accomplished through a planned sale to a private business or an equity sale on the stock market. Keynes is credited with popularizing the term "disinvestment." Privatization is the process by which a government-owned business is sold to a private entity and the government gives the buyer complete ownership control. Disinvestment can take two forms: minority disinvestment, in which the government retains less influence over decision-making when its share of the PSE falls below 50%, or majority disinvestment, in which it keeps more than 50% of the company.

The Central Public Sector Enterprises (CPSEs) in India began their disinvestment process in 1991 when the government implemented a new economic policy. Disinvestment was primarily initiated by selling a minority stake in CPSEs, and it has changed significantly over time as a result of shifting market dynamics. This is carried out on the advice of organizations like the GV Ramakrishna Disinvestment Commission and the Rangarajan Committee in order to close the resource gap. A Disinvestment Commission was established by the Indian government in 1996 and placed under the Ministry of Industries. The commission's task was to evaluate the viability of different PSEs and advise the government on their disinvestment. Numerous significant PSEs were either privatized or disinvested, including Bharat Aluminum Corporation Limited, Videsh Sanchar Nagar Limited, Lodhi Hotel, Computer Maintenance Company, Hindustan Zinc, and many others. The entire disinvestment process in India is managed by the Department of Investment and Public Asset Management (DIPAM), which is part of the Ministry of Finance, Government of India. Disinvestment made significant money available to the government for welfare programs and the funding of infrastructure development projects. Nevertheless, a portion of the money has also been used to pay down the nation's public debt.

The government sets a goal for PSE disinvestment each year. Furthermore, rather than being used for the growth of PSEs and the construction of the nation's social infrastructure, the proceeds from disinvestment are utilized to make up for the government's lack of revenue.

From its cautious beginnings in fiscal 1991–1992, when small stakes in specific CPSEs were divested to financial institutions alone, the Disinvestment program has come a long way. As of January 31, 2018, the market capitalization of companies listed on the BSE and NSE was made up of 10.93% and 11.04%, respectively, of CPSEs. Over time, government disinvestment strategies have evolved and been shaped by political pressures, financial limitations, market dynamics, and the ideology of the center-right ruling party. The government has taken several short cuts in the disinvestment process in its rush to raise money through privatization and disinvestment. It has jeopardized the fundamental goals of the disinvestment program as well as the long-term interests of PSUs that are profitable.

Additionally, there are drawbacks to economic reforms. Reforms result in an excessive reliance on the market, which drives up prices unnecessarily, allocates resources in an unfavorable way, and creates regional disparities in economic growth.

Funds for social welfare, such as health, education, and social security benefits, are available. might go down. Economic reforms make Indian businesses, especially those in small-scale industries, more vulnerable to international competition, which ultimately makes them more difficult to survive over the long term. From the perspective of both national security and political stability, it may be dangerous for multinational corporations to meddle in politics or policies excessively. Reforms may also make the government more inclined to sell profitable public sector companies. Both India and other nations have benefited and suffered from the liberalization and privatization policies that have accompanied the globalization process. According to some academics, globalization presents opportunities for developing countries' large industries to grow into significant players in the international arena, as well as for easier access to global markets and advanced technology. Conversely, detractors contend that industrialized nations use globalization as a tactic to open up new markets abroad. They claim that it has jeopardized the identity and well-being of citizens of developing nations. It has also been noted that the globalization driven by markets has increased the economic divide between different countries and groups of people.

5.10. Industrial Policies of the United States

In addition to passing laws meant to create equitable trading conditions for all parties involved in international trade, the US has put in place industrial policies aimed at boosting home producers' competitiveness. These policies entail the allocation of government funds to particular industries that are deemed crucial for future economic expansion. Low interest loans, loan guarantees, and tax incentives are a few of the strategies used to allocate resources.

Nowadays, practically every country has some industrial policies in place. Even though industrial policies are typically linked to formal, explicit government initiatives (like those in France and Japan) to promote the growth of particular industries (like electronics or steel), other historically free-enterprise countries (like Germany and the US) also have less formal, implicit industrial policies.

What has been the US government's approach to industrial policy? In light of the social, environmental, and safety limitations placed by contemporary society, the US government has made an effort to create a business-friendly environment. The US government has typically placed more emphasis on macroeconomic policies (such as fiscal and monetary policies) that aim to achieve goals like economic stability, growth, and the equitable distribution of the gross domestic product rather than developing a coordinated industrial policy to impact specific industries.

Nonetheless, there is no denying that the US government employs a variety of techniques, known in other countries as "industrial policies," to influence the composition of the economy. Among these policies, agricultural policy stands out the most. When a farmer in agriculture makes a significant innovation, other farmers may copy them and reap the rewards without taking on the same risks. In order to address this issue, the US government is conducting research on agricultural methods and distributing this knowledge to farmers via its agricultural extension service. It is also supporting large-scale initiatives like irrigation systems. In addition, the US government has supported the energy, shipbuilding, and shipping sectors, mostly for reasons related to national security.

Defense spending in the US is frequently mentioned in relation to industrial policy. It makes sense that the United States leads the world in military goods production given that it is the market for these products. American military equipment spending helps domestic producers reach significant economies of scale. Defense spending in the US has benefited civilian industries, particularly electronics, computers, and commercial aircraft. US businesses can apply their expertise gained from military research and development elsewhere.

The US government has helped financially struggling industries in manufacturing. For instance, the government bailed out Chrysler Corporation in the auto industry in 1979 and 1980 by guaranteeing a $1.05 billion loan. In order to lessen the impact of import competition, it also negotiated voluntary export restrictions on automobiles with the Japanese in the 1980s. Additionally, the steel and textile sectors have benefited greatly from trade protection.

5.10.1. Export Promotion and Financing

Export promotion is one more component of US industrial policy. The US government organizes trade missions to introduce new exporters to overseas markets and provides technical support and marketing information to exporters. Additionally, the government encourages exports by funding US product displays at foreign trade shows and setting up foreign trade hubs where US companies can display and sell machinery and equipment.

By enabling its manufacturers to establish export trade associations to facilitate the marketing of US goods overseas, the US also promotes exports. Furthermore, US financial institutions and manufacturers may pool their resources to form joint export trading companies, which they can use to either export their own goods or serve as an export intermediary for other producers. Several companies have established export trading companies, including General Motors, Sears, Rockwell, General Electric, and Control Data.

Furthermore, the US gives its producers export subsidies in the form of affordable loans. The US Export-Import Bank and the Commodity Credit Corporation are responsible for maintaining competitive credit terms for US exporters. The US government established the Export-Import Bank (Eximbank) as an independent organization to promote US companies' exports. The Eximbank provides the following:

- Guarantees of working capital loans for US exporters to cover pre-export costs
- Export credit insurance that protects US exporters or their lenders against commercial or political risks of nonpayment by foreign buyers
- Guarantees of commercial loans to creditworthy foreign buyers of US goods and services
- Direct loans to these foreign buyers when private financing is unavailable
- Special programs to promote US exports of environmentally beneficial goods and services
- Asset-based financing for large commercial aircraft and other appropriate exports
- Project financing to support US exports to international infrastructure projects

EXIM bank has occasionally come under fire for its competitive interest rates when financing exports because a portion of its funding is borrowed from the US Treasury. Some argue that US tax money shouldn't be used to support exports to other nations at interest rates that are less expensive than those offered by private lenders. It is true that tax funds skew trade and redistribute income in favor of exporters to this extent.

Examples of direct loans and loan guarantees provided by EXIM bank are shown in Table 5.5. Aircraft, telecommunications, power-generating equipment, and energy developments have all benefited greatly from EXIM bank credit. Companies like Boeing, McDonnell Douglas, and Westinghouse have reaped significant advantages from these initiatives.

Table 5.5. Examples of Loans Provided by EXIM Bank of the United States (in Millions of Dollars)

Foreign Borrower/U.S. Exporter	Purpose	Loan or Loan Guarantee
Banco Santander Noroeste of Brazil/General Electric	Locomotives	87.7
Government of Bulgaria/Westinghouse	Instruments	81.8
Air China/Boeing	Aircraft	69.8
Government of Croatia/Bechtel International	Highway construction	228.7
Government of Ghana/Wanan International	Electrical equipment	21.1
Government of Indonesia/IBM	Computer hardware	20.2
Japan Airlines/Boeing	Aircraft	212.3
Fevisa Industrial of Mexico/Pennsylvania Crusher Inc.	Glass manufacturing equipment	17.7
Delta Communications of Mexico/Motorola	Communications equipment	11.5

Source: Robert J. Carbaugh. International Economics, 13th Edition. South-Western Cengage Learning. https://wyamaka.wordpress.com/wp-content/uploads/2019/08/international-economics_30.pdf.

The Commodity Credit Corporation (CCC), a government-owned organization run by the US Department of Agriculture, offers officially backed loans for US exports. Financing for export credit is made available by the CCC for qualified agricultural commodities. Generally speaking, the CCC charges interest at a rate that is marginally lower than what private financial institutions are currently charging.

5.11. INDUSTRIAL POLICIES OF JAPAN

While explicit industrial policies have not traditionally been used in the US to support particular industries, they have been in other countries. Examine the situation in Japan. Japan has emerged as a global leader in technology following World War II. Japan's exports in the 1950s were mostly made up of textiles and other low-tech goods. By the 1960s and 1970s, capital-intensive goods like steel, ships, and automobiles constituted the majority of its exports. Japan emerged as a significant global rival in the 1980s and 90s for high-tech products like semiconductors and optical fibers. Proponents of industrial policy claim that the Japanese economy has transitioned from low-tech to heavy industry to high-tech thanks in part to government support for emerging industries.

They contend that RandD subsidies, import barriers, and similar measures encouraged the growth of Japanese industry. Clearly, the Japanese government supported the automobile and machine tool industries in the 1960s, the shipbuilding and steel industries in the 1950s, and the high-tech industries starting in the early 1970s. There have been two distinct phases to Japanese industrial policy: the first began in the 1950s and ended in the early 1970s, when the Japanese government took firm control over the country's resources and the path of economic growth. The government's industrial policy has been more subdued and restrained since the middle of the 1970s. The Ministry of Economy, Trade and Industry (METI) was established by the Japanese government to carry out its industrial policies in the manufacturing sector. This ministry targets particular industries for support in an effort to ease the flow of funds into high-tech industries. METI gathers expert advice on the best course of action from prominent businesses, labor unions, banks, and academic institutions.

The next phase of industrial policy is to raise investment, production, and domestic RandD. Targeted industries have benefited from favorable tax treatment, trade protection, foreign exchange allotments, R&D subsidies, loans with interest rates below market rates, loans that need only be repaid when a business starts turning a profit, and cooperative government-industry research projects aimed at creating innovative technologies.

The Japanese semiconductor, machine-tool, fiber-optic, and telecommunications equipment industries are unlikely to be as competitive without government support. However, as demonstrated by the situations involving computers, aluminum, and petrochemicals, not all Japanese industrial policies have been effective. Long stretches of excess capacity have been observed in industries like steel and shipbuilding, where Japan is competitive in international markets. Furthermore, the Japanese government did not focus its greatest efforts on the TV, stereo, or VCR industries—some of Japan's greatest exports. It's unclear how much industrial policy has helped Japan's economy grow since World War II. High domestic savings rates, educated and driven workforces, positive labor-management relations, labor migration from low-productivity industries (like agriculture) to high-productivity manufacturing, risk-taking entrepreneurs, and similar factors have all benefited Japan. These elements have accelerated Japan's transition from a low-tech to a high-tech country. How quickly this change would have happened in the absence of an industrial policy is up for debate. Japan has the most visible industrial policy among developed countries, but its significance for the country's achievements shouldn't be overstated.

ROLE MODEL

FRIEDRICH LIST

Daniel Friedrich List (6 August 1789 – 30 November 1846) was a German economist and political theorist who developed the nationalist theory of political economy in both Europe and the United States. He was a forefather of the German historical school of economics and argued for the Zollverein (a pan-German customs union) from a nationalist standpoint. He advocated raising tariffs on imported goods while supporting free trade of domestic goods and stated the cost of a tariff should be seen as an investment in a nation's future productivity.

List was a political liberal who collaborated with Karl von Rotteck and Carl Theodor Welcker on the Rotteck-Welckersches Staatslexikon [de], an encyclopedia of political science that advocated constitutional liberalism and which influenced the Vormärz. At the time in Europe, liberal and nationalist ideas were almost inseparably linked, and political liberalism was not yet attached to what was later considered "economic liberalism." Emmanuel Todd considers List a forerunner to John Maynard Keynes as a theorist of "moderate or regulated capitalism."

Biography

Early Life

List was born in the free imperial city of Reutlingen in the Duchy of Württemberg on August 6, 1789. His father, Johannes (1746–1813), was a prosperous master tanner and a city official, and Daniel Friedrich was the second son and youngest child in his family. He was educated at the town's Latin School. In an apprenticeship at his father's tanning business, List showed little interest in manual labor. He was apprenticed as a bureaucratic clerk at Blaubeuren. After passing his examination, he became Taxes and Warehouses Commissioner in Schelklingen.

University of Tübingen

At age 23, List was promoted to a post at Tübingen. While there, he regularly attended lectures at the University of Tübingen and expanded his reading. He also made the acquaintance of the future minister Johannes von Schlayer [de]. In 1816, List's position in the bureaucracy was improved as the succession of King William I of Württemberg ushered in a period of reform. Under minister Karl August von Wangenheim [de], List rose quickly through the bureaucracy and was made the first Professor of Administration and Politics at the University. List had been an advocate for establishing such a position, arguing in 1817: "No one in our University has any conception of a national economy.

No one teaches the science of agriculture, forestry, mining, industry, or trade. [T]he forms of government are in such a truly barbarous state, that if an official of the 17th century rose again from the dead he could at once take up his old work, though he would assuredly be astonished to find the advances that had been made during the interval in the simplest process of manufacture."

As a deputy to the Württemberg chamber, he was active in advocating administrative reforms. He was eventually expelled from the chamber and in April 1822 sentenced to 10 months' imprisonment with hard labor in the fortress of Asperg. He escaped to Alsace, and after visiting France and England returned in 1824 to finish his sentence, and was released on undertaking to immigrate to America.

Move to United States: 1825–1830

Arriving in the United States in 1825, he settled in Pennsylvania, where he became an extensive landholder. He first engaged in farming, but soon switched to journalism and edited a German paper in Reading. He was active in the establishment of railroads. Some argue (e.g., Chang, 2002) that it was in America that he gathered from a study of Alexander Hamilton's work the inspiration which made him an economist of his pronounced "National System" views which found realization in Henry Clay's American System. Others deny this, since he argued for a German customs union already in 1819, when he established the first German union for industry and trade. List's ideas on protectionism predate his American sojourn, and were influenced by liberal protectionists such as Adolphe Thiers. The main theoretical reference approvingly cited by List in his 1827 pamphlet Outlines of American Political Economy, in which he defended the doctrine of pragmatic protection and free trade, was Jean-Antoine Chaptal's De l'industrie française (1819). The discovery of coal on some land which he had acquired made him financially independent.

Return to Europe: 1831–1846

In 1830, he was appointed United States consul at Hamburg, but on his arrival in Europe he found that the Senate had failed to confirm his appointment. After residing for some time in Paris, he returned to Pennsylvania. He next settled in Leipzig in 1833, where for some time he was U.S. consul. He was a journalist in Paris from 1837 to 1843, where he wrote articles for Thiers's center-left paper Le Constitutionnel. He wrote several letters for the Augsburg Allgemeine Zeitung, which were published in 1841 in a volume under the title of Das nationale System der politischen Oekonomie.

In 1841, his ill health had led him to decline an offer to edit the Rheinische Zeitung, a new Cologne paper of liberal views, and Karl Marx took the post. In 1843, he established the Zollvereinsblatt in Augsburg, a newspaper in which he advocated the enlargement of the customs union (German: Zollverein), and the organization of a national commercial system. He strongly advocated the extension of the railway system in Germany. The development of the Zollverein to where it unified Germany economically was due largely to his enthusiasm and ardor. He visited Austria and Hungary in 1844.

In 1846, he visited England with a view to forming a commercial alliance between that country and Germany but was unsuccessful. His last days were darkened by many misfortunes; he lost much of his American property in a financial crisis, ill-health also overtook him, and he killed himself in Kufstein on 30 November 1846. However, since the autopsy revealed that List was "afflicted with such a degree of melancholy that made free thought and action impossible," he could still be given a Christian burial.

CLASS ACTIVITY

Students will learn about and evaluate the current status of US trade. Using the Internet, students will first gather key data and statistics about US trade. Then, in small groups, students will carefully analyze one country that exports to the United States from information downloaded off the Internet. In a role play, these groups will act as trade analysts giving presentations to the US Secretary of Commerce based on their analysis of US imports from that country. They will recommend a US import policy dealing with that particular country. Students will critique all the presentations considering whether any limits should be placed on imports, and if so, how. Finally, students will learn about a 1998 World Trade Organization ruling against the United States' policy of prohibiting the import of shrimp that are caught in nets not safe for endangered sea turtles.

SUMMARY

- Trade regulation is a field of law, often bracketed with antitrust (as in the phrase "antitrust and trade regulation law"), including government regulation of unfair methods of competition and unfair or deceptive business acts or practices. Antitrust law is often considered a subset of trade regulation law.
- Industrial policy is government policy to encourage the development and growth of all or part of the economy in pursuit of some public goal.
- Industrial policies are interventionist measures typical of mixed economy countries. Many types of industrial policies contain common elements with other types of interventionist practices such as trade policy. Industrial policy is usually seen as separate from broader macroeconomic policies, such as tightening credit and taxing capital gains.
- Trade is one of the most crucial concepts in the field of economics. As observed by Ricardo, trade is driven by comparative cost rather than the total cost of producing goods.
- International trade can be defined as the trade where capital, goods, and services are exchanged across international borders or amongst territories because of a specific need for the specific goods or services. In other words, international trades are economic transactions that are made between countries. This trade allows countries to expand their existing markets and access goods and services that are otherwise difficult to avail in the domestic markets. Some of the commonly traded items among consumer goods are clothing, machinery, raw materials, etc.
- United States trade policies have reflected the motivation of many groups, including government officials, labor leaders, and business management.
- United States tariff history has been marked by ups and downs. Many of the traditional arguments for tariffs (revenue, jobs) have been incorporated into U.S. tariff legislation.
- The Smoot-Hawley Act of 1930 raised U.S. tariffs to an all-time high, with disastrous results. Passage of the Reciprocal Trade Act of 1934 resulted in generalized tariff reductions by the United States, as well as the enactment of most favored nation provisions.
- The purposes of the General Agreement on Tariffs and Trade were to decrease trade barriers and place all nations on an equal footing in trading relations. In 1995, GATT was transformed into the World Trade Organization, which embodies the main provisions of GATT and provides a mechanism intended to improve the process of resolving trade disputes among member nations. The Tokyo Round and Uruguay Round of multilateral trade negotiations went beyond tariff reductions to liberalize various nontariff trade barriers.

REVIEW QUESTIONS

1. Define mercantilism.
2. Elaborate on some of the common barriers to International Trade.
3. Define industrial policy.
4. Distinguish between privatization and disinvestment.
5. Define industrial licensing.
6. Explain the meaning of globalization.
7. Define liberalization.
8. Discuss in detail Industrial Policy Resolution, 1956.
9. Give two reasons behind privatization of public sector enterprises.
10. What is meant by the most-favored nation clause, and how does it relate to the tariff policies of the United States?

REFERENCES

1. Ahluwalia, I. J., & Little, I. M. D. (1998). *India's Economic Reforms and Development*. New Delhi: Oxford University Press.
2. Bhaduri, A., & Nayyar, D. (1996). *The Intelligent Person's Guide to Liberalization*. Delhi: Penguin.
3. Bhagwati, J. (2004). *In Defense of Globalization*. Ukraine: Oxford University Press.
4. Bhattacharjee, G. (2020). *Public Sector Enterprises in India: Evolution, Privatization and Reforms*. New Delhi: Sage Publications.
5. Bown, C. P. (2024). Modern industrial policy and the World Trade Organization. *Annual Review of Economics*. doi:10.1146/annurev-economics-100223-041958.
6. Elliott, K. A. (2009). Opening markets for poor countries: Are we there yet? *Center for Global Development Working Paper 184*. Washington.
7. Juhász, R., & Lane, N., & Rodrik, D. (2024). The new economics of industrial policy. *Annual Review of Economics*. doi:10.1146/annurev-economics-081023-024638.
8. Juhász, R., & Steinwender, C. (2024). Industrial policy and the great divergence. *Annual Review of Economics*. doi:10.1146/annurev-economics-091523-044259.
9. Nayar, R. B. (2014). *Globalization and India's Economic Integration*. South Asia in World Affairs Series, Georgetown University Press.
10. Wear, A. (2017). Industry policy emerges from globalization resurgent and more important than ever. *The Mandarin*. Retrieved from: https://www.themandarin.com.au/ (accessed on 3 July 2024).

CHAPTER 6

Trade Policies for the Developing Nations

LEARNING OBJECTIVES

After studying this chapter, you will be able to:

- Discuss on developing-nation trade characteristics
- Describe the tensions between developing and advanced nations
- Define the trade problems of the developing nations
- Identify the stabilizing primary-product prices
- Explain the OPEC oil cartel
- Focus on aiding the developing nations
- Understand the economic growth strategies: import substitution versus export-led growth
- Define the China's transformation to capitalism
- Discuss on India: breaking out of the third world

KEY TERMS FROM THIS CHAPTER

Advanced nations
Cartel
Export-led growth
Flying-geese Pattern of economic growth
Import substitution
International Monetary Fund (IMF)
Organization of Petroleum Exporting Nations (OPEC)
Production and export controls
Buffer stock
Developing nations
Export-oriented policy
Generalized system of preferences (GSP)
International commodity agreements (ICAs)
Multilateral contracts
Primary products
World Bank

INTRODUCTION

For developing countries, trade policies have a significant impact on how their economies grow and how they integrate into the world economy. These policies frequently center on trade liberalization in order to improve trade flows and draw in foreign direct investment, which in turn promotes economic growth. Developing countries can boost their export competitiveness and diversify their economies beyond primary commodities by lowering tariffs and non-tariff barriers. Furthermore, trade agreements and membership in regional trade blocs can boost developing nations' access to markets and bargaining power in international talks. These regulations must, however, be carefully crafted to strike a balance between the advantages of free markets and the requirement to safeguard emerging sectors and preserve food security. To fully take advantage of trade opportunities, effective trade policies should also include measures to develop infrastructure, strengthen governance, and improve workforce skills. Furthermore, trade agreements can support inclusive and sustainable growth by addressing concerns like labor standards, intellectual property rights, and environmental protection. Preferential trade agreements, which offer tariff reductions or exemptions for specific products, may also be advantageous to developing countries. In the end, developing countries must carefully balance trade liberalization, targeted protection, and pro-growth domestic policies in order to maximize the advantages of international trade while minimizing its risks.

6.1. DEVELOPING-NATION TRADE CHARACTERISTICS

Upon analyzing the features of trade between developing and advanced nations, it becomes evident that developing nations rely heavily on advanced nations. Most imports from developing countries come from advanced countries, and most exports from developing countries are sent to these countries. Trade between developing countries is not very large, though it has been growing recently. The export composition of developing nations is another feature, with a focus on primary products (fuels, raw materials, and agricultural goods). Many of the manufactured goods that developing countries export—like textiles, for example—are labor-intensive and use relatively little technology in their production. Table 6.2 shows the output structure for a subset of developed and developing countries.

Table 6.1. Basic Economic and Social Indicators for Selected Nations

	Gross National Product per Capita*	Life Expectancy (years)	Adult Literacy (percent)
United States	$45,840	78	Over 95%
Switzerland	44,410	82	Over 95
Japan	34,750	83	Over 95
Mexico	13,910	75	90
Chile	12,330	78	Over 95
Algeria	7,640	72	70
Indonesia	3,570	71	88
Guinea	1,120	56	65
Burundi	330	49	26

Source: https://wyamaka.wordpress.com/wp-content/uploads/2019/08/international-economics_30.pdf.

The dominance of primary products in developing-nation trade has significantly decreased over the last three decades. In comparison to primary products, many developing countries—such as China, India, Mexico, South Korea, Hong Kong, Bangladesh, Sri Lanka, Turkey, Morocco, Indonesia, Vietnam, and so on—have been able to increase their exports of manufactured goods and services. Significant progress has been made in reducing poverty in countries that have joined the global industrial markets. The ability of developing countries to expand into exporting manufactured goods has been facilitated by investments in factories and human capital. In the developing world, the average level of education and capital stock per worker have increased significantly. Additionally, the production chain can be divided into its component parts thanks to advancements in communications and transportation as well as developing-nation reforms. Developing countries are crucial to the global sharing of production. Additionally, after the mid-1980s, developing countries' competitiveness increased with the liberalization of trade barriers. Particularly for manufactured goods and processed primary products, this increase was observed. In other words, exports of higher technology are becoming more and more prevalent to developing countries. They have, however, been dissatisfied with their meager success in selling these goods to developed countries. With a combined population of about 2 billion, many developing countries, mostly in Africa and the former Soviet Union, have yet to fully integrate into the global industrial economy. Their primary product exports typically consist of a limited selection. These countries have frequently suffered from inadequate trade barriers, widespread corruption, inadequate infrastructure, and inadequate education. Transport costs are an even bigger barrier to integration than rich nation trade policies because they are frequently higher than the tariffs on goods that are exported to advanced nation markets. Over the past 20 years, incomes have been declining and poverty has increased in these developing countries. It is imperative that they expand their export portfolio by exploring international markets for manufactured goods and services whenever feasible.

Table 6.2. Structure of Output for Selected Advanced Nations and Developing Nations, 2007 Value Added as a Percent of GDP

Economy	Agriculture, Forestry, and Fishing	Industry	Services
Advanced Nations			
United States	1	22	71
Japan	2	30	68
Canada	2	33	65
France	2	21	77
Italy	2	27	71
Developing Nations			
Albania	21	20	59
Chad	23	44	32
Pakistan	21	26	53
Tanzania	45	18	37
Mali	37	24	39

Source: https://wyamaka.wordpress.com/wp-content/uploads/2019/08/international-economics_30.pdf.

6.2. TENSIONS BETWEEN DEVELOPING AND ADVANCED NATIONS

Despite developing countries' frustrations with trade, the majority of academics and decision-makers nowadays concur that utilizing international trade is the most effective way for a poor country to grow. Over the last 20 years, numerous developing countries have realized the benefits of this approach and have allowed foreign investment and international trade into their markets. Paradoxically, despite academics' endorsement of this shift, the developed world has occasionally raised its own barriers to imports from these developing countries. Why is that the case? Visualize the global economy as a ladder. Developing countries that produce mostly textiles and other low-tech goods are at the bottom of the economic ladder. The United States, Japan, and other developed countries that produce high-tech software, electronics, and medications are towards the top. The other countries are arranged in a descending order along the middle rungs, producing everything from steel to memory chips to cars. From this angle, economic growth is straightforward: Everyone tries to move up to the next rung. This process is most effective when the leading countries are able to develop new products and industries, which adds another rung to the ladder by allowing older industries to relocate abroad while creating new jobs domestically. However, if innovation stagnates at the top, Americans will have to contend with low-paid laborers in developing countries. Developing countries have the dilemma of having to push out manufacturers of the least developed goods that are still made in developed countries if they are to advance. For instance, Zambia will face competition from European and American manufacturers of clothing and textiles if it decides to produce these items. Producers in developed countries typically seek trade protection to shield themselves from import competition. But this protection keeps developing countries from accessing vital markets, impeding their efforts to develop. As a result, there is prejudice against them catching up to the developed countries. People who are already close to the bottom of the income distribution in advanced nations are typically shielded from competition from developing nations. Many of these individuals have low pay and little skill sets and labor in labor-intensive industries. Programs for income redistribution should help these people, not hinder them. Developed countries have to make some trade-offs between aiding the poor in their own countries and the poor around the world. However, detractors point out that international organizations should guarantee justice to all those living in poverty and that the world as a whole must treat all impoverished people as its own. For instance, the World Trade Organization (WTO) is in charge of making sure that advanced countries' trade policies don't slant excessively in favor of their own citizens and against those of other countries. This explains why tensions between wealthy and impoverished countries have been prevalent in recent WTO meetings. But expanding developing countries' access to the markets of developed countries won't be a panacea for all of their issues. Their economies are plagued by structural weaknesses that are exacerbated by insufficient or nonexistent institutions and policies concerning public services, sustainable macroeconomic management, and law and order.

6.3. TRADE PROBLEMS OF THE DEVELOPING NATIONS

According to the theory of comparative advantage, all countries can profit from free trade if they concentrate on producing the goods in which they have a comparative advantage and trade some of those goods for goods made in other countries.

The market-oriented structure of the international trading system, according to policy makers in the US and many other developed countries, provides an environment in which the advantages of comparative advantage can be realized.

They contend that while there are many advantages to the current international trading system, sensible, gradual changes to it would best serve the trading interests of all countries. Advanced countries also assert that they need to manage their own internal and international economic policies in order to succeed in trade. Some developing countries are skeptical about how trade benefits are shared between them and developed countries based on their trading experiences with these countries.

They contend that many developing countries are unable to industrialize due to the protectionist trade policies of developed nations.

As a result, developing countries have looked for a new system of international trade that would give them better access to developed countries' markets. Developing countries have been beset by a number of issues, including unstable export markets, deteriorating terms of trade, and restricted access to advanced countries' markets.

6.3.1. Unstable Export Markets

A prevalent feature of numerous developing countries is the concentration of their exports within one or a small number of primary products. Table 6.3, which depicts the reliance of a few chosen developing countries on a single primary product, depicts this situation. A bad harvest or a decline in the product's market demand can drastically cut export earnings and have a major negative impact on employment and income levels at home.

Table 6.3. Developing Nation Dependence on Primary Products, 2007

Nation	Major Export Product	Major Export Product as a Percentage of Total Exports
Saudi Arabia	Oil	91%
Venezuela	Oil	90
Burundi	Coffee	89
Nigeria	Oil	88
Zambia	Copper	56
Malawi	Tobacco	50
Ethiopia	Coffee	36
Benin	Cotton	35

Source: https://wyamaka.wordpress.com/wp-content/uploads/2019/08/international-economics_30.pdf.

Economists contend that the low price elasticity of the demand and supply schedules for goods like tin, copper, and coffee is a major contributing factor to the volatility of primary product prices and producer revenues. 1 Keep in mind that the percentage change in quantity demanded (supplied) in response to a 1 percent change in price is known as the price elasticity of demand (supply). A small adjustment to either schedule can result in a significant change in price and revenues to the extent that the supply and demand schedules are relatively inelastic, meaning that the percentage change in price is greater than the percentage change in quantity.

The supply and demand schedules for coffee for the entire market are shown in Figure 6.1. These schedules are assumed to be very inelastic. At point A, where the market demand schedule D0 and the market supply schedule S0 intersect, the market is in equilibrium. The equilibrium price ($4.50) multiplied by the quantity of pounds sold (5 million) yields the producers of coffee's total revenue of $22.5 million.

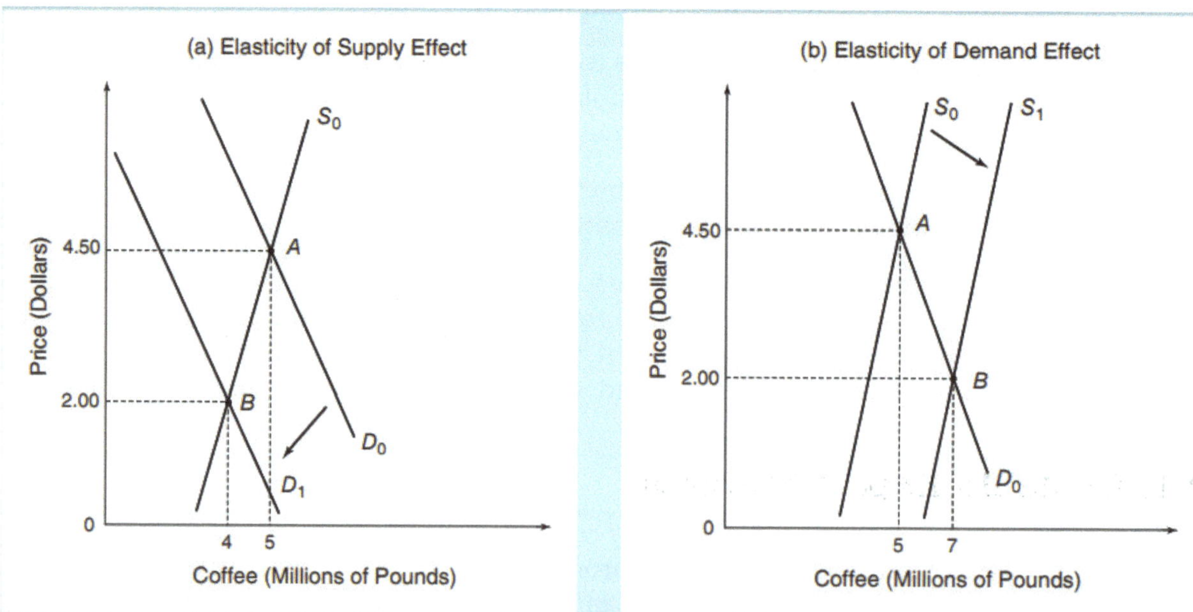

Figure 6.1. *Export price instability for a developing nation.*

Source: https://wyamaka.wordpress.com/wp-content/uploads/2019/08/international-economics_30.pdf.

Assume, with reference to Figure 6.1(a), that the market demand curve for coffee falls to D1 as a result of declining foreign incomes. The market price of coffee drops significantly, from $4.50 to $2.01 per pound, as a result of the decrease in demand due to the inelasticity of the supply. As a result, coffee producers' revenues drop to $8 million. A portion of this decline is due to a decline in producer profit. We conclude that when market supply is inelastic, coffee prices and earnings can be extremely volatile. Not only do shifts in supply cause significant price fluctuations when demand is inelastic, but they also cause significant price fluctuations when demand is not inelastic. Figure 6.1(b) provides an illustration of the latter scenario. Assume that the market supply curve for coffee shifts to S1 to the right due to favorable growing conditions. As a result, the price significantly drops to $2 per pound from $4.50, and producer revenues decrease to $14 million ($2 x $7 million = $14 million). It is evident that when demand conditions are inelastic, prices and revenues can fluctuate greatly.

6.3.2. Worsening Terms of Trade

There has been debate over how trading partners should split up the benefits of global trade, particularly developing countries whose exports are mostly made up of primary goods. These countries typically argue that the developed world benefits disproportionately from international trade. Developing countries claim that during the last century or so, their commodity terms of trade have gotten worse, indicating a decline in the value of their exports compared to imports. Many developing countries have refused to take part in trade-liberalization negotiations, citing worsening terms of trade as justification. Additionally, it has supported the requests of developing countries for preferential treatment in trade agreements with developed countries. Some claim that higher prices are the outcome of the developed nations' manufacturers' monopoly power. Manufacturers benefit from increased productivity not in the form of lower prices, but rather in higher earnings. Moreover, observers argue that competitive markets determine the export prices of developing countries' primary products. These prices exhibit both upward and downward fluctuations. Lower prices are the result of productivity gains that are distributed to international customers. Developing countries argue that their commodity terms of trade have deteriorated because market forces have caused the prices they pay for imports to rise more quickly than the prices they command for their exports. Furthermore, people tend to spend more on manufactured goods than on primary goods as their income increases, which deteriorates the terms of trade for developing countries.

A 1949 United Nations (UN) study corroborated the claims of developing countries regarding deteriorating commodity terms of trade. The study found that between 1876 and 1880 and 1946 and 1947, the prices of primary products fell by 32% when compared to manufactured goods. However, the UN study was hardly conclusive due to data deficiencies and issues with creating price indices. Contrary findings regarding terms-of-trade movements were found in other investigations. In 2004, United Nations economists discovered that, compared to the cost of manufactured goods bought from developed countries, the average prices of agricultural commodities sold by developing countries had decreased by nearly 70% between 1961 and 2001. These reductions in terms of trade were particularly detrimental to Sub-Saharan Africa's poorest countries.

Furthermore, according to estimates from the World Bank, non-oil exporting African countries that experienced declining terms of trade lost revenues totaling 119% of their combined annual gross domestic product between 1970 and 1997. Theoretically, if the terms of trade were to decline, the value of export earnings could be maintained or increased by increasing the quantity produced and exported. In reality, the countries of Africa's export quantities did not increase fast enough to offset the loss.

The declining terms of trade argument seems to have less weight these days when it comes to other developing countries, like China, India, and Russia, as well as other developing world oil exporters. Many of these countries have diversified their economies away from solely relying on oil exports and have been able to achieve economies of scale in the production of certain other primary products, like corn or cotton. Determining whether the terms of trade of developing countries have improved or deteriorated overall is a challenging task. The selection of the base year for comparisons, the challenge of accounting for new products and their attributes, changes in technology and productivity, and the techniques employed to weight the commodities in the index and value imports and exports all muddy the waters when drawing conclusions about terms-of-trade movements.

6.3.3. Limited Market Access

The penetration of developing countries into global markets has improved over the last 20 years. Global protectionism, however, has made it difficult for them to access markets. As Figure 6.2 illustrates, this is particularly true for labor-intensive manufactured goods like textiles and apparel as well as agriculture. Because they account for over half of the exports from low-income countries and roughly 70% of the export earnings from least-developed countries, these goods are crucial to the world's impoverished. The advanced nations often impose higher tariffs on imports from developing nations than they do on goods from other advanced nations. The existence of significant trade blocs like the European Union (EU) and the North American Free Trade Agreement (NAFTA), which have eliminated tariffs for advanced-nation trading partners, is partially reflected in the variations in tariff averages. Additionally, prior to the 1990s, developing countries did not actively participate in multilateral trade liberalization agreements, so their products tended to be excluded from the significant tariff reductions made in those rounds. Put simply, average tariff rates in developed countries are low, but they keep up barriers in precisely the sectors of the economy where developing countries have a comparative advantage: labor-intensive manufacturing and agriculture.

Tariff increases also afflict developing countries. Tariffs in developed countries rise sharply, particularly for agricultural goods. Raising tariffs may limit the market for developing countries' processed imports, preventing them from diversifying into higher value-added exports. Tariff escalation impacts imports of industrial products as well, albeit less frequently, particularly when the products are semi-processed. These products include textiles and apparel, leather goods, wood, paper, furniture, metals, and rubber goods. Many developing nations have a comparative advantage in these markets. Furthermore, developing-nation producers of apparel and textiles have had to forgo significant export revenues due to protectionist barriers. Advanced countries placed import quotas on these goods for many years. Due to high tariff barriers, market access for textiles and apparel will remain limited even after the Uruguay Round Agreement on Textiles and Clothing abolished quotas in 2005.

However, as trade becomes more liberalized on a regional and global scale, traditional trade barriers are gradually being replaced by antidumping and countervailing duties. Developing countries have claimed that because developed countries like the US apply aggressive antidumping and countervailing duties, they have restricted access to their markets. The developing countries claim that as a result of these policies, export volumes and market shares have significantly decreased. In fact, developing countries have looked to the US and Europe to lower trade barriers. Rich countries do, however, point out that poor countries must lower their own tariffs, which are frequently greater than those of their rich counterparts. Developing countries have an average tariff rate of over 20%, while advanced countries have an average tariff rate of less than 6 percent.

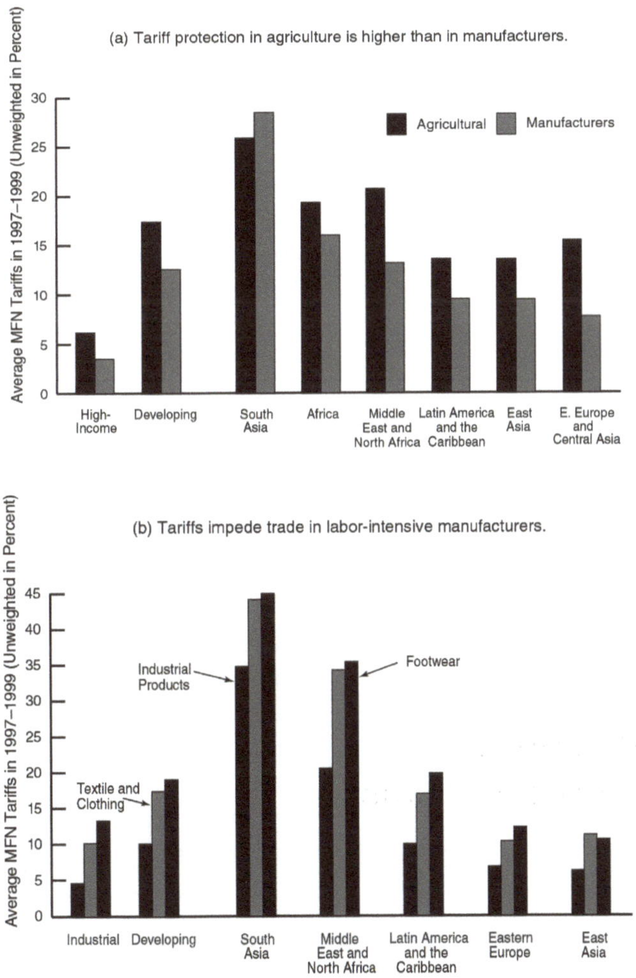

Figure 6.2. *Trade barriers limit export opportunities of developing nations.*

Source: https://wyamaka.wordpress.com/wp-content/uploads/2019/08/international-economics_30.pdf.

Developing countries also frequently apply tariff escalation; on average, their tariffs on fully processed manufactured and agricultural goods are higher than those on unprocessed goods. Average tariffs on manufactured goods are roughly three times higher for trade among developing countries than for exports to developed countries, despite the fact that trade among developing countries makes up a much smaller portion of global trade. Critics point out that they ought to liberalize trade since developing countries are a part of their own issues. Nevertheless, many developing countries find this argument offensive. They argue that cutting tariffs too soon could worsen the already precarious conditions of their economies. Businesses will inevitably shift to the lowest-cost centers, which will result in job losses for some workers, just as it does in wealthy nations that lower tariffs. Poor countries lack reeducation programs and social safety nets to lessen the blow, in contrast to the United States and Europe. The developing world is meant to take note of this and implement some of its own market liberalization. However, it is contradictory for developed countries to advocate for the removal of trade barriers in developing countries, given that developed nations such as the United States and Canada benefited from substantial trade barriers when they were still in their infancy.

6.3.4. Agricultural Export Subsidies of Advanced Nations

For developing countries, global agriculture protectionism is an additional issue. Advanced countries provide their farmers with substantial subsidies in addition to employing tariffs to shield them from import-competing goods. The non-economic advantages of agriculture, such as food security and the upkeep of rural communities, are frequently used to justify subsidies. Subsidies discourage agricultural imports by promoting the production of agricultural commodities, which pushes exports from developing countries to markets in developed nations. Additionally, export subsidies are frequently used to dump the undesirable surpluses of agricultural commodities that arise from government support onto international markets. The prices of many agricultural commodities are lowered by this dumping, which also lowers developing countries' revenue.

For instance, West African rice farmers lament that U.S. and European export subsidies drive down global prices and hinder their ability to compete. 2007 saw an average of one ton of U.S. The cost to sow, tend, and harvest rough rice was $240. When the rice departed a U.S. export-oriented port, U.S. Subsidies brought the price down to $205 for overseas purchasers. On the other hand, a ton of product cost $230 in West Africa. Farmers in West Africa were therefore unable to compete in their own market. As West African rice farmers have gone bankrupt, they have frequently tried to enter Europe illegally in an attempt to find employment. In order to avoid being discovered by European patrols, thousands of people have perished while crossing the Mediterranean at riskier locations. The grievances expressed by rice and cotton farmers in West Africa are similar. They observe that U.S. the cotton export industry has benefited from substantial subsidies. Farmers in West Africa believe that having to compete with American and U.S. farmers makes life unfair authority.

US food aid programs frequently exacerbate this dispute. Indeed, it is true that U.S. Millions of people who would have gone hungry due to farm failure have been spared thanks to food donations to developing nations. However, growers in underdeveloped countries gripe that the U.S. Rather than buying what foreigners grow, the government buys excess grain from American farmers and ships it halfway around the world. With rare exceptions, the United States is required by law to provide food grown domestically rather than paying cash for food imported from abroad. This policy feeds the world's hungry people as well as American farmers, processors, and shippers. Farmers in the United States are not sympathetic to the plight of West Africans, as they oppose U.S. the use of public funds by the government to buy crops abroad. But a lot of developing countries get these subsidies because they are net importers of agricultural products. Eliminating these subsidies would hurt many developing nations because it would lower the prices of the goods they buy on international markets.

6.4. STABILIZING PRIMARY-PRODUCT PRICES

Agriculture and the products of natural resources continue to be the main sources of employment, even though exports of manufactured goods from developing countries have improved somewhat. We now know that there can be significant fluctuations in the export prices and earnings for these goods. International commodity agreements (ICAs) have been attempted by developing countries in an effort to stabilize primary product export prices and revenues. These agreements cover topics like price stabilization, ensuring sufficient supplies for consumers, and fostering the economic development of producers. They are made between the top producing and consuming countries of commodities like coffee, rubber, and cocoa. ICAs have depended on production and export controls, buffer stocks, and multilateral contracts to maintain stability in the commodity markets. It should be noted that other approaches to assisting these countries are required, as these policies have typically had little to no success in improving the economic circumstances of developing countries.

6.4.1. Production and Export Controls

To stabilize export earnings, an ICA's members may decide on production and export limits if the organization produces a significant portion of the commodity's global output, or exports. Controls over production and exports have an impact on the global supply of a commodity, which in turn affects its price. A commodity agreement bases the total amount of production or exports permitted on the target price that each member country has agreed upon. Producing countries will be given a lower production level or export quota if it is anticipated that, for example, the price of tin will fall below the target price in the future. Tin will stay at the target price if scarcity increases. Conversely, producing countries will be permitted to raise their levels of production and exports if it is predicted that the price of tin will rise above the target price in the future.

The distribution of production and export limits among producing nations presents a challenge to any attempt to impose such limits. Small producers might be reluctant to lower their levels of output when prices are declining, so how would a decline in the overall quantity of coffee exports be distributed among individual producers, for example, if a decline in the price is required to offset a falling quantity? The emergence of new coffee producers, who might be lured into the market by artificially high prices, is another issue. Countries that are just starting to produce or export coffee are probably not going to want to cut back on their output at that point. Furthermore, it is difficult to enforce output restrictions, which gives producers an incentive to cheat.

6.4.2. Buffer Stocks

The buffer stock strategy, in which a producers' association (or other international agency) is ready to buy and sell a commodity in bulk, is another way to reduce fluctuations in commodity prices. The producers' association finances and holds supplies of a commodity that make up the buffer stock. When supplies are plentiful and prices are dropping to acceptable levels, the buffer stock manager purchases from the market; when supplies are scarce and prices are rising, they sell from the buffer stock. The International Tin Agreement's hypothetical price-stabilization initiatives are depicted in Figure 6.3. Let us assume that the association establishes a pricing range to direct the buffer-stock manager's stabilization operations, with a floor of $3.27 per pound and a ceiling of $4.02 per pound. Assume the buffer-stock manager observes that the demand for tin is increasing from D0 to D1, starting at equilibrium point A in Figure 6.3(a). The manager must be ready to sell 20,000 pounds of tin to offset the excess demand for tin at the ceiling price in order to defend the $4.02 ceiling price. Conversely, let's say the supply of tin increases from S0 to S1, beginning at equilibrium point E in Figure 6.3(b). The buffer-stock manager must buy the 20,000-pound excess supply that is available at that price in order to defend the floor price of $3.27.

Buffer stock proponents assert that the program has multiple benefits for the primary producing countries. Economic efficiency can be enhanced by a well-managed buffer stock because it allows primary producers to plan investments and expansion knowing that prices won't fluctuate. There is also the argument that rising commodity prices inevitably drive down industrial prices, while falling commodity prices have no equivalent effect. Buffer stocks can reduce the industrialized countries' price inflation by stabilizing commodity prices. In this context, buffer stocks are seen as a way to give primary producers more stability than what the free market will allow.

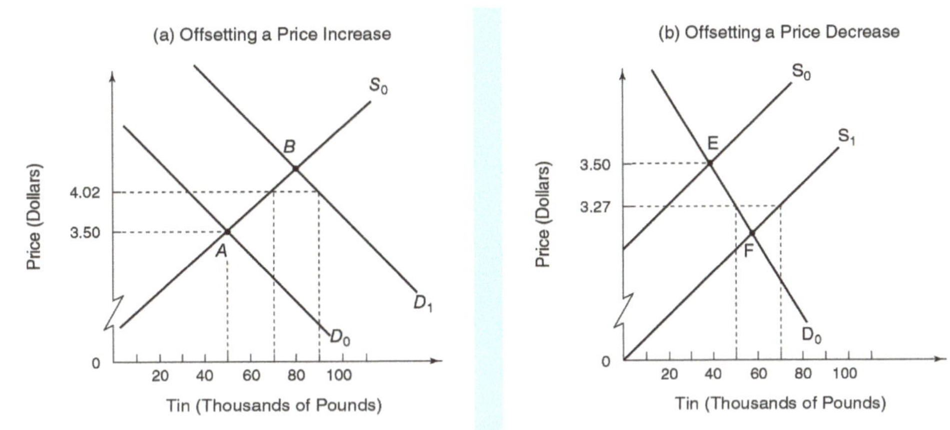

Figure 6.3. *Buffer stock: Price ceiling and price support.*

Source: https://wyamaka.wordpress.com/wp-content/uploads/2019/08/international-economics_30.pdf.

Implementing and managing a buffer-stock program is not without expenses and challenges. Determining a target price that accurately represents long-term market trends is the fundamental challenge in using buffer stocks to stabilize prices. The stock manager will sell the commodity on the open market in an effort to keep market prices in line with the target price if the target price is set too low, depleting the buffer stocks.

The stock manager will have to buy the commodity in bulk in order to support market prices if the target price is set too high. Keeping the stocks can be expensive because it involves paying for labor, insurance, and transportation. Officials in charge of buffer stocks have frequently chosen unwise price targets. If target prices diverge from long-term price trends, buffer-stock officials will periodically adjust them rather than launching large-scale stabilization operations.

6.4.3. Multilateral Contracts

Another strategy for stabilizing commodity prices is the use of multilateral contracts. These contracts typically include a minimum price at which the producing countries will sell the importers guaranteed quantities, and a maximum price at which the importers will buy guaranteed quantities from the producing countries. The goal of these purchases and sales is to keep prices within a predetermined range. Trade between multiple exporting and importing countries has frequently taken place under multilateral agreements, such as the International Wheat Agreement and the International Sugar Agreement. A potential benefit of the multilateral contract as a tool for price stabilization is that it produces less distortion of the market mechanism and resource allocation than buffer stocks or export controls. This is because output constraints are not typically included in multilateral contracts, which means that the emergence of more productive, low-cost producers is not prevented. However, disparities between supply and demand will arise if target prices are not set in close proximity to the long-term equilibrium price. Oversupply would suggest a floor that is too high, while excess demand would point to a ceiling that is too low. Furthermore, because participating members can exit and rejoin multilateral contracts relatively easily, they typically only provide a limited degree of market stability.

6.4.4. Does the Fair-Trade Movement Help Poor Coffee Farmers?

It is evident that producers in developing countries face difficulties due to low commodity prices. Can producers benefit from the help that consumers provide? Take the example of coffee grown in Nicaragua. Santiago Rivera, a coffee farmer in Nicaragua, has ventured far from his mountainside residence to promote the "fair trade" coffee movement. You may soon hear about fair-trade coffee. The goal of the fair-trade coffee movement, which got its start in Europe in the early 1990s, is to raise the income of underprivileged farmers in developing countries by putting in place a system that allows them to sell their beans directly to roasters and retailers, instead of going through local middlemen as is customary.

Thanks to this arrangement, farmers, who grow beans primarily for gourmet stores in high-flavor, high-priced regions of Latin America and other tropical regions with mountains, can now earn up to $1.26 per pound for their beans instead of the $0.40 they were previously receiving from middlemen. Farmers unite into cooperatives with up to 2,500 members under the fair-trade system, which sets prices and organizes exportation directly to brokerage houses and other distributors. Previously, middlemen—referred to as "coyotes" in Nicaragua—were in charge of this duty. Out of the 4 million coffee farmers in the developing world, 500,000 have joined the fair-trade movement thus far. But in some parts of Latin America, the movement has resulted in violent incidents; these have mostly involved middlemen who are being cut out.

The most recent instance of how free-market economics is being used by social activists to promote social change is the fair-trade coffee movement. The movement's organizers claim to have about 120 stores signed up, including major chains like Safeway, Inc., and eight gourmet roasters. Coffee that is fair-trade is marked with a logo. In Europe, where fair-trade coffee is sold in 35,000 stores and generates $250 million in sales annually, fair trade has seen significant success. Up to 5% of all coffee sales in some countries, like the Netherlands and Switzerland, come from fair-trade coffee. European fair-trade organizers are extending their efforts to include other commodities like sugar, tea, chocolate, and bananas in light of these successes. However, proponents of fair trade acknowledge that it will be harder to persuade Americans to purchase coffee with a social message in America than it was in Europe.

They observe that Americans have a tendency to be less conscious than Europeans of social issues in the developing world. Important U.S. corporations still do not support the fair-trade movement. S. coffee shops like Folgers and Maxwell. Still, organizers are attempting to persuade one of Seattle's two dominant coffee companies, Starbucks Coffee Co. as well as Seattle Coffee Co., convincing them to buy a portion of the fair-trade coffee. Critics contest how much "fair-traded" coffee really contributes, though. They point out that the retailers, who occasionally charge exorbitant markups on fair-traded coffee while positioning themselves as corporate citizens, are the real winners—not the farmers. They can get away with it because, in most cases, consumers are not informed about the portion of a product's price that goes to farmers.

6.5. THE OPEC OIL CARTEL

Even though the economies of many developing countries have not significantly improved in recent decades, some have. One such group consists of developing countries that possess oil reserves. Rather than merely creating accords to maintain prices and earnings, countries that export oil have established cartels with the aim of raising prices and making "monopolistic" profits. The Organization of Petroleum Exporting Nations is the most prosperous cartel in recent memory. A collection of countries that sells petroleum on the international market is known as the Organization of Petroleum Exporting Nations (OPEC). To increase member-nation profits, the OPEC countries try to maintain prices higher than they would be under more competitive circumstances. Following a period of relative obscurity during the 1960s, OPEC managed to seize control over petroleum pricing in 1973 and 1974, as the price of a barrel of oil increased from about $3 to $12.

The 1979 Iranian revolution caused an early 1979 double in oil prices, which continued into early 1980. The average price of a barrel of oil was close to $36 by 1981. OPEC's market dominance was a result of its control over roughly half of global oil production and two thirds of global oil reserves, along with a robust and inelastic demand for oil. The world recession and declining demand were major factors in the 1986 drop in oil prices to $11 per barrel, which was followed by a rise. As supply became scarce and demand skyrocketed, the price of an oil barrel was roughly $98 by 2007.

Oil-producing countries acted like independent, competitive sellers before OPEC. Over an extended period, changes in a country's export levels had little effect on international prices because each country was so small in relation to the global market. The oil-exporting countries discovered that they could exert significant control over global oil prices by agreeing to limit competition among themselves through production quotas, as evidenced by the price increases of the 1970s.

6.5.1. Maximizing Cartel Profits

In an effort to boost member profits, a cartel supports prices higher than they otherwise would be under more competitive circumstances. Let's look at some of the challenges a cartel might face as it looks to boost earnings. Assume that there are 10 oil suppliers in the global oil market, each of the same size, and that oil is a standard product. Due to past pricing wars, the prices charged by each supplier are the same as the minimum average cost. Every supplier worries that if it raises its price, the others won't follow suit and all of its sales will be lost. Assume these suppliers decide to band together and create a cartel rather than engage in ruthless price competition. A cartel will act like a profit-maximizing monopolist, restricting output and raising prices in order to maximize the aggregate profits of its members.

The demand and cost conditions of the 10 oil suppliers are shown in Figure 6.4(a) and Figure 6.4(b), which shows the average supplier for the group. The market price of oil under competition is $20 per barrel prior to the formation of the cartel. Economic profit is equal to zero because each supplier can only reach a price that barely covers its average minimum cost. Every vendor in the market turns out 150 barrels a day. The daily production of the industry is 1,500 barrels (150 ×10 = 1500).

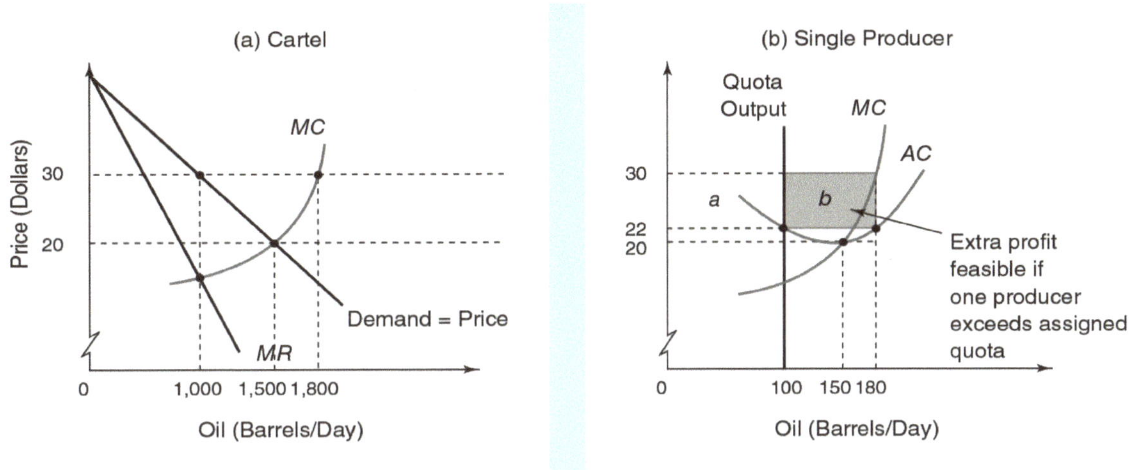

Figure 6.4. *Maximizing OPEC profits.*

Source: https://wyamaka.wordpress.com/wp-content/uploads/2019/08/international-economics_30.pdf.

Assume that the oil suppliers band together to form a cartel, with the primary goal of maximizing the members' combined profits. The cartel must first determine the output level that maximizes profits—that is, the output at which marginal revenue equals marginal cost—in order to achieve this goal. The cartel then establishes production quotas for each supplier in order to distribute the cartel output among its members. The cartel in Figure 6.4(a) will limit output from 1,500 barrels per day to 1,000 barrels per day in order to maximize group profits. As seen in Figure 6.4(b), this implies that each cartel member must reduce its daily output from 150 barrels to 100 barrels. The market price of an oil barrel rises from $20 to $30 as a result of this production quota. For every 100 barrels of oil produced, each member makes $8 per barrel ($30 – $22 = $8), for a total profit of $800 (area a).

Making sure that no cartel member sells more than their quota is the next step. Due to the incentive that each supplier has to sell above its allotted quota at the cartel price, this is a challenging task. However, if every cartel member sells more than their allotted amount, profits will disappear and the cartel price will drop toward the level of competition. Thus, cartels try to impose sanctions on vendors who undercut their allotted quotas. Seling at the allotted quota of 100 barrels per day allows each cartel member to realize economic profits of $800, as shown in Figure 6.4(b). An individual supplier is aware, nevertheless, that if it sells more at the cartel price than this, it will be able to increase its profits. Every single supplier is motivated to raise production to the point where the cartel price of $30 equals the supplier's marginal cost, which happens at 180 barrels per day. The supplier would make economic profits of $1,440 at this output level, which are shown by area a + b. The supplier gains an additional $640 in profits ($1,440 – $800 = $640) by undermining its agreed-upon production quota, as indicated by area b. Keep in mind that this increase in profits only happens if the supplier's additional output represents a small percentage of the industry supply and the price of oil does not drop as the supplier increases output.

It might be possible for a single supplier to produce more than what is required without materially lowering the price of oil on the market. To increase profits, each cartel member can increase its output to 180 barrels per day, which will result in a total output of 1,800 barrels (180 × 10 = 1,800). However, industry output needs to be limited to just 1,000 barrels per day in order to keep the price at $30. The 800 barrels of excess production push prices lower, which lowers economic profits. The cartel is probably going to disintegrate if economic profits return to zero, which is the level of competition.

In addition to the issue of cheating, forming a cartel presents the following additional challenges:

- **Number of Sellers:** Generally speaking, the formation of a cartel is more challenging the more sellers there are. It is easier to coordinate price and output policies among three dominant sellers than it is among 10 sellers, each of whom holds 10% of the market.
- **Cost and Demand Differences:** It is more challenging to reach a price agreement when the costs and product demands of cartel members are different. There is no one price that all members can agree upon because these differences lead to different profit-maximizing prices for each member.
- **Potential Competition:** A cartel's potential for higher profits could draw in new rivals. Their introduction into the market causes the supply of products to rise, which in turn causes prices and profits to decline. Thus, the ability of a cartel to prevent new competitors from entering the market is essential to its success.
- **Economic Downturn:** For cartels, economic downturns are usually problematic. Profits decline in a faltering economy as market sales decline. In an effort to gain sales at the expense of other cartel members, members may believe that by lowering prices, they can avoid significant drops in profits.
- **Substitute Goods:** When consumers can replace the good that a cartel produces (oil) with other goods (coal and natural gas), the cartel's ability to set prices is undermined.

6.5.2. OPEC as a Cartel

The term "cartel" has been widely rejected by OPEC. Nonetheless, a secretariat, a board of governors, an economic commission, and a conference of ministers make up its organizational structure. In an effort to stabilize oil prices, OPEC has made several attempts to develop plans for systematic production control among its members. But OPEC barely has any influence over prices. Less than 40% of the global supply is currently under the group's control, which is insufficient to create a viable cartel. Furthermore, a large number of member countries have broken the agreements by producing more than their allotted quotas, meaning that OPEC's production agreements have not always lived up to expectations. OPEC's actual production levels have nearly always exceeded its target levels since production quotas were first distributed to members in 1983. This means that countries have been selling more oil than has been permitted. In other words, OPEC lacks a club with which to impose its will. Saudi Arabia is an exception, possessing the greatest reserves and the lowest production costs globally. The Saudis invest enormous sums of money to keep their production capacity above their consumption, which gives them the short-term ability to control or threaten to control prices.

The United States and other importing countries may implement policies to raise supply and/or lower demand in order to counteract OPEC's dominant market position. But in order to accomplish these goals, Americans must make some challenging decisions, like the following:

- **Raising the Fuel Economy Standards Mandated by the Federal Government:** According to analysts, the United States could save 1.3 million barrels of oil every day if new cars' gas mileage increased by just one mile per gallon annually and light trucks' mileage increased by half a mile per gallon since 1987. Car manufacturers, however, would oppose higher fuel economy regulations since they would have to increase their production costs as a result of this policy.
- **Increasing the Federal Excise Tax on Gasoline:** The ensuing increase in gas prices would encourage consumers to practice conservation, but this would go against the American desire for inexpensive gasoline. Moreover, consumers with lower incomes and less purchasing power would be disproportionately harmed by rising gas prices.
- Allowing oil companies to drill on federal land designated as wilderness in Alaska, where there is a good chance that oil might be found. Perhaps, but what happens when the wilderness is destroyed, never to return? Who pays for that?
- **Diversifying Imports:** To lessen its reliance on this unstable region, the US may establish closer ties with oil producers outside of the Middle East, despite the potential cost. But doing so would mean that the US would have to collaborate even more with dubious regimes in places like Vietnam, Indonesia, and Angola. It also costs very little to extract OPEC oil from the ground. In the Gulf of Mexico or the North Sea, producing a barrel costs deepwater drillers like ExxonMobil or Conoco $6 to $8, but the Saudis and Kuwaitis only pay $1 or less for the same barrel. OPEC's cost advantage increases its market dominance.
- **Developing Alternate Sources of Energy Such as Biofuels and Wind Power.** Possibly. However, these typically need taxpayer-funded government subsidies.

6.6. AIDING THE DEVELOPING NATIONS

We now know that the countries that export oil are a unique class of developing countries that have experienced significant economic growth in recent years. Not all developing countries, though, are in this advantageous position. Developing countries, dissatisfied with their economic performance and certain that many of their issues stem from the flaws in the current international trading system, have collectively demanded of developed countries institutions and policies that enhance the environment for economic development. The World Bank, the International Monetary Fund, and the generalized system of preferences are a few of the organizations and guidelines designed to assist developing countries.

6.6.1. The World Bank

Two international organizations were founded in the 1940s to facilitate the shift from a wartime to a peacetime setting and to aid in averting a repeat of the unstable economic circumstances that characterized the Great Depression. At the July 1944 United Nations Monetary and Financial Conference in Bretton Woods, New Hampshire, the World Bank and the International Monetary Fund were founded. These organizations are seen by the developing countries as potential funding sources for advancing financial stability and economic growth. An international institution called the World Bank lends money to developing countries with the goal of promoting economic growth and reducing poverty. It makes loans to private companies operating in member countries as well as to member governments and their agencies. The World Bank is not, in the traditional sense, a "bank.." It is one of the specialized agencies of the United Nations, which has 185 member countries. These countries share accountability for the institution's funding sources and expenditures. Five closely related organizations have come to be referred to as the "World Bank Group.." Developing countries can obtain low-cost loans and grants from the International Development Association and the International Bank for Reconstruction and Development. Developing countries that would not otherwise have easy access to capital are given equity, long-term loans, loan guarantees, and advisory services by the International Finance Corporation. The Multilateral Investment Guarantee Agency protects foreign investors against losses resulting from civil unrest, war, and other similar events, thereby promoting foreign investment in developing countries. Furthermore, by offering international facilities for the conciliation and arbitration of investment disputes, the International Center for Settlement of Investment Disputes promotes foreign investment and aids in the development of a mutually trusting environment between developing countries and foreign investors. For developing members who are unable to secure funding from other sources, the World Bank offers grants and loans on reasonable terms. These monies are intended for particular construction projects, like roads, dams, schools, and hospitals. The World Bank works on a wide range of projects, including educating people in Guinea about AIDS, assisting Bangladeshi girls in their education, enhancing health care delivery in Mexico, and aiding India in its reconstruction following a devastating earthquake. The World Bank offers loans to developing countries with little to no ability to borrow money on market terms, often at low interest rates or even interest-free. The World Bank has provided funding for some of the highly indebted developing countries to refinance their debt in recent years. The bank promotes private investment in its participating countries. The World Bank gave developing countries loans totaling more than $24 billion in 2008. Rich industrialized nations provide financial contributions to the World Bank. The World Bank employs 10,000 development professionals in its 109 country offices and at its headquarters in Washington, DC, who come from almost every country on earth. For members, they offer a wide range of technical support services.

The World Bank must deal with the issue of fraud and corruption in addition to helping developing countries combat malaria and construct schools and dams. This is because dishonest government officials and contractors occasionally steal development funds and keep them for themselves rather than allowing them to help the vast majority of the impoverished. The World Bank finds it challenging to track down the money that has been disbursed in order to pinpoint the origin of corruption because money is fungible. Because of financial mismanagement, developing countries lose enormous sums of money from the World Bank, but their taxpayers are still responsible for paying the bank back. Critics claim that from 5 to 25% of the money the World Bank has lent since 1946 has been misappropriated. Millions of impoverished individuals have lost out on chances to enhance their economic, educational, and health conditions as a result of this misuse. Furthermore, the World Bank has poured money into impoverished countries for the past 20 years that they are obviously unable to repay. We'll see if the World Bank can implement measures to guarantee that the money entrusted to it is used wisely and for the intended purpose. Moreover, the World Bank's influence is waning as globalization changes the global economy. There are new rivals who transfer money to developing countries. Wealthy individuals from Singapore to Abu Dhabi are looking for opportunities in far-off locations. In order to secure access to raw materials and export markets, countries like China, Brazil, India, and Russia are also funding industry and infrastructure in even the poorest countries.

6.6.2. International Monetary Fund

The International Monetary Fund (IMF), which has its headquarters in Washington, DC, is another organization that provides assistance to both developed and developing countries. The IMF, which has 185 member countries, can be viewed as a bank for their central banks. Some countries will experience balance-of-payments surpluses over a specific time period, while others will experience deficits. A deficit-ridden country first uses its foreign exchange reserves, like the dollar, which is recognized as payment by other countries. Nonetheless, there will occasionally be insufficient money in the deficit country. At that point, aid from other countries can be extended through the IMF. The surplus countries provide money to the IMF, which then distributes it to countries that are temporarily short of funds. Long-term deficits must be closed, and the IMF works to make sure that this correction happens as quickly and smoothly as feasible. Quotas and loans are the two main sources of funding for the IMF. The majority of IMF funds are generated by member nation-pooled quotas, also known as subscriptions. A member's quota is determined by its financial and economic weight in the world; countries with greater economic weight have larger quotas. The IMF uses the quotas as a way to augment its resources on a regular basis. The IMF also receives funding from member countries through loans. The IMF maintains credit lines with Saudi Arabia and other major industrialized nations.

Every IMF loan has some kind of condition attached to it. This attachment indicates that a deficit country has to consent to implementing the IMF's recommended financial and economic policies in order to receive a loan. The goals of these measures are to reduce the member's deficit in balance of payments and encourage noninflationary economic growth. Nevertheless, deficit countries have frequently resisted the conditionality attached to IMF loans. The IMF has occasionally insisted that deficit countries implement austerity measures, such as significant cuts to imports, private consumption, and public spending, in order to live within their means. The IMF's detractors point out that its bailouts could be a factor in the so-called moralhazard issue, which occurs when countries profit from their choices when things go well but are shielded when they don't. A second area of concern is the contractionary effect of the IMF's restrictive fiscal and monetary policy conditions. If countries do not bear the consequences of their poor decisions, won't they be encouraged to make more bad decisions in the future? Many analysts believe that the answer to this question is yes: won't such circumstances lead to bank and business failures, intensify the recession, and reduce government spending on aiding the impoverished?

6.6.3. Generalized System of Preferences

Developing countries have forced developed countries to lower their tariff walls because they have insufficient access to their markets. Many developed nations have granted nonreciprocal tariff preferences to exports from developing nations in an effort to support these countries in bolstering their industrial base and international competitiveness. Major industrialized nations temporarily lower their tariffs on specific manufactured imports from developing countries below the levels applied to imports from other industrialized nations under the generalized system of preferences (GSP). But because the GSP is made up of numerous separate plans that vary in the kinds of goods they cover and the degree of tariff reduction, it is not a uniform system. In other words, rather than relying on foreign aid, the GSP aims to stimulate economic development in developing countries through increased trade. Advanced countries freely grant trade preferences. They are not required by the WTO. Donor countries set the requirements for eligibility, product coverage, preference margin size, and preference duration. In reality, governments of developed nations hardly ever give developing nations significant export advantages in industries. Therefore, in industries where they have a comparative advantage, developing countries frequently receive only limited preferences. The primary cause of restricted preferences is the strong internal resistance to liberalization in some sectors of developed countries.

From its inception in 1976, the U.S. Duty-free status has been extended to roughly 3,000 items under the GSP program. Eligibility requirements include abiding by international labor, environmental, and intellectual property laws as well as not supporting international terrorism. The U.S. program offers qualified goods from qualified countries total access without tariffs or quotas. Recipients of the U.S. program encompasses about 130 developing countries and the territories they depend on. Similar to other developed countries' GSP initiatives, the U.S. program denies preferential tariff treatment to a number of import-sensitive products. The GSP does not apply to footwear, certain agricultural products, textiles and clothing. Additionally, a country's GSP eligibility for a particular product may be revoked if its yearly exports surpass $100 million or if a domestic industry suffers appreciable harm. As GSP participants have become wealthier over time, they have occasionally been "graduated" out of the program. Hong Kong, Singapore, Malaysia, Taiwan, and Singapore are among the alumni. The GSP program offers preferential access to the markets of developed countries, but its ability to lower trade barriers for developing countries is undermined by a number of factors. First, goods that already have relatively low tariffs are primarily covered by preferences. Second, nontariff measures like antidumping duties and safeguards have the potential to undermine tariff preferences. Moreover, due to lobbying by domestic interest groups in importing nations, certain goods and countries have been excluded from the GSP. Furthermore, preferences don't help most of the world's impoverished. The majority of people who survive on less than $1 per day reside in countries like Pakistan and India, where they are given restricted preferences for goods in which they are comparative advantages. Consequently, the restricted access of developing countries to the markets of developed countries has caused them to become frustrated.

6.6.4. Does Aid Promote Growth of Developing Nations?

There have been decades of debate regarding the effectiveness of aid and whether it fosters growth in developing nations. Opponents argue that aid has simply been wasted or has promoted government bureaucracies, extended unfavorable governments, or benefited the wealthy in developing countries. Despite 40 years of aid, they observe that poverty is still pervasive in South Asia and Africa and draw attention to the unfortunate histories of some of the countries that have benefited greatly from it, including Haiti, the Democratic Republic of the Congo, Somalia, and Papua New Guinea. They believe that aid initiatives should be completely removed, drastically reduced, or changed in significant ways. Supporters argue that these claims are exaggerated, even though they are partially true. They show that while aid has occasionally been ineffectual, it has improved growth and the fight against poverty in some countries and kept others from performing worse. Since a large portion of aid is given to political allies rather than advancing development, donors bear a greater portion of the blame for the shortcomings of aid than do recipients. They list several prosperous countries like South Korea, Indonesia, Botswana, Mozambique, and Tanzania that have benefited greatly from aid. They point out that while indicators of health and education have increased more quickly than they have in any other 40-year period in human history, indicators of poverty have decreased in many countries in the 40 years since aid became widely available.

Researchers in Washington, D.C. at the Center for Global Development have made an effort to settle this dispute by differentiating the aid that is given to developing countries. Aid for the development of infrastructure, which includes banking services, energy production, transportation networks, and communications, is referred to as growth-oriented aid because it is thought to have a significant impact on economic growth. Aid for food supplies, water sanitation, disaster and humanitarian relief, and similar initiatives, however, typically have less immediate effects on economic growth. Over a four-year period, growth-oriented aid was found to yield $1.64 in increased income in the average recipient nation for every $1 invested. This translates to an approximate annual rate of return of 13%. The researchers came to the conclusion that, while not always the case, growth and growth-oriented aid have a positive, causal relationship. In other words, growth-oriented aid flows have yielded results.

6.7. ECONOMIC GROWTH STRATEGIES: IMPORT SUBSTITUTION VERSUS EXPORT-LED GROWTH

Developing countries have pursued two competing approaches to industrialization, in addition to looking to developed countries for financial aid: an inward-looking approach known as "import substitution," in which industries are established primarily to supply the domestic market and foreign trade is given minimal consideration; and an outward-looking approach known as "export-led growth," which promotes the development of industries in which the country has a comparative advantage and heavily depends on foreign countries as buyers of the increased production of exportable goods.

6.7.1. Import Substitution

In developing countries like Argentina, Brazil, and Mexico, the industrialization strategy of import substitution gained popularity in the 1950s and 60s; some of these countries continue to use it today. Using a lot of trade barriers to shield home industries from import competition is known as import substitution. Because trade and industrial incentives prioritize domestic production over exports, the strategy is war-oriented. In the event that fertilizer imports happen, for instance, import substitution necessitates the development of a domestic fertilizer industry to generate import substitutes. Policies that substitute imports could, in theory, result in total self-sufficiency.

The developing countries' perspective on trade provides the justification for import substitution. Many developing countries believe that they are unable to compete with well-established companies in developed nations when it comes to exporting manufactured goods, particularly in light of the high trade barriers that these countries uphold. Developing countries are forced to produce some of the goods they currently import in order to meet the demands of economic growth and development. Tariffs and quotas are used to limit imports, and domestic manufacturers are only allowed to sell their products on the domestic market. This justification is frequently coupled with the infant-industry argument, which holds that by shielding emerging sectors of the economy, they will eventually expand to a level where they can rival those of developed countries. In a certain sense, import substitution makes sense: if a good is in demand and can be imported, why not manufacture it domestically? The economist responds that even though producing a good domestically might be more expensive than importing it, comparative advantage should determine which goods are exported and imported.

The following are some benefits of using import substitution to promote economic development:

- The domestic market for the manufactured good already exists, so there are few risks involved in starting a domestic industry to replace imports.
- A developing country can more easily defend its manufacturers from foreign rivals than it can pressure developed countries to loosen trade restrictions on goods that developing countries export.
- Foreigners have an incentive to locate manufacturing plants in developing nations in order to avoid the import tariff walls, creating jobs for local workers in the process.

There are a few drawbacks in addition to these benefits, which are as follows:

- Trade restrictions prevent foreign competition from reaching domestic industries, so there is no incentive for them to become more efficient.
- Manufacturers in many developing nations face high unit costs because they are unable to take advantage of economies of scale due to the small size of the domestic market.
- Protection of import-competing producers automatically discriminates against all other producers, including potential exporters, because the resources used in the protected industry would have been used elsewhere.
- Any attempt to remove tariffs and quotas is typically met with strong resistance once investment has been made in activities that were profitable solely because of those restrictions.
- Moreover, import substitution encourages corruption. Gains from illegal activities like smuggling are higher in economies that are better protected.

6.7.2. Export-Led Growth

Export-led growth, also known as export-oriented policy, is an additional development strategy. Because it connects the domestic economy to the global economy, this strategy is outwardly focused. The plan calls for encouraging growth through the export of manufactured goods rather than protecting domestic industries that are at a comparative disadvantage. Insofar as export subsidies balance out any export-deterrent effects of import barriers, trade controls are either nonexistent or extremely minimal. Instead of being an aim achieved at the price of the economy's efficiency, industrialization is seen as a natural byproduct of development. Many developing countries were moving away from import substitution strategies and toward export-led growth by the 1970s.

Three benefits come from export-oriented policies: they support labor-intensive manufacturing, an industry where developing countries are likely to have a comparative advantage. They provide domestic manufacturers more opportunity to take advantage of economies of scale by giving them access to a larger market in which to sell. They impose a competitive discipline on domestic firms, compelling them to increase their efficiency, by keeping import restrictions low. The relationship between openness to international trade and economic growth for developing countries is depicted in Figure 6.5. A sample of 72 countries is classified as "globalizers" or "non-globalizers." The 24 countries that saw the biggest increases in their trade to GDP ratio between 1975 and 1995 are referred to as the globalizers. The real income per capita of non-globalizers increased, on average, more quickly in the 1960s and 1970s than that of globalizers. Globalizers, on the other hand, saw significantly faster growth rates in the 1980s; real income per capita increased by an average of 3.5% annually in these countries, while non-globalizers saw growth rates of just 0.8%. In the 1990s, the difference widened even more, with the globalizers experiencing annual growth of 5 points 0 percent compared to the rest's 1 point 4 percent. To put these disparities into context, consider that in 1980, if both the average globalizer and the average non-globalizer had started with an income per capita of $1,000, by 2,000, the globalizer would have increased to $2,300 and the non-globalizer to just $1,240.

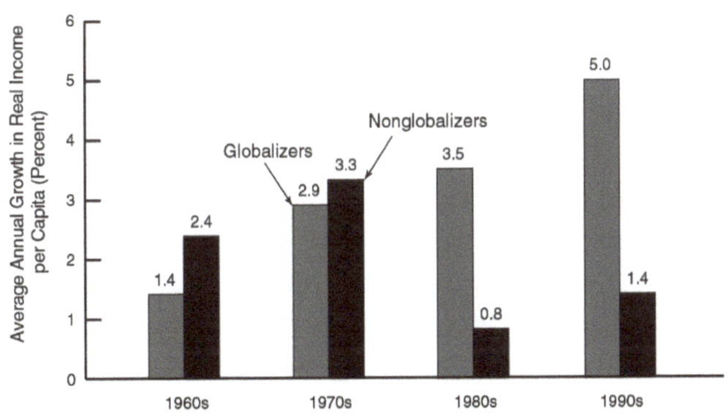

Figure 6.5. *Openness and economic growth.*

Source: https://wyamaka.wordpress.com/wp-content/uploads/2019/08/international-economics_30.pdf.

These results lend credence to the idea that countries adopting export-led growth policies have outperformed countries using import-substitution policies in terms of economic performance. Export-led growth strategies bring foreign competition to home markets, promoting efficient businesses and discouraging inefficient ones. They also encourage increased productivity and, consequently, quicker economic growth by fostering a more competitive environment. On the other hand, trade protectionist import substitution policies shift consumer demand to homegrown goods. The higher cost of domestic inputs in comparison to the price received by exporters, as well as the higher cost of imported inputs, deter exporting.

6.7.3. Economic Growth Good for the Poor

Critics argue that growth tends to be bad for the poor if the growth in question has been promoted by trade or foreign investment. This is true even though the evidence strongly suggests that trade is good for growth. Nevertheless, is growth good for poor workers in developing nations? They contend that increased investment makes economies less stable, putting workers at risk of a financial crisis and drawing the attention of banks in developed nations. Furthermore, they argue that trade-driven growth gives Western multinational corporations a hegemonic role in the development of third-world countries. This is problematic because Western multinational corporations only care about maintaining the status quo in order to increase their profits at any cost to the impoverished. Critics point to the evidence that shows economic inequality rises in tandem with rising national incomes in developed and developing countries, as well as the fact that multinational corporations employ sweatshops to produce their goods. Therefore, even if it's true that trade spurs growth, it misses the mark if workers' welfare is your top priority. Still, there is compelling evidence that growth benefits the impoverished. Developing countries with sustained growth, like those in East Asia, have significantly reduced poverty. The countries with the slowest growth are those with the highest rates of pervasive poverty, particularly those in Africa. While the degree of poverty can be influenced by economic policies, growth ultimately holds greater significance.

6.7.4. Developing Nations Achieve Export-Led Growth

The ability and willingness of developed countries to continue importing significant quantities of goods from developing countries is a prerequisite for exporting to support economic growth in developing nations. Pessimists contend that there is a compositional fallacy at work in this process. If developing countries attempted to export at the same time, the price of their goods would decline on international markets. Moreover, developed countries may impose tariffs to lessen competition from imports if they become wary of foreign competition, particularly in times of high unemployment. If too many developing countries attempt to export at once, will trade liberalization be counterproductive? Despite their large population and geographic size, developing countries are small economically. The combined exports of all the low- and middle-income countries in the world make up just 5% of global production. This is about the same as the United Kingdom's annual production. A coordinated export push by developing nations not already involved in the endeavor would not significantly burden the global trading system, even in the event that the growth of the world's demand for imports were somehow restrained.

Additionally, pessimists frequently underestimate the potential for intra-industry specialization in trade, which opens up new trade opportunities for developing countries. The same holds true for new trade between developing countries and developed countries. Developing countries frequently shift from labor-intensive manufacturing to more advanced forms of production as they expand. This movement creates space for goods from less developed countries in the markets they previously served. For instance, Japan moved away from labor-intensive manufacturing in the 1970s to allow exports from Singapore, Taiwan, and South Korea to take their place. As China started to enter those markets, South Korea, Taiwan, and Singapore followed suit in the 1980s and 1990s. Developing countries' own need for imports increases as a result of their increased exports.

6.7.5. East Asian Economies

Some developing countries have experienced robust and consistent economic growth, despite the general slow performance of their economies. East Asian countries like Singapore, Taiwan, Hong Kong, and South Korea have produced a number of prosperous developing nations. What factors contribute to their success? The natural resources, populations, cultures, and economic policies of the East Asian countries are very diverse. They do, however, share a number of traits that contribute to their economic success, including: (1) high rates of investment and (2) high and rising endowments of human capital as a result of universal primary and secondary education.

East Asian governments have made investments in their citizens and created an environment that is conducive to private enterprise competition in order to promote competitiveness. Additionally, they have maintained open economies to global trade. The economies of East Asia have actively pursued foreign technology, including imports of capital goods, licenses, and training. The economies of East Asia have generally dissuaded trade union formation, whether through policy of laissez-faire (Hong Kong), government paternalism (Singapore), or purposeful suppression (South Korea, Taiwan). The result has been the preservation of free and competitive labor markets as well as the prevention of minimum wage legislation.

With the exception of Hong Kong, the trade policies of the East Asian economies started with an import substitution phase after World War II. These countries imposed high tariffs and quantitative import restrictions in order to grow their consumer goods industries.

A few manufacturing sectors, like textiles, were also supported by them. Despite the fact that these policies at first raised domestic production, over time they caused costs to the economies of East Asia. Large trade deficits for the East Asian economies resulted from import-substitution policies, which encouraged the import of capital and intermediate goods while discouraging the export of manufactured goods.

East Asian economies switched to an export-oriented and outward-oriented strategy in order to secure the foreign exchange required to finance these deficits. By the late 1950s and early 1960s, export-push policies had been implemented in the economies of East Asia.

Close to free trade agreements were established by Singapore and Hong Kong. Policies to encourage exports while shielding home producers from import competition were started by Taiwan, South Korea, and Japan. Thailand, Malaysia, and Indonesia all implemented different measures to promote exports while progressively lowering import barriers. With manufactured exports making up the majority of this growth, these policies helped to increase the East Asian economies' share of global exports. But there are issues as a result of the East Asian economies' extraordinary success. Many East Asian economies are facing serious pollution issues as a result of the industrialize-at-all-costs mentality. Massive trade surpluses have sparked a surge of protectionist sentiment abroad, particularly in the US, where the economies of East Asia rely significantly on the U.S. future export expansion market.

6.7.6. Flying-Geese Pattern of Growth

It is commonly acknowledged that the economies of East Asia have grown according to a flying-geese pattern, in which countries progressively advance in technological development by imitating those of countries that have developed earlier than them. For example, as Japan moves into the higher-technology sectors of automotive, electronics, and other capital goods, Taiwan and Malaysia overtake Japan as the world leaders in apparel and textiles.

About 10 years later, the textile and clothing industries relocate to Thailand, Vietnam, and Indonesia, while Taiwan and Malaysia are able to advance to automotive and electronics products.

The flying-geese pattern is partly due to market forces: labor-rich countries will rise to prominence in labor-intensive sectors like footwear and will eventually advance to more capital- or skill-intensive sectors as savings and education expand the pool of available capital and skilled labor. But as the economies of East Asia have shown, developing flying geese requires more than just markets. Multinational corporations and advanced nation-developed technologies are increasingly influencing even labor-intensive, basic products like electronics assembly. East Asian economies have developed according to a flying geese pattern supported by a robust export platform. East Asian governments have used bonded warehouses, free-trade zones, joint ventures, and strategic alliances with multinational corporations as examples of export platforms. Economic policies that bolstered the incentives for labor-intensive exports were used by governments to support these mechanisms.

6.8. CHINA'S TRANSFORMATION TO CAPITALISM

The People's Republic of China was a minor player in the global goods market at the beginning of the 1970s. It was only the 30th largest exporting country, with less than $15 billion worth of imports and exports. China also made up a very small portion of the global financial markets. China's national output was 60% higher than Japan's and more than half that of the United States by 2005, making it the second largest economy in the world. What led to this change? A revolutionary communist movement took over the country in 1949, marking the beginning of modern China. China adopted the Soviet model of import substitution and central planning shortly after the communist takeover, emphasizing fast economic growth, especially in the industrial sector. The state abolished household farming, collectivizes agriculture, takes control of urban manufacturing, and imposes mandatory production quotas. China's government discouraged markets from functioning, which stunted economic growth and left a large number of people impoverished.

China broke with the Soviet model in the late 1950s, moving from large-scale, capital-intensive industry to labor-intensive, small-scale industry dispersed throughout the countryside. The relationship between individual reward and individual effort received scant attention. Rather, the employees were motivated by a shared commitment to the collective plans' success. This system turned out to be financially unsuccessful. Following the reforms, manufacturing output increased, but production costs were high and product quality was poor. Due to its inability to feed its population, China developed into a major importer of cotton, vegetable oils, and grains. Plant managers, scientists, engineers, and academics who supported reform and material incentives were chastised and forced to work in the fields as a result of this economic downturn.

China witnessed the remarkable growth and prosperity of its formerly impoverished neighbors, namely South Korea, Japan, Singapore, and Taiwan, by the 1970s. As a result, China began to "marketize" its economy by making gradual, tiny adjustments to reduce political unrest and economic disruption. Reforms were implemented in agriculture and industry to lessen the role of state planners and to strengthen individual incentives and the producing unit's role. The majority of goods were sold at prices set by the market, not by the government. More competition was permitted between new businesses and between state-owned businesses; by 2000, nonstate businesses produced roughly 75% of China's industrial output. Furthermore, China allowed joint ventures and foreign investment into its economy. The Chinese government's monopoly on international trade was also broken up, and economic zones were created in its place, allowing businesses to hire and fire employees as well as retain their foreign exchange profits. In other words, China has strayed from the import substitution path, which involves erecting import barriers to promote the growth of indigenous industry. China's economy is heavily dependent on imports, and the country is now remarkably open to international trade.

China had completed all of the simple economic transitions necessary to move toward capitalism by the early 2000s, including allowing farmers to sell their own produce and welcoming foreign investors and salespeople.

There were still other reforms that needed to be addressed, such as:

1. a massive restructuring of state-owned industries that were losing money;
2. cleaning up state banks that had gone bankrupt;
3. establishing a social security system in a society where a job was once guaranteed for life; and
4. creating a monetary system with a central bank independent of the Communist Party and the government.

The closure of financially struggling businesses would result in the mass layoff of millions of workers without benefits, adding to the already unstable pool of over 100 million unemployed individuals in China. Furthermore, if the number of bankruptcies in the state sector rose, the banks that provided loans to the state-run businesses would need additional funding. Such loans have the potential to drive inflation and undermine the monetary policy of a central bank.

Political liberties have not kept up with China's economic decentralization, despite the country having allowed free enterprise to supplant much of its centrally planned economy. Remember the 1989 Tiananmen Square military crackdown by the Chinese government against a pro-democracy demonstration that resulted in fatalities and showed the Communist Party's will to hold onto power? Since there is no freedom of speech under Communist Party rule, independent voices are essentially nonexistent. Thus, China's transition to capitalism has involved a greater application of market forces while maintaining a communist political structure. China now refers to its economic system as a socialist market economy. China's exports have highlighted the country's abundant labor force, which is used extensively in its production process, in relation to international trade. As a result, China is now a hub for low-wage manufacturing, exporting toys, sporting goods, electronics, clothing, textiles, and other items. China is becoming a larger importer of capital goods such as machinery, transportation equipment, and other items requiring more advanced technology than the country can generate on its own. Since 1978, China's economy has grown primarily due to its rapid increase in exports and investment spending.

In 2001, China joined the WTO following 15 years of negotiations. China prioritized membership because it would signal to the world community its increasing economic might, lessen the possibility of export tariffs, and persuade the US to allow China to maintain normal trade relations. But U.S. Trade officials insisted that meaningful conditions for China's membership, including a significant reduction in trade and investment barriers, be met. China committed to the following when it joined the WTO: lowering its average tariff for industrial goods to 8.9 percent and for agricultural goods to 15%; capping export subsidies on agricultural exports at 8.5 percent of farm output value; granting full trade and distribution rights to foreign enterprises operating in China; completely opening the banking system to foreign financial institutions; and protecting foreigners' intellectual property in accordance with internationally recognized standards.

China's economic success is evidence that its economy is now open to foreign investment and trade. The largest issue facing China, though, is bringing its society together in the face of widening gaps in wealth, living standards, and rate of development. Is it possible for the current political structure to handle both domestic and environmental issues? China is forced to seek assistance from market principles. Markets connect it to the rest of the world, but there isn't much internal pressure for market-driven social integration. Because of this, a lot of observers believe that political reform that promotes a multiparty system is ultimately necessary to solve China's problems.

6.8.1. China's Export Boom Comes at a Cost: How to Make Factories Play Fair

China is now a significant exporter of manufactured goods, but this has not come without a price. Retailers like Wal-Mart and The Home Depot are pushing Chinese suppliers to make low-cost goods at the lowest feasible prices, shoving aside worries about labor rights, environmental quality, and product safety. Consumer advocates, for instance, sued Chinese companies in 2007 on the grounds that they were manufacturing dangerous toys, cribs, electronics, and other items. The largest toy company in the world, Mattel, recalled three different toys made in China that included potentially dangerous magnets and lead paint; Disney recalled thousands of Baby Einstein blocks; and smaller companies recalled everything from water bottles and flashlights to children's jewelry, key chains, and notebooks. Children were most disappointed by the double recall of Thomas the Tank Engine toys when it was found that the paint contained dangerously high levels of lead, which can harm a child's brain. Furthermore, it was discovered that the Floating Eyeballs toy was filled with kerosene, leading to its recall. Some who were critical claimed that these instances were a part of a wider trend. The U.S. Due to globalization, an increasing amount of production is being outsourced to countries such as China. Concurrently, the U.S. The government has reduced inspection and regulation of imports. Consequently, a growing number of products that are neither made in the US nor governed by US safety regulations are marketed to US consumers.

China also faces challenges in labor protection. Since U.S. While American consumers can afford cheap clothes and sneakers thanks to retailers like Eddie Bauer and Target, their constant pressure to cut costs from their Chinese suppliers provides Chinese companies with a strong incentive to violate labor standards, which American companies proudly display as a mark of responsible capitalism. In general, these guidelines take into account China's official minimum wage, which varies from $45 to $101 per month and is determined by local or provincial governments. US. Businesses usually also claim to follow the 40–44 hour workweek mandated by the government, after which they must pay overtime. But a lot of Chinese factories are breaching these standards because of the pressure to reduce costs. Their ability to fabricate time sheets and payroll has allowed them to underpay their employees and make them put in long hours at factories that frequently have health and safety issues. Recognizing that labor abuses are not being prevented by the current system of auditing Chinese suppliers, U.S. shops in China are looking for methods to make labor laws better. Whether these efforts prove to be successful is yet to be seen. Another issue facing China is the promotion of safety. In the 20 years since the U.S.S. Businesses started using Chinese factories to produce low-cost T-shirts and jeans, but China's water, land, and air have suffered greatly as a result. The Chinese government and environmental activists acknowledge the role that U.S. Multinational corporations contribute to China's escalating pollution issues by pressuring the country to cut the prices of its goods. The direct disposal of wastewater into rivers has long been a cost-cutting strategy used by Chinese factories. Large factories can save hundreds of thousands of dollars a year by sending waste water directly into rivers, in violation of China's water-pollution laws, as treating contaminated water costs more than 13 cents per metric ton. Because Americans are not bearing the costs of pollution, the outcome is artificially low prices in the US. American businesses that purchase goods from China are frequently criticized for not adopting a stricter stance against their country's polluting suppliers.

6.9. INDIA: BREAKING OUT OF THE THIRD WORLD

Another country whose economy has significantly improved since freer trade policies were implemented is India. India's economy is broad, including manufacturing, agriculture, handicrafts, and a wide range of services. Despite the fact that agriculture still provides a direct or indirect source of income for two thirds of the workforce in India, the country's services industry is expanding. The emergence of the digital era and the abundance of young, educated Indians who speak English well are making India a sought-after location for international outsourcing of technical support and customer services.China and India have developed along distinct routes. China has developed along the same conventional path as countries like South Korea and Japan, resulting in the country becoming a hub for low-wage manufacturing. India came to the conclusion that exporting services was a more viable option after realizing it could not compete with China directly in the manufacturing sector.

According to the Heckscher-Ohlin theory, India's abundant factor has been its relatively educated and English-speaking labor force, which offers an affordable entry point to international services like call centers and data processing operations. India's strategy may prove more beneficial in the long run, even though China's goods-dominated strategy has a better track record thus far due to economic growth rates. Global per-capita income trends show that eventually, services will account for a larger share of a country's wealth than industry.

India adopted an import-substitution model to run its economy and started practicing socialism after gaining independence from Britain in 1947. Following its independence, India developed a fear of all forms of imperialism, which led to both of these. In order to limit competition, India's government implemented protectionist trade barriers, prohibitions on foreign investment, stringent laws governing the financial sector and private industry, a sizable public sector, and central planning. As a result, India experienced isolation from the outside world from the 1950s until the 1980s. India's economy only grew at a slow rate during this time, and the country saw widespread poverty. People in India realized more and more that public sector policy had failed their country.

India's policy makers realized in 1991 that reforms were necessary because their system of import substitution and state controls was stifling the country's economy. As a result, there was a noticeable shift toward a market-based, outward-focused economy. Import tariffs were reduced from an average of 87% in 1990 to 33% in 1994, export subsidies were removed, and the requirement that the government approve industrial investment expenditures was terminated. The rupee was devalued and Indian companies were permitted to borrow on foreign markets. India's economy was closed, agrarian, and underdeveloped before these reforms helped to open it up and make it more progressive, attracting foreign investment and increasing the amount of wealth generated by industry and services. As a result, the rate of poverty has decreased and economic growth has increased dramatically.

The outsourcing industry in India serves as an example of how trade and investment from abroad have helped the country. In the 1990s, companies like General Electric and British Airways moved their back-office operations, including information technology (IT), to India as a result of restrictions on foreign investment being lifted. Other businesses established operations in India as a result of these companies' success, which demonstrated to the rest of the world that the country was a good place for outsourcing. Thousands of Indian workers received training from these multinationals, and many of them went on to work for other burgeoning Indian companies. Put simply, the thousands of new jobs and increased wages brought about by foreign investment benefited Indian workers.

An additional illustration of the advantages of trade and investment liberalization is the Indian automobile sector. Prior to the 1980s, India's state-owned automakers were protected from international competition by import tariffs and restrictions on foreign investment. These companies produced only two models at exorbitant prices using antiquated technology. By the 1990s, foreign investment prohibitions had mostly been lifted and auto import tariffs had been drastically reduced. The upshot was a rise in the number of cars imported into India as well as the arrival of foreign automakers who set up assembly lines there. For Indian auto workers who benefited from higher wages, labor productivity increased more than threefold as competition increased. Additionally, a drop in car prices resulted in a spike in consumer demand, an increase in auto sales, and the creation of thousands of jobs for autoworkers. India exports cars to other countries and its auto industry produces 13 times as many cars now as it did in the early 1980s. Without global connectivity, India's automakers could not have achieved any of this.

But the country's automobile and outsourcing sectors are rapidly expanding, in sharp contrast to the majority of its economy, where trade and foreign investment restrictions stifle competition and encourage the survival of inefficient businesses. The retail of food demonstrates how Indian industry functions in the face of restrictions on foreign investment. In this industry, labor productivity as of 2007 was only 5% of the U.S. degree. The primary reason for this disparity is that the majority of food retailers in India are mom-and-pop counter stores and street markets, as opposed to contemporary supermarkets. Additionally, productivity only accounts for 20% of the U.S. level in Indian supermarkets due to their tiny size and shoddy marketing and merchandising strategies. Global retailers like WalMart have heightened competition in developing nations like China and Mexico, leading to higher productivity. It is not permitted for these retailers to make investments in India.

India cannot afford to sit back and relax despite its economic successes because over 250 million people in the country still live below the official poverty line. The country must concentrate on enhancing its infrastructure, including its ports, rail freight system, roads, and electricity generation, in order to maintain strong economic growth. India has not kept up with economic developments with its recent infrastructure investments. China, on the other hand, has made significant investments to create top-notch infrastructure that can draw in foreign capital and spur economic expansion. By 2030, India is predicted to have the largest population in the world. India benefits greatly from an almost infinite labor supply and consumer demand due to its rapid population growth. However, it also serves as a reminder of the importance of making investments in healthcare, education, and enough job opportunities. The majority of economists believe that India must gradually deregulate industries like banking, retail, and the news media, which are still severely constrained by antiquated laws. Preferences for inefficient, small-scale producers must also end, and laws preventing layoffs in medium- and large-sized businesses must be repealed. Deregulation and market opening would allow for the more easy flow of capital and skilled foreign investments into India, boosting the country's industry and economy. In order to create jobs in rural areas and ensure that India's economic growth reaches every corner of the country, the government must reform the agriculture sector.

Although India has come a long way, more work will be required to maintain its economic expansion. India has a rapidly growing population, and in order to keep its people out of poverty, it will need to create millions of jobs. Whether India's public sector, business community, and society as a whole will exhibit the political will required to collaborate and bring this about is still to be seen.

CASE STUDY

FOREIGN DIRECT INVESTMENT HINDER OR HELP ECONOMIC DEVELOPMENT

Foreign investment brings higher wages, and is a major source of technology transfer and managerial skills in host developing nations. This contributes to rising prosperity in the developing nations concerned, as well as enhancing demand for higher value-added exports from advanced economies.

One of the requirements for economic development in a low-income economy is an increase in the nation's stock of capital. A developing nation may increase the amount of capital in the domestic economy by encouraging foreign direct investment. Foreign direct investment occurs when foreign firms either locate production plants in the domestic economy or acquire a substantial ownership position in a domestic firm. Many developing economies have attempted to restrict foreign direct investment because of nationalist sentiment and concerns about foreign economic and political influence. One reason for this sentiment is that many developing nations have operated as colonies of more developed economies. This colonial experience has often resulted in a legacy of concern that foreign direct investment may serve as a modern form of economic colonialism in which foreign companies might exploit the resources of the host nation.

However, in recent years restrictions on foreign direct investment in many developing economies have been substantially reduced as a result of international treaties, external pressure from the IMF or World Bank, or unilateral actions by governments that have come to believe that foreign direct investment will encourage economic growth in the host nation. This has resulted in a rather dramatic expansion in the level of foreign direct investment in some developing economies.

Foreign direct investment may encourage economic growth in the short term by increasing aggregate demand in the host economy. In the long run, the increase in the stock of capital raises the productivity of labor, leads to higher incomes, and further increases aggregate demand. However, another long-term impact comes through the transfer of technological knowledge from advanced to developing economies. Many economists argue that this transfer of technology may be the primary benefit of foreign direct investment.

It is also often argued that it is necessary to restrict foreign direct investment in a given industry for national security purposes. This reasoning serves as a justification for prohibitions on investment in defense industries and in other industries that are deemed essential for national security. Most governments, for example, would be concerned if their weapons were produced by companies owned by firms in nations that might serve as future enemies. Environmentalists are concerned that the growth of foreign direct investment in developing economies may lead to a deterioration in the global environment since investment is expanding more rapidly in nations that have relatively lax environmental standards. The absence of restrictive environmental standards, it is argued, is one of the reasons for the relatively high rate of return on capital investment in less-developed economies. Technology transfer from the developed economies; however, may also result in the adoption of more efficient and environmentally sound production techniques than would have been adopted in the absence of foreign investment.

CLASS ACTIVITY

VOLUNTARY NATIONAL CONTENT STANDARDS IN ECONOMICS

Voluntary exchange occurs only when all participating parties expect to gain. This is true for trade among individuals or organizations within a nation, and among individuals or organizations in different nations.

- Exchange is trading goods and services with people for other goods and services or money.
- People voluntarily exchange goods and services because they expect to be better off after the exchange.
- When people buy something, they value it more than it costs them; when people sell something, they value it less than the payment they receive.
- When imports are restricted by public policies, consumers pay higher prices and job opportunities and profits in exporting firms decrease.

Materials

- 3 Dum-Dum lollipops per student. Remove any "mystery" flavors. (Note: Buy the original/classic bags of Dum Dums as special or seasonal bags will have different flavors.)
- Post-it notes (1 each for half of students. Ex: 15 post-its for 30 students in class)
- Visual 1 "Trading Results" prepared in slide or on white board.
- Handout 1: Dum Dum Flavor Ranking (1 per student)
- Handout 2: Trading Record (1 per student)
- Handout 3: Tic-Tac-Tariff Cards (1 per half of students, cut into individual cards. EX: 15 copies for students in class, cut to make 90 card)
- Optional: Stamp and ink pad or special colored pen/marker to use as "customs stamp."

Preparation:

- Before class, remove any "mystery flavor" Dum Dum from the bag. While it might seem fun to keep them in the mix, it adds an unnecessary distraction to the game as students will struggle over how to score "mystery" and the discussion could be side-railed into risk and reward. Keep it simple! You want the game focused on trade and the impact of the tariff on trade.
- NOTE: The Dum Dum flavors listed in handout 1 are the 2018 flavors. Check the Dum Dum website for current flavors and update handout 1 if necessary.
- Arrange a place in the front of the room where you can collect and stamp/ initial the Tic-Tac-Tariff cards.

Procedure:

1. Give each student a copy of Handout 1: "Dum Dum Flavor Ranking" and have them rank each of the Dum Dum flavors listed from their favorite (16) down to their least favorite (1). While this may seem backward to students, it's important to go from 16 to 1 as they will be using their rank as a representation of value so high numbers are better than low numbers. (NOTE: Alternately, you could have students place a value of 1 to 10 on each flavor – one low, 10 high. However, while this is a more statistically accurate way to represent their value, you run the risk of some students giving all the flavors a low value and then they don't have much of an incentive to engage in trade and participate in the activity.)
2. While students are ranking the flavors, geographically divide the room in half (EX: left and right sides or front and back) and give half of the students in the room a post-it note to wear as a badge. The badge identifies them as citizens of "Country X." Have the write a large X on their badge and place the badge on their shirt.
3. The other half of the students are from "Country O." Give each of them 1 Tic-Tac-Tariff card to begin with.
4. Give every student a copy of Handout 2: "Trading Record." Instruct them to fold the paper down the middle and only use the left side for round 1.
5. Explain that you will be giving each of them a "basket" of 3 Dum Dum lollipops. They should write the flavors in their basket at the top of their "Trading Record" and then use their values from their "Flavor Ranking" to determine the value of the basket they were given.
6. Pass out the Dum Dums.
7. Display Visual 2 and explain their objective and the rules for round 1. Illustrate with the handouts an example of how they will calculate their basket, record a trade, and play tic-tac-toe during round 1.
8. Display Visual 3. Have one student per table or row add up the values of all the baskets in their table/row and then you can quickly add all their subtotals to come up with a class-wide basket value before trade.

1. **Round 1**

9. Begin Round 1. Allow the round to run for 5–7 minutes or long enough for most students to have traded at least 2 or 3 times.
10. Stop the round and give students time to calculate the value of their current basket of suckers. Expect that some students may end up with more or fewer than 3 suckers in their basket. That's okay. For example, it may have been in their interest to trade two low value suckers for one higher value sucker.
11. Use Visual 3 to record and display the results for the class. Have the same student per row/table get a basket total for their group then add all the group basket totals to come up with the class-wide basket value after trade.
12. Subtract the original basket value from the new basket value to find the increase in the basket value. Explain that this represents the gains from trade in round 1.
13. In the same manner collect and count the number of trades for the whole class and divide by 2 to get the total number of trades. (Each trade will be reported by both parties involved but you only want to count it once, thus the need to divide by 2.)
14. Use the Tic-Tac-Toe Tariff cards you collected as the customs agent to record how many international trades were conducted.
15. Debrief Round 1.
    - How did you do?
    - Raise your hand if the value of your basket increased?
    - Raise your hand if you participated in an international trade?
    - How did it compare to trades you did within your own country? (*International trades take more time/has a higher cost*).
    - Did anyone participate in an international trade for which they did not pay a tariff? Or did anyone change the outcome of a tie game just so they wouldn't have to go through the hassle of playing again?

2. Round 2

16. Congratulate the students on their gains and explain that we're going to do another round. But first, they must put all their Dum Dums from round 1 away. It's important that the Dum Dums from round 1 are out of the game and not used for trading in round 2. (OPTIONAL: You may choose to collect all the Dum Dums and redistribute them randomly for round 2.)
17. Randomly distribute 3 more Dum Dums to each student.
18. Have them calculate their basket values before trade.
19. Collect and display the total value of baskets before trade on Visual 1.
20. Display Visual 3: Rules for Round 2. Explain that in this round they are free to trade with anyone in any country. No Tic-Tac-Toe Tariff required. However, if

they trade with someone from another country, they should record it by checking the "International Trade" box on their transaction record.

Discuss

- How was round 2 different (number of trades, value of baskets, trades with people from other country)? *There will likely be more trades, greater increases in basket value, and more international trades.*
- How did the tariff in Round 1 impact trade, now that you've experienced a round without a tariff? *The tariff reduces the number of trades.*
- Does the tariff eliminate international trade? *It reduces trade. But people will still trade if it's worth it (benefits are greater than costs).*
- Who benefits from a tariff? Government, people (producers) in the domestic country, as more people in their own country will trade with them given that international trades are more costly.
- Who is hurt by a tariff? People who would've traded had the tariff not made it too costly.
- Who bore the cost of the tariff? What are the costs of the tariff? Citizens from both countries bore the costs. Both had to spend time to play the game. Both gave up time they could be trading with other people.

SUMMARY

- Developing nations tend to be characterized by relatively low levels of gross domestic product per capita, shorter life expectancies, and lower levels of adult literacy. Many developing nations believe that the current international trading system, based on the principle of comparative advantage, is irrelevant for them.
- Among the institutions and policies that have been created to support developing nations are the World Bank, the International Monetary Fund, and a generalized system of preferences.
- International commodity agreements have been formed to stabilize the prices and revenues of producers of primary products. The methods used to attain this stability are buffer stocks, export controls, and multilateral contracts. In practice, these methods have yielded modest success.
- The OPEC oil cartel was established in 1960 in reaction to the control that the major international oil companies exercised over the posted price of oil. OPEC has used production quotas to support prices and earnings above what could be achieved in more competitive conditions.
- Besides seeking financial assistance from advanced nations, developing nations have promoted internal industrialization through policies of import substitution and export promotion. Nations emphasizing export promotion have tended to realize higher rates of economic growth than nations emphasizing import-substitution policies.
- The East Asian economies have realized remarkable economic growth in recent decades. The foundation of such growth has included high rates of investment, the increasing endowments of an educated workforce, and the use of export promotion policies.
- By the 1990s, China had become a high performing Asian economy. Although China has dismantled much of its centrally planned economy and permitted free enterprise to replace it, political freedoms have not increased. Today, China describes itself as a socialist market economy. Being heavily endowed with labor, China specializes in many labor-intensive products. In 2001, China became a member of the WTO.

REVIEW QUESTIONS

1. What are the major reasons for the skepticism of many developing nations regarding the comparative-advantage principle and free trade?
2. Stabilizing commodity prices has been a major objective of many primary-product nations. What are the major methods used to achieve price stabilization?
3. What are some examples of international commodity agreements? Why have many of them broken down over time?
4. Why are the developing nations concerned with commodity-price stabilization?
5. Why is cheating a typical problem for cartels?

6. The generalized system of preferences is intended to help developing nations gain access to world markets. Explain.
7. How are import-substitution and export promotion policies used to aid in the industrialization of developing nations?
8. Describe the strategy that East Asia used from the 1970s to the 1990s to achieve high rates of economic growth. Can the Asian miracle continue in the new millennium?

REFERENCES

1. Eaton, J., & Kortum, S. (2002). Technology, geography, and trade. *Econometrica, 70*(5), 1741–1779.
2. Federico, G., & Tena-Junguito, A. (2019). World trade, 1800–1938: A new synthesis. *Revista de Historia Economica–Journal of Iberian and Latin American Economic History, 37*(1), 9–41.
3. International Monetary Fund Research Dept. (1997). *World Economic Outlook, May 1997: Globalization: Opportunities and Challenges*. International Monetary Fund.
4. Krueger, A. O. (2020). *International Trade: What Everyone Needs to Know*. Oxford University Press.
5. Owen, E., & Johnston, N. P. (2017). Occupation and the political economy of trade: Job routineness, offshorability, and protectionist sentiment. *International Organization, 71*(4), 665–699.
6. Peláez, C. (2008). *Globalization and the State: Volume II: Trade Agreements, Inequality, the Environment, Financial Globalization, International Law and Vulnerabilities*. Palgrave MacMillan.
7. Perla, J., Tonetti, C., & Waugh, M. E. (2021). Equilibrium technology diffusion, trade, and growth. *American Economic Review, 111*(1), 73–128.
8. Pugel, T. A. (2003). *International Economics*. Boston: McGraw-Hill.
9. Rodríguez, F., & Rodrik, D. (1999). Trade policy and economic growth: A skeptic's guide to the cross-national evidence. Centre for economic policy research discussion paper No. 2143.
10. Rodrik, D. (2001). The global governance of trade as if development really mattered, October 2001, United Nations Development Program.
11. UNCTAD. (2014). Background note, UNCTAD global commodities forum (7-8 April 2014, Geneva).
12. UNCTAD. (2014). Natural resources sector: Review and identification of opportunities for commodity-based trade and development. Note by the UNCTAD Secretariat, Multi-year Expert Meeting on Commodities and Development (TD/B/C.1/MEM.2/26).
13. World Bank. (2012). *Migration and Development Brief 18*.

CHAPTER 7

Regional Trading Arrangements

LEARNING OBJECTIVES

After studying this chapter, you will be able to:

- Define regional integration versus multilateralism
- Understand the types of regional trading arrangement
- Describe the impetus for regionalism
- Explain the effects of a regional trading arrangement
- Discuss about the European Union
- Describe economic costs and benefits of a common currency: the European monetary union
- Know North American free trade agreement
- Discuss the free trade area of the Americas
- Define Asia-pacific economic cooperation
- Describe transition economies
- Define the China's transformation to capitalism
- Discuss on India: breaking out of the third world

KEY TERMS FROM THIS CHAPTER

Domestic policy	Economic development	Economic integration
Economic union	Environmental regulations	Fiscal policies
General Agreement on Tariffs and Trade (GATT)	Liberalization	Multilateral trading system
Multilateralism	Regional security	Trade barriers
Trade liberalization	Welfare consequences	World Trade Organization (WTO)

INTRODUCTION

Advanced countries have significantly reduced their trade barriers since World War II. Two strategies have led to this trade liberalization. The first is the nondiscriminatory, reciprocal removal of trade barriers. Members of the World Trade Organization (WTO) and the General Agreement on Tariffs and Trade (GATT) agree that any tariff reductions reached by any two members will be applied to all other members. A global strategy like this promotes the progressive lowering of tariffs everywhere.

When a small number of countries, usually on a regional basis, come together to form a regional trading arrangement, that is a second approach to trade liberalization. Members of the system consent to lowering trade barriers within the group as opposed to trade with non-member countries. While each member country is still free to set its own internal policies, all of them include preferential treatment for group members in their trade policies. The World Trade Organization's anti-discrimination principle has not applied to regional trading agreements such as free-trade zones and customs unions.

7.1. REGIONAL INTEGRATION VERSUS MULTILATERALISM

Remember that promoting trade liberalization through international agreements is one of the WTO's main goals. But it can be very challenging to get a lot of nations to agree on reforms. As the WTO struggled to reach a global trade agreement in the early 2000s, nations began to turn more and more to more limited, regional agreements as a substitute. Regional trading agreements' approaches to trade liberalization differ significantly from the multilateral trade liberalization found in the World Trade Organization. Regional trading agreements discriminate against the rest of the world by lowering trade barriers only for a select group of partner countries. Any country that liberalizes its trade with another is allowed to do so without discrimination on the part of the 153 WTO members.

Regional trading blocs are a departure from the WTO system's tenet of normal trading relations and are inherently discriminatory, despite the fact that they can enhance the multilateral trading system. Certain analysts observe that regional trading blocs that curtail member countries' autonomy to pursue trade liberalization with external parties are apt to serve as obstacles to multilateralism. For instance, Malaysia would only be marginally interested in a free-trade agreement with the U.S. if it had already been successful in establishing a market there. However, Argentina, its less prosperous rival, would be keen to sign a regional free-trade agreement and take Malaysia's market share in the U.S.—not by producing a better or more affordable product, but by securing preferential treatment under U.S. trade law. What would be Argentina's motivation to attend WTO meetings and sign a multilateral free-trade agreement that would remove its special privileges once it received its privilege?

Members of a regional trading arrangement may not be very interested in global liberalization, according to two additional factors. First, trade liberalization may not provide trade-bloc members with additional economies of scale because it frequently results in only modest openings to foreign markets. Regional trade blocs, which frequently offer more liberalized trade, might permit domestic companies to run long enough production runs to deplete scale economies. Second, rather than expending time and energy on international negotiations, trade-bloc members might prefer to focus their efforts on forging solid regional ties (Abrego, Riezman, & Whalley, 2006).

However, when regional blocs are organized around openness and inclusivity, they can serve as stepping stones rather than obstacles for international free trade and investment. Regional blocs have multiple ways to promote openings of global markets.

First, due to the greater commonality of interests and the less complicated negotiation procedures, regional agreements may result in deeper economic interdependence among members than do multilateral accords. Second, the creation of a regional free-trade area sets up a self-reinforcing process: as the market that the free-trade area covers grows, it becomes more alluring for non-members to join in order to benefit from the same trade preferences as member countries. Third, regional liberalization promotes workers' partial relocation from import-competing sectors where the country has a significant comparative disadvantage to export-oriented sectors where it has a significant comparative advantage. The labor force's share that gains from trade liberalization increases as adjustment moves forward, while the share that loses decreases. This process fosters political support for trade liberalization in a self-reinforcing manner. For all of these reasons, regional agreements that are established based on openness principles have the potential to overlap and grow, thereby advancing global free trade from the bottom up. (Antràs & Foley, 2009).

7.2. TYPES OF REGIONAL TRADING ARRANGEMENT

Economists have been using the term "economic integration" since the middle of the 1950s. Economic integration refers to the procedure of getting rid of barriers to global payments, trade, and factor mobility. Hence, a regional trading arrangement that unites two or more national economies is the outcome of economic integration. Let's first identify the various kinds of regional trading agreements before moving forward.

An association of trading nations that consents to the removal of all tariff and nontariff barriers among its members is known as a free-trade area. Each member, however, continues to impose its own set of trade barriers on outsiders. The North American Free Trade Agreement (NAFTA), which includes the United States, Canada, and Mexico, is an illustration of this stage of integration. Additionally, the US and Chile have free trade agreements. A further free-trade agreement was made in 1999 when Mexico and the European Union agreed to remove all tariffs on their bilateral trade in industrial goods by the year 2007 (Baier & Bergstrand, 2007).

A customs union is an agreement between two or more trading partners to eliminate all tariff and nontariff trade barriers between themselves, similar to a free-trade association. Furthermore, all of the member countries apply the same trade barriers to non-participants. The common external trade policy equalizes all trade restrictions against outsiders while allowing free trade within the customs union. Benelux, which was established in 1948 and consists of Belgium, the Netherlands, and Luxembourg, is a well-known example.

A common market is a group of trading nations that permits:

1. The free movement of goods and services among member nations,
2. The initiation of common external trade restrictions against nonmembers, and
3. The free movement of factors of production across national borders within the economic bloc.

The common market thus represents a more complete stage of integration than a free-trade area or a customs union. The European Union (EU) achieved the status of a common market in 1992.

After these phases, economic integration may progress to the stage of economic union, where a supranational organization is in charge of coordinating and enforcing national, social, fiscal, and tax laws. In the 1920s, Belgium and Luxembourg united economically. Achieving an economic union is a far more ambitious goal than accomplishing other types of integration. This is so because an economic union necessitates an agreement to transfer economic sovereignty to a supranational authority, whereas a free trade area, customs union, or common market arise primarily from the removal of current trade barriers. The unification of national monetary policies and the adoption of a single currency under the supervision of a supranational monetary authority would represent the pinnacle of economic union. Thus, a monetary union component would be a part of the economic union.

One monetary union example is the United States. Because the 50 states are united in a single monetary union and share a single currency, there are fixed exchange rates between the states. Additionally, the Federal Reserve manages the country's monetary policy and issues currency in its capacity as the only central bank. States are free to trade with one another, and capital and labor are free to flow in the direction of their highest returns. The federal government manages the country's budget and handles issues related to international relations, national defense, retirement and health plans, and other things. State and local governments run other initiatives, like education and police protection, to ensure that states maintain their unique identities within the union.

7.3. IMPETUS FOR REGIONALISM

There are several reasons why people pursue regional trading agreements. Almost all regional trading agreements have been motivated by the hope of increased economic growth. A larger regional market can support specialization and learning-by-doing, facilitate economies of large-scale production, and draw in foreign investment. In addition, regional initiatives can support a range of noneconomic goals, like controlling immigration and enhancing regional security. Additionally, regionalism could strengthen and support domestic economic reforms. For example, countries in East Europe have seen their regional initiatives with the EU as a way to lock in their internal policy shifts toward market-oriented reform and privatization.

When future access to the markets of the larger nations appears uncertain, smaller nations may look to establish safe-haven trading arrangements with them. NAFTA's formation appears to have been motivated in part by this kind of access. Fears of US trade policy shifting toward a more managed or strategic trade orientation drove Mexico to join NAFTA, one of the countries' driving forces in North America. Canada's goal to control the US use of countervailing and antidumping duties was a major driving force behind its pursuit of a free-trade agreement.

The opportunity cost of staying outside of a regional trading arrangement rises as new ones are created or as current ones are deepened or expanded. If their sales are transferred to companies within the member nations, exporters who are not members may experience significant declines in their market share. The prospect of joining a regional trading arrangement could be enough to shift political sentiment in favor of it, since the exporting interests of non-member countries tend to outweigh their import-competing interests. Canada's decision to join NAFTA and stay ahead of the free trade movement in North America seems to have been heavily influenced by the negotiations between the US and Mexico to create a free-trade area.

7.4. EFFECTS OF A REGIONAL TRADING ARRANGEMENT

The potential costs and advantages of such devices can be distinguished from two perspectives. The initial impact of economic integration on consumer welfare and productive efficiency is static. The second aspect of economic integration pertains to the long-term growth rates of member nations and is known as its dynamic effects. The dynamic effects of trade-policy changes can yield substantially larger magnitudes than those based on static models because a small change in the growth rate can result in a substantial cumulative effect on national output. The total welfare gains or losses connected to the establishment of a regional trading arrangement are determined by the interaction of these static and dynamic effects.

7.4.1. Static Effects

The following example shows how lowering tariffs among members of a trade bloc can have static welfare effects. Imagine that there are three nations in the world: the United States, Germany, and Luxembourg. Assume that Germany and Luxembourg decide to create a customs union, with the US remaining a non-member. In order to establish a customs union, Germany and Luxembourg must do away with all tariffs between them while continuing to impose tariffs on the United States.

Assume that Luxembourg has S_L and D_L supply and demand schedules based on Figure 7.1. Additionally, let's assume that Luxembourg is tiny in comparison to Germany and the US. According to this assumption, Luxembourg cannot affect international prices, resulting in perfectly elastic foreign grain supply schedules. Assume that the supply price from Germany is \$3.25 per bushel and the supply price from the US is \$3. Keep in mind that the assumption is that the US is the more efficient supplier.

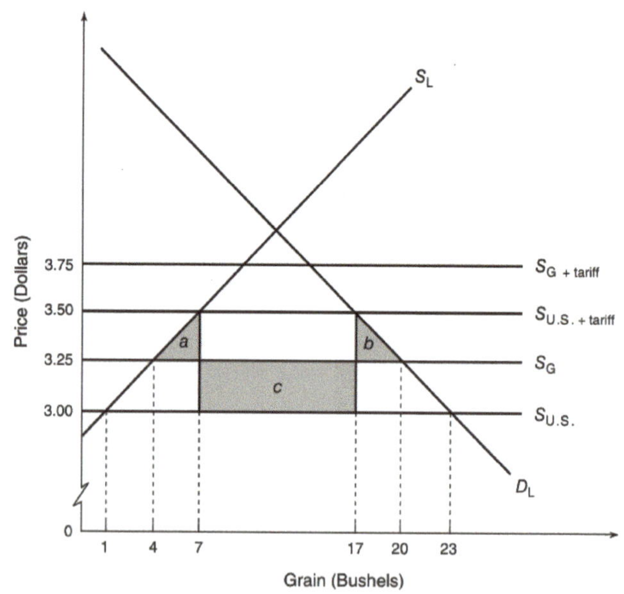

Figure 7.1. *Static welfare effects of a customs union.*

Source: Robert J. Carbaugh, International Economics, ISBN 13: 9781439038949.

The establishment of a customs union has two effects: one that increases welfare through trade creation, and the other that decreases welfare through trade diversion. The relative strength of these two opposing forces will determine how the customs union affects the welfare of its members overall and on a global scale.

Prior to the establishment of the customs union, Luxembourg discovers that, in the context of free trade, it buys all of the imports it needs from the US. Because its supply price is higher than that of the US, Germany does not engage in the market. In a free-trade equilibrium, imports equal 22 bushels, production equals 1, and consumption equals 23 bushels in Luxembourg. The amount of imports from the United States (or Germany) will decrease from 22 bushels to 10 bushels if Luxembourg imposes a tariff of $0.50 cents per bushel.

Suppose that Luxembourg and Germany establish a customs union as a component of a trade liberalization agreement. The import tariff that Luxembourg had imposed on goods from Germany is waived, but it remains in place for goods from non-member states. Germany becomes the low-cost supplier after the tariff is removed. At $3.25 per bushel, Luxembourg currently buys all of its 16 bushels of imports from Germany and imports nothing from the US.

Two opposing effects of the shift toward freer trade under a customs union are trade-diversion that reduces welfare and trade-creation that increases welfare. The relative strength of these two opposing forces will determine how a customs union affects the welfare of its members and the global community overall.

Trade creation happens when lower-cost imports from one member of a customs union replace some of the domestic production of that member. Because trade creation increases production specialization in accordance with the principle of comparative advantage, it improves the welfare of the member countries. There are two components to the trade-creation effect: the production and consumption effects.

Prior to the establishment of the customs union, Luxembourg imported goods at a cost of $3.50 per bushel from the United States, operating under its own tariff regime. Following its admission to the customs union, Luxembourg has eliminated all tariffs imposed on Germany. With the import price down to $3.25, Luxembourg uses three bushels more grain than before. Triangle b in Figure 7.1 represents the welfare gain connected to this rise in consumption.

The creation of the customs union also has a production effect that makes better use of global resources possible. With the tariff barrier against Germany removed, producers in Luxembourg now have to contend with more cost-effective, higher-producing German producers. Three bushels less are produced domestically as a result of inefficient domestic producers leaving the market. Triangle an in the figure represents the decrease in the cost of producing this output. This triangle is an illustration of the beneficial production effect. The overall trade-creation effect is given by the sum of triangles a + b.

A customs union's trade-diversion effect typically indicates a welfare loss, even though it may increase global welfare through the creation of new trade. When purchases from a higher-cost supplier within the union are substituted for imports from a lower-cost supplier outside the union, this is known as trade diversion. This detour implies a less effective reorganization of global production. Figure 7.1 shows that while overall trade volume rises as a result of the customs union, 10 bushels of trade have been transferred from the United States, a low-cost supplier, to Germany, a high-cost supplier. The cost increase of procuring 10 bushels of imported grain is equivalent to area c. This represents the global loss to welfare as well as the loss to Luxembourg. According to our static analysis, if the positive trade-creation effect more than offsets the negative trade-diversion effect, then the creation of a customs union will improve the welfare of both its members and the rest of the world. With reference to the Figure 7.1, this happens when a + b exceeds c.

This analysis shows that the elements promoting trade creation and diversion are critical to a customs union's success. There are a number of variables that affect how big these effects are relative to one another. The types of countries that typically gain from a customs union are one factor. Because the union's formation provides more opportunities for production specialization, countries with highly competitive pre-union economies stand to gain from increased trade.

Additionally, since there is a higher chance that the world's low-cost producers will be union members, the gains are probably going to be greater the larger and more numerous the union is. Only trade creation, not trade diversion, is possible in the extreme scenario where the union is the entire world. Furthermore, when the common external tariff of the customs union is lower rather than higher, the potential for trade diversion is reduced. Reduced tariffs promote increased trade with non-member countries, which reduces the amount of relatively expensive imports from partner countries to replace cheaper imports from non-member countries (Baldwin, 2008).

7.4.2. Did the United Kingdom (UK) Gain from Entering the European Union?

When the UK joined the European Union in 1973, it served as an illustration of both trade creation and trade diversion. Cheaper agricultural produce from Australia, the UK's former colony, was denied entry. Rather, it expanded agricultural production and bought produce from its more costly European neighbors.

The UK was required to abide by the EU's agriculture policy upon joining, which imposed uniform restrictions on agricultural producers from outside the EU. Produce from outside the EU now costs more for UK consumers due to tariffs and quotas. Australia's privileged access to the UK market consequently came to an end. As the UK aligned itself with other more expensive European producers, it was excluded. Customers in the UK paid a hefty price for the shift. The UK had the lowest food costs in Europe prior to joining the EU. However, the UK's food prices increased by 25% on average after it joined the EU due to the higher cost of produce from Europe. Put simply, trade was shifted from low-cost to high-cost producers, and as a result, the UK lost.

As a result of the UK's entry into the EU and the removal of import restrictions, trade in manufactured goods from Europe increased dramatically. By allowing cheaper imports from European trading partners to take the place of more expensive UK output, this trade increased national welfare. It became an empirical question to determine whether the UK's entry into the EU was beneficial or detrimental. Empirical research generally maintains that trade creation was the stronger effect and that the UK's overall welfare improved by joining the EU.

However, did the welfare-expanding effect of trade creation in manufactured goods more than offset the welfare-contracting effect of trade diversion in agricultural products?

7.4.3. Dynamic Effects

The welfare effects of a regional trade agreement are not always constant. Additionally, dynamic gains might have a long-term impact on member-nation growth rates. These dynamic gains result from the movement toward freer trade under customs unions, which opens up larger markets. Any negative static effects may be more than offset by the advantages of a customs union's dynamic gains. Economies of scale, increased competition, and an investment stimulus are examples of dynamic gains.

Expanding markets is one of a customs union's most obvious effects. Producers can benefit from economies of scale that would not have materialized in smaller markets constrained by trade restrictions by freely entering the domestic markets of other members.

Greater specialization of personnel and equipment, the use of the most efficient machinery, and the more thorough utilization of byproducts may all contribute to greater efficiencies in larger markets. There is evidence that the EU has achieved significant economies of scale in the production of steel, cars, shoes, and copper refining, among other products.

The dynamic effects of integration are exemplified by the European refrigerator industry.

Before the European Union was established, Germany, Italy, and France—the three main refrigerator-producing countries in Europe—all provided support to a limited number of producers who catered mostly to their own markets. Less than 100,000 units were produced annually by these manufacturers, which is too few to allow for the use of automated machinery. Low production runs resulted in high costs per unit. The creation of the EU opened up markets throughout Europe and helped large-scale production techniques like spot welding and automated press lines become commonplace. An average Italian refrigerator plant produced 850,000 refrigerators a year by the late 1960s. This volume was more than enough to meet the 800,000 units per year minimum efficient scale of operation. German and French manufacturers produced an average of 570,000 and 290,000 units annually, respectively, in the late 1960s.

Increased competition among producers within a customs union could potentially be facilitated by expanded markets. Trade restrictions are frequently thought to encourage monopoly power, in which a few number of businesses control a large portion of the domestic market.

These businesses might decide to live a quiet life and make agreements not to engage in price-based competition. However, as a customs union moves toward more open markets, the likelihood of successful collusion decreases as the number of competitors rises.

More trade means that domestic producers have to compete or risk going bankrupt. Producers need to reduce waste, maintain low prices, enhance quality, and increase productivity in order to thrive in larger and more competitive markets. In general, competitive pressure benefits the country's consumers and can also be a useful deterrent against the abuse of monopoly power.

Additionally, trade can raise productivity

levels and quicken the rate of technological advancement. Trade can accelerate investment spending in cutting-edge technologies by raising the expected rate of return on successful innovation and more evenly allocating research and development expenses. Increased trade between nations can facilitate the flow of technical knowledge since it allows for greater mobility of capital, both human and physical. These incentives typically speed up an economy's growth, resulting in a sustained increase in income that increases over time rather than just a temporary improvement in economic welfare.

7.5. THE EUROPEAN UNION

Western European nations experienced balance-of-payments deficits in the years following World War II as a result of reconstruction efforts. They established a complex web of tariff and exchange restrictions, quantitative controls, and state trading to protect their businesses and employees from outside competitive pressures. But these trade restrictions were generally seen as ineffective in the 1950s. Therefore, in response to fruitful tariff negotiations conducted under the GATT's auspices, Western Europe started to remove its trade barriers. The 1957 Treaty of Rome established the European Union, formerly known as the European Community, against this backdrop of trade liberalization. Belgium, France, Italy, Luxembourg, the Netherlands, and West Germany were the original six members of the EU.

Denmark, Ireland, and the United Kingdom joined the trade bloc by 1973. In 1981, Greece became a member of the trade bloc; Spain and Portugal joined in 1987. Sweden, Finland, and Austria became members of the EU in 1995. 10 more nations from Central and Eastern Europe—Cyprus, the Czech Republic, Estonia, Hungary, Latvia, Lithuania, Malta, Poland, Slovakia, and Slovenia—joined the EU in 2004. With the admission of Romania and Bulgaria in 2007, the EU now has 27 member states. The European Union sees the current enlargement process as a chance to advance peaceful European integration and stability (Karacaovali & Limao, 2008). The expansion of the European Union has resulted in both winners and losers. The majority of studies concur that countries with strong trade and investment links to Central and Eastern Europe—such as Germany, Italy, Austria, Sweden, and Finland—stand to gain. Given the significant funding they receive from EU programs—especially France's agricultural funds—France, Spain, Portugal, Greece, and Ireland are likely to suffer as the money is distributed among more nations. It is obvious that as the economies of Central and Eastern Europe integrate with those of other European countries, they will benefit the most.

7.5.1. Pursuing Economic Integration

The EU committed in principle to pursue economic integration as a means of eventually transforming into an economic union, as stated in the Treaty of Rome. EU members first eliminated tariffs and created a free-trade zone in 1968 in order to achieve this goal. The value of industrial trade increased fivefold in tandem with this trade liberalization, surpassing that of global trade overall. Because of the free-trade area's success, the EU decided to carry on with its economic integration efforts. When the EU established a unified external tariff system for its members in 1970, it officially became a customs union under the EU Act. Numerous investigations into the general effect of the EU on the welfare of its members in the 1960s and 1970s have been carried out. One study found that while trade diversion was evident in agricultural commodities and raw materials, trade creation was more pronounced in machinery, transportation equipment, chemicals, and fuels in terms of static welfare benefits. A general conclusion was reached, stating that trade creation in the manufactured goods sector during the 1960s and 1970s accounted for 10 to 30% of all manufactured goods imports into the EU. Furthermore, trade creation—estimated at 2 to 15%—surpassed trade diversion by a significant margin. Furthermore, analysts pointed out that the EU benefited dynamically from integration in the form of increased investment, competition, and economies of scale. For example, it has been found that by producing for both the home market and export, numerous businesses in small countries like the Netherlands and Belgium achieved economies of scale. However, individual firms gained significant additional economies of scale after joining the EU, which led to a decrease in the range of products manufactured and an increase in the output of the remaining products.

The EU didn't make much headway toward becoming a common market until 1985, when it established a customs union. Rather than eliminating trade and investment barriers, EU members chose to protect their citizens from outside forces in response to the unfavorable economic environment (recession and inflation) of the 1970s. But by the 1980s, obstacles impeding intra-Block trade had become a source of growing frustration for EU members. Additionally, European officials were concerned that the EU was not as competitive as the US and Japan.

The European Union unveiled a comprehensive plan in 1985 to create a single market. By 1992, this program had eliminated all nontariff trade barriers preventing intra-EU trade. These obstacles included, for instance, conflicting business laws, bureaucratic red tape and border controls, disparate standards and technical regulations, and government procurement policies that were protectionist in nature. After these obstacles were removed, the European Union's economy grew to become the second largest in the world, narrowly behind that of the United States. This led to the creation of the European Common Market.

The leaders of EU governments decided to pursue much deeper levels of integration even as the EU was developing into a common market. Their intention was to start the process of exchanging their national currencies for a single European currency and their central banks for a European Central Bank. The Maastricht Treaty, which was signed in 1991, stipulated that this process would end in 2002. A fully fledged European Monetary Union (EMU) with the euro as its single currency debuted in 2002.

The economic circumstances in each of the EU members varied significantly at the time of the Maastricht Treaty's signature. The treaty stipulated that a nation's economic performance had to be comparable to that of other members in order for it to be deemed ready for monetary union. Naturally, nations with stable currency values cannot pursue varying rates of money growth, have varying rates of economic expansion, and experience varying rates of inflation. Thus, aligning their monetary and economic policies was the first task that needed to be done by the Europeans.

A high degree of uniformity in terms of price inflation, money supply growth, and other important economic factors has resulted from this endeavor, known as convergence. The specific convergence criteria as mandated by the Maastricht Treaty are as follows:

- **Price Stability**: Inflation in each prospective member is supposed to be no more than 1.5 percent above the average of the inflation rates in the three countries with the lowest inflation rates.
- **Low Long-Term Interest Rates**: Long-term interest rates are to be no more than 2 percent above the average interest rate in those countries.
- **Stable Exchange Rates**: The exchange rate is supposed to have been kept within the target bands of the monetary union with no devaluations for at least two years prior to joining the monetary union.
- **Sound Public Finances**: One fiscal criterion is that the budget deficit in a prospective member should be at most 3 percent of GDP; the other is that the outstanding amount of government debt should be no more than 60% of a year's GDP.

Of the 27 member states that make up the European Union, 16 use the euro as their official currency. These nations are Austria, Belgium, Cyprus, Finland, France, Germany, Greece, Ireland, Italy, Luxembourg, Malta, the Netherlands, Portugal, Slovakia, Slovenia, and Spain. Together, they are referred to as the eurozone.

Approximately 327 million Europeans use the euro on a daily basis as a result of its use in five additional European nations. More than 150 million people in Africa and over 175 million people globally use currencies that are pegged to the euro. After the US dollar, the euro is the second most traded and largest reserve currency globally. Further nations that join the European Union are required to do so and to make the euro their official currency. The Maastricht Treaty's convergence requirements must first be met by the accession countries, making membership in the EMU non-automatic. The candidates, however, believe that the low interest rates and exchange-rate stability that accompany full membership in the monetary union outweigh the convergence requirements.

The impetus the EMU offers for political union—a long-standing objective of many European policymakers—is a significant driving force behind the institution. Germany and France founded the EMU. One key strategy for firmly establishing Germany in Europe was monetary union. Furthermore, France was given more authority over European monetary policy through the EMU, something they would be able to accomplish with a single central bank. The German Bundesbank dominated Europe's monetary policy prior to the EMU.

7.5.2. French and Dutch Voters Sidetrack Integration

The EU realized that in order to function well and avoid impasse, it needed to enhance its decision-making procedures and governing bodies as it increased the number of its members. The original governing constitution of the EU was modified by a new constitutional treaty that was finalized in 2004.

The new constitution included provisions to increase the EU's visibility internationally in addition to measures that would make an expanded EU function more efficiently. A new foreign minister will be appointed, the European Parliament's authority will be increased, voting procedures within the EU will be streamlined, and the rotating presidency of the EU will be eliminated in favor of a single person serving as president of the European Council for a maximum of five years. Nearly every amendment to the constitution represented a compromise between members who want to maintain the EU as an intergovernmental organization so that they can continue to better protect their national sovereignty and those who want to see more integration with the EU.

In order to take effect, the constitutional treaty must be ratified by all 25 member countries.

The constitution was ratified by 12 nations, but its future was called into doubt in 2005 when voters in France and the Netherlands rejected it in separate referendums. Voters in both countries were worried that the treaty would support liberal economic trends that could undermine their social protections, such as welfare payments and high minimum wage laws. This is what these voters reacted against. Additionally, voters saw casting a negative vote as a means of protesting against their unpopular national governments, the bureaucracy of the EU, and Turkey's potential membership in the EU. Some in France were concerned that the constitution would lessen French influence within the EU by opening the door for further EU enlargement. Voters in the Netherlands expressed dissatisfaction over the EU's large member states, arguing that some provisions would further entrench their already excessive power.

The rejection undermined the confidence of EU officials, who insisted that the EU could function and grow its membership even in the absence of the constitution. In a swift response, the UK announced that it would put off ratifying the constitution and gave no timeframe. Experts believe that while members grapple with internal reforms and the EU's future identity, the EU may experience a period of stagnation, at least in the near future.

7.5.3. Agricultural Policy

In addition to facilitating unrestricted trade in industrial goods among its constituents, the European Union has eliminated limitations on internal trade in agricultural products. The agricultural-stabilization policies of the individual member states, which varied greatly prior to the EU's formation, have been replaced by a common agricultural policy. The support of farmers' produce prices has been a significant component of the common agricultural policy. For this reason, programs involving direct income payments, output limits, and deficiency payments have been implemented. Additionally, by imposing tariffs on agricultural imports into the EU, the common agricultural policy has supported farm prices within the EU through a system of variable levies. The implementation of export subsidies has ensured the export of any excess produce from the EU.

The fact that different EU members have different agricultural efficiencies presents a challenge for the EU's price-support initiatives. Examine the situation with grains. Due to their high production costs, German farmers have looked for high support prices in order to stay in business. Despite the fact that French farmers are more productive than German farmers and do not require as high of a level of support prices to remain in business, they have discovered that it is in their best interests to advocate for high price supports. High price supports have been imposed on goods like butter, cereals, and beef in recent years. Therefore, the common agricultural policy has restricted food imports from more productive non-member producers and encouraged inefficient farm production by

EU farmers. The EU has seen a decline in welfare as a result of this trade diversion.

7.5.3.1. Variable Levies

A system of variable levies is shown operating in Figure 7.2. Assume that the world price of wheat is $3.50 per bushel and that SE_{U0} and D^{EU0} represent the supply and demand schedules for wheat in the EU. Assume furthermore that the EU wants to ensure that its expensive farmers receive $4.50 per bushel. As long as imported wheat is permitted to enter the EU at the free-market price of $3.50 per bushel, this price cannot be maintained. Let's say the EU introduces a variable tax in order to verify the support price. Instead of the 3 million bushels that would be produced under free trade, EU farmers are allowed to produce 5 million bushels of wheat, given an import levy of $1 per bushel. In addition, rather than 6 million bushels, the EU imports a total of 2 million bushels.

Variable levies have been used by the EU's common agricultural policy to shield EU farmers from low-cost foreign competition. The sliding-scale structure of the variable levy causes the EU's import tariff to automatically rise during times of declining global prices.

Assume that the price of wheat drops to $2.50 per bushel due to higher productivity in other countries. A variable levy system sets a daily levy equal to the difference between the support price and the lowest price on the global market. Due to the variable levy's sliding scale structure, the EU has raised its import tariff to $2 per bushel. Wheat imports and EU production both stay at $4.50 per bushel, the support price. EU farmers are therefore shielded from the effects of fluctuations in foreign supply. In the event that wheat production in the EU declines, import levies may be lowered to promote imports. Then, consumers in the EU are shielded from growing wheat prices.

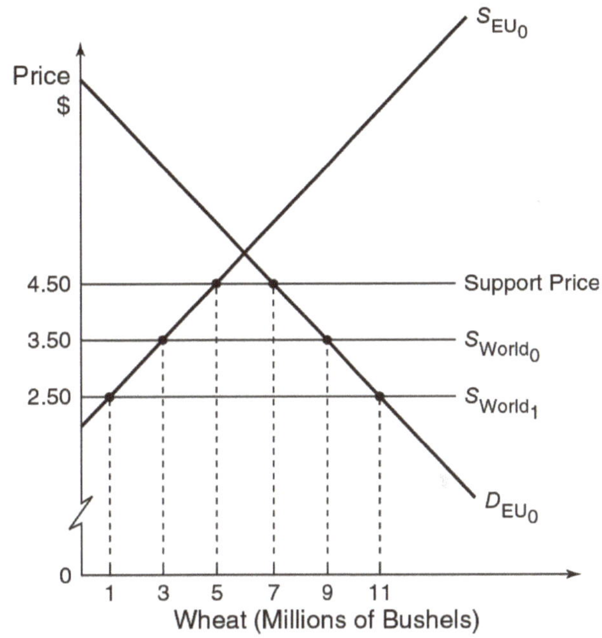

Figure 7.2. *Variable levies.*

Source: Robert J. Carbaugh, International Economics, ISBN 13: 9781439038949.

Generally speaking, a variable import levy is more restrictive than a fixed tariff. It dissuades international manufacturers from lowering prices to sustain export sales and absorbing a portion of the tariff. Reducing prices will only result in increased variable levies. Variable levies deter foreign producers from lowering their export prices in an effort to break into home markets for the same reason.

Regulations governing the application of variable levies were implemented in 1994 with the conclusion of the Uruguay Round trade negotiations. It mandated the conversion of all nontariff barriers into equivalent tariffs, including variable levies. With one exception, the EU's conversion technique preserved the variable levy structure in its entirety. Similar to the previous variable levy, the actual tariff on agricultural imports may change based on global prices. There is currently a cap on the maximum amount that the tariff can increase.

7.5.3.2. Export Subsidies

Additionally, the EU has implemented an export subsidy scheme to guarantee that any excess agricultural production is exported. The common agricultural policy's high price supports have encouraged farmers in the EU to increase production, frequently in excess of demand. However, the global price of agricultural commodities has typically been less than that of the EU. In order to enable its farmers to sell excess produce abroad at a lower price while still receiving the higher international support price, the EU provides export subsidies to these farmers. The government will decrease domestic supply and do away with the need for the government to buy the excess by promoting exports.

Table 7.1. Government Support for Agriculture, 2007

Producer-Subsidy Equivalents	Country as a Percent of Farm Prices
Iceland	61
South Korea	60
Norway	53
Switzerland	50
Japan	46
European Union	26
Canada	18
Mexico	14
United States	10
Australia	5
New Zealand	1

*The producer-subsidy equivalent represents the total assistance to farmers in the form of market price support, direct payments, and transfers that indirectly benefit farmers.

Source: From Organization of Economic Cooperation and Development (OECD), Agricultural Policies in OECD Countries: Monitoring and Evaluation, 2008.

It has cost the EU money to maintain a high standard of living for its farmers. Excessive support costs for dairy, butter, cheese, and meat have resulted in low consumption and increased internal production. Frequently, this has led to enormous surpluses that the EU has to buy in order to maintain the support price. The EU has sold excess produce on international markets for prices far less than the cost of acquisition in an effort to cut these expenses. Farmers in other nations have objected to these subsidized sales. This is particularly true for farmers in underdeveloped, impoverished nations who claim to be disadvantaged when they have to deal with imports whose prices are lower due to export subsidies or when they have to deal with increased competition in their export markets for the same reason.

Almost all industrialized nations subsidize their agricultural output. Table 7.1 illustrates how government programs contributed 26% of the EU's 2007 agricultural product value. In some nations, like Switzerland and Japan, this amount is significantly higher; in other nations, like the US, Australia, and New Zealand, it is far lower. Agriculturally subsidy-heavy countries have been criticized by relatively low-subsidy countries for being overly protectionist.

7.5.3.3. Is the European Union Really a Common Market?

EU members have been working for decades to create a single market with standardized rules for trade, product regulation, and the flow of production inputs.

Think about the Kellogg Co. situation. the cereal manufacturer based in the United States. Kellogg has been pleading with EU members for years to allow it to sell vitamin-fortified cereals across the continent.

However, the firm's requests have encountered many difficulties. Danish government regulators oppose the addition of vitamins because they fear that people who already take multivitamins from cereal may take more than the recommended daily amount, endangering their health. The regulators in the Netherlands do not want folic acid or vitamin D to be included because they do not believe that they are beneficial. Nonetheless, Finland prefers higher vitamin D than other countries in order to help make up for their lack of sun exposure. Thus, Kellogg's UK plants are required to manufacture four distinct kinds of cornflakes and other cereals. The EU was initially intended to be a common market with standardized laws. Producing for a single European market allowed businesses to reach production runs big enough to achieve significant economies of scale.

Rather, long-standing national disparities have forced businesses to bear additional expenses that hinder plant expansion and employment growth.

This inconsistent nature goes far beyond cereal for breakfast. Caterpillar, Inc. distributes tractors across Europe. However, in Germany, the cars have to have lights mounted in different places and a louder backup horn.

Nations must differ, sometimes by only centimeters, in the yield signs and license-plate holders on the backs of tractors and other earthmoving vehicles. Caterpillar officials argue that there is no valid reason for these kinds of regulatory inconsistencies. All they do is complicate efficient mass production.

The EU made an effort to deepen market integration in its service sector in 2005; this sector makes up roughly 67% of its total economic activity. However, Germany and France blocked the attempt to allow companies like law firms and medical practices to more easily expand internationally, arguing that foreign service providers would drive out their own providers.

Plans for company expansion across Europe have also been negatively impacted by persistent regulatory disparities between markets. For instance, the Swedish furniture company Ikea Group is required to foot the bill for research to demonstrate that its entry into new markets won't drive out regional companies. Ikea estimates that the cost of each study is about $25,000, and it takes a year for a decision to be made. Furthermore, only between 33 and 50% of Ikea's petitions are granted.

Despite the fact that over the past 50 years, EU members have moved toward greater economic unification, trade and investment barriers caused by regulatory disparities still exist and impede economic growth. Numerous legal disputes between producers and national regulators, as well as between the European Commission and individual governments, have been brought about by these barriers. In other words, Europe's common market is still unique.

7.6. ECONOMIC COSTS AND BENEFITS OF A COMMON CURRENCY: THE EUROPEAN MONETARY UNION

As we now know, the establishment of the European Monetary Union (EMU) in 1999 led to the creation of the euro, a single currency, and the European Central Bank. Changing to a new currency is very challenging. Imagine the challenge if every one of the 50 U.S. States had to agree on a single currency and financial system with the other 49 states after having their own currency and central bank. That's precisely what people from Europe have done. The European Central Bank, which has its headquarters in Frankfurt, Germany, is in charge of the EMU's monetary and exchange-rate policies. The only entity that sets the short-term euro interest rate, manages the supply of euros, and keeps the member countries' exchange rates permanently fixed is the European Central Bank. Each participating country's central bank operates similarly to the 12 regional Federal Reserve Banks in the US when there is a single central bank.

The advantages of a single currency are clear to Americans. Americans are aware that they can use dollar bills from their wallets and purses to buy hamburgers at any McDonald's or Burger King location across the country. Before the establishment of the EMU, this was not the case in the nations of Europe. French francs had to be exchanged for German marks before a French person could purchase anything in a German store because each country had its own currency. This conversation would resemble that of a St. Louis is required to convert her Missourian money into Illinoisan money every time she travels to Chicago. Worse, the amount of marks the French traveler receives today would probably be different from what he would have received yesterday or tomorrow because marks and francs fluctuated against each other within a range. The traveler had to pay a fee to exchange the currency on top of the uncertainty surrounding the exchange rate, making the cross-border trip a costly endeavor. Because of the tiny amounts of money involved, the costs to individuals can be kept to a minimum, but the costs to businesses can be significantly higher. The EMU can avoid such costs by substituting the euro, a single currency, for the various European currencies. In other words, the euro will result in lower costs for goods and services, easier price comparisons within the EU, and ultimately more consistent pricing.

7.6.1. Optimum Currency Area

The idea of optimal currency areas forms the basis of much analysis of the advantages and disadvantages of a single currency. A region where having a single official currency is more advantageous economically than having multiple official currencies is known as an optimum currency area. One ideal currency area would be the United States, for instance. It is inconceivable that in a monetary system with 50 distinct currencies, the volume of commerce that currently occurs among the 50 states would occur as efficiently. Table 7.2 lists some benefits and drawbacks of creating a common currency region.

The idea of optimum currency areas states that there are benefits to exchanging currencies across national borders. These benefits include more consistent pricing, reduced transaction costs, increased investor certainty, and increased competition. Furthermore, price stability ought to be supported by a single monetary policy administered by a separate central bank.

Table 7.2. Advantages and Disadvantages of Adopting a Common Currency

Advantages	Disadvantages
The risks associated with exchange fluctuations are eliminated within a common currency area.	Absence of individual domestic monetary policy to counter macroeconomic shocks
Costs of currency conversion are lessened.	Inability of an individual country to use inflation to reduce public debt in real terms.
The economies are insulated from monetary disturbances and speculation.	The transition from individual currencies to a single currency could lead to speculative attacks.
Political pressures for trade protection are reduced.	

Source: Robert J. Carbaugh, International Economics, ISBN 13: 9781439038949.

But there can be costs associated with a single policy, particularly if interest rate changes have different effects on different economies. The wider advantages of a single currency must also be weighed against the loss of two policy tools, namely the ability to adjust the exchange rate and an independent monetary policy. Losing these is especially bad if a nation or area is likely to experience recessions or other economic disruptions that impact it differently than the rest of the single-currency area because it will be unable to respond by changing its currency or implementing more expansionary monetary policies.

The theory of optimal currency then looks at different responses to economic shocks and identifies three. The first is labor mobility, which requires that employees in the affected nation be free to relocate abroad. The second is wage and price flexibility: in the event of a disturbance, the nation must be able to modify these. The third is a system that transfers funds automatically to the nation that is impacted.

According to the theory of optimal currency areas, countries participating in a currency area should have comparable business cycles and economic structures in order to maximize its chances of success. Additionally, every participating nation should experience the same effects from the single monetary policy. In addition, there should be wage flexibility, a system of stabilizing transfers, and no legal, cultural, or linguistic restrictions on cross-border labor mobility.

7.6.2. Europe as a Suboptimal Currency Area

For all its shortcomings, creating a monetary union offers benefits for Europe. A monetary union could increase economic efficiency by reducing the costs associated with currency exchange transactions. When visiting Europe, tourists are aware of the cost and duration involved in switching currencies. Reducing transaction costs is advantageous for companies as well as customers. It is also made easier to compare prices honestly within Europe when there is only one currency. Eliminating exchange-rate risk is another benefit; companies will trade and invest in other European nations more readily if they are not burdened with uncertainty about future exchange rates. The European Monetary Union (EMU) fosters competition and enables the expansion and sophistication of European financial markets.

These gains seem to be of relatively modest overall magnitudes. According to estimates from the European Commission, transaction cost savings account for 0.4 percent of the EU's GDP. The efficiency gains are small, but they increase with a country's trade volume with other members of the monetary union. For instance, a monetary union with Germany greatly benefits the Netherlands, whose trade with Germany has historically accounted for more than 20% of its total trade. Conversely, the Netherlands' overall trade with Spain has typically accounted for only about 2% of its total, meaning that the benefits of monetary union with Spain are significantly smaller.

The loss of each member European nation's ability to respond to economic disruptions through monetary policy and exchange rate manipulation is a primary drawback of the EMU. A nation cannot continue to loosen monetary policy or permit its currency to weaken in order to boost its economy when it faces a recession. The requirement to control budget deficits under the EMU may also restrict the use of fiscal policy. Reviving the economy may depend on wage flexibility as well as workers' potential and willingness to relocate. Recovering from a recession can be challenging in Europe due to high wage rigidity and low labor mobility, which can put political pressure on the single monetary policy to be loosened or increase the government debt of the recession-stricken nation. Are the members of the EU an optimum currency area? In other words, do the microeconomic gains of greater efficiency outweigh the macroeconomic costs of the loss of the exchange rate as an adjustment tool? According to some economists, monetary union is not a good idea for all countries because the costs outweigh the benefits for the countries as a whole. Monetary union makes sense for a smaller group of nations, though, where the benefits might outweigh the costs. The efficiency gains are higher because trade within the smaller group of countries is significantly higher than trade with all other countries.

7.6.3. Challenges for the EMU

The economic impact of the European Monetary Union (EMU) on both Europe and the United States will primarily rely on the policy choices made in Europe in the coming years. The actual transition to a single currency won't probably have much of an impact on its own. The ability of the European Central Bank to concentrate on price stability over the long run may be the most significant monetary policy challenge facing the EMU. Because so many nations vote on monetary policy and because strong anti-inflationary measures are not deeply ingrained in nations like Portugal, Spain, and Italy, some worry that monetary policy may eventually become overly expansionary.

There might be certain difficulties in the way monetary policy is implemented. Selecting appropriate short-term interest rates may prove challenging if there are significant disparities in the economic growth rates of the EMU member states. Certain countries may benefit from tightening monetary policy to lower inflationary pressures, while other nations may benefit from loosening monetary policy to boost activity. As a result, it could occasionally be challenging for the European Central Bank to decide on monetary policy for the entire eurozone.

While fiscal policy is still the purview of national governments, the EMU's viability depends on avoiding large budget deficits. Budgetary restraint is recommended because significant budget deficits can result in high interest rates and decreased economic activity. The majority of nations find it extremely challenging to cut their debt and budget deficits in order to satisfy the EMU's convergence requirements. Reducing government spending was and still is politically challenging, particularly when it comes to well-established social programs. The majority of countries' aging populations could put further strain on budgets.

For EMU countries, the necessity of structural reform in European nations poses a challenge as well. Flexible labor markets are arguably the most significant structural problem. Europe's real wage flexibility (adjusted for inflation) is thought to be half that of the US. Furthermore, there is very little labor mobility in Europe, both within and between nations. There are not enough incentives to work hard and learn new skills. Laws restricting employers' ability to fire employees discourage them from recruiting and onboarding new employees. Slow economies are also a result of high taxes and generous unemployment benefits offered by European governments.

Analysts point out that there are various reasons why structural reforms are required. They would first cut the structural unemployment rate in the EU, which has been consistently high. Second, businesses would offer the necessary adaptability in the event of a recession, particularly when it affects one or a few eurozone nations. For instance, if wages and prices were flexible downward, a drop in demand would be followed by a drop in price, which would tend to increase demand. Recession adjustment would benefit greatly from increased labor mobility.

7.6.4. Does the Eurozone Need a Bailout Fund?

The European Monetary Union faced its greatest obstacle since the launch of the euro in 2002 in 2010. The crisis started when Greece's recently elected socialist government disclosed that the country's budget deficit exceeded initial estimates by more than three times. For years, the European Union insisted that Greece's financial figures were falsified. Investors were concerned that Greece would not be able to pay off its mounting debt. The Greek government suggested significant budget cuts, a pay freeze for public employees, pension reforms, higher taxes, and steps to stop widespread tax evasion in order to strengthen its financial position. The markets, however, continued to have doubts about the government's capacity to deliver, in part because they believed that the austerity measures would fail as social and political unrest grew.

Other nations in the eurozone that experienced comparable financial challenges were Portugal, Spain, Ireland, and Italy. Indeed, there were doubts regarding the eurozone's and its currency's long-term viability.

Although the eurozone's members have a common currency and central bank, they lack an organization that can intervene on behalf of financially troubled nations or impose regulations to control government debt and budget deficits.

That is to say, a nation cannot be made to abide by the 3 percent GDP deficit and the 60% GDP total debt ceiling that apply to potential members of the European Monetary Union after it has joined.

More coordination between the government budgets of the eurozone is required, as most economists believe this is necessary to prevent economic crises and ensure the common currency's long-term survival. To put it simply, the stability of the eurozone depends on further fiscal cooperation. Even though the majority of economists believed that the eurozone would eventually break up, they acknowledged that European governments would need to devise a more effective system for handling a financial crisis.

A European Monetary Fund (EMF) could be established as a stopgap measure. The governments of the participating nations may contribute to this bailout fund through assessments. In order to deter excessive debt and deficits, governments that violate the eurozone's deficit limits would be penalized more heavily.

A nation could access funds during a financial crisis up to the amount it had contributed, provided other eurozone members approved of its fiscal policies. Any additional assistance would necessitate an economic adjustment plan under the direction of eurozone participants.

Critics counter that the International Monetary Fund already exists to support nations that are experiencing financial difficulties. However, there are two main reasons why governments in the eurozone might want to have their own fund. It would first give the eurozone autonomy over its own future. Second, the members of the eurozone would have more authority to penalize fiscal miscreants, such as by cutting off regional aid.

On the other hand, should the nation in question fail to live up to its commitments, the IMF's options are limited to withholding further assistance.

The efficacy of fiscal regulations that place a cap on government deficits is another worry raised by critics of the EMF: the bailout of financially irresponsible eurozone members may lead to "moral hazard," or incentives for governments to behave recklessly because they would know they would receive a financial rescue. An EMF, however, might actually make things more difficult for nations who break the rules because careless nations risk punishment from other eurozone members. It may take years before such reforms are implemented. The discussion of a bailout fund and fiscal-policy cooperation in the eurozone had only recently started at the time this text was written.

7.7. NORTH AMERICAN FREE TRADE AGREEMENT

A number of regional free-trade agreements were started by the US as a result of Europe's success in creating the European Union. For instance, talks for a free-trade agreement between the United States and Canada began in the 1980s, and the agreement went into effect in 1989. This made it possible for the United States, Canada, and Mexico to create the North American Free Trade Agreement, which was put into force in 1994. The American visionaries behind NAFTA took a revolutionary risk. The authoritarian political structure, suppressed economy, and ensuing poverty in Mexico were causing issues that would never be able to be solved at the border. Eventually, the unrest in Mexico would spread to the Rio Grande.

The decision was simple: either support Mexico's development as a member of a North America that is integrated, or watch as the economic divide grows and the risks to the United States rise. It was anticipated that the creation of NAFTA would give each member country improved access to the markets, labor, technology, and expertise of the others. There were many striking similarities between the two countries: Mexico would gain from US investment and experience, and the US would gain from Mexico's pool of inexpensive and increasingly skilled labor.

Table 7.3. Winners and Losers in the United States Under Free Trade with Mexico

U.S. Winners	**U.S. Losers**
Higher-skill, higher-tech businesses and their workers benefit from free trade.	Labor-intensive, lower-wage, import—competing businesses lose from reduced tariffs on competing imports
Labor-intensive businesses that relocate to Mexico benefit by reducing production costs	
Domestic businesses that use imports as components in the production process save on production costs.	
Consumers in the United States benefit from less expensive products due to increased competition with free trade.	

Source: Robert J. Carbaugh, International Economics, ISBN 13: 9781439038949.

Negotiating the free-trade agreement, however, was challenging since it called for balancing the economies of a large developing country (Mexico) and two major advanced industrialized nations (Canada and the United States).The stark difference in living standards between the United States, Canada, and Mexico—which has a lower wage scale—was a contentious political issue. Whether developed nations like the United States and Canada would benefit much from trade liberalization with Mexico was one of the key questions surrounding NAFTA. Table 7.3 lists some of the possible benefits and drawbacks of merging the US and Mexican economies.

7.7.1. NAFTA's Benefits and Costs for Mexico and Canada

Because the economies of the US and Canada are so much larger than Mexico's own, the benefits of NAFTA have been comparatively much greater for Mexico. Mexico has a comparative advantage in the production of goods and services, which has increased as a result of trade barriers being removed. Taiwan and Korea, two other low-wage nations, have suffered as a result of Mexico's gains. All things considered, Mexico has produced more low-wage, low-skilled goods—like tomatoes, avocados, fruits, vegetables, processed foods, sugar, tuna, and glass—and more labor-intensive manufactured exports, like economy cars and appliances. In addition to boosting national output, foreign exchange earnings, employment, and wage incomes, rising investment spending in Mexico has also made technology transfer easier.

About a quarter of Mexico's population is employed in agriculture, despite the sector accounting for only four to 5 percent of the nation's GDP. The majority of agricultural laborers in Mexico cultivate small plots of grains and oilseeds for subsistence, a practice that has sustained them for many generations. Mexican producers of chicken, beef, pork, and rice assert that NAFTA-induced US competition in the Mexican market has destroyed their business. They argue that they are unable to compete with US imports because US farmers have an unfair advantage due to easy credit, superior transportation, advanced technology, and significant subsidies.

Since trade with Mexico was far smaller than with the US, Canada's initial concerns about NAFTA had less to do with the flight of low-skilled manufacturing jobs. The main worry was that Canada's European-style social welfare model would be threatened by closer economic integration with the US. This could happen in two ways: either by making certain practices and policies (like universal health care or a high minimum wage) deemed uncompetitive, or by putting downward pressure on the base of personal and corporate taxes in the nation, starving government programs of funding. In stark contrast to the US, Canada's social welfare model is still in place at the moment. NAFTA does not threaten the Canadian way of life, provided that the majority of citizens are prepared to pay the higher taxes required to support extensive government services.

The majority of Canada's gains from NAFTA have come in the form of protections, such as equal access to Mexico's market, preservation of its standing in international trade, and preservation of its present free-trade preferences in the US market. Additionally, Canada wanted to be involved in any process that would eventually increase market access to South and Central America. Despite Canada's long-term hopes for benefits from trade with Mexico, most researchers estimate that the small amount of trade that currently exists between the two countries has resulted in relatively small gains thus far. Another advantage of NAFTA is economies of scale. By exporting to other members, a member of NAFTA can get around the limitations of its own domestic markets and achieve production economies of scale. NAFTA has made it possible for US manufacturing behemoths like General Electric and General Motors to employ economies of scale on their assembly lines. Small quantities of numerous products were assembled in GM's Mexican assembly plants prior to NAFTA, which led to expensive production and somewhat subpar quality. These days, its Mexican plants focus on a small number of high-volume items, which lowers costs and improves quality. Customers in the US and Mexico gain from this outcome.

While it has been successful in encouraging more foreign investment and trade, NAFTA by itself has not been sufficient to modernize Mexico or ensure prosperity. Many Mexicans are disappointed with this outcome. Trade and investment, however, have their limitations. The Mexican government has faced numerous challenges since the start of NAFTA, including low-quality education, red tape, crumbling infrastructure, credit shortages, corruption, and a small tax base.

These elements have a big impact on how economically developed a nation is. Mexico needs improvements to its roads, cheaper electricity, better education, and investment incentives to spur growth in order to become an economically developed country—things that NAFTA is unable to deliver.

Additional wealth is what NAFTA can offer, allowing the Mexican government to use the proceeds for necessities. The benefits of free trade quickly wear off if a government misallocates newly created wealth.

7.7.2. NAFTA's Benefits and Costs for the United States

Proponents of NAFTA argue that by boosting trade opportunities, lowering costs, boosting competition, and helping US businesses achieve economies of large-scale production, the agreement has improved the US economy as a whole. The US has produced more goods, such as chemicals, plastics, cement, advanced electronics and communications equipment, machine tools, and home appliances, that are benefited by substantial physical capital and a highly skilled labor force. Less regulation of foreign insurance companies doing business in Mexico has also helped American insurance companies. American businesses, especially those with greater resources, have found that labor and parts are more readily available. Furthermore, as a result of the country's growing wealth, the United States has profited from a more dependable supply of petroleum, a decrease in illegal immigration from Mexico, and improved political stability in Mexico. Despite these advantages, the US economy is thought to have grown only slightly overall because it is 25 times larger than Mexico's and because many trade barriers between the two countries were removed before NAFTA was put into place.

However, even fierce supporters of NAFTA admit that some sectors of the US economy have suffered as a result of it. Businesses that depend on trade barriers to restrict imports of inexpensive Mexican goods, like sugar and citrus cultivation, have lost out. Workers with low skill levels, like those in the garment industry, stand to lose more because they are more susceptible to competition from low-wage workers overseas.American labor unions have expressed particular concern that US companies may relocate to Mexico as a result of the low wage scale in Mexico, which could lead to job losses in the US. Cities that employ thousands of people to produce simple auto parts like piston rings, like Muskegon, Michigan, are particularly susceptible to low-wage competition from Mexico. In fact, Mexican laborers have received a far smaller hourly wage in the manufacturing sector than have their American and Canadian counterparts. Critics of NAFTA claimed that when US businesses relocated to Mexico to take advantage of the country's cheap labor, there would be a "giant sucking sound." But after more than 10 years, fewer US businesses have moved to Mexico than anticipated. The theory of international trade explains why. Table 7.4 shows that in 2007, the average worker in the United States was productive (gross domestic product per worker) at $94,120, while the average worker in Mexico was productive at $23,409. Thus, the productivity of the US worker was roughly four times that of the Mexican worker. Thus, there would be no difference in the cost per unit of output if employers paid US workers four times as much as they did Mexican workers. Additionally, American businesses benefit from a more stable political and legal framework than that of Mexico. In other words, not many US companies have moved to Mexico due to the lower wages of Mexican labor. Mexico's environmental laws, which have drawn criticism for being laxer than US ones, are another cause for concern. Environmental and labor activists in the United States worry that Mexican plants that pollute the environment could force cleaner, but more expensive, American plants to close. Environmentalists worry that as Mexico grows, pollution of the air and water will also rise. NAFTA proponents respond, however, that a wealthier Mexico might be better able and willing to uphold its environmental laws; additionally, greater economic openness is linked to production nearer cutting-edge technology, which is typically cleaner.

Table 7.4. Gross Domestic Product, Employment and Labor Productivity, 2007

Country	Gross Domestic Product (billions)	Employment (millions)*	Labor Productivity**
United States	$13,751	146.1	$94,120
United Kingdom	2,772	30.2	91,788
Germany	3,317	39.8	83,342
Canada	1,330	16.5	80,606
Australia	821	10.2	80,490
Japan	4,384	63.8	68,714
Mexico	1,023	43.7	23,409
China	3,206	764.0	4,196

*Employment (1 unemployment rate) labor force.

**Labor productivity GDP/number of persons employed. Due to rounding, numbers are not precise.

Source: World Bank Group, Data and Statistics, http://www.worldbank.org/data. See also Central Intelligence Agency, World Fact Book and International Monetary Fund, International Financial Statistics. NAFTA proponents see this as a chance to redistribute productive factors so that each country can contribute to a larger pie, thereby expanding the region's productive base. Nonetheless, a rise in U.S. and Canadian trade with Mexico as a result of NAFTA's lowered trade barriers would partially replace trade between the US and Canada and other countries, such as those in the Caribbean, Asia, Central and South America, and the Caribbean. It is anticipated that a portion of this displacement will lead to a welfare loss from trade diversion, or the switch from a lower-cost to a higher-cost supplier. However, it was anticipated that the displacement would only have a little detrimental impact on the economies of the US and Canada. President Bill Clinton negotiated side agreements with Mexico and Canada to soften the blow of the NAFTA treaty for a skeptical US Congress. In terms of the environment, Canada established an agency to look into environmental violations in any of the three nations. Nations who disregard their own environmental laws may be subject to fines or trade sanctions. In terms of labor, if two of the three nations concur, an agency was founded in the US to look into labor abuses. If nations don't enforce worker safety regulations, child labor laws, or minimum wage standards, they risk fines or trade sanctions. NAFTA has had comparatively little overall impact on the US economy thus far. Among these effects have been rises in the overall U.S. income and a rise in US-Mexico trade, but little effect on the general unemployment rate despite some worker displacement from one industry to another. The effects have generally been more pronounced for specific products or industries that are more exposed to intra-NAFTA trade, including effects on worker displacement.

Table 7.5. Trade Effects of NAFTA: Trade Creation and Trade Diversion (Thousands of Dollars)

Trade Flow	Trade Expansion	Trade Creation	Trade Diversion
U.S. imports from Canada	$1,074,186	$689,997	$384,189
U.S. imports from Mexico	334,912	284,774	50,138
Canadian imports from the United States	63,656	38,444	25,212
Canadian imports from Mexico	167,264	3,321	163,943
Mexican imports from the United States	77,687	50,036	27,651
Mexican imports from Canada	28,001	902	27,099

Source: From David Karemera and Kalu Ohah, (1998). "An Industrial Analysis of Trade Creation and Trade Diversion of NAFTA." Journal of Economic Integration, 419–420. See also Gary Clyde Hufbauer and Jeffrey Schott, NAFTA Revisited: Achievements and Challenges, Washington, DC, Institute for International Economics, 2005.

As Table 7.5 illustrates, between 1994 and 1998, the flow of US imports from Canada was estimated to have increased by $1.074 trillion due to NAFTA. Of that trade expansion,

$690 billion represented trade creation and $384 billion represented trade diversion, or imports that were previously coming into the United States from other lower-cost countries but are now coming from Canada, the higher-cost producer. Overall, the table indicates that trade creation from NAFTA outpaced trade diversion for the US, enhancing the country's welfare. This is in line with most research, which indicates that NAFTA increases trade rather than diverts it. Not in economics, but in politics, NAFTA has had the most impact.

The trade deal has come to represent Mexico and the United States as close allies. This embrace is noteworthy in light of the two nations' long history of hostility. It began when US officials realized that if their southern neighbors were wealthy rather than impoverished, they would have a much better chance of stopping the immigration wave. In other words, through NAFTA, the US bought itself an ally.

7.7.3. NAFTA and Trade Diversion: Textiles and Apparel

Clothing and textiles are one area where NAFTA has caused trade divergence. Mexico's textile industry benefited initially from the trade diversion brought about by NAFTA, but these advantages were short-lived. Despite the fact that other non-member nations could produce textiles more cheaply, Mexican producers were able to compete in the US market after US barriers on imports of Mexican textiles were removed under NAFTA. Mexico overtook China as the country that supplied the majority of textiles to the US for a brief period of time in the late 1990s due to its rapid increase in market share. However, China has grown a fiercely competitive textile export market that has made it the world's lowest-cost producer. Additionally, China's 2001 entry into the World Trade Organization resulted in fewer restrictions on its textile exports. China gained ground on Mexico in US sales as the playing field leveled establishment in 2001. China gained ground on Mexico in US sales as the playing field leveled. To put it plainly, Mexico's textile industry was revived by the early trade diversion brought about by NAFTA, but the benefits could not last. NAFTA ceased to be very beneficial to Mexican textile producers as later trade agreements undermined Mexico's favored status. What will happen to Mexico's textile and clothing industries is difficult to forecast, given that China and other nations now have more access to the US market.

7.7.3.1. Mexico Retaliates After the United States Closes Its Highways to Mexican Cargo Trucks

Reaching a worldwide audience is harder than it seems. Take the conflict between social activists who are worried about highway safety and free traders who want an efficient deregulated trucking system.

For many years, Canadians and Americans have been concerned about the safety of the trucking industry. Both the US and Canada have laws that restrict the amount of time a truck driver can spend on the road in a row; truck drivers also undergo drug and alcohol testing, and their vehicles are inspected for safety standards. On the other hand, neither drug testing nor roadside inspection programs exist in Mexico. There are no truck weighing stations or logbooks required. It does not have a mechanism to check driver licenses or a requirement for the labeling of hazardous or toxic cargo.

The United States, Mexico, and Canada agreed to allow each other's rigs to use their roads as part of NAFTA. President Bill Clinton did, however, place limitations on Mexican trucks in 1995, limiting their use to areas of the United States that were 20 miles or less from the Mexican border. The US Teamsters union was happy with the practice of loading Mexican goods onto American trucks for transportation beyond this arbitrary zone. Furthermore, in 2002, the US government imposed 22 new safety regulations on Mexican trucks, which was a discriminatory measure because these regulations did not apply to U.S.S. and Canadian airlines that conduct business in the US.

A NAFTA arbitration panel determined that the United States was in breach of its treaty obligations as a result of these actions. As a result, a pilot program was established in 2007 and strict safety regulations were placed on the entry of a limited number of Mexican carriers into the United States. The program demonstrated after 18 months that Mexican carriers were just as safe as their U.S.S. and their Canadian counterparts, and that American consumers benefited from the savings on transportation costs. For the Teamsters union, that was bad news.

2009 saw the US government end the pilot program in violation of NAFTA, blocking Mexican truckers from entering the US through its southern border. In retaliation, Mexico published a list of 89 US goods that would now be subject to new tariffs ranging from 10 to 45%. States that exported a range of agricultural products to Mexico, including California, Oregon, and Washington, were among those most severely impacted by Mexico's tariffs. Mexicans began replacing imported American goods with goods from Latin America, Europe, and Canada because the cost of these goods was higher. Undoubtedly, the Teamsters union's protectionism came at a high cost to American farmers. It is unclear at the time of writing this text whether the trucking dispute will be settled.

7.7.3.2. Is NAFTA an Optimum Currency Area?

The discussion of creating an American monetary union and implementing a common currency among Canada, Mexico, and the United States has been sparked by the NAFTA countries' growing convergence. The idea of the ideal currency area is crucial to the viability of such a monetary union economically.

The theory of optimum currency areas states that countries are better suited to adopt a single official currency the more linked they are to one another. The level of economic integration between the three NAFTA members is one example of this relationship. Trade within NAFTA is quite significant, as would be expected. In terms of trade turnover (imports plus exports), Canada and Mexico are the United States' two largest trading partners, in that order. Similarly, Canada and Mexico's biggest trading partner is the United States.

The three NAFTA members' comparable economic structures are another connection. The advanced industrial economies of the United States and Canada are similar. Canada's average real income per person, inflation rate, and interest rate over the last 10 years have all been relatively similar to those in the US. In contrast to Canada and the US, Mexico's economy is growing and strives to maintain financial and economic stability despite having a much lower average real income per capita and much higher inflation and interest rates. Additionally, the peso's value has fluctuated a lot in relation to the US dollar, but it has been more stable in relation to the Canadian dollar. High levels of external debt, balance of payments deficits, and fragile financial markets are some of the other issues Mexico faces.

The benefits of Mexico making the US dollar its official currency are questioned by some analysts. Mexico's economy might become even more fragile if it adopted the dollar because its central bank would be powerless to influence employment and production in the face of economic shocks. Adopting the dollar, however, would provide Mexico with a number of benefits, such as achieving long-term credibility in the country's financial markets, monetary stability over the long run and lower interest rates, and a rise in confidence and discipline as a result of inflation falling to US levels. To put it plainly, the majority of observers believe that there are economic reasons to doubt Mexico's eligibility to participate in a North American optimal currency area. To forge closer political ties with the US, the Mexican government has expressed interest in dollarizing its economy, nevertheless.

In general, Canadians have voiced their displeasure with the US dollar's designation as their official currency. Canadians are especially worried about the policy's potential to undermine their sense of national sovereignty. Furthermore, they point out that since Canada and the US are already committed to achieving low inflation, low interest rates, and a low level of debt relative to gross domestic product, there is no additional benefit of credibility to monetary and fiscal discipline. Politically, the case for Canadian participation in any North American currency area is weaker than the economic one. The possibility of a North American currency area in the near future seemed remote at the time this text was written.

7.8. FREE TRADE AREA OF THE AMERICAS

"Never in America has there been a matter requiring more good judgment or more vigilance, or demanding a clearer and more thorough examination." So said Jose Marti, Cuba's independence hero of the first effort by the United States to unite the two halves of the Americas in 1889. By the first decade of the 2000s, the region's governments were still stumbling on toward that goal, but hardly in step. In an effort to increase the extent of North American economic interdependence, the United States organized the Summit of the Americas in 1994, which was attended by 34 countries from both North and South America, with the exception of Cuba. The proposal for the establishment of the Free Trade Area of the Americas (FTAA) served as the conference's centerpiece. The concept originated in the 1820s when US relations with the emerging Latin republics were being bolstered by Henry Clay, the speaker of the House and secretary of state.

An FTAA would be the world's largest trading bloc if it were to be formed. With a combined income of over $14 trillion, it would generate a market of over 850 million consumers. Additionally, it would level the playing field for US exporters, who faced trade barriers more than three times higher than those of exporters to the US at the beginning of the century.

By signing free trade agreements with Chile in 2003 and five Central American countries in 2005, the United States concretely proved its commitment to this goal and sparked talks with other Latin American countries.

As part of its overall economic platform, Latin America has adopted increasingly more open trade policies over the past 20 years, both within its region and with the rest of the world. Despite their reputation for being heavily indebted, Latin America's larger economies are now regarded as some of the more promising emerging markets for trade and investment in the 2000s.

This new perspective was made possible by three changes in Latin American economic policy: the failure of the import-substitution model of development in the 1960s and 1970s; the use of conventional and generally restrictive macroeconomic policies to promote economic growth and stability; and a reduction in the role of government in managing the economies, with a greater emphasis on markets, private ownership, and deregulation. The principal regional trade agreements in the Americas are listed in Table 7.6.

But in order for the FTAA to become a reality, certain issues must be resolved. The FTAA's acceptance of other trade agreements in the hemisphere presents one difficulty. The hemisphere's nations are parties to four regional customs unions and 21 free trade agreements. Even though these agreements have the potential to accumulate into a "spaghetti bowl" of contradictory clauses, an FTAA offers the chance to consolidate these clauses into a single agreement. The idea that smaller partners in the hemisphere ought to receive extra support raises additional concerns. Critics point out that an FTAA ought to represent more than just the interests of the two biggest economies in the hemisphere, Brazil and the United States.

Table 7.6. Major Western Hemisphere Regional Trade Agreements

Agreement	Members	Year Effective
Free Trade Area of the Americas	34 countries	Negotiating
Central American Free Trade Agreement (CAFTA)	Costs Rica, El Salvador, Guatemala, Honduras Nicaragua, Dominican Republic, United States	2005
North American Free Trade Agreement (NAFTA)	Canada, Mexico, United States	1994
Southern Cone Common Market (MERCOSUR)	Argentina, Brazil, Paraguay, Uruguay	1991
Caribbean Community and Common Market	Antigua, Bahamas, Barbados, Barbuda, Belize, Dominica, Grenada, Guyana, Haiti, Jamaica, Montserrat, St. Kitts, Nevis, St. Lucia, St. Vincent, Surinam, Trinidad, and Tobago	1973
Andean Community	Bolivia, Colombia, Ecuador, Peru, Venezuela	1969
Central American Common Market	Costa Rica, El Salvador, Guatemala, Honduras, Nicaragua	1961

Source: Robert J. Carbaugh, International Economics, ISBN 13: 9781439038949.

The challenges related to agriculture are yet another. The agricultural sector accounts for a considerably larger portion of Latin America's exports and contributes an average of 7% of the region's GDP.

Because the European Union is the largest agriculture subsidizer, the US has refused to reduce tariffs and subsidies that protect US farmers in the FTAA negotiations, arguing that such protections should be negotiated in global trade agreements rather than regional ones. However, Brazil demands that tariffs and subsidies be discussed because it claims that its farmers cannot compete in US markets. But US farmers worry that if trade barriers were lifted, a flood of low-cost agricultural goods from Brazil and other Latin American countries would arrive, destroying them. Respecting intellectual property rights and allowing foreign bidders on government contracts are two more challenging FTAA negotiation topics.

The governments of the region have been unable to bring the two Americas together due to these differences. In 2003, the governments reached a less ambitious compromise in order to maintain the region's progress toward forming an FTAA. The comprehensive agreement that they had spent years negotiating was abandoned. Rather, they were looking for a more adaptable 34-nation deal with a few shared standards and some tariff reductions. Despite this tactic, the FTAA sat dormant in 2005 as its members failed to come to a free trade agreement. Rather, future negotiations were put on hold until the global situation improved.

The FTAA would significantly impact the lives of those who live in the Western Hemisphere and is arguably the most ambitious economic initiative in the region's history. Before it is finished, there will probably be a lot of obstacles to overcome and detours to take.

7.9. ASIA-PACIFIC ECONOMIC COOPERATION

The Asia-Pacific Economic Cooperation (APEC) is a group of countries that includes the United States, Australia, Brunei, Canada, Chile, China, Indonesia, Japan, Malaysia, Mexico, New Zealand, Papua New Guinea, the Philippines, Singapore, South Korea, Taiwan, and Thailand. The APEC was formed in 1989. The leaders of the Asia-Pacific Economic Community (APEC) presented their vision of an Asia-Pacific economic community in 1993, with the goal of removing trade and investment barriers by 2020. Every nation would start liberalizing at the same time, but the rate of implementation would vary according to each APEC economy's stage of development: free trade and investment for industrialized nations would happen no later than 2010, while free trade and investment for developing nations would happen no later than 2020. It is unclear if the economic integration objective of APEC will need to be postponed.

7.10. TRANSITION ECONOMIES

Trade advantages have also been extended to financial and commercial practices in countries that are transitioning from centrally planned to market economies; these countries are referred to as transition economies. Eastern European countries were categorized as nonmarket economies prior to the 1990s economic reforms, whereas Western countries, including the United States, were categorized as market economies.

Both domestic and international trade in a market economy is governed by the commercial decisions made by independent buyers and sellers acting in their own best interests. Prices set by the market allocate scarce resources and place a value on alternatives. Because of this allocation, prices serve as a signaling and rationing mechanism that ensures that the availability of goods is in line with consumer preferences and purchasing power.

Market factors are given less weight in centrally planned economies, or nonmarket economies. International and occasionally domestic trade is governed by state planning and control. The prices and output of goods purchased and sold are frequently governed by the central plan, with little regard for efficiency and cost factors. Prices are set by the state to restrict arbitrary amounts among consumers, and they are mainly unaffected by factors related to international trade. Trade between market economies and centrally planned economies can be challenging because of these disparate pricing mechanisms. The theory of comparative advantage states that market-determined prices form the foundation of trade; therefore, the theory offers limited insight into how nonmarket economies implement their trade policies internationally.

7.10.1. The Transition Toward a Market-Oriented Economy

The nations that were ruled by the Soviet Union were isolated and backward after 50 years of state control, and they required significant change. Numerous of these nations reshaped themselves in 1989 by pursuing economic and democratic reforms. Nations like the Czech Republic and Hungary abandoned their centrally planned state economies in favor of ones where the majority of resources were distributed through markets and private property ownership predominated. After gaining independence from communism, these nations looked to adopt the open, free market economic system of the West in order to achieve prosperity.

The inability of the economies of the 27 former Soviet-controlled nations to produce a high standard of living for their citizens served as the primary driving force behind change in those nations. The failure of these countries' economic policies stemmed from their inability to offer sufficient incentives to producers so they could effectively supply the goods and services that consumers desired to buy. The government's regulation of investment and production, the widespread use of price controls, the reliance on ineffective public enterprises, and the high barriers to international competition all hindered the normal functioning of markets. Entrepreneurial incentives were severely limited by the absence of enforceable property rights.

Production levels in the communist nations were determined by central plans. It was therefore unreasonable to anticipate that the output would satisfy the needs or desires of the populace. There were often shortages and surpluses, but managers were not incentivized to adjust their output as long as quotas were met. Investment decisions made by the government resulted in widespread rationing and underproduction of consumer goods. Except for the defense industry, there were very few incentives for innovation. Despite this, the nations were unable to translate their high levels of defense technology into advances for the general public. Ineffective state-owned businesses were widespread, and public funds were directed toward preferred sectors of the economy regardless of the effects on the economy. With time, it became clear how flawed the political and economic structures of the communist nations were, and how much more successful the market-oriented systems were.

The Eastern European nations that are reforming, nevertheless, have not marched in unison. The countries of the Czech Republic, Lithuania, Estonia, Georgia, Hungary, Slovenia, and Bulgaria have made great strides toward global integration and have shifted significantly toward capitalism.

These nations have gotten very close to the global norm in terms of trade openness, monetary discipline, and the limited role of government in the economy. They have welcomed foreign investment, reduced business red tape, deregulated their financial sector, improved labor market flexibility, safeguarded intellectual property rights, and combated social corruption.

While certain former Soviet states have achieved notable political and economic changes, others are still grappling with the lingering effects of their communist history. Some of the nations that have not undergone significant reform are Turkmenistan, Belarus, Poland, Russia, and Ukraine. Their business practices haven't really altered since the Soviet era. Both ownership and intervention by the government are commonplace. Particularly noticeable are social corruption and the absence of property rights.

The nations that are pursuing economic and political freedom have fared better economically by a number of measures. Since 1989, the per capita incomes of the more liberal nations have exceeded those of the more repressive or unfree nations by a factor of 1.5. Higher rates of economic growth have also been observed in the freer nations. They have also done a better job of controlling inflation, which has kept the value of their currencies stable.

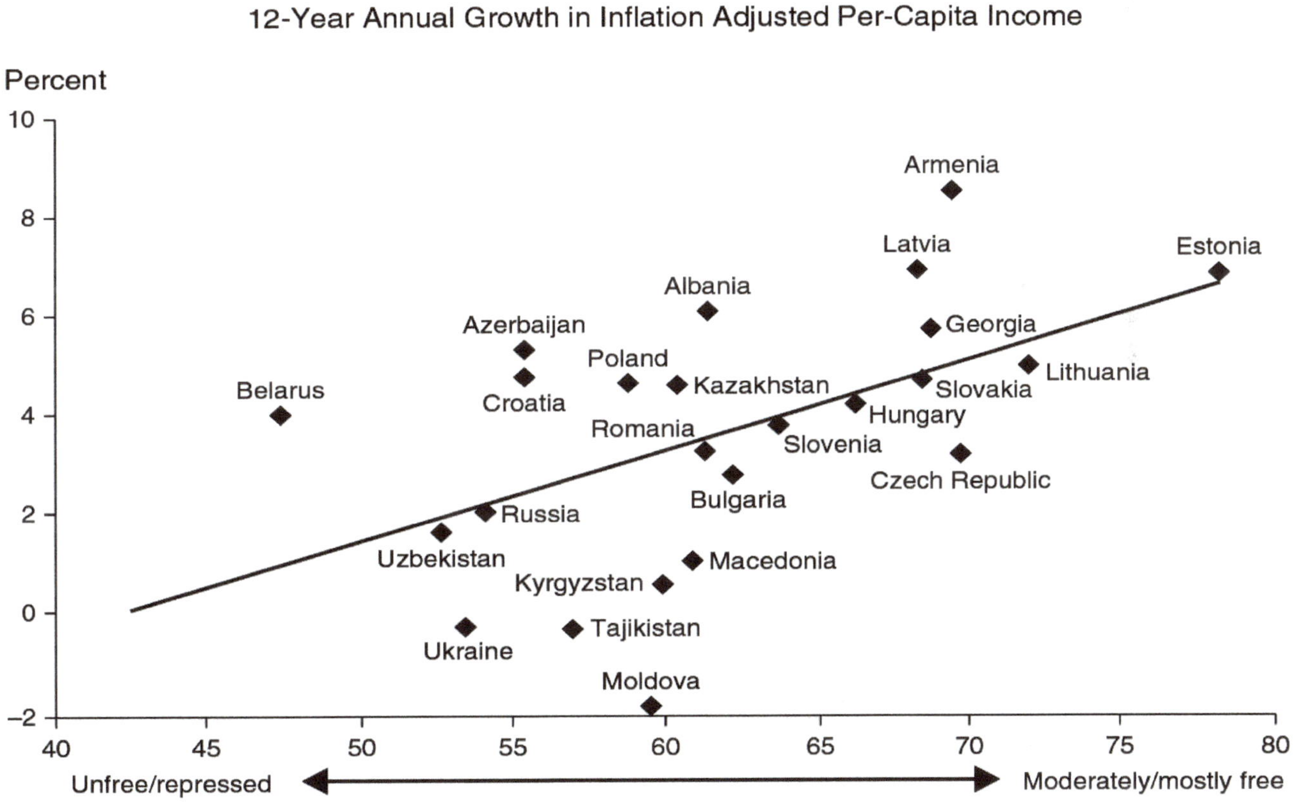

Figure 7.3. *For the former soviet bloc countries, freer economies grow faster.*

Source: Data taken from Julia Carter, (2007). "After the Fall: Globalizing the Remnants of the Communist Bloc," Economic Letter, Federal Reserve Bank of Dallas, p. 5.

For instance, even accounting for their higher productivity, workers from the former Soviet bloc countries are still more expensive than those from China and India, despite the fact that their workers tend to be better educated. In Poland and Hungary, workers receive 73 cents and 58 cents for every dollar earned in the United States. However, at only 20% of US prices, the unit labor costs in China and India are substantially lower. Furthermore, in terms of years of education and instructional quality, workers from the former Soviet bloc do not compare favorably to workers from Western Europe or the United States. As a result, the former communist nations find themselves in a challenging middle ground—they are neither developed enough to compete with the US and Western Europe, nor affordable enough to compete with China and India. In addition, social corruption obstructs significant reforms, and the infrastructure of the former Soviet bloc countries—roads, schools, and hospitals—needs serious improvement. Thus, in order to meet the backlog of development needs, the former Soviet bloc countries frequently postponed or slowed economic reform and globalization (Figure 7.3).

Countries that hope to gain from these ideas in the form of jobs, growth, and improved living standards are more likely to adopt them. Global capitalism does produce results, but not always quickly, as history demonstrates. Due to the legacy of subpar production methods, underemployment, and higher costs brought about by communism, the former Soviet bloc countries encountered difficulties breaking into the international market.

The challenge of eradicating the oppressive legacy of communism has proven to be formidable. Along the border of Russia, an economic divide has developed 20 years after the fall of the Soviet Union. With the exception of the Baltic republics, the economies of the eastern countries remain constrained by the government. Western nations, having advanced further in the direction of economic freedom and globalization, have turned their focus toward Europe and have embraced the European Union. For many years to come, the huge economic region that was formerly the Soviet empire will probably still be affected by this division.

7.10.2. Russia and the World Trade Organization

Russia has been delaying its embrace of capitalism and globalization, but since 1995, it has been negotiating the conditions for joining the World Trade Organization.

Russia's trade policies and its legal and administrative framework for trade have been the subject of extensive examinations during the negotiations, which have resulted in uneven progress toward accession over the years.

There are various reasons why Russia's WTO accession negotiations have been sluggish. Following the dissolution of the Soviet Union, Russia is still in the process of converting its nonmarket economy to a market economy. This involves continuing to restructure its economy, privatize state-owned businesses, and enact market-oriented economic reforms. It has frequently proven challenging and time-consuming to reach political consensus on reforms, especially those that would expose the Russian economy to more capable foreign competitors. Due to a major setback in 1998 brought on by the financial markets losing faith in Russia, Russian policymakers were compelled to make managing the country's economic crisis their top priority. Additionally, since oil is Russia's main export, rising global oil prices starting in 2000 have created a windfall budget surplus and slowed Russia's push for internal economic reforms and integration into the international economy.

After decades of self-imposed isolation by the Soviet Union, the goal of WTO membership has been the cornerstone of Russian economic policies to integrate Russia into the global economy. WTO members have asked Russia to create new laws and regulations that comply with international standards, enhance the enforcement of existing regulations that comply with WTO rules, and consent to terms that will open Russian markets to foreign competition before Russia's application for accession is approved, even though the WTO does not mandate its members to enact specific legislation. Russian agricultural subsidies, the country's customs system, rules governing foreign investment, market access for Russia's service industries, trade barriers posed by Russian technology, and the necessity for Russia to enhance the management and protection of intellectual property rights are among the issues that need to be resolved.

In general, Russia has strong political support for joining the WTO. Reduced tariff and nontariff trade barriers with Russia's trading partners could result in trade gains for Russia worth up to $18 billion over five years after WTO accession, according to Russian officials. Critics, however, worry that an open-trade policy might negatively affect numerous Russian industries, like steel, agriculture, and automobiles, which are not competitive worldwide.

CASE STUDY

AUSTRALIA NEW ZEALAND CLOSER ECONOMIC RELATIONS TRADE AGREEMENT (ANZCERTA)

The Australia New Zealand Closer Economic Relations Trade Agreement (known as ANZCERTA or the CER Agreement) is the main instrument governing economic relations between the two countries. It entered into force in 1983.

ANZCERTA built on a series of earlier RTAs between Australia and New Zealand, including the 1966 New Zealand and Australia Free Trade Agreement (NZAFTA). Each country is a significant investment destination for the other.

Its central provision is the creation of a World Trade Organization (WTO)-consistent Free Trade Area consisting of Australia and New Zealand. The objectives of the Agreement, according to Article 1, are 'to strengthen the broader relationship between Australia and New Zealand; to develop closer economic relations between Australia and New Zealand through a mutually beneficial expansion of free trade between the two countries; to eliminate barriers to trade between Australia and New Zealand in a gradual and progressive manner under an agreed timetable and with a minimum of disruption; and to develop trade between New Zealand and Australia under conditions of fair competition.'

The provisions of the Agreement apply in respect of goods traded in the Free Trade Area, which is defined in Article 2 of the Agreement. The Agreement allows standard exceptions from its provisions, for specified purposes, provided they are not used 'as a means of arbitrary or unjustified discrimination or as a disguised restriction on trade.'

All tariffs and quantitative import or export restrictions on trade in goods originating in the Free Trade Area are prohibited under the Agreement. The rules determining the origin of particular goods are set out in Article 3 of the Agreement. Article 12(1)(a) of the ANZCERTA requires the two countries to 'examine the scope for taking action to harmonize requirements relating to [.] restrictive trade practices.'

Article 22 of the Agreement sets out the review and consultation mechanism to ensure the Agreement's satisfactory implementation. This includes an annual review of the operation of the agreement, and further stipulates that the countries should consult with each other to resolve contentious issues, as there is no dispute settlement procedure under the Agreement.

The process of business law harmonization is aimed at identifying differences in areas that increase the transaction and compliance costs faced by companies operating in both markets. A Steering Committee of Officials, which was established to coordinate the examination of the scope for harmonization, focused on the implementation of a 1988 Protocol, according to which both countries were to eliminate tariffs, quantitative import restrictions and tariff quotas on goods originating in the other country. It was considered that anti-dumping provisions were inappropriate in a free trade area and that anti-competitive business practices by firms operating across the Tasman should be subject to the appropriate competition laws of each country.

It is argued that full trade liberalization was judged necessary but not sufficient to eliminate the need for anti-dumping in the ANZCERTA context. 'Such elimination required active enforcement of similar competition laws and agreement that the jurisdiction of competition agencies extended to matters affecting trade between New Zealand and Australia. In this connection it was agreed that nationals of one state could be made the subject of an enquiry by the competition authorities of the other state and be required to respond to requests for information.'

Competition rules in the two countries were significantly different in 1983 when Australian antitrust laws followed a US model, and NZ followed that of the UK. In 1986, NZ moved to a system that was closer to Australia's.

'Australia and New Zealand eliminated the availability of antidumping actions on goods originating in each other's markets on 1 July 1990. In parallel, Australia and New Zealand simultaneously extended the application of their competition law prohibitions on the misuse of market power. The new provisions (s.46A of the Australian Trade Practices Act 1974 and s.36A of the New Zealand Commerce Act 1986) prohibit the use of substantial market power (Australian law) and dominant position (New Zealand law) in a "trans-Tasman market" for certain anti-competitive purposes.'

'The 1990 Steering Committee report to Governments provided a list of recommended follow-up actions to progress harmonization and a list of matters in respect of which future monitoring and review activity were recommended. In July 1992, the Steering Committee reported to Governments on a number of substantial harmonizing outcomes that had occurred since the signing of the MOU.'

'The Foreign Judgments Act 1991 in Australia and the Reciprocal Enforcement of Judgments Act 1992 in New Zealand provide for more extensive arrangements for enforcing each country's judgments and orders in the other country. Consultation has taken place between Australia and New Zealand about ensuring the compatibility of Australian and New Zealand evidence law, especially in relation to business records and secondary evidence, in the context of enactment of new evidence legislation by Australia and examination of possible evidence reforms by the New Zealand Law Commission.' At the 1995 meeting of the Steering Committee of Officials, focus groups were established in five areas, including competition policy. However, it was decided in the 1996 meeting that 'the Committee would focus on key areas of business law rather than defined "focus group" areas.'

Under ANZCERTA, each country's competition authority and courts have a model of concurrent jurisdiction, whereby each competition authority may control the misuse of market power in the trans-Tasman market. The agreement provides for extensive investigatory assistance, the exchange of information (subject to rules of confidentiality) and coordinated enforcement. The ANZCERTA partners did not formally eliminate the use of CVDs however, even though disciplines on subsidies are included. ANZCERTA includes disciplines on subsidies (Article 11) that are stronger than those contained in the WTO. The 1988 Protocol banned industry-specific subsidies. Export subsidies are also prohibited (these were eliminated by 1987). The OECD (2002) notes that no CVDs have in fact been imposed since ANZCERTA was agreed.

In 1994, the Australian Trade Practices Commission and New Zealand Commerce Commission concluded a bilateral Cooperation and Coordination Agreement to reduce the possibility for inconsistencies in the application of legislation, (Cernat and Laird, 2003). It is worth noting that ANZCERTA does not have dispute settlement provisions pertaining to the RTA as such.

The ANCERTA agreement is very special because of its elimination of anti-dumping. It is clear that there was a direct link between the ending of anti-dumping and the completion of a harmonized and integrated competition regime in this case. The use of anti-dumping appears to have been ended de facto in 1988, but it continued after 1983. Hoekman reports that there were numerous mutual anti-dumping initiations in the period 1983–88 but very few findings that led to measures. Thus the difficulty of using the instrument may have led to a willingness to end its use. Hoekman argues, however, that the key factor was the ability of the two economies to engage in a form of deep integration that went well beyond competition, even though it showed far fewer obviously supranational features than the EU. The comparison springs to mind of the pre-1995 EFTA, where a group of like-minded states were able to practice very free trade with each other due to a very common economic culture. In the case of Australia and New Zealand, the RTA perhaps provided a framework for a joint trajectory from protectionism to openness, with the enhanced role of competition policy in both being an important, but not the only, element.

ACTIVITY

Students will simulate trading under different kinds of trade rules and then reflect on the advantages and disadvantages of each set of rules.

Materials

- How Trade Rules Are Written
- A collection of small items of various values to use as trade goods, such as small pieces of candy, sticks of gum, homework passes, and extra credit points.

Instructional Plan

1. Distribute trade goods to students unevenly, as if the students were countries that specialize: some students get only candy, others get only homework passes,

and so on. When possible, distribute to students goods that they do not want (e.g., if a student has a sweet tooth, give them a homework pass instead of candy) in order to encourage trading.

2. Explain that the students will be allowed to trade but that they first need to come up with ground rules. Divide the class into two groups. One group, simulating the World Trade Organization (WTO), needs to come to a consensus on trade rules and write those rules on the board before anyone can trade. The other group, representing regional trade agreements (RTAs), can make any number of bilateral or "regional" agreements, each of which has to be written on the board (to simulate notifying the WTO). In this group, anyone can trade with anyone else they have an agreement with.
3. Trade agreements must clearly state
   - exchange rates for all products that will be traded under the agreement
   - a dispute resolution mechanism if someone thinks they have been cheated (rock-paper-scissors, mediation by the teacher, etc.)
   - how long the agreement stays in force (only for a few minutes, for the rest of class, the rest of the week, etc.)
4. After the students have made their agreements and traded their goods, lead a reflection:
   a. Which group could start trading more quickly? Why?
   b. Which group was more chaotic? Why?
   c. What are the advantages and disadvantages to trading under the WTO and the RTAs?
   d. How did this exercise differ from how trade agreements work in real life? (One important difference is that in real trade agreements, the exchange rate would be set by market forces and not by the agreement.)

SUMMARY

- Trade liberalization under a regional trading arrangement is very different from the multilateral liberalization embodied in the WTO.
- Under regional trading arrangements, nations reduce trade barriers only for a small group of partner nations, thus discriminating against the rest of the world.
- Since the mid-1950s, the term economic integration has become part of the vocabulary of economists. Economic integration is a process of eliminating restrictions on international trade, payments, and factor mobility.
- A free-trade area is an association of trading nations in which members agree to remove all tariff and nontariff barriers among themselves.
- Regional trading arrangements are pursued for a variety of reasons. A motivation of virtually every regional trading arrangement has been the prospect of enhanced economic growth.
- The formation of a customs union leads to a welfare-increasing trade creation effect and a welfare-decreasing trade diversion effect. The overall effect of the customs union on the welfare of its members, as well as on the world as a whole, depends on the relative strength of these two opposing forces.
- Trade creation occurs when some domestic production of one customs-union member is replaced by another member's lower-cost imports.
- In the years immediately after World War II, Western European countries suffered balance-of-payments deficits in response to reconstruction efforts. To shield their firms and workers from external competitive pressures, they initiated an elaborate network of tariff and exchange restrictions, quantitative controls, and state trading.
- Besides providing for free trade in industrial goods among its members, the EU has abolished restrictions on agricultural products traded internally.
- Much analysis of the benefits and costs of a common currency is based on the theory of optimum currency areas. An optimum currency area is a region in which it is economically preferable to have a single official currency rather than multiple official currencies.
- NAFTA proponents maintain that the agreement has benefited the U.S. economy overall by expanding trade opportunities, reducing prices, increasing competition, and enhancing the ability of U.S. firms to attain economies of large-scale production.
- Textiles and apparel provide an example of trade diversion resulting from NAFTA. Although the NAFTA-created trade diversion initially aided Mexico's textile industry, the benefits were not permanent.
- Trade preferences have also been extended to commercial and financial practices involving nations making the transition from a centrally planned economy to a market economy; such economies are known as transition economies.

REVIEW QUESTIONS

1. How can trade liberalization exist on a non-discriminatory basis versus a discriminatory basis? What are some actual examples of each?
2. What is meant by the term economic integration? What are the various stages that economic integration can take?
3. What are the welfare effects of trade creation and trade diversion for the European Union, as determined by empirical studies?
4. How do the static welfare effects of trade creation and trade diversion relate to a nation's decision to form a customs union? Of what importance to this decision are the dynamic welfare effects?
5. Why has the so-called common agricultural policy been a controversial issue for the European Union?

REFERENCES

1. Abrego, L., Riezman, R., & Whalley, J. (2006). How often are propositions on the effects of regional trade agreements theoretical curiosa? *Journal of International Economics, 68*, 59–78.
2. Antràs, P., & Foley, C. F. (2009). Regional trade integration and multinational firm strategies. In R. Barro & J. Lee (Eds.), *Costs and Benefits of Regional Economic Integration*. Oxford University Press.
3. Baier, S. L., & Bergstrand, J. H. (2007). Do free trade agreements actually increase members' international trade? *Journal of International Economics, 71*, 72–95.
4. Baldwin, R. E. (2008). Sequencing and Depth of Regional Economic Integration: Lessons for the Americas from Europe. *The World Economy, 31*, 5–30.
5. Karacaovali, B., & Limao, N. (2008). The clash of liberalizations: preferential vs. multilateral trade liberalization in the European Union. *Journal of International Economics, 74*, 299–327.
6. Kemp, M., & Wan, H. (1976). An elementary proposition concerning the formation of customs unions. *Journal of International Economics, 6*, 95–98.
7. Krishna, P. (1998). Regionalism and multilateralism: a political economy approach. *Quarterly Journal of Economics, 113*, 227–251.
8. Lee, J. W., & Shin, K. (2006). Does regionalism lead to more global trade integration in East Asia? *North American Journal of Economics and Finance, 17*, 283–301.
9. Limao, N. (2006). Preferential trade agreements as stumbling blocks for multilateral trade liberalization: evidence for the U.S. *American Economic Review, 96*, 896–914.
10. Mansfield, E. D., Milner, H. V., & Pevehouse, J. C. (2008). Democracy, veto players, and the depth of regional integration. *The World Economy, 31*, 67–96.
11. Mansfield, E. D., Milner, H. V., & Rosendorff, B. P. (2002). Why democracies cooperate more: electoral control and international trade agreements. *International Organization, 56*, 477–13.

12. Mansfield, E. D., & Reinhardt, E. (2003). Multilateral determinants of regionalism: the effects of GATT/WTO on the formation of preferential trading arrangements. *International Organization, 57*, 829–862.
13. Mattoo, A., Roy, D., & Subramanian, A. (2002). The Africa Growth and Opportunity Act and its rules of origin: generosity undermined? *The World Economy, 26*, 829–851.
14. Melatos, M., & Woodland, A. (2007). Endogenous trade bloc formation in an asymmetric world. *European Economic Review, 51*, 901–924.
15. Melatos, M., & Woodland, A. (2009). Common external tariff choice in core customs unions. *Review of International Economics, 17*, 292–303.
16. Neary, P. (1998). Pitfalls in the theory of international trade policy: Concertina reforms of tariffs, and subsidies to high-technology industries. *Scandinavian Journal of Economics, 100*, 187–206.
17. Ornelas, E. (2005). Rent destruction and the political viability of free trade agreements. *Quarterly Journal of Economics, 120*, 1475–1506.
18. Ornelas, E. (2007). Exchanging market access at the outsiders' expense: the case of customs unions. *Canadian Journal of Economics, 40*, 207–224.
19. Syropoulos, C. (2002). On tariff preferences and delegation decisions in customs unions: a Heckscher-Ohlin approach. *Economic Journal, 112*, 625–648.

CHAPTER

8 International Factor Movements and Multinational Enterprises

LEARNING OBJECTIVES

After studying this chapter, you will be able to:

- Know the multinational enterprise
- Identify motives for foreign direct investment
- Explain the importance of supplying products to foreign buyers
- Perform country risk analysis
- Understand international trade theory and multinational enterprise
- Focus on international joint ventures
- Know multinational enterprises as a source of conflict
- Describe international labor mobility

KEY TERMS FROM THIS CHAPTER

Centralized model	Country risks	Economic Risk
Efficiency	Employment	Exchange risk
Foreign direct investments (FDI)	Innovative thinking	International joint venture
Multinational corporation (MNC)	Political risk	Public relations
Regionalized model	Sovereign risk	Technical knowledge
Transfer risk	Value-added tax	

INTRODUCTION

Labor, capital, and other factors of production are moved between nations in international economics, and these movements are referred to as international factor movements. There are three ways that international factors move: foreign direct investment, international borrowing and lending, and immigration/emigration. Movements of international factors also bring up social and political issues unrelated to trade in goods and services. Countries frequently impose restrictions on foreign direct investment, capital flows, and immigration.

The international flow of goods and services is driven by almost the same economic forces as the international movement of factors of production. When allowed to, productive factors migrate from countries with high productivity (abundant) to those with low productivity (scarce). As long as returns (like wages and capital yields) are significant enough to surpass the expenses associated with relocating, productive factors will respond to variations in returns. The role of foreign investment and capital flows as a replacement for trade in capital-intensive goods is examined in this chapter. A particular focus is placed on the multinational corporation that manages the global reallocation of capital. The chapter also examines labor mobility across international borders as an alternative to trade in labor-intensive goods.

8.1. THE MULTINATIONAL ENTERPRISE

A multinational corporation (MNC) is a business that conducts business both domestically and internationally. It keeps a central office in one nation that oversees the administration of all of its other offices, including factories or administrative branches. Calling a business that exports its goods to multiple nations a multinational business is insufficient. The multinational must continue to conduct real business and make foreign direct investment in other nations (Jones Ronald, 2005).

8.1.1. Reasons for Being a Multinational Corporation

Companies aspire to become multinational corporations for a variety of reasons. The following are a few of the most typical reasons:

- **Access to Lower Production Costs:** Establishing a production facility abroad, particularly in developing nations, typically results in a substantial reduction in production expenses. While outsourcing can help achieve the goal, it might be even more economical to establish manufacturing facilities abroad. MNCs can benefit from economies of scale and expand their global brand because of their size. Strategic manufacturing and service placement, which enables the company to benefit from undervalued services offered globally, more effective and affordable supply chains, and cutting-edge technological and R&D capacity, is how the company grows.
- **Proximity to Target International Markets:** Establishing a company in a country where its target consumer market resides is advantageous. By doing this, international businesses can obtain consumer intelligence and feedback more easily, as well as lower transportation costs. Because the same brand vision can be used everywhere, international brand recognition eases the transition between various nations and their respective markets and lowers per capita marketing costs.
- **Access to a Larger Talent Pool:** Additionally, multinational firms have a reputation for hiring the brightest talent available, which enables management to give their products and services the best technical expertise and creative thinking.
- **Avoidance of Tariffs:** A company is free from tariffs and quotas if it manufactures or produces its goods in a foreign nation and sells those goods there as well.

8.1.2. Models of MNCs

The following are the different models of multinational corporations:

- **Centralized:** Under the centralized model, businesses establish their executive headquarters in their nation of origin and subsequently construct a number of manufacturing and production facilities in other nations. The executive headquarters is directly in charge of overseeing the establishments and offices abroad.
- **Regional:** According to the regionalized model, a business maintains its head office in one nation while managing a number of offices spread across multiple nations. The regionalized model differs from the centralized model in that it comprises affiliates and subsidiaries that are all accountable to the regional headquarters, which in turn reports to the central headquarters.
- **Multinational:** Under the multinational business model, a parent company maintains operations in its home nation while establishing subsidiaries abroad. In contrast to the first two models, this one grants subsidiaries and affiliates a greater degree of operational autonomy.

8.1.3. Advantages of Being a Multinational Corporation

There are many benefits of being a multinational corporation including:

- **Efficiency:** Because they manufacture in the nations where their target markets are located, multinational corporations can more easily reach those markets in terms of efficiency. They also have easier access to cheaper labor and raw materials.
- **Development:** Multinational firms typically offer higher wages than domestic businesses in terms of development, which makes them more appealing to the local labor force. Due to their large local tax payments, which contribute to the growth of the national economy, they are typically given preferential treatment by the local government.
- **Employment:** Multinational companies employ locals who are familiar with the area's customs and can therefore provide insightful firsthand information about what the community wants.
- **Innovation:** Multinational companies are able to produce more inventive and creative products because they hire both local and foreign labor.

8.1.4. Disadvantages of Being a Multinational Corporation

Despite the benefits of being a multinational corporation, there are also several disadvantages as well:

- **Increased Legal Burden:** Operating in multiple jurisdictions will increase the legal complexity that a multinational corporation must deal with. Laws pertaining to employment, contracts, torts, corporate structures, and the environment vary amongst nations. To handle these complexities, the MNC needs a local legal presence.

- **Increased Tax Compliance:** Operating in numerous countries will also expose an MNC to varying tax regimes. Different regulations may apply to sales tax, value-added tax, tax deductions (e.g., depreciation), the potential to deduct future taxable income from net operating losses, and various tax rates.
- **Public Relations:** A multinational company may be charged with relocating or hiring people outside of its nation of origin, which could damage the company's reputation and influence domestic politics. On the other hand, the MNC might also be charged with abusing local labor, resources, and laws in the other nation.
- **Political Instability:** Political instability may affect a multinational corporation (MNC) based on the locations of its offices and resources. Most multinational corporations (MNCs) operate in less developed nations but are based in politically stable and economically developed nations. The operations of the multinational corporation may occasionally be impacted by political unrest, including local corruption, in the less developed nation.

8.1.5. Examples of Multinational Corporations

The following is a brief list of well-known multinational corporations:

- Apple
- ExxonMobil
- Microsoft
- Proctor & Gamble
- Tesla

8.2. MOTIVES FOR FOREIGN DIRECT INVESTMENT

Foreign direct investments (FDI) are inflows of capital into an economy from outside a foreign nation with the goal of acquiring a long-term managerial stake in a business, apart from the investor's own. It is the total of short capital as shown by the balance of payments, capital reserves, profits reinvested, and other long-term assets. Nearly every economy in the globe acknowledges the significance of foreign direct investment. It should be possible to distinguish between portfolio transfers and FDI. Indirect investments are defined as portfolio transfers. In the increasingly globalized world economy, foreign direct investments are becoming more and more popular for a number of reasons.

8.2.1. Types of Foreign Direct Investment

The three most common categories for foreign direct investments are conglomerate, vertical, and horizontal.

- A company establishes the same kind of business operation in a foreign nation as it does in its home nation through a horizontal FDI. A U.S.-based cellphone provider buying a chain of phone stores in China is an example.
- In a vertical FDI, a business acquires a complementary business in another country. For example, a U.S. manufacturer might acquire an interest in a foreign company that supplies it with the raw materials it needs.
- In a conglomerate foreign direct investment, a company finances a venture that is unrelated to its main business. This frequently takes the form of a joint venture since the investing company lacks prior experience in the field of expertise of the foreign company.

8.2.2. Reasons for Foreign Direct Investments

Foreign direct investments are made for many different reasons. Global corporations make up the majority of FDI, hoping to gain from a number of these benefits:

1. Benefit from reduced operational costs in other nations.
2. Gain from being close to raw materials rather than moving them over the globe.
3. Avoid tariffs and other semi-trade obstacles.
4. Reduce transportation expenses. Nissan, for example, has cheaper transit costs for advertising to the UK market since it manufactures vehicles in the UK.

5. Possibilities for the use of local knowledge to support tapping into domestic markets.

8.2.3. Importance of Foreign Direct Investment

Foreign direct investments come in different forms and at different levels. Even though economies acknowledge the significance of foreign direct investments, corporations' interest in a given economy is determined by the reasons behind these investments. The majority of world economies understand the value of FDI because:

- **Economic Development Stimulation:** FDI will boost a target nation's economic growth, create a further contribution for businesses and investors, and create jobs for the local populace and economy.
- **Direct International Trade:** Because most countries have import tariffs, mercantilism is challenging. In order to achieve sales targets, many economic sectors typically require a presence in international markets.
- **Employment and Economic Boost:** When investors establish new companies abroad, foreign direct investment (FDI) generates new jobs and opportunities. It might increase financial gain and give residents more authority, which would strengthen the targeted economies.
- **Tax Incentives:** Recognizing the value of foreign direct investment, governments offer tax breaks to encourage this kind of investment in projects. Corporations invest in lucrative projects in offshore economies because FDI offers greater tax incentives in these areas.
- **Development of Resources:** One potential major benefit of FDI is the event of human capital resources. The skills acquired via training boost a nation's human capital and general education. FDI benefits nations by fostering the development of their human capital while retaining resource ownership.
- **Resource Transfer:** As FDI promotes resource transfers and the exchange of knowledge, technologies, and skills, there are good reasons for foreign direct investment promotion.
- **Reduced Prices:** FDI can scale back the inequality between revenues and costs. Countries can confirm that production costs will be equivalent and might be sold-out easier.
- **Multiplied Productivity:** The facilities and instrumentality provided by FDI can increase the workforce's productivity within the target country.

8.2.4. Ways to Attract FDI

- **Investment Promotion Agencies (IPA):** A triple-crown IPA might serve as a conduit between suitable foreign investors and the home economy. On the one hand, it should serve as a one-stop shop for the requirements that these investors have of the nation where they are investing. Establishing a seller development program is aided by the IPA. It facilitates the introduction of overseas buyers and domestic vendors. On the other hand, it must stimulate the host country's economy by encouraging it to provide the first-rate facilities and the ready access to skilled laborers, technicians, engineers, and executives needed to attract these kinds of investors.

- **To Strengthen the Capability of the Domestic Economy:** A program like this could give local suppliers financial opportunities to increase their supply in accordance with agreements made with overseas buyers.
- **Set up a Merchant Development Program:** To support the matching method between foreign clients and native suppliers.
- **To Strengthen the Domestic Economy's Capabilities:** It might give local suppliers the chance to get funding for investments they need based on purchase agreements with overseas customers.
- **Improve the Functioning of Monetary Markets Worldwide:** Higher financial market establishments help overcome secondary financial markets in host countries, increasing FDI flows to developing countries even in FDI supply countries. Foreign direct investments, or FDIs, are sums of money that multinational corporations invest abroad in developing or other nations. Transactions involving stocks or portfolios differ from FDI. An indirect investment is a transaction in a portfolio.

8.2.5. Advantages and Disadvantages

Foreign Direct Investment (FDI) has the potential to stimulate and sustain economic growth in both the investing and recipient nations. On the one hand, developing nations have welcomed FDI as a way to fund the development of new infrastructure and the employment of local laborers. However, multinational corporations use foreign direct investment (FDI) to grow their presence in foreign markets. However, one drawback of foreign direct investment (FDI) is that it entails the supervision and control of several governments, increasing political risk.

FDIs come in a variety of forms and levels based on the type of corporation making the investment. Countries profit from lower costs, higher wages, and the exchange of knowledge, skills, and technologies. These are a few explanations for the growing acceptance of foreign direct investments in developing nations. One of the primary causes of the increase in wealth is foreign direct investment (FDI), which also has the ability to empower locals and strengthen specific economies. For this reason, foreign direct investment is valued by the majority of governments across the globe.

8.3. SUPPLYING PRODUCTS TO FOREIGN BUYERS

Once a company is aware that there is a market for its products abroad, it needs to figure out how to supply those products most cheaply. Let's say American company Anheuser-Busch (A-B) wishes to market its Budweiser beer in Canada. Anheuser thinks about the following options: (1) build a brewery in Wisconsin to produce Bud for sale to U.S. consumers in the Upper Midwest and also to Canadian consumers (direct exporting); (2) build a brewery in Canada to produce Bud and sell it to Canadian consumers (foreign direct investment); or (3) license the rights to a Canadian brewery to produce and market Bud in Canada. The degree of economies of scale, the cost of distribution and transportation, and trade barriers between countries all influence which approach A-B decides to use. The following sections go over these things to think about.

8.3.1. Direct Exporting Versus Foreign Direct Investment/ Licensing

Let's look at A-B's approach of directly exporting Bud to Canadians rather than through a license agreement or foreign direct investment. First, we'll examine how economies of scale impact this tactic. When the amount of beer demanded in Canada is relatively small, one would expect economies of scale to encourage A-B to export Bud to Canada; conversely, when the quantity of beer demanded in Canada is relatively large, one would expect Canadian production to be encouraged through a licensing agreement or foreign direct investment. Assume that the average production cost curves for A-B's prospective Wisconsin brewery, A-B's prospective Canadian brewery, and a Canadian brewery that might be granted a license to produce Bud are all the same in order to demonstrate this idea. In Figure 8.1, these cost curves are indicated by AC. The average cost of making a case of beer drops as these breweries expand their production, but then average costs stabilize instead of falling further.

Assume that A-B predicts that U.S. Figure 8.1 illustrates the demand for Budweiser—200 cases per year from consumers. At A-B's Wisconsin brewery, producing this volume enables the realization of significant economies of scale, resulting in a production cost of $8 per case. Additionally, let's assume that the estimated demand for Bud in Canada is for a relatively small amount—100 cases, perhaps. Given that the Wisconsin brewery currently fills 200 cases for the U.S. consumption, the brewery is able to decrease its average cost curve until it produces 300 cases at a cost of $6 per case ($11 – $6 = $5).

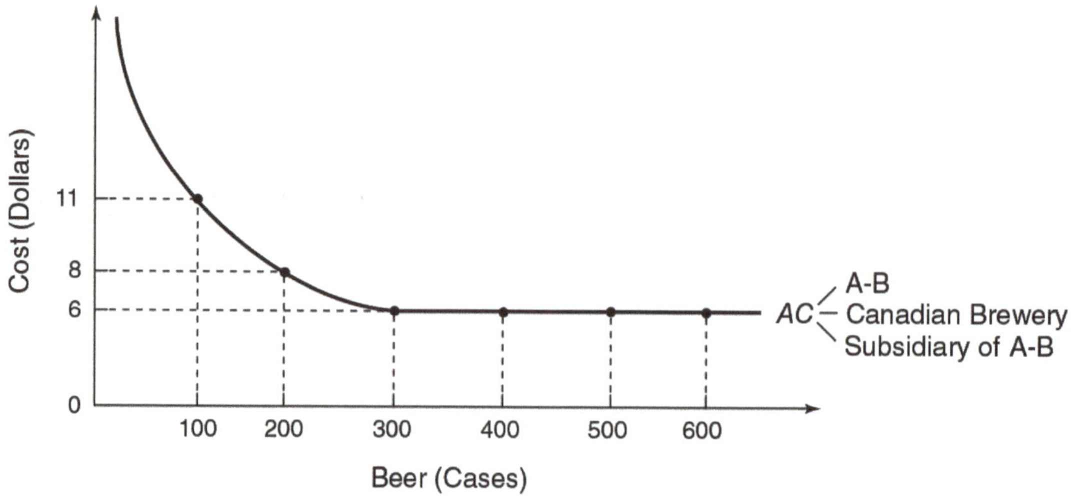

Figure 8.1. *The choice between direct exporting and foreign direct investment/licensing. When the Canadian market's size is large enough to permit efficient production in Canada, a U.S. firm increases profits by establishing a Canadian production subsidiary or licensing the rights to a Canadian firm to produce and market its product in Canada. The U.S. firm increases profits by exporting its product to Canada when the Canadian market is too small to permit efficient production.*

Source: https://wyamaka.wordpress.com/wp-content/uploads/2019/08/international-economics_30.pdf.

This is achieved by increasing output to meet the additional demand in Canada. A-B would maximize profits by exporting Bud to Canada if the cost of shipping and distributing it to Canadians is less than this sum. But if more than 300 cases of Bud are required in Canada, it might make more sense for A-B to use a foreign direct investment or licensing arrangement. To provide an example of this scenario, see Figure 8.1. Assume that 400 cases of Bud are required annually by Canadians, compared to the amount required by U.S. The number of cases remains at 200. A-B is unable to produce Bud at a cost less than $6 per case due to the exhaustion of economies of scale at 300 cases, despite the higher Canadian demand. The licensed Canadian brewery or A-B's Canadian subsidiary brewery could achieve the same level of efficiency as A-B's Wisconsin brewery by producing 400 cases, resulting in a $6 per case production cost for each. A-B reduces overall cost when production costs are equal because it doesn't incur the extra expense of delivering and distributing beer to Canadians. Therefore, A-B boosts its earnings by either purchasing a Canadian brewing company or licensing its beer technology to a Canadian brewer. Trade restrictions have the same potential to offset production-cost advantages as transportation costs. The production-cost advantage of A-B's Wisconsin brewery may be neutralized by high import tariffs in Canada, leaving foreign direct investment or licensing as the only practical means of entering the Canadian market.

8.3.2. Foreign Direct Investment Versus Licensing

After deciding to use foreign production to supply goods overseas, a company must determine if it makes more sense to create a foreign production subsidiary or to give a foreign company a license to use the technology in order to produce the goods.

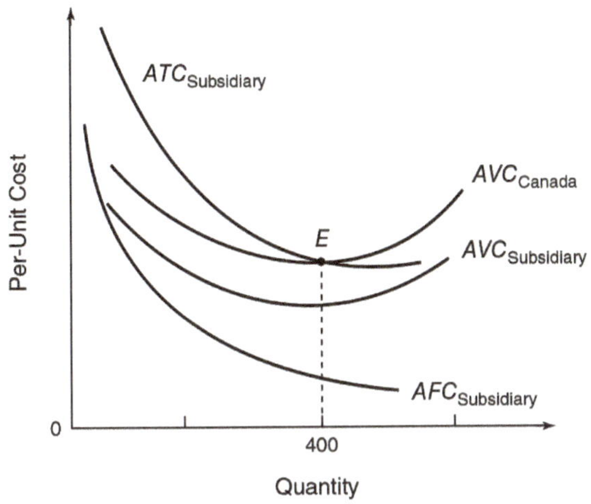

Figure 8.2. *The choice between foreign direct investment and licensing. The decision to establish foreign operations through direct investment or licensing depends on (1) the extent to which capital is used in the production process, (2) the size of the foreign market, and (3) the amount of fixed cost a business must bear when establishing an overseas facility.*

Source: https://wyamaka.wordpress.com/wp-content/uploads/2019/08/international-economics_30.pdf.

There are Kentucky Fried Chicken restaurants in the UK that are locally owned and operated. The parent company U.S. organization only gives its name and operational guidelines in exchange for royalties that the nearby businesses pay. While licensing is a common practice, it requires local businesses to be able to modify their operations to fit the parent organization's production process or technological requirements.

The hypothetical cost scenarios that A-B must consider when deciding whether to invest in a Canadian brewing subsidiary or license Bud production technology to a brewery in Canada are depicted in Figure 8.2. Curve $AVC_{Subsidiary}$ shows the average variable cost of A-B's brewing subsidiary (labor and materials), while Curve AVC_{Canada} shows the average variable cost of a brewery in Canada. Fixed costs associated with starting a foreign brewing subsidiary are also shown by curve $AFC_{Subsidiary}$. These consist of the costs incurred in luring the subsidiary into alignment with the parent company and the pre-existing expenses incurred in evaluating the foreign nation's market potential. $ATC_{Subsidiary}$ provides A-B with the total unit costs associated with establishing a foreign subsidiary.

When comparing $ATC_{Subsidiary}$ and AVC_{Canada}, the Canadian brewery has an absolute cost advantage for a relatively small market of fewer than 400 cases of beer. In this instance, it is more advantageous for A-B to license the technology used in Bud production to a brewery in Canada.

However, A-B's brewing subsidiary has an absolute cost advantage if the Canadian market for Bud exceeds 400 cases; A-B boosts profits by supplying beer to Canadians through foreign direct investment.

The output level at which A-B's brewing subsidiary starts to realize an absolute cost advantage over the Canadian brewery (400 cases in Figure 8.2) is dependent on a number of factors. The variable cost advantage of A-B's brewing subsidiary is greater to the extent that production is capital-intensive and the subsidiary can acquire capital at a lower cost than that paid by the Canadian brewery.

At a lower output level, this benefit offsets the impact of a fixed-cost disadvantage for the subsidiary. This minimum output level is also influenced by the amount of fixed costs incurred by the brewing subsidiary. Reduced fixed costs also translate into lower average total costs for the subsidiary, which again leads to a smaller output at which the subsidiary starts to show an absolute cost advantage.

As mentioned, production costs, fixed costs of setting up shop abroad, labor and capital ratios in the production process, and the size of the foreign market are some of the factors that affect international business decisions. The element of risk and uncertainty is another component. Management considers factors like currency fluctuations and subsidiary expropriations when deciding where to locate production operations.

8.4. COUNTRY RISK ANALYSIS

Risk is present in every business transaction to some extent. There are extra risks associated with business transactions that take place internationally that are not present with domestic transactions. The risks resulting from various national differences in economic structures, policies, socio-political institutions, geography, and currencies are usually included in these extra risks, which are referred to as country risks. The risk of investing in a nation that is reliant on alterations in the business environment that could negatively impact operating profits or the value of assets in a particular nation is known as "country risk."

The goal of country risk analysis (CRA) is to determine whether these risks have the ability to lower the projected return on an international investment. There are numerous ways to define and quantify country risk. Broadly speaking, it refers to the risk arising from those factors that determine or impact a sovereign state's or a country's borrower's ability and willingness "to fulfill their obligations towards one or more foreign lenders and/or investors."

8.4.1. Types of Country Risk

Analysts typically divide country risk into the six primary risk categories listed below. Given the connections between the domestic economy, the political system, and the global community, many of these categories overlap. While there are risk analysts who may disagree with this list in its entirety, most risk ratings from most services tend to include these six ideas.

1. Economic Risk
2. Transfer Risk
3. Exchange Rate Risk
4. Location or Neighborhood Risk
5. Sovereign Risk
6. Political Risk

8.4.1.1. Economic Risk

Economic risk is the substantial shift in growth rate or economic structure that results in a substantial shift in the anticipated return on investment. Risk results from the possibility of unfavorable shifts in the core objectives of economic policy (fiscal, monetary, international, wealth creation, or distribution), or from a notable shift in a nation's comparative advantage (e.g., depletion of resources, downturn in industry, change in the population, etc.). Given that both deal with policy, economic and political risk frequently overlap in certain measurement systems.

Traditional fiscal and monetary policy indicators, such as the amount and makeup of government spending, taxation, the level of public debt, monetary policy, and financial maturity, are examples of economic risk indicators. Measures for longer-term investments center on institutional factors that may influence wealth creation, long-run growth factors, and the level of economic openness.

8.4.1.2. Transfer Risk

The risk associated with a foreign government's decision to impose restrictions on capital movements is known as transfer risk. It is the primary risk under country risk and results from the potential for losses as a result of limitations on out-of-country remittances. Consequently, an obligor may be able to pay in local currency, but may not be able to pay in foreign currency. This kind of risk can arise when a nation's cross-border foreign exchange market is closed or restricted due to a lack of foreign exchange. Restrictions may make capital, dividends, or profits difficult to repatriate. Transfer risk is present in all kinds of investments because governments have the power to modify capital-movement regulations at any time.

The ratio of debt service payments to exports or to exports plus net foreign direct investment, the amount and composition of foreign debt in relation to income, the breakdown of foreign currency reserves by different import categories, and current account status indicators are common examples of transfer risk measures. These quantitative measures' trends show possible imbalances that might force a nation to impose capital flow restrictions on particular kinds of transfers. For instance, an increasing current account deficit relative to GDP suggests a rising requirement for foreign exchange to close the deficit. In the event that the capital account experiences no counterbalancing changes, the likelihood of a transfer issue rises.

8.4.1.3. Exchange Risk

An unanticipated negative shift in the exchange rate is known as exchange risk. Unexpected changes to the currency regime, such as switching from a fixed to a floating exchange rate, are included in the category of exchange risk. Over longer time horizons, exchange rate risk analysis is guided by economic theory. Although economic fundamentals have an impact on short-term pressures, currency traders are best suited to assess currency trading momentum. In the short term, futures contracts and other hedging strategies can be used to eliminate risk for many currencies at a reasonable cost. As a plant or similar direct investment ages, currency hedging becomes unfeasible, increasing exchange risk unless natural hedges can be established. Since a significant decline in value of the currency can alleviate some of the imbalances that cause transfer risk to increase, many quantitative measures used to identify transfer risk also identify exchange rate risk. The exchange rate policy of a nation may aid in separating exchange risk. Compared to fixed or currency board systems, managed floats—where the government tries to keep the currency within a limited trading range—generally carry more risk. Systems with floating exchange rates typically have the lowest chance of causing an unanticipated negative shift in exchange rates. The extent to which a currency is overvalued or undervalued can also be used to separate exchange rate risk.

8.4.1.4. Location or Neighborhood Risk

Spillover effects resulting from issues in a region, a nation's trading partner, or in nations with comparable perceived characteristics are all considered to be part of location or neighborhood risk. While comparable national characteristics (such as the Asian contagion in 1997–1998) and Latin countries in the 1980s may indicate a country's susceptibility to contagion, this category presents analysts with one of the trickier risk assessment problems. Location risk can be measured most simply by geographic position. Location risk can also be defined by trading partners, international trade alliances (like Mercosur, NAFTA, and EU), size, borders, and proximity to politically or economically significant nations or regions.

8.4.1.5. Sovereign Risk

Sovereign risk refers to the possibility that a government will default on loans that it guarantees or be unwilling or unable to fulfill its loan obligations. In a sense, transfer risk and sovereign risk are related if there's a chance that a government will run out of foreign currency as a result of unfavorable developments in its balance of payments. It also has to do with political risk, since a government might choose to break its promises for ideological grounds. Because dealing with a sovereign government presents a special risk for private lenders, sovereign risk is designated as such in the CRA literature. It is unlikely that the private lender can bring legal action against the foreign government without the government's consent, should it choose to default on its obligations. Transfer-risk measurements and sovereign-risk measurements of a government's financial capacity are comparable.

8.4.1.6. Political Risk

Political risk is the possibility that altered political institutions will result from altered social dynamics, governmental authority, or other non-economic factors. This category includes traditional political analysis, the risk of expropriation, and the possibility of internal and external conflicts. An examination of a wide range of factors is necessary for risk assessment, such as the historical background of a nation, the relationships between different groups within it, and the government's decision-making process. Certain political risks can be covered by insurance, which is available from several governmental and international organizations.

There aren't many quantitative tools available to aid in political risk assessment. The range of measurement approaches includes surveys and analyzes by political experts, as well as different classification methods (like type of political structure, range and diversity of ethnic structure, civil or external strife incidents). The majority of services typically employ nation experts who rank or grade a variety of sociopolitical factors and create written analyzes to go along with their scales or grades. Through conversations with regional country agents or visits to other businesses running comparable operations in the nation, company analysts can also create estimates of political risk for their enterprise. Analysts reduce political risk to some kind of index or relative measure in many risk systems.

The risks associated with a multinational enterprise (MNE) building a plant abroad are not the same as those associated with a bank lending to a foreign government. The MNE needs to take a longer view and take into account risks from a wider range of national attributes. Because the MNE is exposed to risk for a longer period of time, certain categories relevant to a plant investment have a much higher degree of risk.

8.4.2. Managing Country Risk

When selecting locations for overseas business, especially if investment is to be made, assessing country risks is an essential task. While some risks can be controlled through financial planning techniques like hedging, insurance, and other financial instruments, other risks are uncontrollable. A risk return analysis can be used to quantify some of these latter risks, with higher returns needed in certain countries to balance the higher risks. In order to create alternative scenarios, it is also essential to study country risks. Although uncertainty will always exist, it can be planned for, leaving no surprises and allowing for backup plans.

Every company faces a different set of national risks. Therefore, we can conclude that a business should consider a wide range of topics and analytical frameworks when developing its own assessment of country risks and formulating its own plan to mitigate the uncertainties associated with those risks.

8.4.2.1. Political Risks

The political risks attached to interventionist governments were significant before the 1990s. These included limits on foreign investment and inefficient government regulations. Numerous nations endeavored to achieve economic autonomy by imposing substantial tariffs and non-tariff barriers on investment and trade. Such political risk has diminished and been replaced in many nations today by a renewed appreciation of free markets and the notion that foreign investment and trade form the cornerstones of economic expansion. Political risks are still present, though.

Political risk may still be a deal-breaker for the natural resource sectors in particular because of the high risk of nationalization, special taxes, or new regulations. Managers in these industries need to think about whether investing is worthwhile given the potential risks. Seeking the opinions of regional political authorities is still beneficial. One method is to distribute a questionnaire to these professionals, gather their responses, and then send the materials back to the participants for additional discussion. This "Delphi" method makes it easier to come to an agreement on the political risks that prospective investors should be aware of.

8.4.3. Managing Political Risk

Political risk analysis and management are now crucial, even when conducting business domestically. Agreements pertaining to international investments aim to reduce political risks. We can use the United States and Canada as an example here. Both nations have signed investment agreements with numerous other nations that guarantee monetary compensation for companies with U.S. or Canadian headquarters if their possessions are taken away.

These agreements guarantee a just and fair process for determining the amount of compensation. The Enron scandal in India serves as an example of how serious political risks can be.

As an added measure of security against particular events like trouble with capital repatriation, expropriation, war, and insurrection, political risk insurance can be bought. For many of these risks, the Export Development Corporation of Canada provides credit insurance.

- **Economic Risks:** When it comes to industry structure, exchange rates, economic volatility, and global competitiveness, economic risks may be especially significant.

8.4.4. Managing Exchange Rate Risks

Both the risk of fluctuations in foreign exchange rates and the possibility that a government won't have the resources to pay back its loans have grown in importance in recent years. There have been persistent budget deficits and fast increases in the money supply in many nations. As a result, these nations continue to have high rates of inflation and occasionally experience devaluation crises. Pressure to devalue the currency of other nations automatically increases when the currency of one nation declines.

Due to large inflows of foreign capital, exchange rates may be kept at unreasonably high levels today. However, these capital inflows could suddenly slow down or even stop. These foreign exchange volatility risks are now recognized by foreign investors. Future capital flows will be more susceptible than past ones to modifications in the financial systems of individual nations and in the overall state of the economy. Future spikes in capital flows could cause some countries' foreign exchange rates to become more volatile. Hedging mechanisms offer some hope for reducing foreign exchange risks, though usually not without some cost, so how can foreign investors protect themselves against these exchange rate risks? Additional strategies for managers to address these country risks are as follows:

1. **Consider the Timing of Investments:** Investors ought to limit their capital transfers to periods when the foreign exchange rate is stable. The "Purchasing Power Parity" theory offers a forecast for probable fluctuations in exchange rates. Examine the cumulative inflation rates of a nation's main trading partners and the nation's own over a period of years. Devaluation is a real possibility if the difference in cumulative inflation rates is greater than the percentage change in the foreign exchange rate.
2. **Borrow Domestically to do Business in the Domestic Country and Avoid Foreign Exchange Rate Exposure:** Remember that this strategy does put the company at risk of interest rate hikes in response to a central bank's devaluation of the foreign exchange market. This strategy also raises the risk of a "run" on deposits for a financial institution that is owned by a foreign entity, as depositors attempt to take money out in order to send it overseas.
3. **Focus on the Devaluation Risk When Choosing Among Countries as Investment Sites:** From this perspective, Chile is currently a less risky region for investment than Argentina or Mexico.
4. **Consider the Amount of Capital Required by Those Activities that are Being Developed in a Country Subject to Devaluation Risk:** For a company in the service or fast-food industries, where capital investment is minimal, the importance of a foreign exchange risk may be low; however, for a company in the manufacturing or natural resource sectors, where significant capital is needed, it may be high.
5. **Spread the Purchase Price Over as Long a Time Period as Possible:**

This makes it possible to buy local currency for less money in the event of devaluation. As an alternative, adjust the projected future payments based on the exchange rate and gear the purchase price to a weighted average of the rate over the course of the next years.

8.4.4.1. Risk of Economic Volatility

A robust banking industry is essential to maintaining economic stability; in its absence, a foreign exchange crisis could have particularly dire consequences. The fact that the time profile for liabilities and assets differs presents a constant problem for financial institutions worldwide. Banks lend long-term and borrow short-term from depositors. This puts the banks at risk for sudden withdrawals from deposits and rapid price drops on fixed assets. Bank loans secured by real estate and stock suddenly face a significant default risk due to sharp declines in their values. This could exacerbate the effects of a foreign exchange crisis and turn it into a wider economic crisis.

8.4.5. Managing Industry Risks

Managers need to assess industry risks in their home country, including the strength of rivals, the possibility of replacements, the capabilities of suppliers and customers, and the risk of new entrants. Creating a matrix where each industry risk is rated as minor, serious, or "show-stopping" and where the various approaches to risk mitigation are examined may be useful in determining the level of risk.

One example of an industry risk for many international corporations might be the challenge of locating suppliers who can provide the necessary degree of quality and service. Disruptions to public utilities could also be dangerous, particularly for businesses that deal in perishable goods. (In certain nations, for instance, power disruptions are frequent. One way for certain Canadian companies to address this issue has been to support other Canadian or U.S. suppliers to launch a company in the same area. Others believe that building one's own utilities—like a power supply—is a way to mitigate the risk associated with power outages. The domestic competitive advantage of a corporation may be strengthened by such actions. Additionally, creating a matrix of industry risks results in strategies and solutions that are particular to each nation and, in some cases, to specific regions within those nations.

8.4.6. Country Risk Strategies

The analysis of country risks has become more important and complex for companies looking to expand into foreign markets, both for suppliers and customers as well as for potential investments. It is now necessary to differentiate between nations and business sectors more carefully. For example, it is now necessary to carefully examine the circumstances that each individual country faces, rather than seeing Southeast Asia as a group of tigers that have been involved in an economic miracle and subsequent downfall.

Managers should get ready by researching interest rates, stock prices, the nation's balance of payments, potential macroeconomic policy scenarios, and deficits in the current and fiscal budgets. To ascertain the risks and rewards associated with specific business opportunities, it is critical to review alternative potential scenarios and projections, assign probabilities to each scenario, and make a determination regarding each one. Price Waterhouse

Coopers has created an index that shows how country risks can be measured in terms of comparable tax rates and rates of return.

Depending on factors like financial strength, experience managing a particular risk, and the nature of the business activity, a corporation's relative importance of different country risks varies. As a result, every company needs to create its own special country risk plans. Analysis and management of country risks are now critical in light of the New Economy, globalization, and the evolving role of governments.

An old proverb states that "no one is an island." This implies that none of us can exist without having an impact on or being impacted by other people. And the same is true for business. No business can function by utterly disregarding the other members of the community. A transaction involving multiple nations is referred to as international business. It gains a sizable share of the world's steadily expanding business. One of the main causes of the enormous expansion of international business is the economy's rapid growth. Companies go global in an effort to grow their clientele and revenue. The domestic market appears too small when a business is doing well. Businesses launch international operations in order to increase sales, establish contacts abroad, and lower the risk of local competition. Businesses that operate overseas need to adopt a more formal approach to conducting business. They ought to understand that doing business internationally differs greatly from doing business domestically. These risks increase when one enters the global business community, and the person needed to handle them needs to be well-versed in business administration. When considering the financial risks associated with conducting business internationally, it is important to remember that a company taking on a foreign customer is also taking on the risk of the nation. A company can reduce country risk by thoroughly investigating the business with which it plans to do international business in the future. The country risk assessment is used to do this.

8.5. INTERNATIONAL TRADE THEORY AND MULTINATIONAL ENTERPRISE

The strategies employed by corporate management may provide the primary explanation for the growth of multinational enterprises. One can summarize the justifications for conducting international business in terms of the comparative advantage principle. Corporate managers perceive opportunities to take advantage of access to new products and technologies, managerial expertise, and factor inputs. The main reason why businesses create foreign subsidiaries is because foreign production offers the best potential for profit. The multinational enterprise analysis is essentially consistent with the comparative advantage principle's predictions when viewed through the lens of trade theory. According to both strategies, a certain commodity will be produced in a nation with low labor costs. The primary distinction between the conventional trade model and the multinational-enterprise analysis is that the latter is predicated on the movement of goods between countries, while the former emphasizes the international movement of factor inputs.

According to international trade theory, when MNEs make foreign direct investments for their own gain, the overall welfare of the source and host countries is improved. It is assumed that if companies can generate greater returns on their foreign investments than on domestic ones, resources will be reallocated from less productive to more productive uses, improving global resource allocation overall. Because conventional trade theory is predicated on the movement of goods between nations, it is essentially the same when analyzing multinational enterprises.

There are some significant distinctions between the multinational-enterprise analysis and conventional trade theory, despite their fundamental similarities. The traditional model assumes that commodities are traded at prices set by competition between autonomous organizations on global marketplaces. However, MNEs are often vertically diversified businesses whose subsidiaries produce both intermediate and finished goods. Sales inside an MNE occur when products are moved from one subsidiary to another. Even though these sales are a component of global trade, variables other than a competitive pricing structure may affect their value.

8.6. INTERNATIONAL JOINT VENTURES

A partnership between two companies with locations in two or more nations is known as an international joint venture (IJV). Establishing a joint venture with a foreign partner is an option for a company looking to explore international trade without taking on all the responsibilities of cross-border business transactions. International investors who form joint ventures reduce the risk associated with buying a company outright. Performing due diligence on the foreign nation and the partner reduces the risks associated with such a business transaction in international business development.

Through the formation of strategic alliances, which are facilitated by IJVs, businesses can obtain a competitive edge by gaining access to a partner's resources, which include people, capital, markets, and technologies. International joint ventures are thought to be a useful tool for transferring knowledge, including technological know-how, from multinational expertise to local businesses. This kind of knowledge transfer can help local businesses perform better. IJVs involve both local and foreign companies, and one or more of the parties are based in the same location as the IJV's operations.

8.6.1. Basic Elements

These include:

- **Contractual Agreement**: IJVs are created through express contracts, which are composed of one or more agreements between two or more people or organizations and are signed with a specific objective in mind for the business.
- **Specific Limited Purpose and Duration**: IJVs can be long-term or have a limited lifespan, and they are created with a specific business goal in mind. IJVs are often created with a finite lifespan because: (a) the complementary activities will only use a small number of assets; (b) the complementary assets will only be used for a short period of time; and/or (c) the complementary production activities will only be partially effective.
- **Joint Property Interest**: Every IJV partner provides assets, money, or other assets, as well as organizational capital, in order to pursue a shared and defined business objective. As a result, an IJV is more than just a set of agreements; rather, the contributions are given to a recently established company, which is typically a partnership, limited liability company, or corporation. As a result, the participants get a shared ownership interest in the IJV's resources and subject matter.

- **Common Financial and Intangible Goals and Objectives**: Regarding the kind and magnitude of anticipated financial and intangible goals and objectives of the IJV, the participants have similar expectations. Since each participant's assets only make up a small percentage of the total resource base, an IJV's goals and objectives are typically very specific.
- **Shared Profits, Losses, Management, and Control**: The participants in the IJV share in certain aspects of the management and control of the IJV, as well as in specific and identifiable financial and intangible gains and losses.

8.6.2. Reasons for Forming

There are many motivations that lead to the formation of a JV (joint venture). They include:

- **Risk Sharing**: Forming a joint venture (JV) is often motivated by the desire to share risks, especially in highly capital-intensive industries where high product development costs are associated with a high probability of product failure.
- **Economies of Scale**: A joint venture (JV) with a bigger business can offer the economies of scale required to compete on a global scale in industries with high fixed costs. It can also be a useful method for two companies to pool resources and reach critical mass.
- **Market Access**: Forming a joint venture with the right partner can give businesses instant access to receptive customer bases and established, efficient, and effective distribution channels, even if they lack the relationship or infrastructure to distribute their products to customers. This is crucial to a business because it can be very challenging, costly, and time-consuming to find new clientele and establish new distribution channels.
- **Geographical Reason**: Partnering with a local business is appealing to foreign companies when there is a compelling business opportunity in a foreign market. This is because entering a foreign market can be challenging due to local obstacles that prohibit foreign-owned or foreign-controlled businesses from operating there as well as a lack of experience in the market.
- **Funding Constraints**: When a company is confronted with high up-front development costs, finding the right JV can provide necessary financing and credibility with third parties.
- **Acquisition:** Partnering in a joint venture (JV) is a desirable choice for companies that wish to acquire one another but are unable to do so because of financial constraints, geographical limitations, legal hurdles, or other issues. Sometimes used as a first step toward a complete acquisition, the JV is much less expensive and riskier than complete acquisitions. With such an agreement, the buyer has the option to buy the remaining portion of the business in specific situations or reduce its losses if the investment isn't as profitable as planned.

8.6.3. Due Diligence

Businesses are advised by business advisers to conduct extensive due diligence on the nation, the company, and the partner before entering into an international joint venture. Due diligence is the process of researching a nation, company, or individual in order to gather important details about the possible advantages, disadvantages, and expenses. It lowers risk and improves profit margins for investors. It entails conducting in-depth due diligence on possible partners via resources like the internet, databases, and media searches; defining roles and responsibilities for each partner; managing control; and reaching an understanding regarding return splits, exit strategies, backup plans, etc. When assisting companies that are thinking about forming a joint venture, international law firms will use a due diligence checklist to make sure the venture is a wise business decision.

8.6.4. Advantages

International joint ventures have many advantages, including giving businesses the chance to expand their capabilities and experience, penetrate new markets, enter related industries, and learn new technologies. Moreover, international joint ventures typically have a brief lifespan, enabling businesses to commit to short-term rather than long-term projects. Companies can gain financial support, create new products, enter new domestic markets, boost profit margins, accelerate revenue growth, share scientists or other professionals with specialized skills that will help the companies, and collaborate internationally through joint ventures.

8.6.5. Structure

International joint ventures are created when two businesses collaborate to achieve a common objective. For instance, Company A and Company B start by looking for and choosing an IJV partner. Numerous steps are involved in this process, including due diligence, market research, partner searching, option evaluation, negotiations, business valuation, and business planning. Every company takes these actions. In addition, there are legal processes like regulatory approvals, ancillary agreements, and IJV agreements. After this is finished, the IJV Company is established, and in this last step, management and formation are done.

When parties are from different cultural backgrounds or legal jurisdictions, structuring joint ventures (JVs) can be difficult. After reaching a consensus on basic issues like the venture's commercial nature, scope, and shared objectives, the parties must choose the location of the venture as well as its legal structure. The structure that is decided upon will typically be between various corporations, partnerships, or limited liability companies.

8.6.5.1. Limited Liability

Limited liability makes it possible to restrict debts and losses to the venture's assets while shielding member assets from personal liability for the venture's obligations. The partners in an limited liability partnership (LLP) are only liable to the amount of their capital contributions and have limited liability. Within the U.S., the law mandates that every limited partnership have at least one general partner with unlimited liability in addition to limited liability partners. Any and all liabilities of the limited partnership may be attributed to the general partner. A common solution to this issue is for businesses to create a special purpose organization, such as a corporation or limited liability company, which serves as the general partner.

By granting limited liability to each member, a joint venture established as an LLC offers protection to the partners. It is not necessary to have a general partner with unlimited liability who can be held accountable for all liabilities, unlike in a limited liability partnership (LLP). Both limited partnerships and limited companies in the U.S. enjoy the advantage of being pass-through entities for U.S. tax purposes. There are no taxes due by the limited partnership. Rather, the venture's tax liability is distributed among the LLP members in accordance with their stake in the venture.

8.6.6. Management

International joint ventures can be divided into two categories: shared management and dominant parent. All projects in dominant parent IJVs are overseen by a single parent that also selects all of the venture's functional managers. The executives from each parent company comprise the board of directors, which is responsible for all operational and strategic choices made for the venture. When a foreign joint venture parent is chosen for reasons other than managerial input, a dominant parent enterprise is advantageous.

Conversely, joint management businesses have both parents running the business. The executives and functional managers who will make up the board of directors are arranged by each parent. There are two different kinds of shared management ventures in this management style. The first kind is a 50:50 IJV, in which each partner contributes 50% of the equity and receives 50% of the participating control. The second kind involves an agreement between the partners that one partner will have a greater role in the IJV than the other and that not all shared management ventures will be 50:50.

8.6.7. Finance

In order to facilitate management and control, it is imperative that partners in an international joint venture agreement make an early decision regarding the financial structure. Establishing the funds needed to launch the IJV, the significance of finding a reliable strategic alliance partner, and financial reporting are a few of the steps. A tax-planned joint venture will be established following the agreement, helping to maximize the after-tax returns.

8.6.7.1. Factors affecting International Joint Ventures

8.6.7.1.1. Economic Factors

- **Formation and Planning:** Joint venture issues are typically the consequence of inadequate planning or hasty establishment by one or more of the parties. For instance, if a product was unsuitable for the joint venture or if the parties involved did not properly evaluate the relevant factors, a marketing strategy might not succeed. Parties need to consider a number of analyzes regarding the target market and the environment in which they intend to operate. If this isn't done, the business will take a negative turn and run into more issues later.
- **Financial Performance:** Tensions over money are one of the quickest paths to failure for a joint venture. This typically occurs when sales are below budget, expenses exceed

budget, or other factors result in lower-than-expected financial performance. Inadequate planning by the parties prior to forming the joint venture, a lack of managerial rigor in the market approach, and unforeseen shifts in the market environment could also contribute to poor financial performance. An effective way to address this is to conduct a thorough assessment of financial conditions both prior to and during the joint venture.

- **Manager:** Ineffective management blending—a problem that can hinder joint venture success—occurs when managers with completely different approaches to organizational issues or who are not accustomed to working together. A common reason why joint ventures fail is miscommunication about leadership techniques. A successful joint venture requires mutual respect, understanding, and compromise in addition to the integration of each party's strengths to strengthen the alliance and overcome its weaknesses.
- **Management Structure:** There may be a mismatch in the managers who attempt to gain equal rights in the venture. The outcome is a significant slowdown in the decision-making process. There is now a "committee" in place to ensure that both parties support every decision, which slows down daily operational decisions that are best made quickly for more business efficiency. This could divert attention from the wider picture and eventually cause serious issues.

8.6.7.1.2. Economic Environment of IJV

More clients and a more powerful organization are the ultimate objectives of a fruitful JV partnership. Viewing joint ventures (JVs) from the perspective of their customers can help to ensure that they are as profitable as possible. In order to maximize value for customers and stakeholders, a JV partnership should strive to have the following features: downplaying weaknesses and putting on a united front, while channeling the expertise and strengths of both parties.

8.6.7.1.3. Cultures of IJV

A joint venture is an attempt to combine two or more cultures with the goal of utilizing each partner's unique strengths. If left unchecked, a lack of awareness of each party's culture presents a challenge. One prevalent issue in these multicultural businesses is that culture is often overlooked when they are first being formed. It is typically believed that after the new unit has been established, the cultural issues will be addressed. Usually, agreements are reached, and some cultural practices from both sides are maintained while others are either completely abandoned or changed.

8.6.8. Potential Disputes and Agreements When Entering IJV's

Disagreements may occur when two or more partners decide to form an international joint venture. In some cases, a neutral governing law and jurisdiction is selected in order to avoid problems between the partners, especially in International Joint Ventures (IJVs), who are likely to want their home country's governing law and jurisdiction to apply to any disputes that may arise. Arbitration is a common method of resolving disputes in IJVs; however, because the legal system has greater authority, it is frequently given precedence. Litigation and mediation are two more techniques used in conflict resolution. Selecting partners is the first step in entering into an international joint venture agreement. Usually, this process continues until both parties sign a Memorandum of Understanding or a Letter of Intent. A memo outlining an understanding between parties is called a memorandum of understanding. A Letter of Intent, on the other hand, is a written agreement between the parties that is not yet finalized. Aspects of an IJV such as applicable law, shareholding, share transfer, board of directors, dividend policy, funding, access, confidentiality, and termination must all be addressed before signing.

8.7. MULTINATIONAL ENTERPRISES AS A SOURCE OF CONFLICT

An organization or collection of companies that operate across multiple countries but are managed from a single nation is known as a multinational corporation, or MNC for short. European industrialization gave rise to this type of cross-border trade, which was then facilitated by globalization and liberalization. Multinational corporations (MNCs) typically have a central office in one nation where all of their other offices, branches, or factories are managed in unison. Due to their scale and involvement in multiple markets, multinational corporations (MNCs) typically possess greater financial resources than small businesses, leading to distinct market relationships.

MNCs' distinct organizational structure has benefits and drawbacks for all parties involved. Due to their extensive global reach, MNCs currently control a significant portion of FDI and dominate markets around the world in the 21st century. It is important to recognize that MNCs facilitate investment into less developed nations, which is crucial for those nations to grow in order to assess their contribution to national development. This argument states that there is a discrepancy between a nation's level of savings and the best possible investment. FDI is one way to reduce this gap, i.e., transfer of resources in the form of financial infusions from a foreign source. This essay addresses the system's detractors as well as how it impacts developing nations. Additionally, it investigates how MNCs' immense financial and political power can either cause or prevent conflict.

- **Limitations:** Since it is uncommon to find incriminating documentation, information regarding the detrimental effects of MNCs is limited. Development data is also skewed because organizations such as the OECD only cover member countries, while UNCTAD projects estimates without including any coverage from ground zero. More contributions to this field of study are needed from non-governmental organizations and impartial, non-aligned groups.

8.7.1. Elaboration and Analysis

As previously stated, a multinational corporation (MNC) is a company that possesses valuable assets or facilities in at least one country other than its country of origin. These corporate entities typically engage in a variety of activities, i.e., sales, transportation, distribution, and so forth—and that too across a number of industries. It is only reasonable to assume that they must have an impact on the target country's markets, rivals, and resources, either positively or negatively.

- **Development of Nations Involved:** Developing nations pursue MNC taxation because local businesses are not sufficiently established to enable them to secure the necessary financial resources to accelerate national development. This justification is based on the fact that multinational corporations (MNCs) manage over 50% of global exports, with their foreign-based affiliates accounting for 33% of those exports. This raises the gross domestic product of the host nation, which gains from MNC taxes as well. According to a 1999 study by academics from Europe, local businesses' initial profits are typically lower due to competition in the product and factor markets, but these profits typically increase as long as they remain connected to their supplier industries. But the existence of a massive corporation has other unintended consequences besides a financial struggle. Studies indicate that the technology employed by multinational corporations (MNCs) can influence domestic firms when they observe how they use it; this phenomenon is referred to as the demonstration effect. Additionally, their presence opens up three avenues for knowledge transfer to domestic businesses.
  - Imitation of production methods through reverse engineering process;
  - Competitive optimization of services by domestic firms; and
  - Employee turnover from MNCs, which joins domestic firms and shares knowledge.

  Local businesses can rebuild their organizational structures to better compete in a globalized market thanks to these three effects. They might only gain, though, if they are able to take in spillover data. Emerging Markets Multinationals have consequently grown in significance across practically all industries. China's Haier is a global leader in the appliance industry, India's Infosys and TCS are leaders in the IT sector, and ZTE has emerged as one of the top producers of telecom equipment. Therefore, it can be concluded that the expansion of multinational corporations (MNCs) in their home countries or their entry into a host country benefits both parties in a number of ways, such as higher employment rates, infrastructure investments, knowledge and technology transfer, higher gross productivity, higher revenue, and highly competitive industries that aim to become more efficient.

- **Involvement in Conflict Creation:** With the intention of colonizing underdeveloped communities under the guise of trade, the British East India Company was the first multinational corporation (MNC) to enter new markets. Their Dutch and French counterparts followed closely behind. While the end of imperialism rendered such direct invasions unnecessary, the rise of neo-colonialism allowed both state-owned and private multinational corporations (MNCs) to freely operate in economically vulnerable countries endowed with natural resources. Although the development of host countries is a byproduct of this dominance, their main goal is to regulate the supply and demand for goods. A business firm that has the ability to produce and distribute goods also attracts certain political value, which it may use for its own benefit. Through the "divide and rule" tactic, varying degrees of distributional conflict provide incentives for various patterns of cooperation or conflict between the internal player and the MNC, thereby increasing the revenue dependence of all political parties on the MNC.

These incidents are hard to record since, if proven, they could result in harsh penalties for the offenders. However, a few significant occurrences have been documented and made public globally. It was established that US multinational corporations (MNCs) provided the rebels with inexpensive weapons and financial support during the 1909 revolution in Nicaragua against President Zelaya. There has been evidence to support the claim that Royal Dutch Shell combined funded armed conflicts against the Mexican government in order to safeguard its commercial interests. The MNC Transit Company's use of the Costa-Rican army against Nicaragua to undermine US trade with the Nicaraguan government is the most egregious example of MNCs abusing their political power.

MNCs thus foment strife among important national stakeholders, who then turn to them for assistance, thereby increasing their bargaining power. This holds true for regional conflicts involving rival or adjacent states as well as internal conflicts. One could argue that underdeveloped nations with autocratic governments or those that have just gained independence are more vulnerable to these kinds of conflicts. For instance. both countries are endowed with large oil reserves, but Nigeria, a recently formed nation, was rife with political and economic unrest involving MNC meddling, while Norway, a developed democracy, has not experienced conflict as a result of the absence of oil exporting MNCs.

8.8. INTERNATIONAL LABOR MOBILITY: MIGRATION

The ease with which workers can migrate both within and between economies is referred to as labor mobility. It is significant to the study of economics because it examines the relationship between growth and production and labor, one of the primary factors in production. Geographic and occupational labor mobility are the two main categories. While occupational mobility refers to a worker's ability to change job types, geographic mobility refers to a worker's ability to work in a specific physical location. A worker relocating to France from the United States, for instance, serves as an illustration of the idea of geographic mobility. Conversely, an auto mechanic who decides to become an airline pilot exemplifies the idea of occupational mobility.

In general, higher labor mobility benefits the economy. Increased freedoms typically result in happier employees who fill jobs, even the less glamorous ones, which increases output and productivity in the economy.

8.8.1. Importance of Geographic Mobility

From the standpoint of policymakers, geographic mobility can have significant effects on a nation's economy. This is due to the fact that lowering immigration requirements has multiple benefits:

- **Boost the Labor Supply:** The labor supply generally rises as more people enter the workforce. Wage rates may decline if there is a static labor demand combined with an increase in the labor supply.
- **Boost Unemployment:** An increase in the labor supply could result in a labor glut if employers don't demand more workers. This would raise unemployment. There are thus more workers than there are open positions.
- **Boost Productivity:** Skilled workers will not make up the entire labor pool of new hires. If new workers bring specialized skills to the workplace, they can boost productivity; conversely, they may drive out less productive current workers.

Getting geographic mobility involves more than just economic considerations. It might also have to do with government authority and state sovereignty. Ultimately, governments are also worried about security, and when borders are entirely open, governments have no idea who or what is entering their territories. Furthermore, even though more people moving around has a positive effect on the economy overall, it is also one of the first things that people and their representatives get angry about. Immigration is a contentious issue, both domestically and internationally.

One can achieve a reduction in geographic constraints in multiple ways. Treaties or economic agreements between nations are used to achieve this. Additionally, nations have the power to lower the requirements for obtaining a worker visa or raise the number of them that are offered. Improved geographic mobility will ultimately rely on how well each worker performs. An employee is less likely to want to move if there are no economic opportunities in another country or in a different area of their current country.

8.8.2. Importance of Occupational Mobility

The rate at which an economy can grow is determined by the ease with which workers can transition from one industry to another. For instance, we probably would still be hunter-gatherers if there was no occupational mobility since nobody could have become a farmer or specialist. There are various benefits to reducing occupational mobility restrictions:

- **Boost the Labor Supply in Specific Industries:** When barriers to entry are lowered, workers may find it easier to transition to other industries, potentially meeting the demand for labor.
- **Reduced Wage Rates:** When labor enters an industry more easily, there will be more labor available to meet demand, which drives down wage rates until equilibrium is reached.
- **Give Emerging Industries Room to Expand:** When an economy is moving toward new sectors, there needs to be a workforce to manage the companies in those sectors. Because there aren't enough workers to operate the machinery needed to make the product or provide the service, a labor shortage may have a detrimental effect on overall productivity.

Regulations have the power to limit an employee's mobility at work. Requirements for education, training, and licensing prohibit the free movement of labor between industries. For instance, because working as a physician requires specific training and licensure, there are restrictions on the number of physicians available. Because there is a limited supply of physicians and a high demand for their services, the equilibrium wage is raised, allowing physicians to command higher wages. By directing unfit workers into sectors of the economy with less regulations, this keeps wages low by increasing the labor supply relative to the demand for labor.

8.8.3. Labor Mobility: Two Perspectives

Labor mobility affects workers on two levels: the aggregate level and the personal level.

1. **Personal Level:** Increased labor mobility offers employees the chance to better their financial circumstances on an individual basis. Employee satisfaction can lead to increased productivity if they are given the freedom to

relocate, train for new positions, or pursue higher pay. It will also be easier for new industries to draw in the best candidates by providing better benefits because many workers who do not feel permanently restricted to low pay or jobs with minimal benefits will look for better positions.

2. **Aggregate Level:** The economy as a whole is referred to as the aggregate level. The degree of labor force mobility can influence the speed at which technological advancements are embraced by an economy, the ease with which competitive advantages can be capitalized upon, and the rate at which novel industries emerge. Restrictions on the movement of labor, whether geographical or occupational, can hinder growth by making it more challenging for companies to hire skilled employees. Unrestricted labor can also lead to unemployment and lower wages in some industries.

8.8.4. Types of Labor Mobility

Geographic mobility, or the degree of flexibility and freedom that workers have to relocate to another nation or continent in search of gainful employment, and occupational mobility, or the ease with which workers can change careers, are the two main categories of labor mobility.

8.8.5. Restrictions Placed on Labor Mobility

Not all labor mobility is popular. For instance, expanding borders and promoting migration may, in severe circumstances, result in overcrowding in some areas, placing a burden on public services and raising the cost of living there. This could then stoke animosity and provoke social unrest. Reducing restrictions on occupational mobility can occasionally have the opposite effect. Certain jobs have specific training requirements, so hiring anyone can lead to inefficiencies and expensive errors.

Global worker welfare improves in tandem with increased labor mobility. Less restriction on where they can move and what professions they can apply for generally helps workers find better-paying jobs and improve their living conditions. Businesses also benefit from better training for employees and the ability to hire the right person at the right time. Productivity increases lead to better economies.

CASE STUDY

WAGE CONVERGENCE IN THE AGE OF MASS MIGRATION

The truly heroic age of labor mobility occurred in the late 19th and early 20th centuries, when immigration significantly contributed to population growth in some countries while emigration led to population declines in other countries, despite the fact that there are significant cross-national movements of people in the modern world. Tens of millions of people traveled great distances in search of a better life in a world economy that was only recently integrated by railroads, steamships, and telegraph cables and was not yet subject to many legal restrictions on migration. Indians migrated to Africa and the Caribbean, Chinese to Southeast Asia and California, and a sizable Japanese population migrated to Brazil. Most notably, people from the European periphery—Sweden, Ireland, Italy, and Eastern Europe—moved to the United States, but also to Canada, Argentina, and Australia, where land was plentiful and wages were high.

Indeed, this process led to the real wage convergence that our model predicts. The table that goes with it displays real wages in 1870 for four significant "origin" countries and four significant "destination" countries, as well as the change in these wages up to the eve of World War I. Real wages were substantially higher in the destination countries than in the origin countries at the start of the period, as the table illustrates. Real wages increased during the next 40 years in every country, with the notable exception of Canada, where they did so much more quickly than in the countries of destination. This suggests that migration did, in fact, contribute to the global trend toward wage parity, if not quite there.

	Real Wage, 1870 (U.S. = 100)	Percentage Increase in Real Wage, 1870–1913
Destination Countries		
Argentina	53	51
Australia	110	1
Canada	86	121
United States	100	47
Origin Countries		
Ireland	43	84
Italy	23	112
Norway	24	193
Sweden	24	250

Source: Jeffrey G. Williamson, "The Evolution of Global Labor Markets Since 1830: Background Evidence and Hypotheses," Explorations in Economic History 32 (1995), pp. 141–196.

CLASS ACTIVITY

ASSESSING LEVEL OF RISK

Group Activity

1. Ask the students to make a list of the typical enjoyable and social activities they enjoy doing that don't involve alcohol. Talk about all the advantages and disadvantages of taking part in these activities.
2. Request that the students make a list of the riskier activities (e.g., bungee jumping, surfing). Talk about the advantages and disadvantages of engaging in these activities once more.
3. Take a look at every activity on the list and have a discussion about the class's perception of acceptable risk as well as the risk that would prevent them from engaging in an activity.

Teacher Information: This should give the teacher a chance to show the class that most alcohol-free activities have fewer negative effects and that the "good times" are more enduring. It would also be helpful to talk about how different we are from one another when determining what level of risk is acceptable, but the most crucial thing is that we make a deliberate choice and weigh the risks.

Benefits

- Students practice risk assessment, and consider what comprises a "reasonable" level of risk.

SUMMARY

- A multinational corporation (MNC) is a company that operates in its home country, as well as in other countries around the world. It maintains a central office located in one country, which coordinates the management of all of its other offices, such as administrative branches or factories.
- Foreign direct investments (FDI) are investment inflows in an economy from a foreign country to accumulate an enduring management interest in an enterprise, except that of the investor.
- Foreign direct investments are commonly categorized as horizontal, vertical, or conglomerate.
- Once a firm knows that foreign demand for its goods exists, it must ascertain the lowest-cost method of supplying these goods abroad.
- Once a firm chooses foreign production as a method of supplying goods abroad, it must decide whether it is more efficient to establish a foreign production subsidiary or license the technology to a foreign firm to produce its goods.
- Country risk analysis (CRA) attempts to identify the potential for these risks to decrease the expected return of a cross-border investment.
- Evaluating country risks is a crucial exercise when choosing sites for international business, particularly if investment is to be undertaken. Certain risks can be managed through insurance, hedging and other types of financial planning, but other risks cannot be controlled through such financial mechanisms.
- International trade theory suggests that the aggregate welfare of both the source and host countries is enhanced when MNEs make foreign direct investments for their own benefit.
- An international joint venture (IJV) occurs when two businesses based in two or more countries form a partnership. A company that wants to explore international trade without taking on the full responsibilities of cross-border business transactions has the option of forming a joint venture with a foreign partner.
- MNCs create conflict in key stakeholders of a nation, who in turn approach them for help, giving them higher bargaining power. This applies not only for internal conflict, but to regional conflicts between neighboring or competing states.
- Labor mobility refers to the ease with which laborers are able to move around within an economy and between different economies. It is an important factor in the study of economics because it looks at how labor, one of the major factors of production, affects growth and production.

REVIEW QUESTIONS

1. What are international resource movements?
2. What is international mobility of factors of production?

3. How does production factor movement affect international trade?
4. What motivates foreign direct investment?
5. What are the advantages and disadvantages of foreign direct investment?
6. How to supply goods to other countries?
7. What is the country risk analysis method?
8. What are the major issues involving multinational enterprises as a source of conflict for source and host countries?
9. What is international labor mobility?
10. What are the main types of labor mobility?

REFERENCES

1. Asiedu, E., & Lien, D. (2011). Democracy, foreign direct investment and natural resources. *Journal of International Economics, 84*(1), 99–111. https://doi.org/10.1016/j.jinteco.2010.12.001.
2. Bah, A., Xie, K., & Izuchukwu, O.-O. (2015). Strategies and determinants of foreign direct investment (FDI) attraction. *International Journal of Management Science and Business Administration, 1*(5), 81–89. http://dx.doi.org/10.18775/ijmsba.1849-5664-5419.2014.15.1007.
3. Buckley, P. J. (2011). The theory of international business pre-Hymer. *Journal of World Business, 46*(1), 61–73. https://doi.org/10.1016/j.jwb.2010.05.018.
4. Dunning, J. H., & Pitelis, C. N. (2008). Stephen Hymer's contribution to international business scholarship: An assessment and extension. *Journal of International Business Studies, 39*(1), 167–176. https://doi.org/10.1057/palgrave.jibs.8400328.
5. Ežmale, S. (2016). Attracting foreign direct investments: The case of Latgale region. *SOCIETY. INTEGRATION. EDUCATION. Proceedings of the International Scientific Conference, 4*, 256. http://dx.doi.org/10.17770/sie2016vol4.1556.
6. Friedberg, R., & Hunt, J. (1995). The impact of immigrants on host country wages, employment and growth. *Journal of Economic Perspectives, 9*(2), 23–44. https://doi.org/10.1257/jep.9.2.23.
7. Jones, R. (2005). Immigration vs. outsourcing: Effects on labor markets. *International Review of Economics and Finance, 14*(2), 105–114. https://doi.org/10.1016/j.iref.2004.08.004.
8. Kraja Boriçi, Y., & Elezi Osmani, E. (2015). Foreign direct investment and economic growth in Albania. *ECONOMICS, 3*(2), 27–32. http://dx.doi.org/10.1515/eoik-2015-0014.
9. Ozga, M. (2009). The influence of the foreign direct investments on the regional disproportions in Poland. *Equilibrium, 3*(2), 111–123. http://dx.doi.org/10.12775/equil.2009.025.

10. Sarkodie, S. A., Adams, S., & Leirvik, T. (2020). Foreign direct investment and renewable energy in climate change mitigation: Does governance matter? *Journal of Cleaner Production, 263*, 121262. https://doi.org/10.1016/j.jclepro.2020.121262.

11. Yulek, M., & Gur, N. (2017). Foreign direct investment, smart policies and economic growth. *Progress in Development Studies, 17*(3), 245–256. https://doi.org/10.1177/1464993417713272.

CHAPTER 9

The Balance of Payments

LEARNING OBJECTIVES

After studying this chapter, you will be able to:

- Determine the global phenomena of balance of payments:
- Write the main purpose of balance of payments
- Discuss on balance of payments (BOP) accounting

KEY TERMS FROM THIS CHAPTER

Economic transactions	Exchange rate system
Financial account	Financial instruments
Foreign investment	International buying
International Monetary Fund (IMF)	International monetary system
International transactions	National assets
Unilateral transfers	Value-added tax

INTRODUCTION

Trade in capital, goods, and services, as well as transfer payments like remittances and foreign aid, make up the balance of payments (BOP) transactions. A nation's international accounts are made up of its net international investment position and balance of payments. Transactions are separated into two accounts by the balance of payments: the capital account and the current account. A distinct, typically very tiny, capital account is listed separately, and the capital account is sometimes referred to as the financial account. Transactions involving products, services, investment income, and current transfers are all included in the current account. In general, transactions involving financial instruments and reserves held by central banks are included in the capital account. Strictly speaking, it pertains solely to financial instrument transactions. While the capital account is not taken into account when calculating national output, the current account is. When an item is paid for through export (a current account transaction), the exporting nation effectively imports foreign capital. A nation must use its reserves to pay for its imports if capital exports are not an option. Since central bank reserves are not included in the narrow definition of the capital account, this condition is frequently referred to as a balance of payments deficit. However, in practice, the broadly construed balance of payments must by definition add up to zero.

9.1. BALANCE OF PAYMENTS: THE GLOBAL PHENOMENA

The difference between all money coming into the country in a specific time period (e.g., a month) and the total amount of money leaving the country at the end of that period is the balance of payments, also known as the balance of international payments or BoP in international economics (e.g., a quarter, or a year) and the money that is sent to other countries.

Put differently, it refers to the exchange of goods and services between nations over a given duration. Individuals, businesses, and governmental entities engage in these financial transactions in order to compare receipts and payments related to the exchange of goods and services. The current account, capital account, and financial account make up the three parts of the balance of payments. A nation's net income is shown in its current account, and its net change in national asset ownership is shown in its capital account.

9.1.1. History

Prior to the 19th century, gold was used as the medium of exchange for international transactions, which gave nations with trade deficits little flexibility. Since growth was slow, the main strategy for improving a country's financial situation was to promote a trade surplus. However, because national economies were not well integrated, trade imbalances were rarely a catalyst for crises. International economic integration grew as a result of the industrial revolution, and balance of payment crises became more common. The Bretton Woods system, which ruled from the end of World War II until the 1970s, introduced a gold-convertible dollar with fixed exchange rates to other currencies. However, the Great Depression forced countries to abandon the gold standard and engage in competitive devaluation of their currencies. While the U.S. money supply rose and the country's trade deficit widened, but the system was abandoned when the government was unable to completely convert the dollar reserves of foreign central banks into gold. Currencies have floated freely since the Nixon shock, which is recognized as the end of the dollar's convertibility to gold. This means that a nation facing a trade deficit can artificially depress its currency—by stockpiling foreign reserves, for example—in order to increase exports and make its goods more appealing. The increased cross-border movement of capital can lead to balance-of-payments crises and severe currency devaluations, like the ones that hit Southeast Asian nations in 1997. A number of nations engaged in competitive currency devaluations during the Great Recession in an effort to increase exports. In response to the global financial crisis at the time, all of the main central banks implemented sharply expansionary monetary policies. As a result, the value of other countries' currencies increased relative to the U.S.S. pound and other significant currencies. In response, a large number of those countries further loosened their monetary policies to boost exports, particularly those whose exports were being pressured by the Great Recession's stagnant global demand.

9.1.2. Exchange Rate Regime

A central bank accommodates those flows under a fixed exchange rate system by purchasing any net inflow of funds into the nation or by supplying foreign currency funds to the foreign exchange market to match any outflow of funds abroad. This keeps the funds flows from impacting the exchange rate between the nation's currency and other currencies. The balance of payments surplus or deficit is then occasionally used to describe the net annual change in the foreign exchange reserves held by the central bank. A managed float, in which some exchange rate fluctuations are permitted, or, at the other extreme, a fully floating exchange rate (also referred to as a purely flexible exchange rate) are alternatives to a fixed exchange rate system. In a pure float, the central bank lets the market determine the rate, maintains constant foreign exchange reserves, and maintains a zero balance of payments by not intervening in any way to defend or devalue its currency.

9.1.3. Components

When a nation's income is in surplus, the current account displays it; when it is in deficit, it displays the net amount of spending. It is the total of three components: unilateral transfers, factor income (earnings on foreign investments less payments to foreign investors), and balance of trade (net earnings on exports less payments for imports). These things include financial assets or the exchange of goods and services between the home nation and the rest of the world. Gifts given to foreigners by private citizens and non-governmental organizations are referred to as private transfer payments. Gifts or grants given by one government to foreign nationals or governments are referred to as "governmental transfers." The current account balance is obtained by adding unilateral transfers and investment income to the balance of goods and services. Because it covers transactions that occur in the present and don't result in future claims, it is known as the current account. The net change in foreign asset ownership is documented in the capital account. It comprises the reserve account, which is the foreign exchange market activities of a country's central bank, as well as loans and investments made within the nation and abroad (but not the dividends and interest that the loans and investments will generate in the future; those are earnings and will be recorded in the current account). A nation's capital account is said to be negative or in deficit if it buys more foreign assets with cash than it sells to other nations for cash.

The term "capital account" is also used in the narrower sense that excludes central bank foreign exchange market operations: Sometimes the reserve account is classified as "below the line" and so not reported as part of the capital account.

Expressed with the broader meaning for the *capital account*, the BoP identity states that any current account surplus will be balanced by a capital account deficit of equal size – or alternatively a current account deficit will be balanced by a corresponding capital account surplus:

Current account + broadly defined capital account + balancing item = 0

The balancing item, which can be positive or negative, is just a figure that guarantees that the sum of the current and capital accounts is zero while accounting for statistical errors. According to the rules of double entry accounting, a transaction in the capital account results from an entry in the current account, and the two accounts automatically balance when combined. Not all reported figures reflect a balance; for example, the current and capital accounts may report a surplus for both accounts. When this occurs, however, it always indicates that something has been missed, usually the nation's central bank's operations, and that something is recorded in the statistical discrepancy term (the balancing item). The main divisions on an actual balance sheet usually have a number of subheadings.

For example, entries under Current account might include:

- **Trade:** buying and selling of goods and services
    - *Exports* – a credit entry
    - *Imports* – a debit entry
        - *Trade balance* – the sum of Exports and Imports
- **Factor Income:** repayments and dividends from loans and investments
    - *Factor earnings* – a credit entry
    - *Factor payments* – a debit entry
        - Factor income balance – the sum of earnings and payments.

Visible and invisible entries were often divided, particularly in older balance sheets. Imports and exports of tangible goods were documented by visible trade; entries for trade in tangible goods, excluding services, are now frequently referred to as the merchandise balance. International service purchases and sales would be recorded under invisible trade, which is occasionally combined with factor and transfer income to represent invisible earnings. The balance of the surpluses in the current account and the specifically defined capital account (not including changes in central bank reserves) is referred to as the balance of payments surplus (or deficit; a deficit is just a negative surplus). The relevant identity is, denoting the balance of payments surplus as BoP surplus.

BOP surpluCs = current account surplus + narrowly defined capital account surplus.

9.1.3.1. Measurements and Definitions

Payments for a nation's imports and exports of financial capital, goods, services, and financial transfers are included in the balance of payments. It is made using just one currency, usually the relevant nation's domestic currency. The systematic records of all a country's economic transactions, both visible and invisible, with all other countries over a specified period of time are maintained by the balance of payments accounts. All foreign receipts are recorded as credits in the BoP accounts, and all foreign payments are recorded as debits. The accounts demonstrate that the balance of payments accounts are consistently balanced because they are kept up to date through double entry bookkeeping. Funding sources for a country, like exports, loans, and investments, are reported as positive or surplus items. Funds used for things like imports or overseas investments are recorded as negative or deficit items. The BoP accounts' total must be zero, with neither an overall surplus nor deficit, when all of its components are included. A country's trade balance, for instance, will be in deficit if it is importing more than it is exporting. This means that other means must be used to make up the difference, such as using funds from foreign investments (but not the investments themselves, as they are deficit items), depleting currency reserves, or obtaining loans or investments from other nations.

Individual components of the balance of payments (BoP) may exhibit imbalances, such as the current account, the capital account (excluding the reserve account of the central bank), or the sum of the two. However, the overall BoP accounts will always balance when all forms of payments are included.

When the latter total is out of balance, surplus countries may accumulate wealth while deficit countries get more indebted. This amount is commonly referred to as a country's balance of payments. If sources of funds (such as sales of bonds and export goods) exceed uses of funds (such as paying for imports and purchasing foreign bonds) by a certain amount, the balance of payments is said to be in surplus (i.e., positive).

If the former are less than the latter, there is a balance of payments deficit, or a negative balance of payments. The central bank accumulates (or decumulates) foreign exchange reserves in tandem with a BoP surplus (or deficit).

9.1.3.2. Variations in the Use of Term Balance of Payments

Author J. specializes in economics. Orlin Grabbe cautions that because people have different ideas about what the term "balance of payments" means, it can lead to misunderstandings. According to Grabbe, the term is occasionally used incorrectly by individuals who are unaware of its accepted meaning, not only in everyday speech but also in financial and economic literature. Whether or not the reserve account entry, which is a component of the capital account, is included in the BoP accounts is a frequent source of confusion. The reserve account keeps track of the national bank's activities. If it is removed, the BoP may be in deficit (meaning the central bank is borrowing from outside or depleting its reserves) or surplus (meaning the central bank is increasing its foreign exchange reserves). Occasionally, non-economists misapply the term "balance of payments" to refer to only relatively narrow components of the balance of payments (BoP), such as the trade deficit, thereby omitting portions of the current account and the entire capital account. The various naming conventions in use are another source of confusion. Prior to 1973, the BoP sheet had no set format, with the main divisions occasionally being made into visible and invisible payments. Although the IMF's standards for BoP accounting are identical to the standard definition, they employ different terminology, particularly in regards to how the term "capital account" is defined.

9.1.3.3. The IMF definition of the Balance of Payments

The United Nations System of National Accounts (SNA), the Organization for Economic Co-operation and Development (OECD), and the International Monetary

Fund (IMF) all use the same set of definitions for the BoP accounts. The primary distinction in the nomenclature used by the IMF is that transactions that, according to other definitions, would be recorded in the capital account are captured under the term "financial account." The term "capital account" is used by the IMF to refer to a group of transactions that were previously only a minor portion of the current account as a whole. These transactions are divided up by the IMF to create an additional top-level division of the BoP accounts.

Expressed with the IMF definition, the BoP identity can be written:

The IMF uses the term *current account* with the same meaning as that used by other organizations, although it has its own names for its three leading sub-divisions, which are:

- The goods and services account (the overall trade balance)
- The primary income account (factor income such as from loans and investments)
- The secondary income account (transfer payments)

9.1.4. Uses

For the first, the balance of payments influences the supply and demand of a nation's currency, making it a crucial component of international financial management. If outflows surpass inflows, for instance, then, under all other circumstances, the domestic market's demand for the currency is likely to surpass the foreign exchange market's supply. This suggests that there would be pressure on the currency to weaken in relation to other currencies. On the other hand, its currency would probably increase if inflows outpaced outflows. Second, information about a nation's balance of payments may indicate that nation's suitability as a global business partner. It might not be possible for a nation experiencing severe balance of payments issues to increase imports from outside. Instead, in an effort to strengthen the balance of payments, the nation may implement policies that limit imports and deter capital flight. However, a nation with a sizable balance of payments surplus would be less inclined to impose restrictions on foreign exchange and more likely to increase imports, providing foreign businesses with marketing opportunities. Third, information on the balance of payments can be utilized to assess how well a nation is performing in the global economy. A nation's persistent trade deficits may indicate a lack of international competitiveness in the nation's domestic industries.

9.1.5. Imbalances

Even though the BoP must balance overall, imbalances between nations can result from surpluses or deficits on any one of its constituent elements. Current account deficits are a source of general concern. Debt will accumulate or foreign ownership of assets will rise in countries with current account deficits. These are the kinds of deficiencies that usually cause concern.

- A visible trade deficit where a nation is importing more physical goods than it exports (even if this is balanced by the other components of the current account.)
- An overall *current* account deficit.
- A basic deficit which is the current account plus foreign direct investment (but excluding other elements of the capital account like short terms loans and the reserve account.)

During the Washington Consensus era, sentiment began to shift in favor of the idea that imbalances are not something to be concerned about. Following the 2007–2009 financial crisis, public opinion turned back the other way. Leaders of surplus and deficit countries, as well as prominent economists and members of the financial press, the IMF, and other international organizations, have all reaffirmed the belief that significant current account imbalances are important. For example, the current account deficit of Armenia increased from \$0.7 billion to \$1.3 billion in 2020 during the COVID-19 pandemic. Nonetheless, some economists continue to express little concern regarding imbalances, and some have even made claims—like Michael P. Dooley, David Folkerts-Landau, and Peter Garber argue that in order to address imbalances, countries should resist the urge to turn to protectionism. Other countries' current account deficits and surpluses are correlated, leading to an increase in the latter's debt. This is defined as an excess of costs over revenues in Wolfgang Stützel's book Balances Mechanics. Since 2007, growing disparities in international trade have been extensively examined as a potential contributor to the global financial crisis. Many Keynesian economists, including Heiner Flassbeck, Paul Krugman, and Joseph Stiglitz, believe that the Euro Crisis is primarily the result of the discrepancies between the current accounts in the eurozone.

9.1.5.1. Causes of BoP imbalances

There are differing opinions about what causes the biggest imbalances in the balance of payments (BoP), with the US receiving the most attention due to its current large deficit. The prevalent perspective posits that current account factors—which encompass the exchange rate, the government's fiscal deficit, business competitiveness, and individual behaviors like consumer willingness to incur debt in order to finance increased consumption—are the root cause. The main cause of excess consumption and asset price inflation, according to a different theory put forth in-depth in a 2005 paper by Ben Bernanke, is the capital account. This is because savers in surplus countries create a global savings glut that outpaces available investment opportunities and is pushed into the US.

9.1.5.2. Reserve asset

The currency or other store of value that countries primarily use for their foreign reserves is known as the reserve asset in the context of the Bretton Woods and international monetary systems. BoP imbalances typically show up as surplus countries hoard reserve assets, while deficit countries incur debts denominated in reserve assets or at least deplete their supply. Gold serves as the reserve asset for all standard participants in a gold standard. When it comes to the Bretton Woods system, gold or the U.S.S. dollar could function as the reserve asset, but its smooth operation required non-US nations to decide to maintain the majority of their holdings in US dollars. There hasn't been a de jure reserve asset since the end of Bretton Woods, but the US dollar has remained by far the main de facto reserve. The 1997 Asian Financial Crisis, which forced several countries to accept deals on unfavorable terms when they ran out of foreign currency needed for necessities, contributed to the sharp increase in global reserves in the first 10 years of the 21st century. According to estimates from the International Monetary Fund (IMF), official reserves increased from \$1,900 billion to \$6,800 billion between 2000 and mid-2009.

After reaching a peak of roughly $7,500 billion in the middle of 2008, global reserves decreased by roughly $430 billion as nations without reserve currencies used them to protect themselves from the worst consequences of the financial crisis. Global reserves started growing again in February 2009, and by the end of 2010, they had approached $9,200 billion. About 65% of the $6,800 billion global total as of 2009 is held in U.S.S. dollars, with about 25% being paid in euros. Precious metals, the Japanese yen, the UK pound, and IMF special drawing rights (SDRs) are also relevant. The governor of the People's Bank of China, Zhou Xiaochuan, suggested in 2009 that the national currencies supporting SDRs be expanded to include the currencies of all major economies, as well as a gradual shift towards a greater use of SDRs. Although the US benefits from the dollar's current central role in terms of lower borrowing costs, it also adds to the pressure that the U.S.S. cause a current account deficit as a result of the Triffin conundrum. In a piece that appeared in Foreign Affairs magazine in November 2009, economist C. Fred Bergsten contended that both the United States and the rest of the world would benefit from Zhou's proposal or a change to the international monetary system along similar lines. The number of new bilateral agreements that allow international trades to be conducted using a currency other than a traditional reserve asset—like the renminbi—as the settlement currency has increased noticeably since 2009.

9.1.5.3. Balance of Payments Crisis

A country experiences a balance of payments (BoP) crisis, also known as a currency crisis, when it is unable to pay for necessary imports or make its external debt repayments. Usually, this is followed by a sharp drop in the value of the currency of the impacted country. Large capital inflows, which are initially linked to rapid economic growth, typically precede crises. But there comes a time when foreign investors decide to withdraw their money because they are worried about the amount of debt their incoming capital is creating. Because of herd effects, it occasionally only takes the withdrawal of one or two significant investors to cause a widespread panic. The consequence and outflow of capital is linked to a sharp decline in the value of the currency of the affected country. Due to the fact that the impacted nation's businesses primarily generate revenue from domestic sources but frequently have debts denominated in reserve currencies, this presents problems for the affected nation's businesses that have received the inbound investments and loans. The government's options for policy are severely constrained once it has used up all of its foreign reserves in an attempt to maintain the value of the national currency. It can attempt to stop further drops in the value of its currency by raising interest rates, but while this helps people who have debts in foreign currencies, it usually makes the local economy worse. This kind of crisis is more likely to strike lower-income nations, but it can be avoided in particular with economic growth and foreign exchange piling.

9.1.6. Balancing Mechanisms

Providing tools to address imbalances is one of the three core purposes of an international monetary system. In general, there are three ways to address BoP imbalances; however, in actuality, a combination of the first two approaches is typically employed to some extent. These techniques include rules-based adjustment, adjustments to exchange rates, and adjustments to a country's internal prices in line with demand levels. Enhancing exports through other channels and raising productivity and competitiveness can also be beneficial; however, it is generally believed that a country always strives to produce and market its goods as effectively as possible.

9.1.6.1. Rebalancing by Changing the Exchange Rate

A country's current account surplus will generally be corrected by an increase in the value of its currency relative to other countries, which will reduce the competitiveness of exports and drive down the cost of imports. It will also aid in a surplus there because it tends to make investment flows into the capital account less alluring. In contrast, a decline in a country's currency value makes imports more expensive for its people to purchase and makes exports more competitive, which helps close a deficit (though the Marshall–Lerner condition often means that the solution doesn't work right away). When allowed to fluctuate freely in the market, exchange rates also have a tendency to move in the direction that will restore equilibrium. Exchange rates can also be modified by the government under a rules-based or managed currency regime. The demand for a nation's currency tends to rise when it sells more than it imports because other nations eventually need the selling nation's currency to pay for the exports. The increased demand usually results in a rise in the price of the currency in relation to other ones. When a nation imports more than it exports, it attempts to exchange its own currency for foreign currency to pay for its imports, which tends to increase supply of the currency on the international market and drive down prices. Exchange rates are impacted by a variety of market factors, including speculation and variations in national interest rates, in addition to BoP effects.

9.1.6.2. Rebalancing by Adjusting Internal Prices and Demand

Making adjustments to the home economy is the standard procedure for resolving imbalances that arise when members of a currency union, like the Eurozone, have differing exchange rates set by a strict gold standard. For the surplus country, the change is largely optional, but for the deficit country, it is required. When it comes to a gold standard, the process is mostly automated. A nation with a positive trade balance will see a net inflow of gold because it will sell more than it purchases. This will inevitably lead to an increase in the money supply, which in turn causes inflation and price increases. As a result, its goods will become less competitive, reducing the trade surplus. Nonetheless, the country can choose to remove gold from the economy (thereby neutralizing the inflationary effect), accumulating gold reserves, and maintaining a positive balance of payments. However, unless it decides to abandon the gold standard, a nation with an unfavorable balance of payments will suffer a net loss of gold, which will inevitably have a deflationary effect. Prices will drop, increasing the competitiveness of its exports and reversing the imbalance. Although the gold standard was widely regarded as successful until 1914, the large imbalances that resulted from World War I necessitated painful correction through deflation. Deflationary policies contributed to prolonged unemployment but did not restore equilibrium. By the middle of the 1930s, most former members—aside from the US—had abandoned the gold standard.

When exchange rate adjustment is not appropriate, surplus nations like Germany may be able to support rebalancing efforts by raising their level of internal demand (i.e., its expenditures on merchandise). Although the excess of earnings over spending is the common definition of a current account surplus, another way to put it is the excess of savings over investment.

That is:

CA = NS – NI

Where; *CA* is the current account; *NS* is the national savings (private plus government sector); and *NI* is the national investment.

A country's savings will increase if its income exceeds its expenditures, unless those savings are being used for investments. Any current account surplus will typically decrease if consumers are encouraged to spend more rather than save, if the government creates a budget deficit to counteract private savings, or if businesses allocate a larger portion of their profits to investment. Fears that the 2010s would not be an easy decade for the eurozone increased, however, when Germany amended its constitution in 2009 to forbid running a deficit greater than 0.35% of GDP. Calls to reduce this surplus by increasing demand have not been well received by officials. The IMF published a study in their April 2010 World Economic Outlook report that demonstrated how governments can move away from a sustained current account surplus without hurting growth or increasing unemployment by selecting the appropriate policy options.

9.1.6.3. Rules Based Rebalancing Mechanisms

Countries can decide to set their exchange rates against one another, and then use other strategies and rule-based, negotiated exchange rate adjustments to address any imbalances that result. One system that was based on rules was the Bretton Woods system, which had fixed but flexible exchange rates. One of the designers of the Bretton Woods system, John Maynard Keynes, had advocated for more regulations to push surplus nations to shoulder more of the rebalancing burden because he believed that they were better positioned to do so and that their surpluses were a burden that was placed on the world economy. Keynes proposed that the threat of seizing a portion of the surplus revenue should be added to the traditional balancing mechanisms in case the surplus country decided not to use it for further imports. Nevertheless, at the time, the Americans did not embrace his ideas. American economist Paul Davidson had been pushing his redesigned version of Keynes's plan in 2008 and 2009 as a potential remedy for global imbalances. He believed this would boost growth globally without carrying the negative risk of other rebalancing techniques.

9.1.7. Post-Washington Consensus Developments

Following the 2009 G-20 summit in London, Gordon Brown declared the end of the Washington Consensus. There is currently widespread consensus that significant disparities between nations—such as the mainstream U.S.S. economist C. According to Fred Bergsten, the U.S. deficit and the corresponding substantial inflows of foreign capital into the U.S.S. was among the factors that contributed to the 2007–2010 financial crisis. Since the crisis, governments have intervened more frequently in BOP areas, such as capital controls and foreign exchange market intervention, and have generally received less criticism from economists, international organizations like the IMF, and other governments. When the crisis started in 2007, there were $1,680 billion in annual BoP imbalances worldwide. On the credit side, the biggest current account surplus was China with approx. $362 billion, followed by Japan at $213 billion and Germany at £185 billion, with oil producing countries such as Saudi Arabia also having large surpluses. With a current account deficit of over $1,100 billion, the US led the world in debit balances, with the UK, Spain, and Australia combined accounting for nearly another $300 billion.

Despite warnings of impending public spending cuts, deficit countries generally did not implement them in 2009; rather, as part of global efforts to boost demand, public spending increased and helped to accelerate the recovery. Instead, the focus has been on the surplus countries, with the IMF, EU, and countries like the U.S. Russia and Brazil requesting their assistance in making the necessary corrections to the imbalances. Increased use of pooled reserves, according to economists like Gregor Irwin and Philip R. Lane, may help emerging economies avoid needing such large reserves and hence reduce their need for current account surpluses. In a January 2009 article for the Financial Times, Gillian Tett states that she anticipates policymakers' concerns regarding exchange rates to grow over the course of the upcoming year. A sustained recovery will require rebalancing the global economy by reducing both sizable surpluses and deficits, according to a June 2009 article by IMF chief economist Olivier Blanchard.

There was a slight decrease in imbalances in 2008 and 2009, but there were early signs at the end of 2009 that significant imbalances like the U.S. The current account deficit is expected to start growing once more. Japan's aging population has limited her ability to contribute to the rebalancing efforts, despite the country having allowed its currency to appreciate through 2009. The value of the euro, which Germany uses, is permitted to fluctuate fairly freely; however, additional appreciation would present challenges for other currency union members with significant deficits, like Greece, Ireland, and Spain. Instead, Germany has been asked to help by increasing domestic demand, a request that German officials have not warmly received. Up until 2010, China had declined requests to allow the renminbi, or Chinese Yuan, to appreciate. Wen Jiabao, the premier of China, stated that calls to allow the currency's value to rise have been made out of a desire to impede China's development, and that China has been contributing to the global recovery by maintaining the renminbi's stable value relative to the US dollar. However, following China's positive export results for December 2009, the Financial Times reported that analysts believe China will permit some currency appreciation by mid-2010.

A Chinese official indicated in April 2010 that the government is thinking about allowing the renminbi to appreciate. However, by May, analysts were predicting the appreciation would probably be postponed because of the declining value of the Euro as a result of the European sovereign debt crisis of 2010. In June 2010, China declared that the renminbi would no longer be pegged to the US dollar. This move was warmly received by the markets and eased concerns about imbalances ahead of the 2010 G-20 summit in Toronto. Nonetheless, the renminbi is still subject to management, and its increased flexibility allows it to fluctuate in value. Just two months after the end of the peg, the renminbi's value had only increased by roughly 0.8 percent compared to the US dollar. The renminbi was up 3.7 percent against the US dollar by January 2011, which indicates that nominal growth of 6 percent annually is expected. When accounting for China's higher inflation, this represents a real appreciation of 10%, meaning that the U.S.S. Treasury refused to designate China as a currency manipulator in their report to Congress that was submitted in February 2011. Treasury officials did advise that, for the benefit of the world economy, the rate of appreciation was still too slow. Although there is a strong case for an upward revaluation, Moody's analyst Alaistair Chan predicted in February 2011 that an increased rate of appreciation against the US dollar is unlikely in the near future. Furthermore, China's currency had been rising for a year and a half as of February 2012, despite receiving remarkably little attention. Even though some of the top surplus nations, like China, have been increasing domestic demand, these efforts have not yet been enough to cause their current account surpluses to balance out. June 2010 saw the U.S.S. The current account deficit for the month had increased to $50 billion, a level not observed since the middle of 2008. There are growing concerns that the US may enact protectionist policies given its high unemployment rate and reluctance to take on more debt.

9.1.7.1. Competitive Devaluation After 2009

International tensions over imbalances had escalated even more by September 2010. According to Guido Mantega, the finance minister of Brazil, there is a currency war going on in the world, with nations vying with one another to lower their values in an effort to increase exports. Brazil's real has increased by 25% versus the US dollar since January 2009, making it one of the few major economies without a reserve currency to refrain from major currency intervention. According to some economists, competitive devaluation might be beneficial because it will essentially have the same effect as expansionary global monetary policy, like Barry Eichengreen has suggested. Others, like Martin Wolf, warned that tensions might rise even further and argued that the G20 meeting in November should decide on a coordinated plan of action to correct imbalances. Most commentators concurred that the G20 in November 2010 produced little real progress on imbalances. After the summit, an IMF report was made public, cautioning that if no further progress is made, imbalances could roughly double and return to pre-crisis levels by 2014.

9.1.8. Economic Policy and the Balance of Payment

International headcount and balance of payments data are essential for developing national and global economic policies. For a nation's policymakers to look for answers, foreign direct investment (FDI) and imbalances in the balance of payments are essential.

The balance of payments data shows how national and international policies have affected things. For instance, a nation might put policies into place to draw in foreign investment. To encourage exports, however, a different nation might wish to maintain a relatively low value of its currency.

There will be disparities between a nation's accounts even though its balance of payments will bring its capital and current accounts into balance. The United States' current account deficit in 2019 is $498 billion, according to data from The World Bank.

Let's say a nation consistently experiences balance of payments deficits. In that scenario, as the nation's foreign exchange reserves run out, it might experience a decline in confidence. However, it also increases the nation's susceptibility to cyclical, seasonal, or erratic changes in other nations. That might cause excessive inflation in the country. As a result, currency stability offers a solid guarantee for the economy's long-term growth. Through the annual balance of payments, countries can assess the state of the economy both domestically and globally and develop effective monetary policies that take into account the political influence of multilateral and international relations. In theory, the goals of economic policy could be used as the benchmark for balance of payments strategies. Exchange rate policy is handled similarly to income policy at the same time. In the event of stable exchange rates, the balance of payments policy can only be based on the equilibrium of the balance of payments.

The degree of domestic economic stability serves as the criterion in the case of flexible exchange rates.

9.2. PURPOSE OF BALANCE OF PAYMENTS

A systematic record of all economic transactions between citizens of one country and citizens of other countries over a given period of time is known as the balance of payments. Even though the definition of balance of payments given above is fairly clear, there are some terms that might need further explanation. There is no specific system mentioned in the phrase "systematic record." Nonetheless, double entry bookkeeping is the method most often used. All such transactions involving the transfer of ownership or title are considered economic transactions. While some transactions include the actual transfer of goods, services, money, and assets in addition to the transfer of title, other transactions do not. Let's take an example where a foreign undertaking's subsidiary is profitable and operating in India. This company has two options: it can reinvest its profits in India rather than paying dividends to its parent company overseas, or it can pay all of its profits as dividends to shareholders abroad. The balance of payments accounts contain records of both types of transactions. There is no set time frame for the balance of payments; it can be any amount of time. Typically, the time frame is one calendar years' worth of finances. The balance of payments is very helpful because it provides information that is needed to formulate future domestic monetary, fiscal, and foreign trade policies.

Following are the important uses of balance of payments:

- It offers helpful information for analyzing a nation's economic strengths and weaknesses as a trading partner internationally. A comparison of the balance of payments statements over a number of years can be used to determine whether the country's international economic position is getting better or getting worse. If things are getting worse, you can take the appropriate action.
- It reveals the changes in the composition and magnitude of foreign trade. The changes that curb economic well-being of a country are taken care by the government.
- On the basis of a nation's historical trade performance, it also forecasts potential future consequences. A persistent and significant deficit in the balance of payments over time is indicative of rising foreign indebtedness, which eventually results in financial insolvency. In a similar vein, persistently high balance of payments surpluses, especially when they exceed the nation's ability to absorb them, portend imminent inflationary risks.
- Detailed balance of payments accounts also reveal weak and strong points in the country's foreign trade relations and thereby invite government attention to the need for corrective measures against the weak spots.

9.2.1. Balance of Payments Accounts

The economic transactions between a country and the rest of the world may be grouped under two broad categories:

1. **Current Transactions:** Current transactions pertain to export and import of goods and services that change the current level of consumption in the country or bring a change in the current level of national income.
2. **Capital Transactions:** Capital transactions are those that, rather than having an impact on the current level of national income or consumption, increase or decrease a country's total stock of capital. Stated differently, transactions arc flow current transactions. The balance of payments account is split into two main accounts based on the two types of transactions:
   i. **Current Account:** The Table 9.1 presents the items that are entered into the current account of the balance of payments in the order of their significance. The items listed in the table's categories were released by the IMF and are presently used in India. It is entered that values payable are in the "debt" column and values receivable are in the "credit" column. The difference between each item's credit and debit is displayed as the net balance, which can be either positive (+) or negative (-). There is an additional way to categorize the items in your current account: visible and invisible items. Trade in merchandise, i.e., exports and imports of goods are included in the list of visible items. Everything else, including banking, insurance, and shipping, that is paid for with the current account and received in exchange for services, is referred to as invisible. Sometimes a different category, i.e., un-required transfer is designed to treat gifts, donations, military support, and technical assistance differently than other items. Given that they entail unilateral transfers, these are distinct from other invisible items. The items that are visible's net balance, i.e., trade balance refers to the difference between merchandise imports (M_g) and exports (X_g). "Balance on Current Account" refers to the total balance on the current account when $X_g < M_g$, which is an unfavorable situation. "Balance on the Current Account" refers to the excess or deficit that is transferred to the Capital Account.

Table 9.1. The Current Account of Balance of Payments

Transactions	Credit	Debit	Net Balance
I. Merchandise	Export.	Import	–
2. Foreign travel	Earnings	Payments	–
3. Transportation	Earnings	Payments	–
4. Insurance (premium)	Receipts	Payments	–
5. Investment	Dividend	Dividends	–

6. Government (purchases and sales of goods and services)	Receipts	Payments	–
7. Miscellaneous*	Receipts	Payments	–
Current Account Balance	–	Payments	Surplus (+) Deficit (-)

* Includes motion picture royalties, telephones and telegraph services, consultancy fees, etc.

Source: https://www.mbaknol.com/managerial-economics/balance-of-payments-bop/.

ii. Capital Account: As mentioned earlier, the items entered in the capital account of balance of payments are those items, which affect the existing stock of capital of the country. The broad categories of capital account items are: (a) short-term capital movements; (b) long-term capital movements; and (c) changes in the gold and exchange reserves.

a. Buying short-term securities like acceptance bills, commercial bills, and treasury bills is one example of a short-term capital movement.; (ii) the speculative acquisition of foreign exchange; and (iii) foreigners' cash holdings, which they may have done out of fear of conflict or unstable political conditions. A short-term capital item is typically the outcome of the current account's net balances, either positive or negative.

b. The following are examples of long-term capital movements: (i) direct investments in stocks, bonds, real estate, and tangible assets like machinery, buildings, and plants that investors control; (ii) portfolio investments, which include all other stocks and bonds like government securities and company securities that do not grant the holder controlling power; and (iii) amortization of capital. i.e., repurchasing and reselling securities that were previously bought or sold to foreigners. Direct investment includes both the import and export of capital goods directly. It is important to remember that while exporting goods is a credit item, exporting capital is a debit item. While the export of capital results in the outflow of foreign exchange, or a withdrawal from the foreign exchange reserves, the export of goods causes an inflow of foreign currency, which is an addition to the circular flow of money income.

c. Reserves of foreign currency and gold comprise the third main group of items in the capital account. Maintaining gold and foreign exchange reserves helps to keep the home currency's exchange rate stable and enables payments to creditors in the event that there are payments outstanding on all other accounts.

The double-entry bookkeeping system, which allows for the recording of both sides of a transaction, is the foundation of balance of payments accounting, i.e., payments and receipts are kept on file. For instance, exports involve the inflow of foreign currency and the outflow of goods. In the same way, imports and exports involve the inflow and outflow of goods and currency. In this system, both inflow and outflow are recorded. Lender credit and borrower debit result from international borrowing and lending. Both are noted in the payments balance. On the other hand, gifts, aids, donations, and assistance are unilateral transfers that do not entail the transfer of money of a comparable amount. Since these items are not refundable, there is only credit and no debit associated with them. Nonetheless, the donor is credited for record-keeping purposes and the receiving nation is debited to maintain the record of nonrefundable amounts. These entries are valuable for non-commercial purposes as information. Additionally, these transactions help the reporting nation's current account deficit decrease. Given that both the debit and credit sides of international transactions are recorded in this balance of payments accounting system. From an accounting perspective, the balance of payments is consistently in balance.

9.2.2. Significance of Balance of Payments (BoP) Data

Each year, the balance of payments keeps track of every financial transaction that takes place between a nation and the rest of the world. The current account, capital account, and financial accounts are the two separate components that make up the balance of payment. The current account records transactions like income, transfers, and the export and import of goods and services. However, the capital and financial accounts record the transactions pertaining to the portfolio and foreign direct investments. The balance of payments, which represents a nation's performance in both foreign trade and investments, is a crucial gauge of that nation's economic health. Therefore, sources of funds are recorded as positive and uses of funds as negative in the Balance of Payment. When all else is equal, the balance of payments is zero, meaning there is neither a deficit nor a surplus. However, a trade balance will be in surplus if a nation exports more goods than it imports, or decrease if it imports more than it exports. Government officials, international business managers, investors, and consumers place a high value on balance of payments data between the home and host countries. This is because these data both influence and are influenced by other important macroeconomic variables, such as GDP, employment, price levels, exchange rates, and interest rates. As a result, the balance of payments can serve as a gauge for both political and economic stability. One indication that there may be substantial foreign investment in a nation is if its BoP is continuously positive. It might also indicate that not much of the nation's currency is exported.

The International Monetary Fund (IMF) published the Balance of Payment Manual, i.e., The main global source of BoP and related statistical data is the IMF. The balance of payments manual is prepared by it and published in a balance of payments year book. The national balance of payments must be considered in monetary and fiscal policy. In order to assess the health and growth of particular trade or financial transactions by nation and region of the world relative to their home country, multinational corporations use a variety of balance of payments (BOP) measures.

Businesses require balance of payments data in order to predict changes in the host nation's economic policies that are prompted by balance of payment events. The following factors may make balance of payments information significant:

1. BoP indicates a country's financial position vis-Ã -vis foreign countries, thereby a country's ability to buy foreign goods or services.
2. BoP is important indicator of pressure on a country's exchange rate, and thus on the potential of a firm trading with or investing in that country to experience foreign exchange gains or losses. Changes in BoP may presage the impositions of foreign exchange controls.
3. BoP data helps in knowing the changes in a country's BoP may also signal imposition (or removal) of controls over payments, dividends, and interest, license fees, royalty fees, or other cash disbursements to foreign firms or investors.
4. BoP data helps to forecast a country's market potential, especially in the short- run. A country experiencing a serious BoP deficit is not likely to import as much as it would if it were running a surplus.
5. BoP data can also signal increased riskiness of lending to particular country and it also helps to in the formulation of trade and fiscal policies.

9.2.3. The Current Account Component in Balance of Payments (BoP)

The Current Account records a nation's total exports of goods, services and transfers, and its total imports of them. The current account is subdivided into two components (1) balance of trade (BoT), and (2) balance of invisibles (BOIs).

Structure of Current Account in India's BOP Statement:

1. Current Account
   - i. Merchandise (BOT): Trade Balance (A-B)
     - a. Exports, f.o.b.
     - b. Imports, c.i.f.
   - ii. Invisibles (BOI): (a + b + c)
     - a. Services
       - Travel
       - Transportation
       - Insurance
       - Govt. not elsewhere classified
       - Miscellaneous
     - b. Transfers
       - Official
       - Private
     - c. Income
       - Investment Income
       - Compensation to employees

Total Current Account = I + II

1. **Balance of Trade (BoT).** The term "balance of payments" describes the difference between a nation's imports and exports of goods. BOT, which refers to transactions involving movable goods and ownership transfers between residents and nonresidents, is another name for "general merchandise." Thus, merchandise imports and exports—aside from ships, airline stores, and other establishments—are covered by the balance of trade. purchased

by non-resident transport operators operating in the relevant nation, as well as comparable goods acquired abroad by operators operating in that nation, purchases made by foreign tourists, and purchases made by domestic missions. Export and import data are derived from trade statistics and reports on payments and receipts that businesses and individuals submit. Export valuations ought to take the form of f. o. imports are valued using c and the b (free on board) basis. I. f (pricing, coverage, and fear). Credit entries are exports. The information for these goods is gathered from exporters' various forms, which they fill out and submit to the appropriate authorities. Debit entries are made during imports. An advantageous (surplus) balance of trade is indicated by a surplus of exports over imports, whereas an unfavorable (deficit) balance of trade is indicated by a surplus of imports over exports. We can determine whether a nation has a deficit or a surplus by looking at its current account balance. Is the economy always strong or weak based on the presence of a deficit or surplus? These conclusions are not always true. However, in order to fully comprehend the importance of this portion of the BOP, we must first examine the current account's constituents: income, goods, services, and current transfers.

i. **Goods** – These are physical, movable items, and a change of ownership from a non-resident (in a foreign country) to a resident (in the local country) is required for a transaction to be recorded under "goods." General merchandise, items used to process other goods, and non-monetary gold are examples of movable goods. Money coming in from an export is indicated as a credit, and money leaving the country is indicated as a debit.

ii. **Services** — The export and import of services is known as "service trade." Common services include construction, tourism, and financial services that banks offer to foreign investors. These deals come about as a consequence of an intangible activity like travel, business services, royalties, or licensing. When money is received, it is recorded as an export (credit) and when it is paid for a service, it is recorded as an import (a debit).

iii. **Current Transfers** – Financial settlements related to the transfer of ownership of tangible assets or money. A current transfer is any one-way payment made between nations, including pensions, gifts, grants, worker remittances, donations, official assistance, and grants. Present transfers are given out unilaterally and come with no compensation. Current transfers are not regarded as actual resources that have an impact on economic production because of their nature.

iv. **Income** – The majority of current income from investments made in earlier periods. The pay and salaries given to non-resident employees are also included. Put differently, income refers to the amount of money that comes into (or leaves) a nation through salaries, investments (such as dividends) from portfolios, direct investments, and other types of investments. Income, goods, and services all work together to fuel an economy. Items falling under these categories are therefore real resources that are moved to and from a nation in order to produce goods and services.

2. **Balance of Invisibles (BoI).** These transactions are the outcome of intangible activities like travel, business services, insurance, banking, unilateral services, royalties on foreign-held patents or trademarks, and transportation. Every cash receipt that a resident receives from a non-resident is recorded under invisibles. The income received by residents for the services they render to non-residents, the interest and dividends they receive on their foreign investments, the income they receive for granting permission to use their own patents and copyrights, and the cash and in-kind gifts they receive from non-residents are all included in the receipts. Conversely, when a resident pays a non-resident, the debits of invisible items consist of the same items. When basic debit items are used, the roles of residents and nonresidents are switched. Current Account Balance (CAB) is the total of the credit and debit entries under the two headings, merchandise and invisibles, that add up to the net balance. Symbolically, it is surplus when the credits exceed the debits, and deficit when the credits fall short of the debits (CAB = BOT + BOI).

9.2.3.1. Use of Current Account

Although it is unlikely in practice, the balance should be zero in theory. A surplus or deficit in the current account balance tells us something about the health of the economy both overall and in relation to other global markets. The current account credit balance (surplus) of a nation signifies that the economy of that nation is net creditor to the other nations with which it has transacted. It also demonstrates the amount of money a nation saves as opposed to investing. It suggests that the nation owes other economies money for the abundance of resources it provides. A nation with a current account balance surplus offers receiving economies the opportunity to boost productivity while running a deficit by sending these resources overseas. The term "financing a deficit" describes this. Conversely, a nation's current account debit (deficit) balance indicates that its economy is in net debt relative to the rest of the world. In order to meet its domestic consumption and investment needs, it is utilizing resources from other economies and investing more than it is saving. As an illustration, suppose an economy determines that, rather than saving money, it should invest it overseas in an investment project in order to generate investment income in the future. Future returns would be recorded as investment income (a credit) in the current account under the income section, but this would be indicated as a debit in the financial account of the balance of payments at that point in time. Depletion of foreign exchange assets is typically associated with a current account deficit because those reserves would be utilized for foreign investments. The local economy may be responsible for paying the foreign economy's investment income in the future if the deficit indicates a rise in foreign investment in the local market. Knowing the source of a deficit or surplus is crucial because examining the current account as a whole may not always be accurate.

9.2.4. Balance of Payments (BOP) and Exchange Rates

The BOP is defined by the International Monetary Fund (IMF) as a statistical statement that methodically summarizes an economy's trade with the rest of the world for a given time period. Economic transactions such as capital flows, exports and imports of goods and services, gifts, and other comparable one-sided transfer payments are all measured by BOP data. A shift in the nation's foreign exchange reserves equals the net amount of all these transactions. Since the introduction of floating exchange rates, the significance of a deficit or surplus in the BOP has evolved. BOP metrics have historically been used to demonstrate pressure on a nation's foreign exchange rate. The government was compelled to make compensatory transactions as a result of this pressure because it had to close the deficit or risk devaluation.

1. **Exchange Rate Impacts:** The relationship between the BOP and exchange rates can be illustrated by use of a simplified equation that summarizes BOP data:

$$BOP = (X-M) + (CI-CO) + (FI-FO) + FXB$$

Where; X is exports of goods and services; M is imports of goods and services; (X-M) is known as Current Account Balance; CI is capital outflows; CO is capital outflows; (CI-CO) is known as Capital Account Balance; FI is financial inflows; FO is financial outflows; (FI-FO) is known as Financial Account Balance; and FXB is official monetary reserves such as foreign exchange and gold.

The effect of an imbalance in the BOP of a country works somewhat differently depending on whether that country has fixed exchange rates, floating exchange rates, or a managed exchange rate system.

i. **Fixed Exchange Rate Countries:** In a fixed exchange rate regime, it is the duty of the government to maintain a BOP close to zero. The government is expected to buy or sell official foreign exchange reserves in order to intervene in the foreign exchange market if the total of the current and capital accounts does not approach zero. If the total of the first two accounts is higher than zero, there is global excess demand for the local currency. The government would then need to step in and buy back foreign currencies or gold with domestic money in order to maintain the fixed exchange rate. This would return the BOP to almost zero. There is a domestic currency exchange supply on international markets if the total of the current and capital accounts is negative. Then, the government must step in and purchase the national currency using its gold and foreign exchange reserves. To enable effective intervention, a government must, of course, maintain sizable foreign exchange reserve balances. The nation will have to devalue its currency if its foreign exchange reserves run out before it can be used to purchase back its own money. Business managers utilize balance-of-payments statistics to predict changes in the official exchange rate, particularly in countries with fixed exchange rates. Technically speaking, a change in floating exchange rates is referred to as either depreciation or appreciation, whereas a change in fixed exchange rates is typically referred to as devaluation– or revaluation.

ii. **Floating Exchange Rate Countries:** A floating exchange rate system absolves a nation's government of the duty to fix the foreign exchange rate. The exchange rate will (in theory) automatically adjust in the direction required to achieve a BOP close to zero because the current and capital account balances do not add up to zero. A nation with a significant current account deficit and a balance of zero in its capital and financial accounts, for instance, would have a net BOP deficit. There will be an overabundance of the local currency on international markets. Like any other good that is in excess supply, the market will correct the imbalance by driving down prices. As a result, the value of the home currency will decline, and the BOP will return to zero. This theory is not always followed by exchange rate markets, especially in the short-to-intermediate term.

iii. **Managed Floats:** Countries with managed floats frequently find that they must take action to maintain their desired exchange rate values, even though they still depend on market conditions for daily exchange rate determination. Therefore, rather than directly intervening in the foreign exchange markets, they aim to change the market's valuation of a particular exchange rate by influencing the driving forces behind market activity. These governments primarily alter relative interest rates, which affects the economic principles that govern how exchange rates are determined. A shift in domestic interest rates is an attempt to correct the imbalance brought about by the current account deficit by adjusting the capital account balance, particularly the short-term portfolio component of these capital flows. Changes in interest rates can have a significant impact on global capital flows and exchange rate movements. In order to draw in more foreign capital, a nation with a managed float that wants to protect its currency may decide to increase domestic interest rates. This will change the dynamics of the market and raise the demand for local currency. Through this procedure, the government notifies players in the exchange market of its plans to take action to keep the value of the currency within predetermined bounds. However, the procedure also increases the cost of local borrowing for businesses, so domestic opponents of the policy are rare. Business managers in managed-float nations use BOP trends to predict shifts in the national interest rate policy of the government.

9.3. BALANCE OF PAYMENTS (BOP) ACCOUNTING

A balance of payments (BoP) is a methodical statement that methodically compiles an economy's monetary transactions with the rest of the world over a given time period. To put it simply, a country's balance of payments is an organized record of all the transactions that take place between its "residents" and the rest of the world (Table 9.2).

Three main elements of actual process of measuring international economic activity are:

1. Identifying what is/is not an international economic transaction;
2. Understanding how the flow of goods, services, assets, money create debits and credits; and
3. Understanding the bookkeeping procedures for BoP accounting.

Every transaction is documented in compliance with double-entry bookkeeping guidelines. In other words, accounting principles are used to record every transaction. These entries are debited in one case and credits in the other.

The net balance of all entries in the statement is zero, and the total of all credit and debit entries is equal in theory. Exports are recorded as debits when there is a decrease in foreign financial assets or an increase in foreign financial liabilities, and imports are recorded as credits when there is an increase in foreign financial assets or a decrease in foreign financial liabilities.

Put another way, decreases in holdings are recorded as credits and increases in holdings are recorded as debits when it comes to assets, whether they be financial or real. Conversely, liabilities are recorded as debits when they decrease and as credits when they increase. In actuality, the figures hardly ever balance to the point of mutual cancellation. This is the outcome of mistakes or oversights during the statement compilation process. To balance the credit or debit, a different balancing item is utilized. Nonetheless, there is no bookkeeping requirement that the totals on the two sides of a specific number of balance of payments accounts match, and it happens that analysts and government officials are quite interested in the balances displayed by specific combinations of accounts. In the balance of payments, these amounts are frequently referred to as "surpluses" or "deficits." The reader can better understand how accounting principles are applied to balance of payments accounting by referring to the following few straightforward guidelines.

1. A transaction resulting in a cash outflow, whether it be individual or corporate, that raises the demand for foreign currency (exchange) must be recorded as a debit. Conversely, a transaction that increases the supply of foreign currency (exchange) should be recorded as a credit entry.

2. Credit entries should be made for any transactions that result in an immediate or future payment from the rest of the world (RoW) to the nation. Conversely, transactions that lead to a payment—actual or potential—from the nation to the RoW ought to be noted as debits.

Table 9.2. Actual Process of Measuring BoP Activity

Credit	Debit
1. Exports of goods and services	1. Imports of goods and services
2. Income receivable from abroad	2. Income payable to abroad
3. Transfers from abroad	3. Transfers to abroad
4. Increases in external liabilities	4. Decreases in external liabilities
5. Decreases in external assets	5. Increases in external assets

Source: https://www.mbaknol.com/international-finance/balance-of-payments-bop-accounting/.

Therefore, credits in the balance of payments indicate a decrease in foreign assets or an increase in foreign liabilities, whereas debits indicate a decrease in foreign liabilities or an increase in foreign assets. The accrual accounting principle controls the timing of transaction recording in balance of payments accounting. As a result, whenever economic value is produced, changed, transferred, or eliminated, a transaction is recorded. A shift in ownership gives rise to obligations and claims. To put it simply, balances of payments are typically prepared for a year, though they can also be split into quarters.

9.3.1. The Capital Account Component in Balance of Payments (BoP)

Lending and public and private investment activities are recorded in capital accounts. It is the overall shift in foreign ownership of assets held in the country. A domestic country has a surplus in its capital account if foreign ownership of its assets has grown faster in a given year than domestic ownership of foreign assets. On the other hand, a domestic nation has a capital account deficit if domestic ownership of foreign assets has grown faster in a given year than foreign ownership of domestic assets. The term "financial account" refers to it. Many items are listed under the capital account in the IMF manual. However, in order to accommodate its unique institutional structure and analytical requirements, India, along with many other nations, has combined the accounting classification. The capital account included the following important sectors up until the end of the 1980s: (i) private capital, (ii) banking capital, and (iii) official capital. The relevant dividing line between the two categories of private capital was loans with an initial maturity of one year or less. The first category was long-term, and the second was short-term.

According to the regular BOP data, long-term private capital included foreign investments (both direct and portfolio), long-term loans, foreign currency deposits (FCNR and NRE), and an approximate share of unclassified receipts that were credited to the capital account. The movements in the external financial assets and liabilities of commercial and cooperative banks that were permitted to deal in foreign exchange were essentially covered by banking capital. Official capital transactions were categorized as (i) loans, (ii) amortization, and (iii) miscellaneous receipts and payments, with the exception of transactions with the IMF and changes in RBI's holdings of foreign currency assets and monetary gold (the government holds SDRs).

Components of Capital Account: From 1990–91 onwards, the classification adopted is as follows:

1. **Foreign Investment**: Foreign investment is bifurcated into Foreign Direct Investment (FDI) and portfolio investment. Direct investment is the act of purchasing an asset and at the same time acquiring control on it. The FDI in India could be in the form of inflow of investment (credit) and outflow in the form of disinvestment's (debit) or abroad in the reverse manner. Portfolio investment is the acquisition of an asset, without control over it. Portfolio investment comes in the form of Foreign Institutional Investors (FIIs), offshore funds and Global Depository Receipts (GDRs) and American Depository Receipts (ADRs). Acquisition of shares (acquisition of shares of Indian companies by nonresidents under section 5 of FEMA, 1999) has been included as part of foreign direct investment since January 1996.
2. **Loans**: Loans are further classified into external assistance, medium and long-term commercial borrowings and short-term borrowings, with loans of original maturity of one-year or less constituting the relevant dividing line. The principal repayment of the defense debt to the General Currency Area (GCA) is shown under the debit to loans (external commercial borrowing to India) for the general currency area since 1990–91.
3. **Banking Capital**: The foreign assets and liabilities of commercial and government banks that are permitted to deal in foreign exchange, as well as the balances of international organizations like the World Bank, IDA, ADB, and IFC that are kept on file with the RBI, make up banking capital. Deposits from non-residents (NRIs) are a significant part of bank capital.
4. **Rupee Debt Service**: Rupee debt service includes principal and interest repayment for the former rupee payments area (RPA). This is carried out in accordance with the high-level committee on balance of payments' recommendation.
5. **Other Capital**: As a residual item, other capital generally refers to the following: funds raised and held overseas by Indian corporations, delayed export receipts, India's subscriptions to international organizations, and IMF quota payments. The primary cause of delayed export receipts is the lead time that elapses between the actual shipment of goods that customs records and the bank channel's receipt of funds. It also includes the rupee value of the

gold that the RBI has purchased (monetized gold).

6. **Movement in Reserves**: Movement in reserves includes adjustments to the Indian government's SDR balances and the Reserve Bank of India's foreign exchange holdings. These are recorded after adjustments for valuation-related changes are subtracted. Changes in valuation result from the fact that foreign exchange assets are denominated in US dollars and take into account the appreciation or depreciation of non-US currencies held in reserves, such as the Euro, Sterling, Yen, and others. Moreover, there is no reserve position with the IMF included with this item.

9.3.2. Use of Exchange Controls

A set of limitations placed on international payments and transactions by the government or an exchange control authority is referred to as an exchange control.

Depending on the needs of the nation, exchange control can be total, encompassing all types of international transactions, or partial, limited to specific types of transactions or payments. A fully functional exchange control system has the following primary characteristics.

- The government acquires, through the legislative measures, a complete domination over the foreign exchange transactions.
- The government monopolizes the purchase and sale of foreign exchange.
- Law eliminates the sale and purchase of foreign exchange by the resident individuals. Even holding foreign exchange without informing the exchange control authority's declared illegal.
- All payments to the foreigners and receipts from them are routed through the exchange control authority or the authorized agents.
- Foreign exchange payments arc restricted, generally, to the import of essential goods and service such as food items, raw materials and some other essential industrial inputs like petroleum products.
- A system of rationing is adopted in the foreign exchange allocation for essential imports.
- To ensure the effectiveness of the exchange control system and to prevent the possible evasion, strict, stringent laws arc enacted.
- The circuitous legal procedure of acquiring import and export licenses is brought in force. In the process, the convertibility of the home currency is sacrificed.

9.3.2.1. Why Exchange Control?

Using the exchange control system, an unfavorable balance of payments can be adjusted. The exchange control system necessitates a laborious bureaucratic system of checks and balances, in contrast to the self-sufficient and automatic operation of the market system. However, due to a lack of other options, many nations with balance of payment deficits choose to implement exchange control. Indeed, the following prerequisites must be met for the balance of payments to automatically adjust.

- International competitive strength of the deficit countries.
- A fairly high elasticity of demand for imports.

- Perfectly competitive international market mechanism.
- Absence of government intervention with the demand and supply conditions.

There has always been uncertainty about these conditions' existence. Countries differ in their economic strength and their industries lack competitiveness due to differences in resource endowments, technology, and the rate of industrial growth. Different nations' protectionist policies tamper with the functioning of the global market. Furthermore, the automatic method of adjusting the balance of payments necessitates rigorous discipline, strong economic backing, and political resolve to withstand the destabilizing shocks that the automatic method is predicted to bring to a nation undergoing adjustment. The effectiveness of international market mechanisms to bring about automatic balance of payments adjustment is frequently questioned because these conditions are rare. Because of these factors, exchange control is still the last choice for nations experiencing severe balance of payments deficits. Exchange controls contribute to a higher level of efficacy in solving the deficit issue. Additionally, it shields a nation's economy from the effects of economic hardships in other nations. The efficiency with which exchange control handles the issue of capital movements is another benefit. By merely refusing to release foreign exchange for capital transfers, the government's monopoly on foreign exchange can effectively halt or reduce capital movements. Because of this benefit, many nations implemented exchange control during the Great Depression of the 1930s. While exchange control is unquestionably a better way to handle balance of payments disequilibrium, it does not offer a long-term fix for the underlying causes of the deficit problem.

9.3.2.2. Issues with Exchange Control

Exchange control may no doubt provide solution to balance of payment deficits, but it also creates following problems:

- When restrictions on exchange control becomes wide spread then large number of currencies are rendered nonconvertible. This restricts foreign trade and the gains from foreign trade are either lost or reduced to a minimum.
- Even after an economy's interest is protected, i.e., the exchange-control countries feel it is better to direct their internal monetary and fiscal policies toward the promotion of economic growth, achieving full employment, and its maintenance, rather than giving up exchange control, now that the external deficit has been recovered and the economy is fully insulated against external influence. They implement fiscally stimulative and easy monetary policies as a result. As a result, prices and income tend to increase, setting off an inflationary trend in the economy.
- Prices also typically rise because import-competing industries are less motivated to control cost increases and boost productivity in a damaged economy. As a result, exports tend to decrease and imports tend to increase as exports become relatively more expensive and imports relatively less expensive. These are the initial effects of home currency overvaluation. Undoubtedly, the equilibrium of the balance of payments is maintained; however, the initial benefit gradually wanes.

A dual exchange rate policy could exist under the multiple exchange rate system. Under a dual exchange rate policy, all other types of transactions are subject to the market rate, while authorized private and official transactions are subject to the official rate. The multiple exchange rate system is not without its drawbacks, though. International transactions become more complex and uncertain as a result of the system. Additionally, it needs an honest and effective administrative apparatus; otherwise, resources are frequently used inefficiently. Therefore, before choosing a course of action, it is preferable for the deficit countries to assess the effectiveness and viability of exchange control. According to some, exchange control should only be implemented sparingly and temporarily until a fundamental solution to the balance of payments deficit is found. Since exchange control alone cannot permanently solve the balance of payments deficit, it should only be implemented with careful consideration.

9.3.3. Disequilibrium in Balance of Payments

As we have already mentioned, from an accounting perspective, the balance of payments is always in balance. Additionally, in the accounting process, a capital account surplus—which comes from either borrowing from outside or depleting gold and foreign exchange reserves—counterbalances a current account deficit. Similar to this, a deficit in the capital account brought on by loans and bills to the debtor nation, or by a reduction in its reserves of foreign exchange and gold, balances a surplus in the current account. Nonetheless, because total receipts during the reference period do not always equal total payments, disequilibrium in the balance of payments does occur. There is an imbalance in the balance of payments when total receipts do not equal total payments for the accounting period. The process outlined below is used to obtain the final balance of payments position. The total receipt and total payment resulting from the transfer of goods and services, as well as long-term capital movements, are considered in evaluating the overall balance of payments position. Every transaction is now divided into induced and autonomous transactions. Self-executing transactions occur due to individuals' inclination to increase their consumption or generate higher profits. For instance, the goal of exporting and importing current account items is to increase consumption or profit. Donations or gifts are another independent item in the current account. They are purposeful and voluntary. The import and export of long-term capital are separate transactions in the capital account. Furthermore, autonomous transactions include short-term capital movements driven by the desire to invest overseas in order to increase returns. Therefore, the autonomous transactions are all exports and imports of goods and services, as well as long- and short-term capital movements driven by the desire to make gifts and donations or to earn higher returns abroad. No matter what other transactions are included in the balance of payments accounts, exports and imports still occur. These are therefore independent transactions. There won't be any more transactions if the value of the imports and exports (X_g and M_g) is equal. However, short-term capital movements result if X_g is less than M_g, (e.g., overseas lending or borrowing). These kinds of foreign loans or borrowings are made to offset the trade imbalance rather than for their own purpose. These are known as induced transactions as a result. They entail making room for capital flows. However, the movement of short-term capital, viz. gold movements and allowing for capital movements due to the induced transactions that occur in the autonomous transactions. The nation's gold and foreign exchange reserves decrease as a result of these transactions. Only independent transactions are taken into consideration when evaluating the balance of payments position. The balance of payments' surplus or deficit is determined by the total amount received and paid as a result of the autonomous transaction. The balance of payments is out of balance if total receipts and payments are not equal. The balance or payment indicates a deficit if the total payments exceed the total receipts. Conversely, there is a surplus in the balance of payments if the receipts from autonomous transactions exceed the payments for autonomous transactions. Obviously, when both are equal, there is no surplus or deficit and the balance of payments is in balance. From a policy perspective, the government is concerned because the reduction of gold and foreign exchange reserves is typically interpreted as a sign that the balance of payments is going into deficit. But, if reserves are ample and the government has made a conscious effort to deplete them, then the balance of payments deficit is not encouraging for the economy. Furthermore, the surplus-nature disequilibrium—aside from the one that could lead to inflation—is not as dangerous as the deficit-nature disequilibrium. As a result, the deficit type of disequilibrium in the balance of payments will be our primary concern here.

9.3.3.1. Causes of BOP Disequilibrium

When a nation's autonomous payments exceed its autonomous receipts, a balance of payments deficit kind of imbalance results. The export of capital and the import of goods and services are the sources of the autonomous payments. Similarly, the import of capital and the export of goods lead to autonomous receipts. Therefore, it is possible to argue that disequilibrium of a deficit type occurs when total imports surpass total exports. Imports and exports, however, do not decide for themselves. Numerous other factors affect the quantity and value of imports and exports. Regarding the factors influencing imports, the total amount of goods imported by a nation is determined by three factors: (i) the demand within the nation for foreign goods, which is primarily based on the purchasing power of its citizens overall; (ii) the cost of imports relative to domestic alternatives; and (iii) the preference of the populace for foreign goods. Analogously, a nation's overall export is determined by three factors: (i) foreign demand for its products and services; (ii) price and quality competitiveness; and (iii) exportable surplus. These factors don't change when things are static. As a result, once reached, equilibrium in the balance of payments stays steady. But in dynamic environments, the variables that impact imports and exports are constantly shifting—sometimes subtly, but more frequently abruptly and violently. From time to time and from nation to nation, the changes vary in length and intensity. Disturbances both domestically and internationally bring about changes that lead to an imbalance in the balance of payments.

9.3.3.1.1. Price Changes and Disequilibrium

The shift in price level is the primary factor contributing to the balance of payment's disequilibrium. Price movements could be either deflationary or inflationary. Generally, deflation results in a surplus in the balance of payments. From the perspective of the nation, the balance of payments surplus is not a major cause for concern. It might, however, result in misallocation of resources and unnecessary spending. Conversely, fluctuations in prices due to inflation result in deficits in the balance of payments. Gold reserves are depleted and debt levels rise as a result of the balance of payments deficit. loss of jobs and changes to the home economy lead to additional economic issues in the deficit countries. Thus, the only effect that inflationary price changes will have on the balance of payments position will be covered. The relative prices of imports and exports fluctuate as a result of inflation. When inflation increases domestic prices relative to import prices, imports rise even when the exchange rate stays constant. On the other hand, as domestic prices rise and foreign demand declines, inflation results in a decline in exports. The price-elasticity of domestic market demand for imports influences the rise in imports, while the price-elasticity of international demand for domestic products influences the fall in exports. There will inevitably be more imports than exports if the price elasticity of imports and exports is not zero. Consequently, the balance of payments will experience a deficit. Long-term disequilibrium will result if inflationary conditions continue. A large deficit and an inflexible state of disequilibrium are referred to as fundamental disequilibrium. Prices may fluctuate locally, within a single nation or a small group of nations, or globally, as was the case in the global economy during the 1930s. In most countries, depression and inflation occur almost simultaneously if price fluctuations take the form of a business cycle. The impact on imports varies depending on the economic size of the respective countries. Balance of payments deficits and surpluses range from modest to significant. In the inflationary phase of the trade cycle, the countries with a higher marginal propensity to import accumulate larger deficits; in the depression, they accumulate a moderate deficit or even a surplus. This kind of unbalance is referred to as cyclical disequilibrium. But this is merely a hypothetical scenario. Any generalization would be foolish because the marginal propensities to import are poorly understood.

9.3.3.1.2. Structural Changes and Disequilibrium

A country's inability to keep up with technological advancements can lead to structural changes in its economy. Examples of these factors include the depletion of inexpensive natural resources. e. technological lag and (iii) shifts in consumer preferences and tastes. Due to either a lack of foreign demand or a high cost of production, these changes render exporting nations incapable of competing in the global market. Demand and supply dynamics are altered by all of these modifications. The balance of payments is negatively impacted if the volume of foreign trade is fairly high. Disequilibrium in the balance of payments is the final outcome. We refer to it as structural disequilibrium. The discovery of new resources may also be the source of the structural disequilibrium, as this may significantly attract foreign capital. The significant capital inflow could cause the deficit in the balance of payments to reverse to a surplus.

9.3.3.1.3. Other Factors

In addition to the fundamental factors responsible for disequilibrium in the balance of payments, there are certain other factors, which may cause temporal disequilibrium, Some of them are as follows:

- Disturbances or crop failure particularly in the countries, producing primary goods.
- Rapid growth in population leading to large-scale imports of food materials.

- Ambitious development projects requiring heavy imports of technology, equipments, machinery and technical know-how.
- Demonstration-effect of advanced countries on the consumption pattern of less developed countries.

9.3.4. Correction of Balance of Payments (BoP) Deficit

A variety of international transactions are likely to result in short-term and minor balance of payments deficits. There is no need for quick remedial action to address these deficiencies. More significantly, the economy may suffer more negative effects than positive ones from sporadic short-term adjustments to domestic economic policies intended to close short-term balance of payments deficits. Due to the fact that these modifications result in short-term economic fluctuations and disruptions in the process of reallocating resources. As a result, the policy makers do not take smaller-scale short-term deficits seriously. A persistent deficit suggests that the nation's imports are outpacing its exports, or that its gold and foreign exchange reserves are declining. These nations become less credible and liquid internationally. This circumstance frequently results in compromises with these nations' political and economic independence. July 1990 saw a similar circumstance in India. As a result, a nation that consistently experiences significant balance of payments deficits must take corrective action, like altering its internal economic policies, in order to eliminate the deficit or at the very least reduce it to a manageable level. It is commonly acknowledged that there are no prerequisites for the existence of an automatic corrective mechanism based on the international price mechanism and visualized under the gold standard. As a result, the government's only choice is to use the tools at its disposal to alter the supply and demand in the market. Remember that the right combination of policies in this area can differ from nation to nation and periodically based on the state of the economy. The following are the different ways that balance of payments deficits are corrected:.

- **Indirect Measures to Correct Adverse BoP:** A free trade system results in balance of payments deficits because either domestic prices are much higher than foreign prices or there is a larger aggregate domestic demand for goods and services than there is supply of those goods and services. Therefore, the deficit can be closed by either lowering excess demand, raising domestic production at a cost of production that is comparable to that of other countries, or doing both at once. Short-term output increases can be exceedingly challenging, particularly in cases where a nation is almost at full employment or where other factors are impeding industrial growth. Therefore, lowering the demand for imports is the only way to lower the deficit.
- **Income and Expenditure Policies:** Here, we'll talk about how declining income can cause demand to decline and how that helps close the balance of payments deficit. Monetary and fiscal policies are the two tools available to policymakers to alter disposable income. Fiscal policy is based on people's disposable income, whereas monetary policy is based on the supply and demand for money. The following describes how these policies function and how effective they are at resolving balance of payment issues.

- **Monetary Policy:** Open market operations, statutory reserve ratios, selective credit controls, discount and bank rate policy, and open market operations are some of the tools used in monetary policy. The first two of these are used in relation to the policy for balance of payments. But this shouldn't imply that other instruments aren't important. The government is able to select any or all of these tools and implement them at the same time. A "tight money policy," also known as a "dear money policy," is implemented to address the issue of the balance of payments deficit. The "dear money" policy raises bank and discount rates by the central bank. As a result, the demand for institutional funds for investments declines under normal circumstances. The decline in investments and their subsequent multiplier effect cause a decline in people's income. A higher marginal propensity to consume than zero results in a lower demand for products and services. When everything else stays the same, a decline in imports is also implied by the decline in demand. This is the method by which "a tight money policy" makes up a balance of payments deficit. However, in the following scenarios, the effectiveness of a "tight money policy" is questionable: (i) when rates of return are significantly higher than the higher bank rate because of inflationary conditions; (ii) when investors have already made changes to their investments in anticipation of an increase in the interest rate. Next, open market operations are paired with the tight money policy, i.e., the auction of government securities and bonds. Together, these two tools contribute to a decline in the demand for money and other products. As a result, the balance of payments deficit will inevitably shrink if everything goes according to plan.
- **Fiscal Policy:** As a means of controlling income, fiscal policy involves making changes to public spending and taxation. Taxes lower the disposable income of households. While indirect taxes achieve the same goal by raising the price of the commodities they tax, direct taxes transfer household income directly to the public reserves. While indirect taxes have a relatively smaller effect, direct taxes cause a greater direct reduction in personal savings. Taxation lowers a household's disposable income, which in turn lowers aggregate demand, which includes the demand for imports. Taxation, by taxing capital at progressive rates, also contributes to the reduction of investment. By implementing the surplus budgeting policy, which maintains government spending below revenue,

the government can also lower income and demand. Taxes decrease a household's disposable income while public spending raises household income and purchasing power. However, compared to taxes, public spending has a multiplier effect that is one greater. Therefore, this fact should be taken into account when adopting a surplus-budget policy. This fact must be explained by a surplus so great that the total cumulative impact of taxes on disposable income is greater than the impact of public spending. The foreign trade multiplier determines the amount of income that must be decreased in order to reduce the balance of payments deficit to a specific level.

9.3.4.1. Exchange Depreciation and Devaluation

Changing the relative prices of imports and exports is one way to reduce excess demand through price measures. Exchange depreciation and devaluation can alter the relative prices of imports and exports. A decline in the value of one's own currency expressed in foreign currency is referred to as exchange depreciation, while a decline in the value of one's own currency expressed in gold is referred to as devaluation. But in terms of buying power, devaluation and depreciation turn out to be equal, and their effects on foreign demand are likewise equal. As a result, in their capacity to correct an unfavorable balance of payments, we will regard them as a single entity. Exchange depreciation and devaluation alter the relative costs of imports and exports, i.e., export prices fall and import prices rise, but not always in the same ratio as the devaluation. When the relative prices of imports and exports fluctuate, the country's demand for imports declines, devaluing its currency and increasing demand for its goods abroad—as long as that demand is price elastic. Therefore, if exchange depreciation or devaluation is successful, exports will rise and imports will fall. The nation's export revenue would rise while its import payments would fall. In due course, this reduces the balance of payments deficits in the end. However, the following circumstances determine whether or not the anticipated outcomes of devaluation or exchange depreciation are realized.

- The Marshall-Lerner condition is the most significant requirement in this context. According to the Marshall-Lerner condition, devaluation won't help the balance of payments unless the total of the domestic and international demand for imports and exports is more elastic than unity. Revaluation rather than devaluation can improve the balance of payments if the total of the elasticity is less than unity.
- Devaluation can be successful only if the affected countries do not devalue their currency in retaliation.
- Devaluation must not change the cost-price structure in favor of imports.
- Finally, the government ensures that inflation, which may be the result of devaluation, is kept under control, so that the effect of devaluation is not counter-balanced by the effect of inflation.

CASE STUDY

CAN DSS HELP MASTER CARD MASTER THE CREDIT CARD BUSINESS?

Credit (change) cards have been very big business for several decades. In 2001, over $30 trillion in payments for goods and services were charged using credit cards. The cards have made life easier for many people because they do not need to carry large amounts of cash for most purchases. Many people also use the cards as a way to borrow money because they need only pay a small percentage of the amount they owe each month, although they are usually charged very high interest rates for the unpaid balance. The interest goes to the issuing bank, making credit cards a very profitable service for them. However, the credit card industry is intensely competitive, highly fragmented, and growing at a rate of 3 to 4 per year, making those profits difficult to achieve.

Visa and MasterCard are associations of banks that issue the credit cards. They market their cards, often several different cards, and provide support for the transactions, making networks available to collect and use the data. The most popular credit card has been Visa, with 44.5% of the business in 2001, while MasterCard is number two with 31.6%. Being very much second to Visa, MasterCard is trying to overtake it. While it had been number two since the beginning, MasterCard began to emerge from "its doldrums" in 1997, according to Robert Selander, MasterCard's CEO. It began to realize it might really be able to overtake Visa and become number one. To reach that goal, MasterCard needed to present itself so that potential user will choose a MasterCard rather than a Visa. It also had to spur the bank issuers to promote MasterCard cards rather than those of their competition.

In 1998, when MasterCard had only 28.8% of the credit card charge volume while Visa's was over 50%, MasterCard decided it needed a new computer center, partially to handle all the data as the company's business expanded as a result of its drive to overtake Visa. It also foresaw growth as a result of its change in strategy. The company's new strategy required a system that would be able to keep a record of every transaction of every customer for three years. The strategy included ways MasterCard and its member banks could use that data to increase their credit card business. MasterCard wanted to increase its daily volume of 30 million transactions in 1977. At the time it had three separate computer centers on four floors in the suburbs of St. Louis, Missouri, and it wanted to consolidate the computer centers while enlarging the new center so that it would be able to handle both the current volume and the planned volume as it expanded. At that time it was storing nearly 50 terabytes (50 trillion numbers and letters) of data, including the dollar amount, merchant, location, and card number. MasterCard also planned to add other data fields, such as ZIP codes, to make the data more useful. However, to protect MasterCard users, it did decide not to include demographic data such as incomes and ages.

Nonetheless, "The credit card business lives and dies by data," said Ted Iacobuzio, director of consumer credit research for the consulting and research firm, TowerGroup.

While both Visa and MasterCard had already been warehousing so much data, they were both moving toward providing reports to their member banks. MasterCard's goal was to give its members (the banks) direct access to their customers' data as well as tools to analyze all of this data, all in order to persuade the banks to choose MasterCard over Visa. For example, if banks could use MasterCard tools to improve their analysis of the profitability of the cards in their portfolios or gain more customers and transactions to process, they would be inclined to push MasterCard more often. Such analysis could help banks determine the types of customers that were most profitable or find ways to appeal to more potential MasterCard customers. Many banks issue both Visa Cards and MasterCard cards (sometimes several of each), and if the banks can use this information from MasterCard while Visa does not have or make available such information, the MasterCard company can gain a strategic advantage. For example, in 2001, MasterCard persuaded Citigroup, the largest issuer of credit cards, to push MasterCard over Visa so that 85% of its credit cards came from MasterCard versus only 15% from Visa. J. P. Morgan Chase likewise was convinced to use MasterCard for 80% of the cards it issued.

MasterCard hoped it could persuade banks to use these data if they could see value (increased profit) in the process. Joseph Caro, MasterCard's vice president of Internet technology services, said that "little percentages" can be very profitable to banks. In one case, a bank was requiring its merchants to verify the whole process by using the telephone to call in one transaction out of 50 for approval (rather than using a telecommunications method), while most banks were requiring only one transaction in 500. Because call-ins cost about $3 each, that bank could save $300,000 a year by switching over to the one in 500 method. Another bank was turning down one transaction out of five because so many call-ins were timing out. The bank was able to discover that most of the customers turned down were actually creditworthy. By changing its set up, the bank would be able to eliminate thousands of unnecessary lost transactions. About 28,000 banks and financial service companies issue MasterCard credit cards. To draw these customers into using its credit card transaction data, MasterCard needed not only to make each bank's data available to them, but it also needed to make available appropriate analytic software. MasterCard assigned 35 full-time developers to the task of identifying and creating software tools to accomplish this task. Drawing on Business Objects Web Intelligence software in 2001, these developers created and programmed 27 tools for the banks to use. (These tools are not free and they are not available to merchants.) One of MasterCard's new tools, called the Business Performance Intelligence, is for operational reporting and includes a suite of 70 standard reports that banks can use to analyze their daily, weekly, or monthly transaction. The banks can then compare the results from one market (such as a United States state or region, or a single country) with that of another market. MasterCard also works with individual banks to create their own custom reports, enabling them to concentrate on their own issues and concern. Subscribing banks access the MasterCard business intelligence system via a secure extranet.

The developers also created MarketScope, which are applications that have the goal of helping banks and merchants work together to generate more purchases from the merchants if they are paid for by MasterCard. One example they give is to enable Wal-Mart stores to determine how many MasterCard holders spend $25 or more on sporting goods in January and February. Then, MasterCard's vice president of systems development, Andrew Clyne, suggested that Wal-Mart could send these card-holders the right to obtain tickets to their closest major league baseball team based upon future sporting goods purchase above a certain dollar minimum. Lacobuzio said that such a strategy should appeal to state and regional banks. However, he believes it is likely that national and international banks would have already developed and are using their own analytical software. But even they would have a use for MasterCard's software as a kind of benchmark against which to measure the effectiveness of their own systems.

Moreover, despite the increasing volume, the processing was much faster. As Caro said, "If we can do thing faster, little percentages start moving in our direction."

Visa, however, is not sitting still, and is managing about 100 trillion terabytes of data for its clients. Until recently, it mainly supplied the data online or on disks to its bank customers, who used their own software and computers to analyze the data. Recently, Visa started to run analyzes for the banks on its own computers. In May 2002, Visa also introduced a Web service called Resolve Online to help banks deal with disputed payments and is working on providing banks with online analytic tools. "If MasterCard is ahead of the game in any of this," says Iacobuzio, Visa "will have it in six months."

MasterCard's new data storage site, which was opened in May 2002, is also in St. Louis, in a single 525,000-square – foot building. The complex, which was built on open land, cost MasterCard $135 million. The changeover to the new site happened over a weekend with almost no problem, despite the purchases of about $4 billion each day.

ACTIVITY

Prepare a project report on the impact of trade policies on the balance of payments which are based on a comparative study of developed and developing countries. Also provide recommendations for policymakers in both developed and developing countries to improve their BoP positions.

SUMMARY

- The balance of payments (BOP) transactions consist of imports and exports of goods, services, and capital, as well as transfer payments, such as foreign aid and remittances. A country's balance of payments and its net international investment position together constitute its international accounts.
- The term "capital account" is also used in the narrower sense that excludes central bank foreign exchange market operations: Sometimes the reserve account is classified as "below the line" and so not reported as part of the capital account.
- The balance of payments takes into account payments for a country's exports and imports of goods, services, financial capital, and financial transfers. It is prepared in a single currency, typically the domestic currency for the country concerned.
- When exchange rates are fixed by a rigid gold standard, or when imbalances exist between members of a currency union such as the Eurozone, the standard approach to correct imbalances is by making changes to the domestic economy.
- Balance of payments and international headcount data is critical to the formulation of national and international economic policies. The balance of payments imbalances and foreign direct investment (FDI) is crucial for a country's policymakers to seek solutions.
- The balance of payment is defined as a systematic record of all economic transactions between the residents of a country and residents of foreign countries during a certain period of time. Although the above definition of balance of payments is quite revealing certain terms used in the definition may require some clarification.
- The balance of payments accounting is based on the double-entry book-keeping system in which both sides of a transaction, i.e., receipts and payments are recorded. For example, exports involve out-flow of goods and inflow of foreign currency.
- Balance of payment records all economic transactions between a county and the rest of the countries around the world annually. The balance of payment is made up of two distinguished components respectively the current account, capital and financial accounts.
- The Current Account records a nation's total exports of goods, services and transfers, and its total imports of them. The current account is subdivided into two components (1) balance of trade (BoT), and (2) balance of invisibles (BOIs).

REVIEW QUESTIONS

1. What are the various types of exchange rate regimes, and how do they impact international trade and economic stability?

2. How does the IMF define the Balance of Payments, and what are the key components of this definition?
3. Why is Balance of Payments data crucial for policymakers, and how can it influence economic decision-making and policy formulation?
4. How do fluctuations in the Balance of Payments affect exchange rates, and what mechanisms link these two economic indicators?
5. What is the role of the Capital Account in the Balance of Payments, and how does it interact with other components to reflect a country's economic transactions?

REFERENCES

1. Anderlini, J. (2009). *China Calls for New Reserve Currency*. Financial Times. Archived from: http://www.ft.com (accessed on 3 July 2024).
2. Camba-Crespo, A., García-Solanes, J., & Torrejón-Flores, F. (2021). Current-account breaks and stability spells in a global perspective. *Applied Economic Analysis, 30*(88), 1–17. https://doi.org/10.1108/AEA-02-2021-0029.
3. Davidson, P. (2009). *The Keynes Solution: The Path to Global Economic Prosperity*. Palgrave Macmillan.
4. Giles, C. (2009). *Surplus Nations Urged by IMF to Take up Baton*. The Financial Times. https://www.ft.com/content/ceeff158-ade6-11de-87e7-00144feabdc0
5. Helleiner, E., Pauly, L. W., & Ravenhill, J. (2005). *Global Political Economy*. Oxford University Press.
6. Prasad, E. S., Rajan, R. G., & Subramanian, A. (2007). *Foreign Capital and Economic Growth.* Peterson Institute. Brookings Papers on Economic Activity, 1, 153-230
7. Rachman, G. (2010). *Bankruptcy Could be Good for America*. The Financial Times. https://www.ft.com/content/a8486284-fee9-11de-a677-00144feab49a
8. Wolf, M. (2010). *Currencies Clash in New Age of Beggar-my-Neighbor*. The Financial Times. Archived from: http://www.ft.com (accessed on 3 July 2024).
9. Wolf, M. (2010). *The Eurozone's Next Decade Will be Tough*. The Financial Times. https://www.ft.com/content/19da1d26-fa2f-11de-beed-00144feab49a

CHAPTER 10

Foreign Exchange

LEARNING OBJECTIVES

After studying this chapter, you will be able to:

- Meaning of foreign exchange
- Learn about functions of foreign exchange market
- Discuss the types of foreign exchange market
- Explain the forex market participants

KEY TERMS FROM THIS CHAPTER

Cash payment	Electronic trading platforms
Financial instruments	Foreign currency
Forex market	Global economy
Global financial system	Infrastructure
Physical exchange	Risk management

INTRODUCTION

The international exchange market where currencies are traded is known as foreign exchange, or simply forex or FX. It is essential to the global economy because it makes currency conversions possible for businesses, which in turn facilitates investment and trade across borders. This interchange is essential for cross-border transactions, allowing nations to easily take part in the global economy. The foreign exchange market is open for business five days a week, 24 hours a day, in the world's principal financial hubs. Because it is decentralized, all transactions don't happen in a single physical location. Rather, trade takes place electronically via computer networks involving dealers, banks, businesses, and governments. Fundamentally, trading foreign exchange entails purchasing one currency and selling another. Pairs of currencies, like USD/EUR or GBP/JPY, are quoted. The base currency is the first one in the pair, and the quote currency is the second. The amount of the quote currency required to buy one unit of the base currency is shown by the exchange rate.

Central banks, commercial banks, hedge funds, companies, and individual traders are among the participants in the forex market. Central banks, like the US Federal Reserve and the European Central Bank, are important because they have the power to affect currency values through changes in interest rates and other monetary policy decisions. Commercial banks serve as middlemen for people and companies in need of foreign exchange services. They help to make transactions easier and give the market liquidity. Hedge funds and big businesses trade foreign exchange to control their exposure to currency fluctuations and protect themselves from the currency risk associated with their global operations. Through brokerage firms, individual traders—from professionals to retail investors—also engage in forex trading. Leverage gives traders the ability to manage bigger positions with a smaller initial investment, but it also raises the possibility of suffering sizable losses.

Trillions of dollars are exchanged on the forex market every day, indicating its high liquidity. Trader ability to purchase and sell currencies without materially influencing exchange rates is ensured by liquidity. But it also means that market sentiment, geopolitical developments, and the release of economic data can all have an impact on exchange rates. To maintain stability and control currency fluctuations that could affect their economies, governments and central banks keep a close eye on the foreign exchange market. Interventions may be made to stabilize exchange rates or accomplish policy goals, such as buying or selling currencies in bulk.

A vital component of the global financial system, foreign exchange facilitates the flow of capital and trade between countries. It has a significant impact on everything from individual investment plans to the decisions made by multinational corporations due to its constant operation and enormous liquidity. Anyone working in the financial markets or international trade needs to understand its dynamics.

10.1. MEANING OF FOREIGN EXCHANGE

The foreign exchange market is where buyers and sellers exchange foreign currencies for one another. Stated differently, a foreign exchange market is a marketplace for the purchase and sale of currencies from various nations (Chen James et al., 2009).

Central banks, commercial banks, brokers, exporters, importers, immigrants, investors, and tourists make up the foreign exchange market's structure. The Figure 10.1 illustrates the positions and positions of the major players in the foreign market.

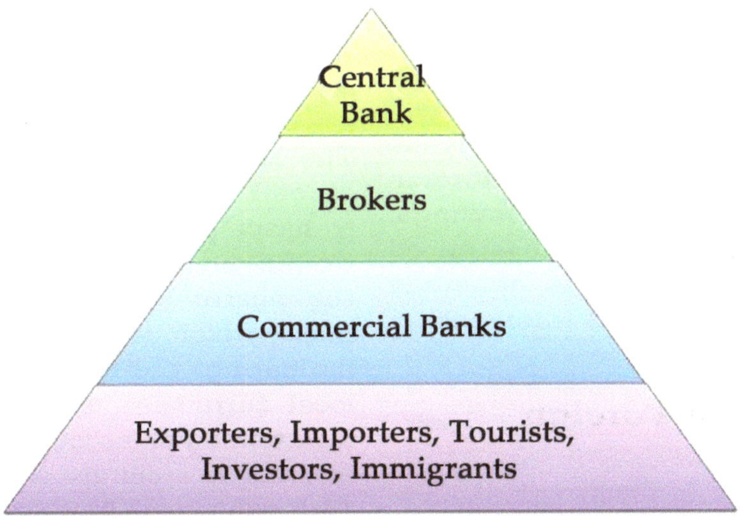

Figure 10.1. *The structure of the foreign exchange market constitutes central banks.*

Source: https://i0.wp.com/theintactone.com/wp-content/uploads/2018/07/foreign-exchange-market.jpg?resize=500%2C358&ssl=1.

The actual buyers and sellers of foreign currencies—exporters, importers, tourists, investors, and immigrants—are at the base of a pyramid. They approach commercial banks to purchase the currencies because they are the real users of them. The second-most significant player in the foreign exchange market is the commercial banks. The banks that deal in foreign exchange play the role of "market makers" because they quote the exchange rates for buying and selling foreign currencies on a daily basis. Additionally, they serve as clearing houses, which helps to eliminate the discrepancy between the supply and demand of currencies. These banks purchase currencies from brokers and then resell them to customers.

The foreign exchange brokers are the third rung of a pyramid. These intermediaries serve as a conduit between the real buyers and the commercial banks as well as between the central bank and the latter. They are the main repository for data on the market. These are the people who broker a deal between the buyer and the seller on a commission basis rather than actually purchasing the foreign currency.

The highest authority in the exchange market's structure is the central bank of each nation. They serve as the nation's last-resort lender and keeper of its foreign exchange. To ensure that the foreign exchange market operates in an orderly manner, the central bank has the authority to regulate and control it. One of the main duties of the central bank is to intervene directly, if needed, to stop the foreign exchange market's aggressive swings. Seling the currency when it is overpriced and purchasing it when it is generally undervalued is an example of intervention.

10.1.1. History of Foreign Exchange

10.1.1.1. Ancient

Exchanges and trades of currencies started in antiquity. At the time of the Talmudic writings (Biblical times), money-changers—those who assist others in changing money while also receiving a commission or charging a fee—were a common sight in the Holy Land. These individuals, also known as kollybistės, utilized city stalls and, during feast days, the Temple's Court of the Gentiles. In more recent ancient times, goldsmiths and/or silversmiths were also money changers. The Byzantine government maintained a monopoly on currency exchange throughout the fourth century AD. PCZ I 59021 Papyri (c. 259/8 BC), demonstrates the instances of currency exchange in ancient Egypt. In the ancient world, trade was facilitated by the use of currency and exchange, which allowed people to purchase and sell goods like food, ceramics, and raw materials. A merchant could exchange fewer Greek gold coins for more Egyptian ones or for more tangible goods if a Greek coin contained more gold than an Egyptian coin because of its size or composition. This is the reason that the majority of the world currencies that are in use today had their value fixed to a certain amount of a recognized standard, such as gold or silver, at some point in their history.

10.1.1.2. Medieval and Later

The Medici family had to establish banks abroad in the 15th century in order to transact currency exchange on behalf of textile merchants. The bank developed the nostro (Italian for "ourse") account book, which featured two-column entries indicating the amounts of foreign and local currencies as well as details about maintaining an account with a foreign bank, in order to facilitate trade. In the 17th and 18th centuries, Amsterdam had a thriving foreign exchange market. Foreign trade occurred in 1704 between representatives of the County of Holland and the Kingdom of England.

10.1.1.3. Early Modern

Alex. Around 1850, Brown and Sons became one of the major currency traders in the United States. In the year 1880, J. M. do Espírito Santo de Silva (Banco Espírito

Santo) requested authorization to operate a foreign exchange trading business, and was granted it. According to at least one source, the introduction of the gold standard in 1880 marked the start of modern foreign exchange. International trade was subject to far less regulation before World War I. The start of a war served as a catalyst for nations to abandon the gold standard monetary system.

10.1.1.4. Modern to Post-Modern

Gold holdings increased at an annual rate of 6 point 3 percent between 1903 and 1913, while foreign exchange holdings of countries increased at an annual rate of 10 point 8 percent from 1899 to 1913. By the end of 1913, the pound sterling was being used for almost half of all international trade. In 1860, there were only three foreign banks operating in London; by 1913, there were 71. There were only two foreign exchange brokers in London in 1902. Britain was mainly excluded from currency trading until 1914, when it peaked in Paris, New York City, and Berlin at the beginning of the 20th century. In London, there were 17 foreign exchange brokers between 1919 and 1922, and 40 companies were engaged in exchange business by 1924. The Kleinwort family was regarded as the industry leaders in foreign exchange during the 1920s, while Japheth, Montagu and Co. and Seligman still deserve to be acknowledged as important FX traders. London's trade started to take on characteristics of its current form. By 1928, the city's financial operations relied heavily on the Forex market. For those living in London in the 1930s, attempts at achieving wholesale prosperity from trade were hindered by continental exchange controls as well as other factors in Europe and Latin America.

10.1.1.5. After World War II

Following the signing of the Bretton Woods Accord in 1944, currencies were permitted to fluctuate within a range of ±1 percent of their par exchange rate. The Foreign Exchange Bank Law was first introduced in Japan in 1954.

As a result, the Bank of Tokyo became a center of foreign exchange by September 1954. Japanese law was amended between 1954 and 1959 to permit transactions in foreign exchange using a greater number of Western currencies.

U. S. The Bretton Woods Accord and fixed exchange rates are said to have been terminated by President Richard Nixon, which led to the eventual creation of a free-floating currency system. The Smithsonian Agreement permitted rates to vary by up to ±2 percent after the Accord ended in 1971. 1961–1962:

The amount of overseas operations carried out by the U.S. The Federal Reserve was not very high. The people in charge of managing exchange rates decided that the Agreement's bounds were unrealistic, and they stopped doing so in March 1973.

At some point thereafter, no major currency was kept with the ability to be converted into gold, and institutions had to rely on currency reserves.

The amount of trading in the market tripled between 1970 and 1973. Some of the markets were split at some point (according to Gandolfo in February and March 1973), and a two-tier currency market with dual currency rates was subsequently introduced. That was done away with in March 1974. In June 1973, Reuters replaced the telex and phones that were previously used for trading quotes with computer monitors.

10.1.1.6. Markets Close

Due to the ultimate ineffectiveness of the Bretton Woods Accord and the European Joint Float, the forex markets were forced to close sometime during 1972 and March 1973. The largest purchase of US dollars in the history of 1976 was when the West German government achieved an almost 3-billion-dollar acquisition. This event indicated the impossibility of balancing of exchange rates by the measures of control used at the time, and the monetary system and the foreign exchange markets in West Germany and other countries within Europe closed for two weeks (during February and, or, March 1973. *Giersch, Paqué, & Schmieding* state closed after purchase of 7.5 million Dmarks "*Brawley* states." ...Exchange markets had to be closed. When they re-opened.... March 1 that is a large purchase occurred after the close).

10.1.1.7. After 1973

The full floating and relatively free market conditions of the modern era began in 1973, marking the end of state control over foreign exchange trading in developed nations. According to other accounts, the initial exchange of a currency pair by the U.S. retail customers in 1982, and by the following year, more currency pairs would be accessible. As part of modifications that started in 1978, the People's Bank of China permitted some domestic businesses to trade foreign currencies as of January 1, 1981.

The South Korean government lifted its restrictions on foreign exchange and first permitted free trade in 1981. The government of the nation agreed to accept the IMF quota for foreign trade in 1988.

Intervention by European banks (especially the Bundesbank) influenced the Forex market on 27 February 1985. In 1987, slightly more than 25% of all trades made anywhere in the world took place in the United Kingdom. The second-highest trading involvement was exhibited by the United States. Iran switched from oil-barter to foreign exchange in some international agreements during 1991.

10.2. FUNCTIONS OF FOREIGN EXCHANGE MARKET

The market where buyers and sellers transact in foreign currencies is known as the foreign exchange market. To put it simply, a foreign exchange market is a marketplace where various national currencies are bought and sold. Three primary functions that are essential to any foreign exchange are the main categories into which the foreign exchange operations fall (Figure 10.2).

They are as follows:

1. Transfer Function
2. Credit Function
3. Hedging Function

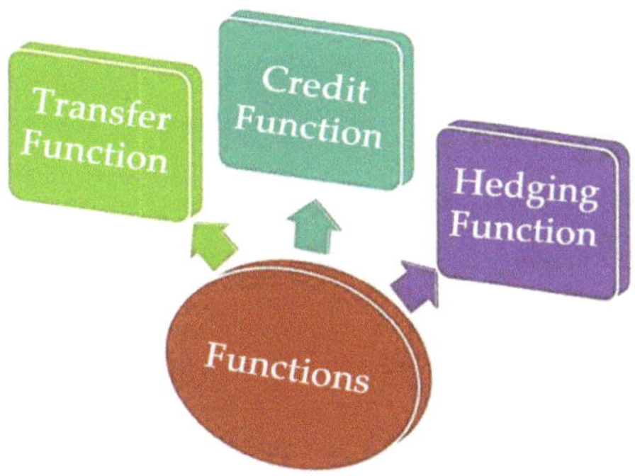

Figure 10.2. *Functions of foreign exchange market.*

Source: https://i0.wp.com/theintactone.com/wp-content/uploads/2018/07/functions-of-foreign-exchange.jpg?resize=500%2C376&ssl=1.

10.2.1. Transfer Function

The movement of money, or foreign currency, from one nation to another for the purpose of payment settlement is the fundamental and most obvious use of the foreign exchange market. In essence, it involves exchanging one currency for another, with FOREX serving as a means of transferring purchasing power between nations. For instance, FOREX will help convert the rupee to the dollar if an Indian exporter imports goods from the USA and the payment is to be made in dollars. Credit instruments like bank drafts, foreign exchange bills, and phone transfers are used to carry out the transfer function.

10.2.2. Credit Function

To promote a seamless transfer of goods and services between nations, OREX offers importers a short-term credit. Credit can be used by an importer to finance their overseas purchases. For example, if an Indian business wishes to buy machinery in the United States, it can pay for the purchase by using the foreign exchange market to issue a bill of exchange with a three-month maturity.

10.2.3. Hedging Function

Hedging facilities are one of the foreign exchange market's other significant roles. Foreign exchange transactions are risk-free when exchange rates are set and controls are implemented. Covering import and export risks is referred to as hedging. It gives importers and exporters a way to protect themselves from losses brought on by changes in exchange rates. An investment that shields your money from a hazardous circumstance is called a hedge. Using hedges reduces or neutralizes the risk that the value of your assets will decline. In the event that the asset loses value, it also caps your loss at a predetermined sum. Like house insurance, it's comparable. Every month, you pay a set sum of money. Your loss is only the known amount of the deductible if a fire destroys your home's entire worth. In finance, hedging refers to a risk management tactic. Its focus is on mitigating or completely removing the uncertainty risk. This strategy aims to lock in profits and limit losses that might result from unanticipated fluctuations in investment prices. It operates according to the offsetting principle. e. adopting an equal and opposing stance in two distinct markets. To put it simply, it's the act of hedging one investment by making another. People typically try to protect themselves against a negative event when they make plans to hedge. This lessens the impact of the event but does not stop it from happening. This hedging strategy is used by large corporations and portfolio managers in addition to individual investors to reduce exposure to different kinds of risks and their associated negative effects.

10.3. TYPES OF FOREIGN EXCHANGE MARKET

The foreign exchange market, commonly referred to as the forex market, is an international currency trading platform. The decentralized market enables the buying and selling of foreign exchange. Since the market is over-the-counter, it will have the final say over foreign exchange rates. It entails exchanging, buying, and selling currencies at the going rate. The forex market has the highest trade rate globally (Figure 10.3).

Let us take a look at different types of foreign exchange markets:

- Spot Markets
- Forward Markets
- Future Markets
- Option Markets
- Swaps Markets

Figure 10.3. *Types of foreign exchange market.*

Source: https://i0.wp.com/theintactone.com/wp-content/uploads/2018/07/types-of-fx-transactions.jpg?resize=500%2C265&ssl=1.

10.3.1. Spot Markets

A spot market is a type of financial market where commodities and financial instruments are exchanged for immediate delivery. The physical exchange of a financial instrument or commodity for cash consideration is referred to as delivery. Because there is an actual physical exchange of assets and cash payments are processed instantly, the spot market is also referred to as the cash market or physical market. Delivery and cash payments typically occur on the spot in a spot market. Nonetheless, settlement—the actual delivery of the instrument or commodity and the transfer of funds—typically takes two working days in the majority of organized markets (i.e., T+2). The buyer and seller perform the terms of the contract on the spot at the going rate and quantity, even with the T+2 settlement date (Figure 10.4).

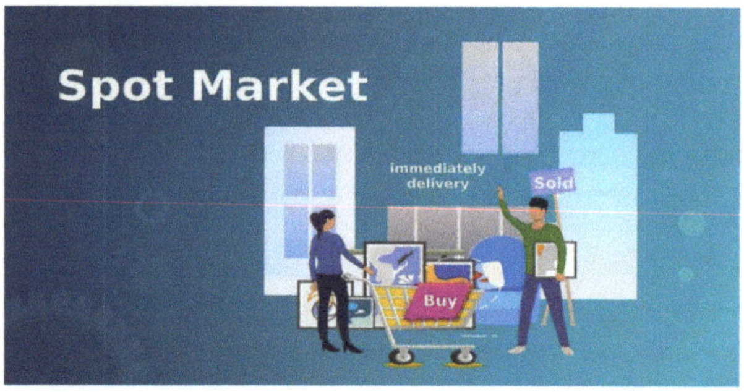

Figure 10.4. *A spot market is a financial market.*

Source: https://cdn.educba.com/academy/wp-content/uploads/2020/05/Spot-Market.jpg.

In contrast, in forward and futures markets, delivery is also anticipated in the future and parties agree to trade at a forward/future price of the underlying asset. For this reason, forward/futures markets, in contrast to spot markets, create a contract today, but settlement is anticipated later. Spot markets can occur anywhere there is a system in place to facilitate this kind of trade. One instance of a trade on the spot market is when a shareholder (Mr. Jones) desires to purchase 1,000 IBM shares through the NYSE. He'll get in touch with his broker to purchase the shares at the going rate, which in this case is $117.60. At a consideration of $117,600, the broker instantly transfers the funds to the seller. As soon as the money clears and is received by the seller, Mr. Jones becomes the owner of the shares.

10.3.1.1. Assets Traded on Spot Markets

Spot markets are used to trade fixed-income instruments like bonds and treasury bills, foreign exchange, and equity. Spot markets are dominated by commodities due to the trading of metals, energy, livestock, and agriculture. Both perishable and non-perishable commodities are traded on spot markets. The foreign exchange market is the most actively traded asset in the world, with traders exchanging different currencies on one of the biggest spot markets in the world, with a daily turnover exceeding $6 trillion. Standardization of commodities allows for effective trading on spot markets. The most traded commodity is crude oil. Lately, technology has been included in spot markets alongside commodities, such as mobile minutes and bandwidth.

10.3.1.2. Characteristics of Spot Markets

Certain features are associated with spot markets. Below are the most apparent:

- Transactions are settled at the ruling price known as the spot price or spot rate.
- Delivery of the asset takes place immediately or otherwise at T+2.
- Transfer of funds is instantaneous; otherwise, settlement can be at T+2.

10.3.1.3. Trading Mechanism

Also referred to as the spot price or spot rate, the price on the spot market is the going rate for a trade that is executed on the spot. Prices are set by buyers and sellers using supply and demand in the economy. The spot price is primarily a function of supply and demand, as opposed to the forward price, which is determined by the time value of money, the yield curve, and/

or storage costs. For a transaction to take place, both buyers and sellers must consent to pay and receive the spot price for the typical quantity of assets on offer.

10.3.1.4. Types of Spot Markets

There two main types of spot markets – over-the-counter (OTC) and organized market exchange (Figure 10.5).

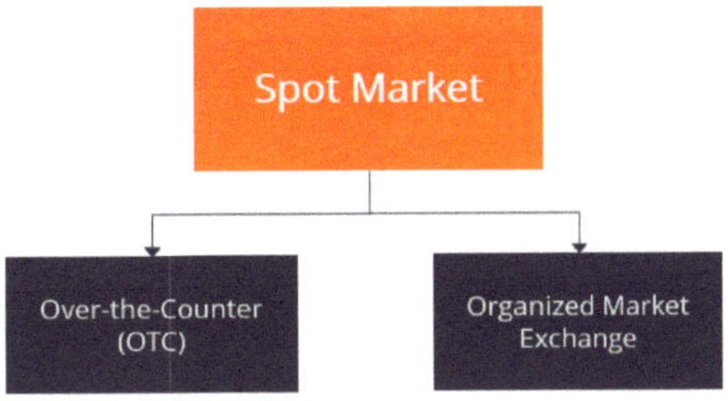

Figure 10.5. *Types of spot markets.*

Source: https://cdn.corporatefinanceinstitute.com/assets/spot-market1.png.

1. **Over-the-Counter (OTC):** In an over-the-counter (OTC) setting, buyers and sellers come together to conduct bilateral trade by consensus. There is no central exchange organization to oversee trades or a third party to supervise transactions. Unlike what is typically seen on organized exchanges, the assets being traded might not be standardized in terms of quantity, price, or other terms.

   As a result, all terms of trade are negotiated and transactions take place immediately. Since most trades in OTC markets are private, prices may not be disclosed. The most popular and active over-the-counter market is the currency exchange market.

Figure 10.6. *An organized market exchange.*

Source: https://carlosandcompany.com/wp-content/uploads/2023/03/when-does-the-forex-market-open-2.jpg.

2. **Market Exchanges:** Buyers and sellers get together in an organized market exchange to place bids and offer commodities and financial instruments that are available. Either a trading floor or an electronic trading platform can be used for trading. Because there are so many trades on some exchanges, prices are decided instantly, which has made trading more efficient thanks to electronic trading platforms (Figure 10.6).

Exchanges may specialize in particular asset classes or deal in a variety of commodities and financial instruments. Market makers, or exchange brokers, are typically used to facilitate trade. According to the exchange standard, assets traded on exchanges are standardized. Minimum contract prices for traded assets, or assets in particular quantities and values, are probably in place. Many bids (prices offered to buy) and offers (prices offered to sell) from sellers determine prices.

Spot prices are subject to minute or even millisecond fluctuations. Exchanges are governed, with standard operating procedures and trading. The New York Stock Exchange (NYSE), which primarily trades stocks, and the Chicago Mercantile Exchange Group, which primarily trades commodities and allows trading in options and futures, are two examples of well-known exchanges.

- Advantages of Spot Markets
  - Spot markets facilitate trading in a transparent environment, where transactions occur at prevailing prices that are public information and known to all parties. Basically, it is easier to execute spot market contracts.
  - Traders in spot markets can hold and find a better deal if they are not satisfied with current prices and terms.
  - Trades are done and completed on the spot.
  - There may be no minimum capital requirements in spot market transactions compared to some contracts on the futures market that have minimum investment amounts for a single contract.
- Disadvantages of Spot Markets
  - Due to the volatility of some financial instruments and commodities, investors can buy on the spot at inflated prices before assets find their "true price." Hence, trading on the spot market can present significant risks, especially for volatile assets.
  - There may be no recourse if a party notices some irregularities in the trade after the spot market transaction is concluded.
  - There is usually a lack of planning in spot trades, as opposed to forwards and futures trading where parties agree on settlement and delivery at a future date.
  - The spot market is not flexible in terms of timing, as parties will have to handle physical delivery on the spot.
  - The interest rate spot market is affected by counterparty default risk.
  - Currency trading in spot markets is prone to

counterparty risk due to the solvency of the market maker.

10.3.1.5. Managing Risk in Spot Markets

1. **Understand the Market:** Investors and traders must comprehend the spot market in which they plan to conduct business. It entails being aware of the spot market's trading terminology, price discovery process, supply and demand function, and jargon.

   Traders also need to be aware of the characteristics of other market players and the rules governing a spot market exchange. To lower the risk of counterparty default, participants in OTC spot markets should assess the counterparty. It is simpler to reduce potential risks by being aware of how the market operates.

2. **Develop a Trading Strategy:** Before deciding to transact, parties that trade in the spot market must establish a trading strategy. Before opening a position, traders should ascertain their own entry and exit points on particular assets.

   Other tactics that can be used include the use of price floors and limits as well as the quick detection of counterparty or trade risk. A trader can make more informed decisions about whether to engage in a trade, hold onto it, or proceed with it by using stops and limits.

Various stops and limits, such as the following, are helpful:

- **Limit Order:** Closes your position once the price breaches your chosen level.
- **Normal Stop:** Position is closed automatically if the market moves adversely against your position.
- **Guaranteed Stop:** Closes position at exactly the specified price, which eliminates the risk of slippage.
- **Trailing Stop:** Follows a positive price movement and closes if the price begins to move against the target position.

3. **Manage Emotions:** When trading in spot markets, emotions can be impacted by the volatility of financial markets. To ensure a successful trade, it is crucial to control these emotions. Trading can be hampered by a variety of emotions, such as fear, doubt, greed, anxiety, and temptation. Such feelings have the potential to impair judgment and decision-making, which could lead to a bad trade outcome.

4. **Be Up-To-Date on Current Events and News:** Additionally, it is essential for investors to stay informed about events and news that have an impact on the commodities or instruments traded on spot markets, especially if they intend to make a trade. For an investor in the spot market, it is important to monitor market sentiment, stay up to date on financial and economic news, and pay attention to announcements from political and regulatory bodies. When deciding whether to place a spot trade, one should take into account any news that could influence the target asset's price.

10.3.1.6. Examples of Spot Market

Example #1

John, who runs a fabric company in New York, is searching for vendors who offer high-quality textiles at reasonable prices. He searches online and discovers a Chinese supplier who offers bulk orders totaling more than $10,000 at a discount of nearly 40%. Naturally, the payment must be made in CNY, and if the market rate for USDCNY is high right now, John could save a lot of money.

He checks the current USD CNY rate, which is 7.03, higher than the usual value. But looking at the discount the supplier is giving, John decides to execute a foreign exchange to convert the CNY equivalent of $10,000.

- USDCNY = 7.03
- Purchase amount = $ 10,000
- CNY amount = $ 10,000 * 7.03
- CNY Amount= 70,300

The foreign exchange spot transaction settles or is delivered after two days (T+2), and John can make the payment, which allows him 40% savings on his purchase.

Example #2

Steve wants to put $5,000 into the stock market, but he's not sure where to begin. He opens a Demat account with a bank he trusts and investigates the different stocks that are traded on the market. Steve wants to invest only in blue-chip stocks because he is afraid of losing his money.

At $200.47 per share, he purchases 100 Apple shares. He pays for it and expedites the transfer of Apple stock into his account; the spot market permits prompt settlement as well. It makes it possible for Steve to acquire Apple stock that same day. In addition, Steve searches for additional penny stocks that he believes have the potential to perform well. He puts $2,000 into each of two distinct penny stocks.

With his $1,000 now in hand, Steve chooses to make currency investments. In light of the news about China's economic expansion, he invests in the Chinese yuan, anticipating a rise in value based on his analysis of market trends. He invests the remaining $1,000 in currency, believing that the Chinese Yuan will appreciate in value over time.

10.3.2. Forward Market

An over-the-counter derivatives market that deals in these instruments and commits to accepting delivery at a predetermined price and time in the future is known as a forward market. Furthermore, the contract can be tailored with respect to the price, amount, and date. Aside from standard securities markets or commodities dealings, the foreign exchange market is the primary context in which the forward markets are used. In the forward market, asset prices are solely determined by interest.

Figure 10.7. *The forward market is the marketplace.*

Source: https://cdn.educba.com/academy/wp-content/uploads/2021/01/Forward-Market.jpg.

The market that determines the price of financial instruments and assets (such as bonds, swaps, equity, caps, futures, forward rate agreements, bills of exchange, etc.) is known as the forward market.) for future delivery and it is utilized for trading financial instruments. To put it simply, the forward market is the place where we can buy and sell assets and financial instruments for future delivery (Figure 10.7).

10.3.2.1. Classification of Forward Market

The types of forward market that exist in the financial sector are as follows (Figure 10.8):

- **Closed Outright Forward**: Under this type of contract, the exchange rate is fixed between the two parties upon an agreement as per the prevailing spot rate plus the premium.
- **Flexible Forward**: Under this method, the parties can tend to exchange funds which are usually on or even before the maturity date.
- **Long Dated Forward:** They are similar to the short-dated contracts except that the maturities are usually for distant dates
- **Non-Deliverable Forward:** Under this method, there is no physical delivery except that the parties agree to settle only the difference between the spot rate and the exchange rate.

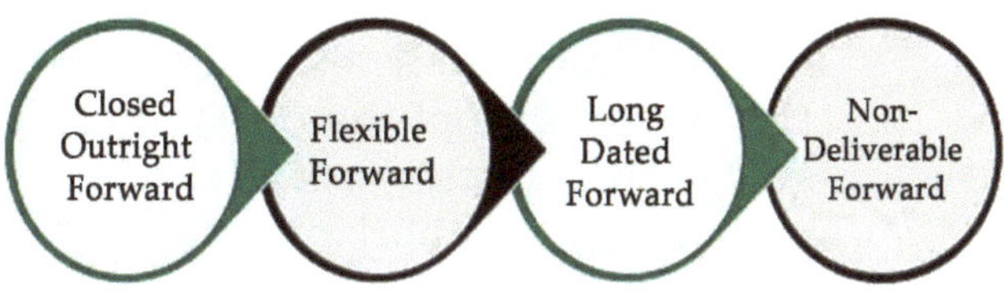

Figure 10.8. *The types of forward market that exist in the financial sector.*

Source: https://www.wallstreetmojo.com/wp-content/uploads/2020/03/Classification-of-Forward-Market.jpg.

Features of Forward Price

The features of the forward market are given below:

- In the forward market, the delivery price is the forward price.
- The contract size depends upon needs and requirements.
- The settlement of the contract is made on the date which is agreed between the parties.
- All the terms of the contracts are negotiated by the parties.
- All the transactions of such a market are done by telephone, with a particular broker.
- All the transactions are made based on the principal-to-principal concept.
- All the participants should examine the credit risk and maintain the credit limit for all the opposite parties.
- If there is any transaction which is made through a broker, a certain amount of commission is charged from buyer and seller otherwise no commission is charged.
- The participants normally deal with one another but some parties are entered into the contracts through one or more dealers.
- There is no money transaction until delivery but a small margin deposit may be required of non-dealer customers on certain occasions.
- In the forward market, trading is mostly unregulated.

Example

Let's take the case of a farmer who harvests a particular crop but doesn't know how much it will cost three months later.

The farmer can fix the price at which he will sell his crop in the following three months by entering into a forward contract with a specific third party. The forward market is the name given to the market for such transactions (Figure 10.9).

Figure 10.9. *Forward market refers to a market that deals in over-the-counter derivative instruments.*

Source: https://www.wallstreetmojo.com/wp-content/uploads/2020/03/Forward-Market-Main.jpg.

Importance

- It helps the parties to the contract to fix the future price at which a particular underlying will be exchanged.
- It helps the individual or corporation to hedge against uncertainties in the future.
- It helps individuals who look for customization in their contract and do not want to directly deal in the futures market where there is standardization for each contract or the underlying product.
- It also helps certain corporations to hedge their FX exposure when there are payments to be received/ paid in the future.

Benefits

- **Offers Complete Hedge:** Whenever a certain seller has certain commodities to exchange in the future for which the price is uncertain, or there happens to be an exporter who wishes to lock in the exchange rate at which the payment must be received, he may do so in the forward market by entering into such contracts. Such contracts, therefore, happen to provide complete hedge and try the maximum to go on to avoid such uncertainties so that parties are assured of the payment rates.
- **Customization:** At times, one party may not be willing to enter into such contracts through futures as the terms and conditions of the contract are well stated and standardized, and it is only forward markets that provide such flexibility to customize the forward contracts. The parties at their own will may decide on the quantity, time, and also the rate at the time of delivery as per their needs and specifications. This adds a lot of convenience to both the parties owing to the flexibility options that this market provides. They happen to be tailor-made for the parties and can thus be adjusted for any duration and amount.
- **Matching of Exposure:** Owing to the feature of flexibility and customization, the parties can now match their exposure with the time-frame of the period during which they decide to enter into the contract. If the horizon happens to be for a period of 2 months rather than the standard of 3 months in the futures contract, the parties can enter into such contracts as per their will so that their exposure is hedged in accordance with their

time-frame. Owing to the contracts being tailor-made to suit the parties, they can be customized to suit any party and thus modify the duration.

- **Over-the-Counter Products:** The products generally tend to be dealt over the counter, and thus owing to the flexibility that they provide, huge institutional investors such as hedge funds tend to prefer to deal with them rather than entering into a standardized futures contract. Over the counter, products give them the advantage of the flexibility to suit their strategy, duration and contract size as per their needs and requirements.

Limitations

- **Difficulty in Cancelation:** At times, the contract, once entered into may not be canceled, and sometimes the parties often do default as they are not so regulated, unlike the futures contract
- **Difficulty in Finding a Counterparty:** Since they are OTC products at certain times, there may be difficulty in finding a similar counterparty to contract with for the forward contract

10.3.3. Future Markets

A futures market is an auction platform where traders purchase and sell futures contracts for delivery on a predetermined future date, as well as commodities. Futures are derivatives contracts that are traded on an exchange that guarantee the delivery of a good or service at a predetermined price in the future. The New York Mercantile Exchange (NYMEX), the Minneapolis Grain Exchange, the Kansas City Board of Trade, the Chicago Mercantile Exchange (CME), the Chicago Board of Trade (CBoT), and the Chicago Board Options Exchange (CBOE) are a few examples of futures markets.

In the past, trading pits—which were situated in major financial centers like New York, Chicago, and London—were used for open outcry and hand signals. As with most other markets, futures exchanges have transitioned to a largely electronic format in the 21st century (Figure 10.10).

Figure 10.10. *A futures market is an auction market.*

Source: https://www.investingtips360.com/wp-content/uploads/2019/03/Futures_market.jpg.

- **Major Futures Markets:** Big futures markets operate their own clearinghouses, where they can profit from both the trades that are executed and the trade processing that occurs afterwards. A few of the largest futures markets that run their own clearing houses are Eurex, the ICE, and the Chicago Mercantile Exchange. Options Clearing Corporation and LCH are external clearinghouses used by other markets such as CBOE and LIFFE. Trades are settled by Clearnet, respectively. The Commodities Futures Trading Commission (CFTC), the primary U.S. agency, is registered with the majority of futures markets. S. organization in charge of futures market regulation. The regulatory body of the nation in which an exchange is headquartered typically oversees it.

- **Futures Market Example:** They will want to keep those costs at a set rate, for example, if a coffee farm sells green coffee beans to a roaster for $4 per pound and the roaster sells the roasted beans for $10 per pound and both are profitable at that price. The investor consents to reimburse the coffee farmer for any difference in price above a predetermined threshold. The investor keeps profits if coffee prices rise above a predetermined threshold. The investor covers the difference and the roaster receives the coffee at a fixed rate if the price of green coffee exceeds a predetermined threshold. The roaster pays the same price and the investor keeps the profit if the price of green coffee is less than the predetermined rate.

10.3.4. Option Markets

- **What Are Options?:** An "option" is a contract that permits (but does not require) trading between two parties to purchase, sell, or trade financial instruments such as stocks, exchange-traded funds (ETFs), or index funds at a set price within a predetermined time frame. The name of this market is the options market. Call and put options are the two different kinds of options. When an investor wishes to buy financial instruments in the future, they refer to the call option. The trader's sale of the share in the option contract runs counter to this put option.
    - o **How Options Work?:** If you buy any shares, you should invest in those whose price projections indicate future profit. To profit from this investment strategy, you must purchase the stock at a lower price and sell it later for a higher price. However, given the nature of volatile and unpredictable markets, this prediction could be incorrect. You can include a put option in the contract, which enables you to sell the share at a predetermined price, to protect yourself from these kinds of possible losses. That being said, this transaction must be completed by the expiration date.
- **Factors of How Options Work:** Following are a few factors which can determine the options prices:
    - o **Existing Price**: When figuring out the price of an option, the stock's current price is very important. The cost of the option premium and the stock's current price are directly proportionate. The value of the options increases in tandem with an increase in the stock price, and vice versa.
    - o **Strike Price:** Strike price is the future selling price at which the security. It is different for different security. The cost of the option increases when the difference between the existing price and strike price is not much and vice versa.
    - o **Expiration Period:** The option contracts have an expiration

date, as was previously mentioned. The option contract's cost increases with a longer expiration period. This is because there is a greater likelihood of a profitable price fluctuation when the trader has more time on their hands.

- **Dividends:** When the dividend increases the value of the put option increases while the value of the call option decreases.
- **Volatility:** High volatile stocks yield higher profits hence options highly volatile are expensive as compared to the less volatile ones.

Figure 10.11. *The concept of options trade is a bit complicated than stock trading.*

Source: https://media.licdn.com/dms/image/D4E12AQGYtPV-6vAb4Q/article-cover_image-shrink_600_2000/0/1685807661341?e=2147483647&v=beta&t=6WZw2kIsai9kpxDy7-OXlg4PTW_JvN2RHW8QZbpn79s.

- **What Is Options Trading?:** With options trading, you can buy or sell securities within a predetermined time frame at a predetermined price. When trading options, buyers can choose not to buy the security at the designated price before the expiration period.

Although the idea of trading options is a little more complex than that of stock trading, you can profit more from it should the price of the stocks rise. You are not required to pay the full price of the security when trading options. Hedging is the process of using options trading to guard against losses in the event that the value of the security declines (Figure 10.11).

- Terms Related to Option Trade
  - **Strike Price:** The predetermined value of the stock at which it will be bought or sold in the future.
  - **Open Interest:** Open interest refers to the total number of option contracts that are currently out there in the market at any given point in time. Open Interest for a contract becomes zero past the expiration date.
  - **Strike Price Intervals:** An option contract can be sold at different strike prices; all these different strike prices are referred to as strike price intervals. These prices are decided by the exchange on which the securities or assets are traded.
  - **American & European Options:** The two distinct underlying asset types and the contract execution date are denoted by the terms "American" and "European." Deals involving American options may be completed on or prior to their expiration date. In contrast, a deal involving

"European options" can only be completed on the day of expiration and not earlier.

- o **Lot Size:** The Lot size indicates the set of units of the underlying asset that are part of a single contract. The typical lot size depends on the stock and is determined by the exchange on which the stock is traded.
- o **Expiration Date:** The pre-decided future date on or before which the options contract can be implemented. There are three different durations viz. 1 month, two months or 3 months.

- Types of Options in Trading
  - o **Call Option:** With a call option, an investor can buy a predetermined number of shares in stocks, bonds, or other financial instruments such as indexes and exchange-traded funds (ETFs) at any time prior to the contract's specified expiration date. If you choose a call option, the share price or stock price must rise in order for you to profit. The call options contract gives you the option to buy that security at a predetermined price that is less than the stock's current market value. Therefore, when you make a purchase, you can profit from a call options contract. Additionally, call options are known to continuously suffer from "time decay," or an increase in value with passing time.
  - o **Put Option:** A put option contract, in contrast to a call option, grants the investor the right to sell securities, assets, or commodities at a predetermined price prior to the contract's expiration date. Investing in put option contracts can result in future profits in the event that the assets' value declines. You can use the put option to sell shares that are underperforming and at a predetermined price that is closer to the original price in the future in order to profit. Put options provide additional protection against a person's net loss. It also experiences time decay, just like the call option.

10.3.5. Swap Market

A swap is a type of derivative contract in which two parties exchange pre-arranged cash flows from one financial instrument for another. Typically, the notional principal amount—a preset nominal value—is used to calculate the cash flows. A "leg" is any one of the cash flow streams. Swaps represent a relatively new class of derivative, having been introduced in the late 1980s. They are among the most widely traded financial contracts despite being relatively new due to their ease of use and wide range of applications. Swap contracts are a useful tool for corporate finance professionals to reduce uncertainty and hedge risk associated with specific operations. For instance, a currency swap contract may be used by the company's CFO as a hedging tool when a project is subject to exchange rate risk. Swaps are exchanged over-the-counter rather than on exchanges, in contrast to futures and options. Additionally, because there is always a chance of counterparty default in swap contracts, counterparties in swaps are typically corporations and financial institutions rather than private individuals.

Typically, a few financial institutions take part in swap markets as market makers. By matching counterparties, the organizations—also referred to as swap banks—allow the transactions to occur (Figure 10.12).

1. **Types of Swaps:** Modern financial markets employ a wide selection of such derivatives, suitable for different purposes. The most popular types include:
   i. **Interest Rate Swap:** Based on a fixed notional principal amount, the parties agree to swap one stream of future interest payments for another. Interest rate swaps typically entail the swapping of a fixed interest rate for a variable interest rate.
   ii. **Currency Swap***:* The principal amount and interest payments made in various currencies are exchanged by the parties involved. Swaps like these are frequently used to protect another investment position from changes in currency exchange rates.
   iii. **Commodity Swap:** These derivatives are intended to swap floating cash flows based on the spot price of a commodity for fixed cash flows established by a commodity's pre-agreed price. Commodity swaps, despite their name, do not entail the exchange of the actual commodity.
   iv. **Credit Default Swap:** A CDS offers protection against a debt instrument's default. The premium payments are transferred from the buyer to the seller in a swap. Should the asset default, the asset will be transferred from the buyer to the seller, and the seller will pay the buyer back the face value of the defaulted asset. Credit default swaps gained some notoriety as a result of their role in the global financial crisis of 2008.
2. **Applications of Swaps:** Nowadays, swaps are an essential part of modern finance. They can be used in the following ways:
   i. **Risk Hedging:** Hedging risks is one of the main purposes of swaps. For instance, currency swaps are used to protect against fluctuations in currency exchange rates, and interest rate swaps can protect against changes in interest rates.

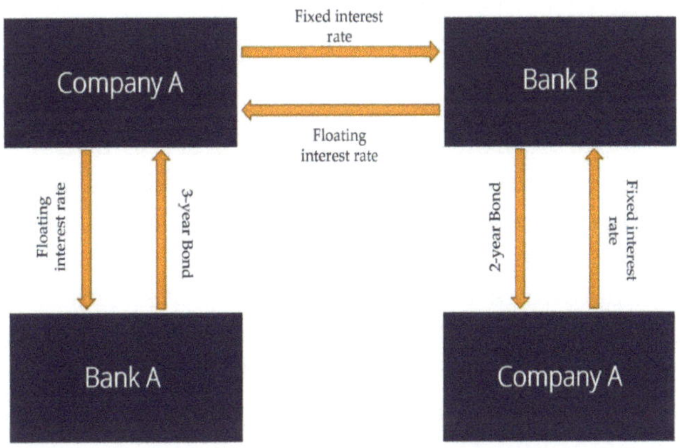

Figure 10.12. *Modern financial markets employ a wide selection of such derivatives.*

Source: https://cdn.corporatefinanceinstitute.com/assets/swaps1.png.

ii. **Access to New Markets:** Swaps are a tool that companies can use to gain access to markets that were previously closed off. For instance, a US business may choose to swap currencies with a British business in order to benefit from the more desirable dollar-to-pound exchange rate, as the UK-based company would be able to borrow money at a lower cost domestically.

10.4. Forex Market Participants

Commercial banks that execute orders from importers, exporters, investment firms, insurance and retirement funds, hedgers, and individual investors make up the majority of those involved in the forex market. Additionally, commercial banks engage in trading activities on their own dime and in their own best interests. The biggest banks frequently have daily turnover of several billions of U.S.S. Dollars and many other currencies are primarily profitable through currency speculation. In addition, brokerage houses serve as a vital intermediary between a multitude of banks, funds, commission houses, dealing centers, etc.

Commercial banks and brokerage houses actively influence price formation and market dynamics by setting their own rates in addition to executing currency exchange transactions at prices set by other market participants. They are known as market makers for this reason. As opposed to the aforementioned, passive players are unable to establish their own quotes and execute deals at rates that active market participants provide. The following are typical goals of passive market participants: paying export-import contracts; making foreign industrial investments; branching out or forming joint ventures overseas; speculating on exchange rate differentials; hedging currency risks (insurance against losses in the event of unfavorable price changes), etc.

The participants' makeup bears witness to the fact that serious businesses actively use this market for serious objectives. That is, not every trader is involved in the Forex market for speculative reasons. As was already mentioned, significant losses in export-import transactions could result from changes in currency exchange rates. Exporters and importers are compelled to use hedging instruments such as forward deals, options, futures, etc., in an effort to mitigate currency risk. Furthermore, a company that is not involved in export-import activities could still suffer losses if currency exchange rates fluctuate. For this reason, learning Forex is essential to running a profitable business.

10.4.1. Forex Market Players

Forex market players can be divided into several groups:

1. **Central Banks:** Their primary responsibility is to maintain the balance between exports and imports and prevent economic crises by preventing spikes in the value of national currencies on the foreign exchange market. The Forex market is directly impacted by central banks. They can exert direct influence by intervening in currency markets, or they can exert indirect influence by controlling the money supply and interest rates.

A central bank may intervene in the market independently to affect the value of the country's currency or in concert with other central banks to implement a joint monetary policy or make joint interventions. Central banks typically enter the foreign exchange market to ensure the stability or adjust the current national currency exchange rate because it has a big impact on the domestic economy, rather than for financial gain. Because central banks can be both bullish and bearish depending on the specific difficulties they are currently facing, they cannot be classified as either bulls or bears. Through commercial banks, central banks can also participate in the currency market. While profit is not the primary motivation of these banks, they are also not drawn to unprofitable operations, so central banks typically intervene covertly through multiple commercial banks at the same time. Occasionally, central banks from various nations collaborate to conduct coordinated interventions.

The greatest influence on world currency markets were:

- U.S. Central Bank – US Federal Reserve (Fed)
- European Central Bank (ECB)
- Bank of England (also known as the Old Lady)
- Bank of Japan

2. **Commercial Banks:** Most foreign exchange operations are carried out by them. Through accounts opened in commercial banks, other market players conduct conversion and deposit-lending operations. Banks gather the total market demand for currency conversions, as well as for fundraising or investment to satisfy them in other banks, through transactions with clients. Banks may function independently and at their own expense in addition to attending to the requests of their clients.

Since the foreign exchange market is ultimately a market for interbank transactions, when we discuss the movement of exchange rates or interest rates, we are referring to the interbank foreign exchange market. Major international banks dominate the foreign exchange market, with daily transaction volumes estimated to be in the billions of US dollars. These include Standard Chartered Bank, Citibank, Chase Manhattan Bank, Union Bank of Switzerland, Deutsche Bank, and Barclays Bank. Their primary distinction is the volume of transactions they handle, which frequently results in notable variations in quotations.

Big players may act as either "Bulls" or "Bears."

- "Bulls" are those market participants who are interested in enhancing the value of currency.
- "Bears" are interested in reduction of currency value.

The market is permanently in equilibrium between the bulls and the bears, so currency quotations fluctuate within fairly narrow limits. However, when either of the group prevail, exchange rates change in a rather dramatic and significant way.

3. **Firms Performing Foreign Trade Operations:** Businesses that engage in international trade continuously place or attract free currency volumes in the form of short-term deposits, as well as demand (from importers) or supply (from exporters) foreign currency. These participants use commercial banks to complete their conversion and deposit transactions because they lack direct access to the currency market.
4. **Firms Carrying out International Investment:** Investment funds,

money market funds, and international corporations, as well as companies represented by a variety of international investment funds, carry out the policy of diversified asset portfolio management by investing capital in securities issued by foreign governments and corporations. In dealer jargon, they are simply referred to as funds. The most well-known funds are Dean Witter's and George Soros' Quantum, which both executed profitable exchange bets. This group also includes major international corporations that invest in foreign industries through joint ventures, subsidiaries, and the like. Examples of these companies are Xerox, Nestle, GE (General Electric), BP (British Petroleum), and others.

5. **Currency Exchange:** There are currency exchanges in some transitional economies; they serve businesses by exchanging currencies and adjusting market exchange rates. Because of the size of the exchange market, the state typically actively regulates the exchange rate (Figure 10.13).

Figure 10.13. *Some countries with transition economies there are currency exchanges.*

Source: https://cdn.britannica.com/87/191987-131-6D09155D/currency-exchange-rate-background-LED-display-board.jpg.

6. **Brokerage Firms:** Brokerage firms facilitate the exchange of foreign currency between buyers and sellers, perform conversions, and handle lending and depositing activities. Brokers take a percentage of each transaction as commission for acting as an intermediary. The term "ECN" (Electronic Communication Network) brokers has gained a lot of traction lately. ECN is a trading platform that gathers requests for currency exchange from different contractors. Large banks, brokerage houses, and individual customers make up their clientele. Because of the high standards, most private investors do not have access to such brokers. It is assumed that ECN brokers only charge a commission and do not function as counterparties with their clients, i.e., they are not market makers (Figure 10.14).

Figure 10.14. *Brokerage firms are bringing together buyers and sellers.*

Source: https://forsahub.com/wp-content/uploads/2022/02/brokerage.jpg.

7. **Individuals:** People engage in a variety of non-trade activities, such as purchasing and selling cash, transferring salaries, pensions, and royalties, and traveling abroad. Since margin trading was introduced, people have had the chance to invest free money in the Forex market in an attempt to turn a profit.

CASE STUDY

HEDGING FOREIGN EXCHANGE RISK

Background

Company X is a multinational corporation based in the United States that manufactures consumer electronics. It sources raw materials globally, including from suppliers in Japan and South Korea. The company exports its finished products to Europe and Asia, generating revenue in multiple currencies, including Euro (EUR) and Japanese Yen (JPY). Fluctuations in exchange rates can significantly impact its profitability and financial stability.

Challenge

Over the past year, Company X has faced increasing volatility in exchange rates. The USD has strengthened against the Euro and weakened against the Yen, affecting both its import costs and export revenues. This volatility has made it challenging to forecast profitability accurately and manage cash flow effectively.

Strategy

To mitigate foreign exchange risk, Company X decides to implement a hedging strategy using forward contracts. Here's how they approach it:

1. **Assessment of Exposure:** Company X assesses its exposure to foreign exchange risk by analyzing its imports (costs in JPY) and exports (revenue in EUR). They estimate their future currency requirements and potential exposures based on historical data and current market conditions.
2. **Hedging with Forward Contracts:** Company X enters into forward contracts with its banks or financial institutions. For imports from Japan, they enter into JPY/USD forward contracts to lock in a favorable exchange rate for converting Yen into Dollars at a future date. Similarly, for exports to Europe, they enter into EUR/USD forward contracts to secure a minimum acceptable exchange rate for converting Euros into Dollars.
3. **Execution and Monitoring:** The finance team monitors exchange rate movements closely and adjusts their hedging strategy accordingly. They may roll over existing forward contracts or enter into new ones to ensure they are adequately covered against adverse movements in exchange rates.
4. **Benefits and Challenges: Benefits**
   - **Stabilized Costs:** Hedging allows Company X to stabilize its costs for imported raw materials, reducing the impact of adverse currency movements on profitability.

- **Predictable Revenues:** By hedging export revenues, the company can predict its USD-denominated earnings from sales in Europe, providing more certainty for financial planning and budgeting.
- **Enhanced Financial Stability:** Overall, effective hedging helps Company X maintain financial stability and protect its bottom line from currency fluctuations.

Challenges

- **Costs:** There are costs associated with entering into and managing forward contracts, which can impact overall profitability.
- **Effectiveness:** Hedging strategies are not foolproof and may not always perfectly offset losses from adverse exchange rate movements.
- **Complexity:** Managing multiple currency exposures and hedging strategies requires expertise and resources, which smaller companies may find challenging.

Conclusion

Through proactive management of foreign exchange risk using forward contracts, Company X mitigates the impact of currency volatility on its financial performance. This case study underscores the importance of strategic hedging in multinational operations to enhance stability, manage costs, and support sustainable growth in a globalized economy.

CLASS ACTIVITY

In this class activity on foreign exchange, students will engage in a dynamic discussion about currency markets and exchange rate dynamics. Using real-time data or hypothetical scenarios, students will analyze factors influencing exchange rates, such as economic indicators, political events, and market sentiment. They will explore the implications of currency fluctuations on international trade, investment decisions, and global economic stability. Through group discussions and presentations, students will apply their knowledge to assess strategies for businesses and investors to manage foreign exchange risk effectively. This interactive session aims to deepen understanding of forex markets and their role in the interconnected global economy.

SUMMARY

- The Foreign Exchange is a market where the buyers and sellers are involved in the sale and purchase of foreign currencies.
- The basic and the most visible function of foreign exchange market is the transfer of funds (foreign currency) from one country to another for the settlement of payments.
- The foreign exchange market, also known as the forex market, is a global marketplace for trading in currencies. It is a decentralized market that allows you to buy and sell foreign exchange.
- A spot market is a financial market where financial instruments and commodities are traded for instantaneous delivery.
- Financial instruments traded on spot markets include equity, fixed-income instruments such as bonds and treasury bills, and foreign exchange. Commodities also dominate spot markets through the trading of energy, metals, agriculture, and livestock.
- In an organized market exchange, buyers and sellers meet to bid and offer financial instruments and commodities available.
- It is crucial for parties that trade in the spot market to adopt a trading strategy before they decide to transact. Traders should determine their own entry and exit points on specific assets before a position is opened.
- Options trading enables you to purchase or sell securities at a predetermined price within a pre-decided period. In options trading, buyers have the privilege and flexibility of not purchasing the security at the specified price before the expiration period.

REVIEW QUESTIONS

1. What is foreign exchange and why is it important in the global economy?
2. Explain the difference between spot and forward exchange rates.
3. What factors influence exchange rate movements?
4. How do central banks intervene in foreign exchange markets?
5. What are the benefits and risks of using leverage in forex trading?
6. Explain the concept of currency hedging and provide examples of hedging strategies.
7. Compare and contrast the roles of speculators and hedgers in the forex market.
8. How does interest rate parity affect exchange rates?
9. Discuss the challenges and benefits of a floating exchange rate regime compared to a fixed exchange rate regime.
10. What are the implications of a strong or weak currency for a country's economy?

REFERENCES

1. Baker, J. (2002). *The Bank for International Settlements—Evolution and Evaluation*. Quorum Books.
2. Chen, J. (2009). *Essentials of Foreign Exchange Trading*. John Wiley & Sons. ISBN 978-0470464007.
3. Cornell, B., & Reinganum, M. R. (1981). Forward and futures prices: Evidence from the foreign exchange markets. *Journal of Finance, 36*, 1035–1045.
4. DeRosa, D. F. (2000). *Options on Foreign Exchange*. John Wiley & Sons.
5. DeRosa, D. F. (2001). *In defense of Free Capital Markets—The Case Against a New International Financial Architecture*. Bloomberg Press.
6. Desai, P. (2003). *Financial Crisis, Contagion, and Containment: From Asia to Argentina*. Princeton University Press.
7. Dunbar, N. (2000). *Inventing Money: The Story of Long-Term Capital Management and the Legends Behind it*. John Wiley & Sons.
8. Fourcans, A., & Franck, R. (2003). *Currency Crises—A Theoretical and Empirical Perspective*. Edward Elgar.
9. Hakala, J., & Wystup, U. (2002). *Foreign Exchange Risk: Models, Instruments and Strategies*. Risk Books.
10. Hull, J. C. (2006). *Options, Futures, and Other Derivatives* (6th ed.). Prentice-Hall.
11. Kritzman, M. P. (2000). Puzzles in finance: Six practical problems and their remarkable solutions. In J. Clark Francis, W. Toy, & J. G. Whittaker (Eds.), *The Handbook of Equity Derivatives* (Rev. ed., Chapter 1, pp. 1–21). John Wiley & Sons.
12. Lipton, A. (2001). *Mathematical Methods for Foreign Exchange: A Financial Engineer's Approach*. World Scientific Publishers.
13. Lipton, A. (2003). *Exotic Options: The Cutting-Edge Collection Technical Papers Published in Risk 1999–2003*. Risk Books.
14. Lowenstein, R. (2000). *When Genius Failed: The Rise and Fall of Long-Term Capital Management*. Random House.
15. McKay, P. A. (2005). Scammers operating on periphery of CFTC's domain lure little guy with fantastic promises of profits. *The Wall Street Journal*. (Dow Jones and Company). Retrieved 2007-10-31.
16. Neftci, S. (2000). *An Introduction to The Mathematics of Financial Derivatives* (2nd ed.). Academic Press.
17. Ong, L. L. (2003). *The Big Mac Index: Applications of Purchasing Power Parity*. Palgrave Macmillan.
18. The Bank for International Settlements. (2010). *The $4 Trillion Question: What Explains FX Growth Since the 2007 Survey?*
19. Triennial Central Bank Survey. (2016). *Foreign Exchange Turnover in April 2016*. Basel, Switzerland: Bank for International Settlements.

20. Weisweiller, R. (1986). *Arbitrage: Opportunities and Techniques in The Financial and Commodity Markets*. John Wiley & Sons.
21. Weithers, T. (2000). Options fundamentals. In J. C. Francis, W. Toy, & J. G. Whittaker (Eds.), *The Handbook of Equity Derivatives* (Rev. ed., Chapter 1). John Wiley & Sons.

Index

A

Absolute advantage 44, 45, 46
Adjustment costs 114
Administrative hurdles 122
Ad valorem tariffs 59, 85
Agriculture 21, 23, 38, 50, 51, 53, 56, 70, 92, 120, 178, 179, 186, 192, 198, 202, 204, 218, 220, 241, 245, 247, 264, 281, 289, 295, 390, 407
American Civil War 164, 169
American Depository Receipts (ADRs) 366
Antidumping duty 121
Asia-Pacific Economic Cooperation (APEC) 291
Assistive policies 124, 157
Autonomous organizations 322

B

Balance of payments (BOP) 341, 342, 359, 378
Bananas 30, 181, 225
Banking 8, 9, 15, 30, 55, 194, 234, 243, 247, 320, 356, 361, 365, 366
Bilateral agreements 18, 21, 36, 71, 178, 349
Boost productivity 332, 361, 368
Buffer stocks 222, 223, 224, 253
Buffer stock strategy 223

C

Call option 398, 399, 400
Capital account 316, 342, 343, 344, 345, 346, 347, 348, 350, 357, 358, 363, 365, 366, 369, 378
Capital flows 8, 9, 304, 319, 362, 363, 369
Capitalism 41, 191, 241
Capital stock 211
Cash payment 381
Caterpillar 97, 273
Central banks 231, 268, 342, 343, 344, 382, 383, 402, 403, 407
Centralized model 303
Central Public Sector Enterprises (CPSEs) 197
Chicago Board of Trade (CBoT) 397
Chicago Mercantile Exchange (CME) 397
Chocolate 225
Civil War 170
Closed Outright Forward 395
cocoa 222
Coffee 20, 24, 56, 68, 70, 96, 155, 216, 217, 222, 224, 225, 398
Commercial banks 382, 402
Commodities Futures Trading Commission (CFTC) 397
Commodity Credit 161, 199
Commodity Credit Corporation (CCC) 200
Commodity prices 223, 224, 253
Commodity Swap 401

Comparative advantage 3, 5, 6, 14, 29, 36, 42, 45, 46, 47, 49, 50, 51, 58, 82, 83, 84, 108, 112, 113, 163, 164, 165, 215, 218, 232, 235, 236, 253, 258, 263, 281, 292, 315, 322
Comparative disadvantage 49, 83, 115, 131, 236, 258
Competitive market 100, 129, 151
Competitive pricing structure 322
Compound tariff 87, 118
Concentration 115, 192, 196, 215
Consumer protection 161
Consumer surplus 100
Contractual Agreement 323
Costs 46, 48, 104, 109, 110, 112, 275, 276, 281, 282, 289, 301, 305, 405, 406
Country risk analysis (CRA) 315
Country risks 303, 315, 318, 319, 320, 321, 337
Credit Default Swap 401
Credit Function 387, 388
Currency Swap 401
Current account 194, 316, 342, 343, 344, 345, 346, 347, 348, 349, 350, 351, 352, 353, 356, 357, 358, 359, 360, 361, 362, 363, 369, 378
Current account deficits 347
Customer services 245
Customs procedures 124
Customs union 15, 76, 203, 204, 259, 260, 262, 263, 264, 265, 267, 268, 300, 301

D

Demand allocation 121
Demand dynamics 3
Direct cash payments 138
Disinvestment 161, 197
Domestic consumption 96, 102, 103, 105, 113, 361
Domestic content 136
Domestic market 6, 78, 87, 133, 145, 148, 149, 163, 167, 175, 193, 235, 236, 265, 321, 347, 371
Domestic policy 255
Domestic production subsidy 121
Dumping 121, 142, 147, 148

E

Economic activity 1
Economic development 255
Economic downturns 228
Economic efficiency 223
Economic growth 1, 13, 17, 18, 37, 42, 49, 50, 51, 52, 53, 61, 72, 73, 82, 117, 176, 189, 191, 197, 201, 209, 210, 213, 230, 232, 234, 235, 236, 237, 238, 241, 245, 246, 247, 248, 253, 254, 261, 274, 278, 288, 293, 300, 309, 310, 338, 339, 349, 368
Economic integration 1, 259, 300
Economic nationalism 1, 3
Economic profit 227
Economic Risk 303, 315
Economic theory 1
Economic transactions 341, 362
Economic union 16, 255
Education 7, 11, 27, 29, 50, 198, 211, 231, 234, 238, 239, 247, 260, 282, 294, 309, 333
Efficiency 29, 84, 303, 306
Electronic trading platforms 381
Employment 109, 192, 283, 303, 306, 309
Energy 113, 152, 162, 190, 191, 193, 198, 200, 234, 257, 339, 390, 407
Entrepreneurial incentives 292
Environmental Protection Agency (EPA) 180
Environmental regulations 255
European Central Bank 268, 275, 278, 382, 403
European currency 268
European Monetary Fund (EMF) 279
European Monetary Union (EMU) 268, 275, 277
Exchange brokers 384, 385, 392
Exchange Rate Risk 315
Exchange rate system 341
Exchange risk 303
Exchange-traded funds (ETFs) 398, 400
Export dependence 115
Export-led growth 209, 236, 237
Export-oriented policy 209, 236
Export promotion 199

Export quotas 121
Export subsidy 121
Export taxes 85
External debt 41
Exxon 97

F

Fair-trade 111, 224, 225
Fast-track authority 188
Financial account 341, 342, 343, 347, 361, 365
Financial instruments 341, 381, 407
Financial services 15, 20, 55, 70, 360
Fiscal policies 255
Fixed exchange rates 9, 260, 343, 362, 363, 385
Flexible Forward 395
Foreign competition 102
Foreign currency 381
Foreign direct investment 15, 49, 210, 248, 303, 304, 305, 308, 309, 310, 311, 312, 313, 316, 338, 347, 353, 366, 378
Foreign direct investments (FDI) 303, 308, 337
Foreign Exchange Regulation Act 161, 192
Foreign Institutional Investors (FIIs) 366
Foreign investment 55, 58, 72, 248, 341, 366
Forex market 381, 385, 386, 402, 404
Forward market 394, 395, 396
Forward Markets 389
Free trade agreements (FTAs) 73
Free trade area (FTA) 15
Free Trade Area of the Americas (FTAA) 288
Free-trade equilibrium 101
Free Trade Zone (FTZ) 98
Future Markets 389, 397

G

General Agreement on Tariffs and Trade (GATT) 6, 77, 174, 255, 256
General Currency Area (GCA) 366
General Electric 97, 199, 246, 282, 404
Generalized system of preferences (GSP) 209
General welfare 72
Geographic mobility 332, 333, 334
Global agriculture protectionism 220
Global Depository Receipts (GDRs) 366
Global economy 1, 2, 7, 13, 25, 30, 32, 36, 37, 42, 43, 50, 72, 93, 150, 164, 194, 213, 231, 236, 295, 347, 352, 371, 381, 382, 406, 407
Global financial system 381
Globalization 1, 2, 7, 8, 11, 25, 37, 38, 69, 84, 161, 164, 167, 194, 207, 254
Global liberalization 13, 257
Global market environment 51
Global marketplaces 69, 322
Global oil production 226
Global quota 121
Global supply chains 2, 52, 120
Global trade 13, 159, 167
Global value chains (GVCs) 1, 2
Governmental organizations 151
Government regulation 161
Great Depression 10, 107, 151, 172, 173, 174, 230, 343, 368
Gross domestic product (GDP) 41

H

Healthcare 247
Heckscher-Ohlin theory 245
Hedge funds 382
Hedging Function 387, 388

I

Immigration/emigration 304
Import duties 85
Import license 121
Import licensing 122, 123, 157, 177, 192
Import penetration 115
Import quota 121, 127
Import substitution 6, 209
Import-substitution-industrialization (ISI) 162
Inadequate education 212
Inadequate infrastructure 212
Inadequate planning 327
Inadequate trade barriers 212

Industrial licensing 161, 195
Industrial policy 161, 162, 206, 207
Industrial revolution 189, 195, 343
Industrial Revolution 163, 189
Ineffective management blending 327
Inflation 19, 31, 32, 33, 34, 35, 36, 88, 166, 184, 193, 223, 242, 268, 269, 276, 278, 286, 287, 293, 319, 348, 350, 352, 353, 370, 371, 374
Information technology (IT) 246
Infrastructure 381
Infrastructure investments 246, 330
Innovation 49, 306
Innovative thinking 303
Insurance 11, 19, 21, 30, 55, 71, 88, 118, 120, 199, 224, 282, 317, 318, 337, 356, 361, 388, 402
Insurance policies 138
Intellectual property 19, 20, 55, 72, 74, 178, 179, 186, 210, 233, 243, 290, 293, 295
Interest Rate Swap 401
International agreements 1, 3, 20, 70, 257, 386
International borrowing 304, 358
International brand recognition 305
International Business Machines (IBM) 97
International buying 341
International Chamber of Commerce (ICC) 21, 41, 71
International commodity agreements (ICAs) 209, 222
International conflicts 3
International economic law 57
International economy 1, 2, 37, 163, 295
International exchange market 382
International finance 1
International institutions 1
International joint venture 303
International joint venture (IJV) 323, 337
International market 20, 25, 28, 63, 226, 294, 350, 368
International marketing 25, 41, 158
International monetary 1, 341
International Monetary Fund 9, 12, 84, 193, 209, 230, 231, 253, 254, 279, 283, 341, 347, 348, 358, 362
International Monetary Fund (IMF) 193, 209, 231, 341, 347, 348, 358, 362
International Monetary Fund's (IMF) 9
International negotiations 3, 67, 257
International political economy 3
International price discrimination 143
International relations 1, 3, 60, 260, 354
International sanctions 3
International Sugar Agreement 224
International trade 3, 21, 37, 49, 51, 53, 57, 62, 67, 68, 69, 70, 72, 77, 78, 83, 206, 337, 385
International Trade Commission (ITC) 145
International trade law 57, 83, 184
International transactions 341, 369
International travel 55
International Wheat Agreement 224
Investment liberalization 246
Investment Promotion Agencies (IPA) 309

J

Job Creation 51
Job Displacement 51
Joint Property Interest 323
Joint venture issues 326
Joint venture (JV) 324

L

Labor costs 5, 14, 29, 32, 93, 110, 111, 135, 165, 294, 322
Labor market conditions 52
Labor mobility 276, 277, 278, 303, 304, 332, 333, 334, 335, 338
Latin American economic policy 288
Legal system 328
Liberalization 194, 207
Licensing 28, 124, 195, 311, 312
Limited liability partnership (LLP) 325, 326
Loans 10, 35, 55, 138, 198, 199, 200, 201, 230, 231, 232, 242, 317, 319, 320, 344, 345, 346, 347, 349, 365, 366, 369
Long Dated Forward 395
Lot size 400
Lowering tariffs 210, 262

M

Macroeconomic policies 161
Macroeconomics 1
Major Futures Markets 397
Marginal rate of transformation (MRT) 48
Market access 72, 122, 132, 219, 281, 295, 302
Market demand curve 100, 217
Market economy 155, 156, 242, 253, 291, 294, 300
Marketing plan 63, 68
Market makers 392
Market rates 138, 201
Mercantilism 44, 164, 207, 309
Ministry of Economy, Trade and Industry (METI) 201
Mixed economy 161
Most favored nation (MFN) 173
Multilateral contracts 209
Multilateralism 255, 257
Multilateral trading system 255
Multinational business model 306
Multinational-enterprise analysis 322
Multinational enterprise (MNE) 317
Multinational firms 306
Multinational trade blocs 12
Mundell-Fleming model 12

N

National assets 341
National income 166
National security 3, 87, 108, 113, 114, 119, 198, 199, 248
Natural resources 5, 28, 42, 50, 53, 113, 165, 167, 222, 238, 330, 338, 371
Neighborhood Risk 315, 317
Neomercantilism 164
New Industrial Policy 193, 194
News media 247
New York Mercantile Exchange (NYMEX) 397
Non-Deliverable Forward 395
Non-protectionist policies 124
Non-tariff barriers (NTBs) 72
North American Free Trade Agreement (NAFTA) 218, 259, 289

O

Offshore-assembly provision (OAP) 93
Open interest 399
Optimum currency area 276, 277, 300
Optimum tariff 85
Option Markets 389, 398
Organization for Economic Co-operation and Development (OECD) 346
Organization of Petroleum Exporting Nations (OPEC) 209, 226
Organized market exchange 391, 392, 407
Over-the-counter (OTC) 391

P

Persistent dumping 121
Physical exchange 381
Policy decisions 2
Policy responses 51, 52
Political instability 307
Political risk 303, 317, 318
Predatory dumping 121
Price agreement 228
Prices 69, 142, 222, 272, 291, 292, 309, 350, 368, 371, 390
Product failure 324
Protectionism 61, 74, 85, 114
Protectionist trade barriers 124
Public relations 303
Put option 398, 399, 400

Q

Quotas 3, 7, 19, 20, 21, 43, 55, 58, 59, 60, 62, 70, 73, 75, 87, 118, 121, 122, 126, 127, 128, 129, 130, 131, 132, 133, 134, 135, 139, 153, 163, 166, 167, 168, 176, 178, 192, 218, 219, 226, 227, 229, 232, 233, 235, 236, 241, 253, 264, 292, 296, 305

R

Ratification 41, 57
Regional blocs 257
Regionalized model 303
Regional security 255
Regional trading blocs 257
Retail 99, 246, 247, 382, 386
Retaliatory trade barriers 181
Revenue effect 85
Risk management 381
Rubber 20, 70, 218, 222
Rupee debt service 366
Rupee payments area (RPA) 366

S

Sanitary and phytosanitary measures (SPS) 122
Scientific tariff 85
Selective quota 121
Self-executing transactions 369
Shared management ventures 326
Smoot-Hawley Act 161, 171, 172, 173, 206
Social preferences 183
Social regulation 121, 152
Societal costs 114
Sovereign risk 303, 317
Special drawing rights (SDRs) 349
Specific tariff 85
Sporadic dumping 121
Spot Markets 389, 390, 391, 392, 393
stock's current price 398
Strike price 398
Strike Price 398, 399
Strike price intervals 399
Structural Adjustment 51
Subsidy 79, 113, 138, 139, 140, 164, 166, 167, 182, 183, 272, 273
Sugar 24, 56, 132, 133, 225, 281, 282
Swap Market 400

T

Tariff avoidance 85, 94
Tariff escalation 85, 92, 218
Tariff evasion 85, 94
Tariff liberalization 85, 119
Tariff-rate quota 121
Tariff rates 85
Tariffs 6, 7, 19, 21, 38, 58, 59, 60, 61, 70, 72, 75, 76, 77, 78, 85, 86, 87, 89, 94, 95, 96, 104, 112, 116, 118, 119, 120, 127, 130, 131, 139, 158, 163, 170, 174, 175, 177, 182, 206, 218, 235, 255, 256, 305
Tax breaks 6, 68, 112, 138, 309
Tax laws 19, 183, 259
Tax-planned joint venture 326
Tea 96, 225
Technical barriers to trade (TBTs) 122
Telecommunications 77, 113, 162, 200, 201, 376
Tensions over money 326
Textile industry 163, 178, 285, 300
Textiles 5, 109, 129, 134, 163, 164, 179, 201, 211, 213, 218, 219, 233, 239, 242, 285, 394
the Chicago Board Options Exchange (CBOE) 397
Trade 1, 2, 3, 6, 7, 13, 15, 17, 18, 19, 20, 21, 22, 23, 28, 29, 30, 36, 39, 41, 42, 43, 44, 45, 46, 48, 49, 50, 51, 52, 53, 54, 55, 56, 57, 58, 60, 61, 63, 64, 67, 68, 69, 70, 71, 72, 73, 74, 75, 77, 83, 84, 85, 91, 92, 97, 98, 108, 109, 111, 112, 116, 120, 121, 123, 126, 127, 130, 131, 132, 133, 136, 138, 145, 146, 150, 151, 152, 156, 157, 158, 159, 160, 161, 162, 163, 164, 165, 166, 167, 168, 173, 174, 175, 176, 179, 180, 182, 183, 184, 186, 188, 194, 201, 205, 206, 207, 209, 211, 214, 215, 217, 218, 219, 224, 236, 242, 252, 254, 255, 256, 257, 259, 263, 265, 266, 280, 282, 284, 285, 286, 288, 289, 291, 292, 294, 296, 297, 298, 299, 300, 309, 312, 322, 342, 345, 356, 359, 397, 399, 403
Trade agreements 52, 299
Trade barriers 21, 72, 74, 75, 108, 123, 159, 167, 219
Trade diversion 263, 264, 265, 268, 271, 284, 285, 300, 301
Trade liberalization 183, 255, 300

Trade regulation law 162
Trade restrictions 60, 61, 108, 109, 168, 236, 265, 312
Trade theory 3, 29, 42, 43, 47, 66, 83, 108, 303, 322, 337
Trade war 85
Trading system 13, 73, 74, 122, 164, 172, 179, 215, 230, 238, 253, 257
Transfer Function 387
Transfer risk 303, 316
Transfer Risk 315, 316
Transformation curve 41
Transformation schedule 47
Transport costs 212

U

Unilateral transfers 341
United Auto Workers (UAW) 135
United Nations Commission on International Trade Law (UNCITRAL) 21, 71

V

Value-added tax 303, 341
Voluntary export restraints (VERs) 7, 122
Voluntary restraint agreements (VRAs) 7

W

Welfare consequences 255
Wheat 38, 84, 224, 271
Widespread corruption 212
World Bank 7, 38, 84, 92, 158, 209, 218, 230, 231, 248, 253, 254, 283, 353, 366
World Trade Organization (WTO) 1, 2, 6, 18, 20, 42, 56, 57, 61, 70, 73, 77, 123, 133, 157, 174, 184, 214, 255, 256, 296, 299

Y

Yield curve 390

FSC
www.fsc.org
MIX
Papier | Fördert gute Waldnutzung
FSC® C083411

Kolibri 360 GmbH
Ferdinand-Jühlke-Straße 7
99095 Erfurt, Deutschland
produktsicherheit@kolibri360.de